After the Cataclysm

After the Cataclysm:

Postwar Indochina and the Reconstruction of Imperial Ideology

The Political Economy of Human Rights:
Volume II

Noam Chomsky
and Edward S. Herman

Haymarket Books
Chicago, Illinois

Copyright © 1979 by Noam Chomsky and Edward S. Herman

First Edition published by South End Press, Boston, Massachusetts

This edition published in 2014 by
Haymarket Books
P.O. Box 180165
Chicago, IL 60618
773-583-7884
www.haymarketbooks.org
info@haymarketbooks.org

ISBN: 978-1-60846-397-8

Trade distribution:
In the US, Consortium Book Sales and Distribution, www.cbsd.com
In Canada, Publishers Group Canada, www.pgcbooks.ca
In the UK, Turnaround Publisher Services, www.turnaround-uk.com
All other countries, Ingram Publisher Services International, IPS_Intlsales@ingramcontent.com

This book was published with the generous support of Lannan Foundation and Wallace Action Fund.

Cover design by Josh On.

Entered into digital printing August 2018.

Library of Congress Cataloging-in-Publication data is available.

Contents

Preface to the 2014 Edition   vii

Preface xv

1 The Setting   1
    1.1   The U.S. Impact on Indochina   1
    1.2   The United States in Vietnam: A Partial Victory   8
    1.3   Picking Up the Pieces: A Return to   20
          Counterrevolutionary Intervention

2 Precedents   25
    2.1   The Intelligentsia and the State   25
    2.2   In the Light of History   35

3 Refugees: Indochina and Beyond   55

4 Vietnam   69

5 Laos   137

6 Cambodia   155

7 Final Comments   339

Notes   347

Index   447

Preface to the 2014 Edition

Our study *The Political Economy of Human Rights*, originally published 25 years ago, consists of two volumes, closely inter-related. The first, entitled *The Washington Connection and Third World Fascism*, reviews the horrendous reign of terror, torture, violence and slaughter that Washington unleashed against much of the world in the 1960s and 1970s, primarily in the western hemisphere and Southeast Asia, including U.S. aggression in Indochina, surely the worst crime of the post-World War II era. The second volume, *After the Cataclysm*, reviews the immediate aftermath in Indochina along with some relevant but overlooked comparative and historical material.

As discussed in the preface to the original publication, the two volumes are devoted to both facts and beliefs: the facts insofar as they could be obtained, and beliefs arising from the way facts were selected and interpreted through the distorting prism of a very powerful ideological system, which gains much of its power from the belief that it is free and independent.

The earlier history of *PEHR*, reviewed in a prefatory note to the first volume, illustrates some of the interesting features of the doctrinal system. In brief, an earlier version was published by a small but successful publisher, owned by a major con-glomerate. An executive of the conglomerate was offended by its contents, and in order to prevent its appearance shut down the publisher, effectively destroying all its stock. With very rare exceptions, civil libertarians in the U.S. saw no problem in these actions, presumably because control of expression by concentrated private power, as distinct from the state, is considered not only legitimate but even an exercise of "freedom," in a perverse sense of "freedom" that finds a natural place in the prevailing radically anti-libertarian ideology (often called "liberal" or even "libertarian," a matter that will not surprise readers of Orwell).

Elsewhere, we have discussed the general character of the doctrinal system more explicitly, reviewing its consequences in a wide array of domains.[1]

One useful perspective on the ideological system is provided by a comparison of treatment by media and commentary of *their* crimes and *our own*—both the reporting of the facts and the propaganda system's reaction to each. There was a highly revealing illustration at the time we were writing in 1977-78: the Indonesian invasion of East Timor in December 1975, and the Khmer Rouge takeover of Cambodia in April 1975. Our two longest and most detailed chapters review these two cases: East Timor in Volume I, Cambodia in Volume II.

In both cases, information was quite limited. In the case of East Timor, knowledge of the facts was limited by design: a good deal was quite accessible, including coverage in the Australian press. In the case of Cambodia, in contrast, reliable facts were very hard to obtain.

There was, however, extensive information about the second element of our inquiry: the belief systems that were constructed. In the case of East Timor, the U.S. reaction was brief: silence or denial. In the case of Cambodia, as we reviewed in detail, the reaction was unrestrained horror at the acts of unspeakable brutality, demonstrating the ultimate evil of the global enemy and its Marxist-Leninist doctrines.

The comparison is revealing. In both cases, it was clear that terrible crimes were in process, in the same area of the world, in the same years. There was one striking difference between the two cases. The crimes underway in Cambodia could be attributed to an official enemy (at least if U.S. actions, directly death-dealing and also helping lay the basis for further deaths are overlooked, as they were) and no one had a suggestion as to what might be done to mitigate or end them. In the case of East Timor, the crimes unequivocally traced back to Washington, which gave the "green light" for the invasion and provided critical military and diplomatic support for the vast atrocities (with the help of its allies), and they could have been ended very easily, simply by orders from Washington. That conclusion, never seriously in doubt, was demonstrated in September 1999, when President Clinton, under intense domestic and international pressure, quietly informed the Indonesian generals that the game was over. They instantly abandoned their strenuous claims to the territory and withdrew, allowing a UN peace-keeping force to enter. In a display of cynicism that mere words cannot capture, this was interpreted as a "humanitarian intervention," a sign of the nobility of the West.[2]

Our chapter on East Timor was far and away the most important in the two volumes, precisely because the huge ongoing crimes could have so readily been ended. It passed without mention in the doctrinal system—as, indeed, did our detailed review of many other U.S. crimes. In dramatic contrast, a sizable literature has been devoted to our chapter on Cambodia, desperately seeking to discover some error, and with unsupported and unjustifiable claims about our alleged apologetics for Pol Pot. We reviewed those that were even mildly serious in *Manufacturing Consent*, and there should be no need to do so again.

While evidence about Cambodia in 1978 was slim, enough existed to make it clear, as we wrote, that "the record of atrocities in Cambodia is substantial and often gruesome," with "a fearful toll," though the available facts bore little relation to the huge chorus of denunciation of the genocidal Marxist rulers. Not all joined in the chorus, including some of the most knowledgeable and respected correspondents, among them Nayan Chanda of the *Far Eastern Economic Review*. The most striking exceptions were the few people who actually had some significant information about what was happening: the State Department Cambodia specialists, who stressed the limited nature of evidence available at the time we wrote and estimated that deaths from all causes were probably in the "tens if not hundreds of thousands," largely from disease, malnutrition, and "brutal, rapid change," not "mass genocide."

Such sources, however, were not useful for the task of ideological reconstruction, so they were ignored. And the tasks were serious ones. One crucial task was to suppress the hideous crimes that the U.S. had committed in Indochina, and even justify them by invoking the catastrophe when the U.S. finally withdrew. That includes Cambodia, where the U.S. air force executed Henry Kissinger's orders (originating with Nixon) for "A massive bombing campaign in Cambodia. Anything that flies on anything that moves" in rural Cambodia. A related task was to turn the anti-war movement into the guilty parties by charging them with denying enemy crimes and even for preventing (non-existent) Western efforts to overcome them. Amazingly, Western intellectuals even rose to these demands.[3]

When some information about East Timor finally seeped through the ideological filters, it became necessary to explain why the U.S. government had been so fully engaged in these terrible crimes—which went on through 1999—and why the Free Press had failed to bring them to public attention while focusing attention on crimes of the official enemy that were beyond our control. The obvious explanation, confirmed in innumerable other cases, could not be accepted. A "more structurally serious explanation" was offered by the respected correspondent William Shawcross: "a comparative lack of sources" and lack of access to refugees. In short, the extensive information in the Australian media was unavailable to Western journalists in comparison to the very scattered data about Cambodia; and it is far more difficult to travel to Lisbon or Melbourne to interview the thousands of refugees there than to trek through the jungle on the Thai-Cambodia border.

Most chose a different approach. James Fallows explained that the U.S. "averted its eyes from East Timor" and "could have done far more than it did to distance itself from the carnage"—the carnage that it was purposefully implementing. Later, in her famous study of our failure to respond properly to the crimes of others, current UN Ambassador Samantha Power wrote that "the United States looked away" when Indonesia invaded East Timor, killing perhaps one-fourth of its population. In fact, the U.S. looked right there from the first moment, and continued to for 25 years until finally deciding to end the criminal aggression by its favored client.[4]

The basic facts were never obscure, at least to those interested in their own responsibility for what happens in the world. When Indonesia invaded, the UN sought to react but was blocked by the United States. The reasons were explained by UN Ambassador Daniel P. Moynihan, widely lauded as a dedicated advocate of international law and morality. In his 1978 memoirs, he wrote with pride about his achievements after the Indonesian invasion and its grim aftermath, of which, he makes clear, he was well aware. In his words: "The United States wished things to turn out as they did, and worked to bring this about. The Department of State desired that the United Nations prove utterly ineffective in whatever measures it undertook. This task was given to me, and I carried it forward with no inconsiderable success."[5]

Khmer Rouge atrocities peaked in 1978, and were ended when Vietnam invaded and drove the Khmer Rouge out of the country. The U.S. immediately turned to supporting the Khmer Rouge under the name "Democratic Kampuchea," while continuing its support of Indonesia's ongoing crimes in East Timor. The reasons were candidly explained by the State Department: the "continuity" of Democratic Kampuchea with the Pol Pot regime "unquestionably" made it "more representative of the Cambodian people than the [Timorese resistance] Fretilin is of the Timorese people."[6]

The doctrinal system remained unaffected.

The pattern is pervasive. To move to another area, consider Latin America, the traditional U.S. "backyard." In Volume I, we reviewed some of the horrifying consequences of U.S. policies there from the early 1960s. The plague of repression that spread over the continent hit Central America with full force after we wrote, always with crucial U.S. participation and initiative. The general picture is well known to scholarship. John Coatsworth observes that from 1960 to "the Soviet collapse in 1990, the numbers of political prisoners, torture victims, and executions of non-violent political dissenters in Latin America vastly exceeded those in the Soviet Union and its East European satellites,"[7] including many religious martyrs, and mass slaughter as well, consistently supported or initiated in Washington. Needless to say, the conventional picture within the ideological system is reversed.

Another and related reversal is even more dramatic. In recent years, much of Latin America has broken free from U.S. domination, a development of enormous historical significance, illustrated in many ways. One has to do with the topic of our study. During the period we reviewed, Latin America was a primary center of torture worldwide. No longer. The extent to which that has changed is revealed in an important study by the Open Society Foundation that reviewed global participation in the CIA program of extraordinary rendition. This program, initiated by George W. Bush, sends suspects to favored dictators so that they can be tortured and might provide some testimony—true or false, it doesn't much matter—that can be used to expedite U.S. terror operations.[8] Virtually the entire world participated: the Middle East, of course, because that was where the selected torturers were, and most of Europe. In fact only one region was absent from the record of shame: Latin America.[9]

The implications are evident, and have reached the doctrinal system in much the same fashion as those reviewed at length in these two volumes.

Preface

This is a companion volume to *The Washington Connection and Third World Fascism*. The final chapter of Volume I examined U.S. intervention in Vietnam up to the collapse of the Saigon regime in April 1975, including its real and nominal purposes, the balance and interplay of terror and violence, and the images constructed by the propaganda system. The main body of this volume (chapters 4, 5, 6) is devoted to the postwar condition of the three states of Indochina: Vietnam, Laos and Cambodia (Kampuchea) respectively. The time frame of the discussion is from mid-1975 to the end of 1978. As in Volume I, the discussion has a double focus: on Indochina itself and on the West (primarily, the United States) in relation to Indochina. We will consider the facts about postwar Indochina insofar as they can be ascertained, but a major emphasis will be on the ways in which these facts have been interpreted, filtered, distorted or modified by the ideological institutions of the West.

Chapter 1 presents the general background. In chapter 2, we review some historical precedents reflecting our dual concern: specifically, we will consider the treatment of the defeated enemy during and after other conflicts, and the ways in which the Western intelligentsia have tended to relate to state power in the past. In chapter 3 we turn to the interesting pattern of responses in the West to the plight of refugees during the period under review. In this preface, we will take note of several themes that will be developed in detail in chapters 4-6 and also consider the Vietnam-Cambodia conflict and the invasion of Cambodia by Vietnamese forces in December 1978-January 1979, which brought to an end the first phase of the postwar era and set the stage for a new period which, we suspect, will bring renewed agony and bloodshed to Indochina.

The ferocious U.S. attack on Indochina left the countries devastated, facing almost insuperable problems. The agricultural systems of these peasant societies were seriously damaged or destroyed. Much of the population was driven into urban slums, in part, in a conscious effort to destroy the social base of the revolutionary movement, in part as an inevitable consequence of the unleashing of advanced military technology against defenseless rural peoples. With the economies in ruins, the foreign aid that kept much of the population alive terminated, and the artificial colonial implantations no longer functioning, it was a condition of survival to turn (or return) the populations to productive work. The victors in Cambodia undertook drastic and often brutal measures to accomplish this task, simply forcing the urban population to the countryside where they were compelled to live the lives of poor peasants, now organized in a decentralized system of communes. At a heavy cost, these measures appear to have overcome the dire and destructive consequences of the U.S. war by 1978.

Vietnam, in contrast, actually diverted very scarce resources in an effort to maintain the artificially inflated living standards of the more privileged sectors of Saigonese society, while encouraging migration to "new economic zones" in which productive work could be undertaken. "For almost three years, the capitalist heart of southern Vietnam remained largely untouched by the country's new communist rulers,"[1] a dependent and unproductive economic sector that the country could hardly tolerate for long. In March 1978 private businesses were closed in Saigon and measures were introduced to eliminate cash hoarding: "Convinced that a harsh life of agricultural labour awaits them in Vietnam's 'new economic zones,' thousands of ethnic Chinese from Cholon have fled the country in small fishing boats..."[2] The exodus was accelerated by intensifying conflict between Vietnam and China and by the disastrous floods of the fall of 1978, which had an extremely severe effect throughout the region, leading to serious food shortages except in Cambodia, which was apparently able to overcome the disaster effectively. In a sense, the refugee flow from Vietnam in 1978 is comparable to the forced resettlement of the urban population of Cambodia in 1975. Meanwhile in Laos, efforts to return peasants to their homes in areas devastated by the U.S. attack appear to have been fairly successful, and there has also been an exodus of more privileged urban elements to Thailand, along with a far larger flight of mountain tribesmen who had been organized by the CIA to fight against the Lao revolutionary forces that are now in power.

The West has generally assigned all the tribulations and suffering of Indochina to the evils of Communism, without, however, suggesting some different and more humane way to deal with problems of the sort that the West has never faced. Or to mention a still more significant lapse, while the West sanctimoniously deplores the failure of the people of Indochina to solve the problems and overcome the suffering that are in large measure a result of Western intervention, it feels no compulsion to offer assistance, either guided by the humanitarianism that is constantly preached or as reparations. Occasionally, one finds some recognition of this failure. Thus the editor of the *Far Eastern Economic Review*, while denouncing the "cynical policies" that have created a "loathsome" society in Communist Vietnam, adds, parenthetically, that "if the blame is to be traced further back to its source—Vietnam's switch to doctrinaire socialism and its economic crisis (and thus its

present dependence on Moscow) are attributable to those countries who have denied any aid or other encouragement to the
increasingly desperate appeals of the now-defeated moderates."[3]
He does not name these countries, but primary among them is
the United States, which has refused aid and sought to block it
from other sources, and has even rejected normal trade relations
while rebuffing all Vietnamese efforts at normalization.

The editor's formulation betrays a certain naiveté, typical of
Western journalism and scholarship. He does not consider the
background in policy for this denial of aid and encouragement.
A major thrust of U.S. policy has been to create harsh conditions
for its victims struggling to rebuild viable societies, transferring
to them the blame for their distress even when this is very directly related to imperial violence. This is the fate that a country
in the U.S. sphere must endure if it successfully exits from the
Free World and tries to use its resources for its own purposes
rather than adopting the dependency model favored by the privileged in the industrial societies. The policy of imposing hardship
was followed in the case of China and Cuba, and is now being
implemented once again to punish Indochina. While extremely
ugly, the policy is rational enough from the standpoint of the
leadership of the Free World.

Two interesting contrasts come to mind. After World War
II, Germany and Japan were given substantial aid, although they
were aggressor nations, with many of their leaders tried and executed for this crime, rather than victims of an unprovoked foreign attack. They were, however, under U.S. control. The aid
flowed because of their reintegration into the Free World and
serviceability to U.S. interests. A second contrast is between
Indochina and, say Indonesia or Paraguay. As discussed in Volume I, these and other countries in the U.S. sphere are major
human rights violators, but although Human Rights is the "Soul
of our foreign policy,"[4] these states are not only recognized by

the United States and trade freely with it, but they are also recipients of aid and special financial privileges. They only abuse
their own citizens or the victims of their aggression, while carefully protecting the rights and privileges of substantial foreign
interests. They have the "property rights" priorities that have *real*
significance in explaining the "human rights" pretense discussed
in Volume I. The contrast to U.S. Indochina policy could hardly
be more dramatic.

The media response to the travail of the people of Indochina
is discussed at length in this volume. The Free Press has fulfilled
its primary obligations to the state by averting Western eyes from
the carnage of the war and effacing U.S. responsibility. As noted,
all problems are attributed to the evils of Communism. The propaganda barrage has not only been highly selective, but has also
involved substantial falsification. All in all, the performance of
the Free Press in helping to reconstruct a badly mauled imperial
ideology has been eminently satisfactory. The only casualties have
been truth, decency and the prospects for a more humane world.

While all of the countries of Indochina have been subjected
to endless denunciations in the West for their "loathsome" qualities and unaccountable failure to find humane solutions to their
problems, Cambodia was a particular target of abuse. In fact, it
became virtually a matter of dogma in the West that the regime
was the very incarnation of evil with no redeeming qualities, and
that the handful of demonic creatures who had somehow taken
over the country were systematically massacring and starving
the population. How the "nine men at the center" were able to
achieve this feat or why they chose to pursue the strange course
of "autogenocide" were questions that were rarely pursued. Evidence suggesting popular support for the regime among certain strata—particularly the poorer peasants—was ignored or
dismissed with revulsion and contempt. The fact that peasants
in cooperatives were reported to work a 9-hour day, sometimes

more, evoked outrage and horror on the part of commentators who seem to find no difficulty in coming to terms with the far more onerous conditions of labor, often near-slavery, that are common within the U.S. sphere of influence, such as those of Iranian slum-dwellers or Latin American Indians described in Volume I. At the same time, any scrap of evidence that would contribute to the desired image was eagerly seized (and regularly amplified), no matter how unreliable the source. Ordinary critical examination of sources, indeed, any effort to discover the truth, was regarded as a serious moral lapse. Furthermore, there was substantial fabrication of evidence. We will review these matters in detail in chapter 6.

There has been remarkably little serious effort to try to determine or comprehend what really happened in Cambodia during the period we are considering, although a few serious scholars concerned with Cambodia have, as we shall see, tried in vain to bring a measure of sanity and understanding to the discussion. Some have also warned of the consequences of the hysteria that was being whipped up in the West. Charles Meyer, a conservative French specialist on Cambodia, who was close to Prince Sihanouk for many years, warned that the accusations against the regime in Cambodia might "become the pretext of a Vietnamese invasion for a pretended liberation of the Khmer people."[5] He urged a more rational stance, with an attempt to evaluate evidence and to consider the historical and cultural context. His advice and warning were ignored. Those who failed to heed such warnings by Meyer and others, preferring to join in the international hysteria whatever the facts, undoubtedly contributed to exactly the consequence Meyer feared.

Some well-informed observers give considerable weight to this factor. Nayan Chanda, analyzing the background for the Vietnamese invasion, suggests that of the many factors involved the most crucial may have been "Hanoi's feeling that politically it was this dry season or never," since the "international image" of Cambodia was slowly changing: "Some observers are convinced that had the Cambodian regime got a year's reprieve, its internal and international image would have been improved enough to make any Vietnamese drive difficult if not impossible."[6] But relying on the international image that had been created as of late 1978, Vietnam could still assume that it would escape serious censure. As the London *Economist* observed: "If Vietnam believed that, because the Cambodia regime was almost universally condemned, criticism of the invasion would be muted, its belief was correct." The *Economist* then indicated that it shared this attitude.[7] Whether peasants of Cambodia share it as well is another question, but one which is naturally of little concern to the West.

When the fall of Phnom Penh was imminent, the Pol Pot regime dispatched Sihanouk to present its case at the United Nations. Sihanouk had been kept under house arrest by the regime and obviously had little use for its leadership; nor they for him, given the long history of bitter struggle prior to the Lon Nol coup of 1970 as Sihanouk's government sought to destroy them while suppressing the peasant rebellions with violence and brutality. Nevertheless, Sihanouk declared his loyalty to that government and condemned the Vietnamese-imposed regime as mere puppets:

> I did not participate in [the Pol Pot] government. I was virtually their prisoner for three years and now I must come and represent them. I am a patriot. They are patriots...They are courageous fighters, I cannot say for freedom but for national independence.[8]

While under house arrest, Sihanouk obviously had little opportunity to observe what was happening in the country. Nevertheless, his reactions are of some interest. He presented a dual picture: on the one hand, oppression, regimentation and terror; on the other, constructive achievements for much of the population. As for the latter, he informed the press in Peking that:

When Pol Pot organized the working people, it was good. The progress in agriculture was tremendous and in industry it was good...I do not make propaganda for Pol Pot, he is not my friend. But I do not want to criticize without justification.[9]

Sihanouk reported that he was taken 5 or 6 times on trips through the countryside:

[The people] work very hard, but they are not unhappy. On the contrary, they smile. On their lips we could hear songs, revolutionary songs naturally, not love songs. I prefer love songs. I was a crooner, I composed many love songs, but the revolutionary songs are not so bad. And the children, they played. They had no toys but they could run, they could laugh. They could eat bananas, which they had in the gardens of the cooperatives, and the food of the cooperatives was not bad, naturally not as good as my food in Phnom Penh, but good... They are not fat like me, but they are not skinny.[10]

Suppose there was a reign of terror. How could they laugh? How could they sing? How could they be so very gay?...It seems that they are not terrorized. If the regime forced them to smile, we would see immediately that [the] smile is not natural, but I know my people well and the smile is quite natural.[11]

Speaking before the United Nations, Sihanouk described Democratic Kampuchea as a nation "in full economic upswing, possessing vast rice paddies ever more admirably and fully irrigated and innumerable fields where fruit trees, maize, sugar cane, all kinds of vegetables and other crops grow in great profusion ..." Discounting for rhetorical excesses in the context of an attempt to construct a case against the Vietnamese invasion, and noting the limitations on his information, still it is noteworthy that Sihanouk was offering a positive picture of the achievements of the regime he despised, rather than, for example, seeking to associate himself with the Cambodian group placed in power in Phnom Penh by the Vietnamese army, as he might have done once he had left China, or simply dissociating himself at once from the conflict.

Sihanouk balanced this positive account with critical comment. He qualified his remarks in Peking by adding that he was
speaking only about "basic rights" in praising the regime: "we are
not animals like oxen and buffalo which work in the fields making
rice. Yes, we make rice too, but we are not just animals."[12] He also
objected to restrictions on free practice of religion and "the right to
travel very freely, not to be confined to the cooperatives, to be able
to go to France for vacation, to roam freely...And the right to love
and be loved, the right to choose your wife and be with your wife
and children all the time, and not be separated."[13] At the United
Nations he expanded on the "subject of violations of human rights
by Pol Pot," describing his suffering under confinement despite the
privileges afforded him and his loss of contact with his children and
grandchildren, whose fate he does not know.[14] Sihanouk's children
by his present wife were allowed to stay with him, "but his two
daughters by a previous marriage were married and had to accompany their husbands to the countryside"; "He was unable to protect
them from the draft of workers for the rural cooperatives."[15] That is,
they became peasants, as did virtually everyone in Cambodia. Sihanouk also reported that he had heard stories of terrible atrocities
over BBC and Voice of America, but naturally was unable to verify
these accounts, which he said he hoped were not true.

Though Sihanouk's evidence was very limited, what information is now available—and it is neither extensive nor very reliable
for the most part—indicates that his dual picture may well be
accurate, as we shall see when we review the evidence in detail.
The positive side of his picture has been virtually censored out of
the Western media, at least until the visit by two U.S. journalists
in December 1978. The negative side, much of which Sihanouk
heard on the foreign radio, has been presented to a mass audience in a barrage with few historical parallels, apart from wartime
propaganda. It may well be that elements of both pictures are accurate. As for the negative side there can be little doubt that the

war was followed by an outbreak of violence, massacre and repression, and it seems that bloody purges continued throughout the period under review. It is also beyond question that the entire population was compelled to share the lives of the poorer peasants. The first of these consequences is an atrocity by anyone's standards, though, as we shall see, there are unanswered questions as to its character, scale, and locus of responsibility. The second is an atrocity by Western standards, though it is worth noting that the peasants may not regard it as an atrocity if others are compelled to live as they do, just as it is unclear how much they miss the opportunity to have vacations in France.

It is quite important to stress, in this connection, that while the West is appalled that privileged urban elements are compelled to live the life of peasants, it does not regard peasant life in itself as an atrocity. Rather, this is the normal state of affairs. It is not regarded as a continuing atrocity, for example, that "malnutrition is 'a chronic condition that seems to many to be getting worse' in areas like South Asia, stunting millions of lives by retarding physical and mental development, and indirectly causing millions of deaths."[16] While Western scorn and ire are focused on Indochina and its continuing misery, we hear little condemnation of neighboring Thailand, a potentially rich country that has suffered neither colonialism nor war—in fact, "for over a decade, Thailand's economy had experienced an artificial boom, due mainly to American military spending which accounted for half the growth of gross national product in the 1960s."[17] A confidential report of the World Bank gives a "damning indictment" of the policies of the ruling elite that have left nine million people—a third of the population—in "absolute poverty, while real incomes particularly in the north and northeast, have stagnated or declined." The report "may finally bury any vestiges of official optimism" on the situation in rural areas, where poverty is increasing to near starvation levels among rice farmers, while incomes of unskilled rural workers, a rapidly expanding group as Thai agriculture becomes commercialized, "are as low as those of subsistence rice farmers of the northeast." And as a further "price of 'modernisation,' in 1973 there were 400,000 drug addicts, 300,000 prostitutes, and 55,000 children under five who died of malnutrition." The World Bank study also explains the social structure and relations of power that lead inexorably to these consequences.[18]

As we have discussed in Volume I, these conditions, now extended over a large part of the Third World, are the direct result of U.S. intervention over many decades. It is an important part of Western ideological self-protection to present these effects as unexplained natural phenomena, not atrocities. Thus, no condemnation is leveled at the Thai elite for creating this situation and maintaining it by force. Nor has the United States become an international pariah because of its direct responsibility for the worsening conditions of the millions of peasants who are suffering in this relatively favored country.

It is hardly to be expected that peasants in Southeast Asia or elsewhere will be much impressed by the discriminating judgments of Western moralists. It is perhaps more likely that they would be impressed by the positive side of the developments in Cambodia described by Sihanouk.

The conflict between Vietnam and Cambodia, which entered a new phase in January 1979, had its roots in historical antagonisms exacerbated by imperial conquest. Although there were periods of cooperation in the war against French and later U.S. aggression, the relations between the Vietnamese Communists and the Cambodian revolutionaries were frequently strained and often bitter.[19] In the post-1975 period, the border conflict became the focus of these antagonisms, though the dispute ran far deeper. As Heder points out, "behind the current conflict between Kampuchea and Vietnam and their governing communist parties lie differences so profound that each revolution stands as an implicit critique of the other." With regard to the border issue, Heder points out that it

> is at once secondary and crucial to the conflict. It is secondary, because it is only a symptom of wider disagreements and because only a relatively small area is in dispute, despite the propaganda charges made at times by both sides. It is crucial, however, because of its role as a barometer for the Kampucheans. The government uses it to gauge Vietnamese attitudes, and the population employs it to measure the regime's nationalist credentials.

From the Cambodian point of view, the border conflict raises "intense fear of racial and national extinction...Although the Kampucheans may have fired the first shots, they considered their action a response to *de facto* Vietnamese aggression by long-term occupation of Kampuchean land."[20]

For the Vietnamese, Cambodian incursions had been a serious irritant since 1975, causing destruction and death, and sometimes massacre of civilians, and hampering projects of economic development. The problem became far more severe as the simmering conflict with China, which was easily detectable years earlier,[21] grew to significant proportions. This conflict, combined with the closing off of other options by the United States as described above, compelled the Vietnamese to ally more closely with the Soviet Union, while Cambodia allied itself with China. Thus the local conflict was further embittered as it gained an international dimension.[22] The U.S.-China agreements must have further increased Vietnamese concern over the unsettled and often bloody border conflict. Ideological differences no doubt also played a role, as did the very different character and process of the social revolution in the two countries.

A limited Vietnamese invasion was beaten back in December 1977. The full-scale invasion of December 1978 was successful in conquering the roads and towns of Cambodia and imposing a pro-Vietnamese government in Phnom Penh. Apart from that, its prospects and consequences seem quite unclear.

The 1978-79 invasion began, as had been predicted, with the advent of the dry season in December. U.S.-government sources reported on December 2 that "a full-scale dry season offensive by Vietnamese troops has shattered a Cambodian Army division in the worst setback the Phnom Penh Government has suffered in the 18-month-old conflict."[23] On the same day, a drive to establish a "liberated zone" was announced in Hanoi, in the name of the Kampuchean National United Front for National Salvation (KNUFNS) consisting of Cambodian refugees organized and trained by Vietnam.[24] Shortly after, Cambodian Premier Pol Pot announced a policy of "protracted war" in the face of the overwhelming military superiority of the Vietnamese.[25] An all-out invasion took place on December 25, and according to Western sources, succeeded in entrapping almost half of Cambodia's 30,000-man army, who were "believed to have been decimated by a concentration of artillery fire and aerial bombing."[26] A 100,000-man Vietnamese force backed by 15-20,000 KNUFNS troops and equipped with aircraft, tanks and other advanced weaponry proceeded to take military objectives throughout Cambodia, as the Cambodian forces retreated into the jungle, where preparations had begun months earlier, under Chinese guidance, "for a long-drawn-out guerrilla resistance."[27]

Credible evidence is so sparse that it is difficult to assess the prospects for this guerrilla resistance. As we write (early February, 1979), Western analysts are reporting substantial successes for guerrilla forces throughout much of the country, with the Vietnamese troops controlling the towns and roads and the Pol Pot forces moving freely in much of the countryside.[28] It is clear that the Vietnamese do not believe that the regime they have placed in power in Phnom Penh can control the situation. They have not withdrawn any forces, and in fact may have supplemented them.

According to the approved version in the Soviet Union and the West, the Cambodian people who have been groaning under their persecution should have welcomed the KNUFNS as liberators and turned on the handful of oppressors who had been subjecting them to systematic programs of massacre and starvation. Apparently, that did not happen. In a lame attempt to deal with their problem, some commentators point out that "although the Cambodian army is fighting fiercely, the farmers in the countryside are not resisting the advancing Vietnamese and rebel troops."[29] This is supposed to show that the farmers did not support the Pol Pot regime. Perhaps they did not, but this will hardly serve as evidence, unless the same commentators are willing to conclude that French farmers did not support their government in 1940—not to mention the fact that France was not outnumbered seven to one by Germany (or ten to one, if we believe the accounts of systematic massacre circulated in the Soviet bloc and the West) nor was it vastly inferior in armaments. Exactly how farmers are to "resist" armored columns remains unexplained as well.

Some commentators, apparently troubled by the failure of the population to turn against their genocidal leaders and to rally to the support of the new Cambodian regime that has liberated them from their torture, have sought other explanations. Henry Kamm, one of the major proponents of the theory of "auto-genocide," writes that "fear of revenge is believed to be inhibiting the growth of widespread popular support for the Vietnamese and the new Cambodian regime of President Heng Samrin that has been installed in Phnom Penh," a fact that will require Vietnam "to commit major forces indefinitely to prop up the Heng Samrin Government."[30] How the "nine men in the center" are to exact this revenge, given the assumption that the population subjected to their genocidal programs opposed them with near unanimity, Kamm does not explain.[31] In fact, the historical precedent is for a conquered population to accommodate quickly and without great difficulty to the rule of a foreign enemy or of imposed Quislings, as in France during World War II. Surely one would have expected an overwhelming and joyous welcome for the Heng Samrin regime by virtually the entire population if the version of recent history that Kamm and his colleagues in the Free Press have been propounding had any merit. The limited evidence currently available suggests a rather different picture.

The Cambodian resistance to the Vietnamese invasion of December-January lends credence to the dual picture described by Sihanouk. The Vietnamese invasion can be explained, but it cannot be justified. What its consequences will be, one can only guess. It may succeed in establishing in power a friendly regime that will be accepted by the population, or it may lead to the virtual extinction of Khmer nationalism, or it may set the stage for a long and bloody war, with agonizing consequences for the tormented people of Indochina and serious implications beyond.

The United Nations Security Council debate was a depressing scene. The *New York Times* reported an "anomalous air of jollity," quoting a diplomat who was enjoying the "wit and restraint" and who commented that "perhaps the world has grown up a little since those days" when the atmosphere was one of "grim tension."[32] To appreciate the "anomaly," one must bear in mind that the delegates taking part in the jollity accepted Sihanouk's analysis that the Vietnamese invasion was comparable to the Nazi invasion of France.

It is an open question whether the consolidation of nation-states in Indochina will proceed at anything like the level of barbarism and violence that characterized the same process in Europe or the United States over the past several centuries. Given the major and continuing Western role in contributing to misery in Indochina, the barely concealed pleasure over continuing tragedy is as contemptible as the deep hypocrisy of typical Western commentary.

1

The Setting

1.1 The U.S. Impact on Indochina

The U.S. war in Indochina began as one of innumerable examples of counterrevolutionary intervention throughout the world. As a result of the wholly unanticipated level of resistance of the Vietnamese revolutionaries, and later their allies when the United States spread the war to the rest of Indochina, it was gradually transformed into one of the most destructive and murderous attacks on a civilian population in history, as the world's most powerful military machine was unleashed against peasant societies with extremely limited means of self-defense and lacking the capacity to strike back at the source of aggression.

The main outlines of the U.S. war are well documented. After World War II, the United States determined to back French imperialism in its effort to destroy what planners clearly recognized to be an indigenous nationalist movement in Vietnam, which declared independence in 1945 and vainly sought recognition and aid from the United States. The French-U.S. repacification effort failed. In 1954, France accepted a political settlement at Geneva, which, if adhered to by the United States, would have led to independence for the three countries of Indochina. Unwilling to accept the terms of this settlement, the United States undertook at once to subvert them. A client regime was established in South Vietnam which immediately rejected the basic framework of the agreements, launched a fierce repression in the South, and refused to permit the elections to unify the two administrative zones of the country as laid down in the Geneva Accords (see Volume I, chapter 5). In the 1950s, the United States still hoped to be able to reconquer all of Vietnam; later, it limited its aims to maintaining control over South Vietnam and incorporating it into the Free World by any necessary means. Direct involvement of U.S. armed forces in military action against the South Vietnamese began in 1961-62.

Meanwhile in Laos the United States also successfully undermined the Geneva political settlement and prevented any sharing of power by the Pathet Lao, the left wing resistance forces that had fought the French and won the 1958 election despite a major U.S. effort to prevent this outcome. The United States then turned to subversion and fraud, setting off a civil war in which, as in South Vietnam, the right wing military backed by the United States was unable to hold its own. Meanwhile, Cambodia was able to maintain independence despite continual harassment by U.S. clients in Thailand and South Vietnam and an unsuccessful effort at subversion in the late 1950s.

By the early 1960s, virtually all parties concerned, apart from the United States and its various local clients, were making serious efforts to avoid an impending war by neutralizing South Vietnam, Laos, and Cambodia; that is, removing them from external (overwhelmingly U.S.) influence and control. Such an outcome was anathema to the U.S. leadership. President Johnson informed Ambassador Lodge in 1964 that his mission was "knocking down the idea of neutralization wherever it rears its ugly head." The United States was deeply concerned to prevent any negotiated political settlement because, as is easily documented, its planners and leaders assumed that the groups that they backed could not possibly survive peaceful competition.

Once again the United States succeeded in preventing a peaceful settlement. In South Vietnam, it stood in opposition to all significant political forces, however anti-Communist, imposing the rule of a military clique that was willing to serve U.S. interests. By January 1965, the United States was compelled to undermine its own puppet, General Khanh; he was attempting to form what Ambassador Taylor called a "dangerous" coalition with the Buddhists, who were not acting "in the interests of the Nation," as General Westmoreland explained. What is more, Khanh was apparently trying to make peace with the NLF, quite possibly a factor that lay behind the elimination of his predecessors. At that point, the United States, which stood alone in understanding "the interests of the Nation" in South Vietnam, had no alternative but to extend its already substantial military campaign against the rural society of the South, where the overwhelming majority of the population lived. The United States therefore launched a full-scale invasion in a final effort to destroy the organized popular forces in the South. The invasion was accompanied by the bombing of North Vietnam, undertaken to lay some basis for the claim that the United States was "defending the South against external aggression," and in the hope that the DRV would use its influence to bring the southern rebellion to a halt and permit the United States to attain its goals. This maneuver failed. The DRV responded by sending limited forces to the South, as most U.S. planners had anticipated. Meanwhile, the United States began the systematic bombing of South Vietnam, at three times the level of the more publicized—and more protested—bombing of the North.

The war also intensified in Laos, with U.S. bombing from 1964 and military operations by a "clandestine army" of Hmong tribesmen, organized and directed by the CIA to supplement the inept "official" army trained and armed by the U.S. military. U.S. outposts in northern Laos were guiding the bombing of North

Vietnam from Thai bases. By this time Thai and North Vietnamese forces were also engaged, though on a considerably smaller scale. By 1968, the United States was conducting a bombing campaign of extraordinary severity in northern Laos, far removed from the war in South Vietnam. By 1969 the sporadic U.S.-Saigon attacks on Cambodia had escalated to intensive bombardment, and after the coup of March, 1970, which overthrew the Sihanouk government, Cambodia too was plunged into the inferno. U.S.-Saigon military actions began two days after the coup and a full-scale invasion (called a "limited incursion") took place at the end of April—"limited," as it turned out, largely because of the unprecedented demonstration of protest in the United States. This invasion and the subsequent bombing, particularly in 1973, led to vast suffering and destruction throughout the country.

All of these efforts failed. In January 1973 the United States signed a peace treaty in Paris which virtually recapitulated the NLF program of the early 1960s. This was interpreted as a stunning diplomatic victory in the United States. The United States government announced at once that it would disregard every essential provision of this treaty, and proceeded to do so, attempting again to conquer South Vietnam, now through the medium of the vastly expanded military forces it organized, trained, advised, and supplied. In a most remarkable display of servility, the Free Press misrepresented the new agreement in accordance with the Kissinger-Nixon version, which was diametrically opposed to the text on every crucial point, thus failing to bring out the significance of the U.S.-Thieu subversion of the major elements of the agreement. This misrepresentation of the actual terms of the agreement set the stage for indignation at the North Vietnamese response and the sudden collapse of the puppet regime.[1]

All of these U.S. efforts dating back to the 1940s eventually failed. By April 1975, U.S. clients had been defeated in all parts

of Indochina, leaving incredible carnage, bitterness, and near in-
soluble problems of reconstruction. The United States thereafter
refused reparations or aid, and exerted its considerable influence
to block assistance from elsewhere. Even trade is blocked by the
United States, in a striking display of malice.[2]

Historical comparisons are of only limited value—too
many factors vary from case to case—but it nevertheless may
be suggestive to compare the situation in Indochina after 1975
with that of Western Europe as World War II came to an end.
Western Europe was, of course, a group of advanced industrial
countries which had, furthermore, suffered much less damage
than the peasant societies brutalized by the United States in
Indochina. Nevertheless, substantial U.S. assistance was provided to reconstruct industrial capitalism and to tame the labor
movement and the popular resistance forces.[3] The harsh winters
of the early postwar years brought Great Britain almost to its
knees, and years went by before the effects of the war in Western
Europe were overcome. The early years were marked by brutal
massacres, forced labor and "reeducation" for prisoners of war,
and other measures of retribution. (See chapter 2, section 2.)

In Indochina, the problems of reconstruction after 1975
were incomparably more severe. The destruction of the land
and the social structure far surpassed anything in the industrial
democracies subjected to Nazi attack and occupation. There are
still no reparations or aid from the United States, and only very
limited assistance from elsewhere. The most severe natural ca-
tastrophes in many decades have caused further havoc, as have
conflicts of an extremely serious nature between Vietnam and
Cambodia, and Vietnam and China. These conflicts the United
States regards with satisfaction. As Secretary of Defense Harold Brown explained in an address to the Trilateral Commission (composed of elite groups in the United States, Japan, and
Western Europe), the Cambodia-Vietnam conflict "does take

the pressure off ASEAN [the U.S. Southeast Asian allies]" while in the long run the "Vietnamese attempts at minor league hegemonism is [sic] likely to preoccupy the Communist powers in Southeast Asia for some time to come."[4] These conflicts are also helpful to U.S. policy by further impeding the difficult tasks of reconstruction and creating still more destruction in the lands ravaged by the U.S. military machine.

Vast social changes are imperative in Indochina to overcome centuries of injustice and oppression exacerbated by French colonialism, with its brutal and destructive impact on the peasant society, little recognized or appreciated in the West. Still more urgent, even a matter of sheer survival, is the need to return to the countryside the millions of people driven into urban concentrations by U.S. violence. The artificial Western implantations which survived on a foreign dole must be dismantled, and quickly, if the population is to survive. On this matter, all competent authorities agree. It is difficult to imagine how the task might be accomplished without considerable further suffering and disruption under the best of circumstances. Certainly, the far wealthier Western societies, which had suffered much less from World War II, would have had great difficulty in dealing with their far more limited problems without enormous foreign assistance, and would no doubt have been compelled to resort to Draconian measures.

It is worth noting that despite their enormous wealth and advantage, the Western powers have never conceived of undertaking serious programs directed to the welfare of the impoverished majority in the underdeveloped countries under their domination and influence, and would have no idea how to proceed even if, in some stunning reversal of history, they were to devote themselves to these ends. While Western elites are always keen to denounce injustice beyond their reach—from their position of privilege that derives from centuries of brutal exploitation—the task of overcoming degradation and poverty within their own realms merits nothing more than occasional rhetorical flights, and they have demonstrated their talents and concern primarily in devising new forms of brutality and oppression when their own interests are threatened.

Under existing conditions, it is not clear that the tasks facing the postwar regimes in Indochina can be accomplished at all. By the standards of Western European or U.S. history, one should expect brutality, oppression, and recurrent warfare as these problems are confronted.

While the countries of Indochina face their perhaps insuperable tasks, the United States and its allies have tasks as well. One is to reconstruct recent history so as to present their past role in a better light. A second is to ensure that the countries that have freed themselves from Western dominion face harsh and severe conditions. The reasons are primarily two: to teach the lesson that exit from the Free World in the interest of national autonomy is the worst fate that a subject people can endure, and to provide a *post hoc* justification for U.S. intervention by showing the awful consequences of its defeat. It is obvious that the most severe consequences have followed directly from the original U.S. intervention. It is beyond question that Indochina would be a far happier place if the United States had refrained from backing the French imperial conquest, or had been willing to accept the political settlement of 1954, the neutralization proposals advanced by everyone from de Gaulle to the NLF in 1962-64, or the Paris Accords of 1973. It is both irrational and deeply immoral for the propaganda systems of the West to pretend that Western sensibilities are shocked by postwar atrocities and suffering, a transparent effort to efface its own record of barbarism—primarily, though not solely, that of the leader of the Free World. But total irrationality has never offered much of an impediment to propagandists in the past, and as we shall see, it is no more of a problem in the present case. As usual, a fair degree of fabrication and deceit also comes in handy. Given the mono-lithic character of the media and scholarship, which tolerate little dissent, these efforts have achieved extraordinary success.

We will now turn to a more detailed discussion of some particular aspects of this amazing story and will see how these various themes run their predictable course in connection with each of the countries of Indochina, observing how the West is proceeding to come to terms with its crimes. In the course of this discussion, we will also consider some relevant background.

1.2 The United States in Vietnam: A Partial Victory

The war in Vietnam ended with a defeat for U.S. imperial vi-olence, but only a partial defeat—a significant fact. The U.S. Expeditionary Force of over half a million men in South Viet-nam became "a drugged, mutinous and demoralised rabble"[5] and was withdrawn. U.S. leaders had painfully learned a lesson familiar to their predecessors: a conscript army is ill-suited to fight a colonial war with its inevitable barbarism and incessant atrocities against helpless civilians. Such a war is better left to hired killers such as the French Foreign Legion or native merce-naries, or in the modern period to an advanced technology that leaves some psychic distance between the murderers and their victims—although even B-52 pilots reportedly began to object when Nixon and Kissinger dispatched them to devastate Hanoi in December, 1972 in a final effort to compel the North Viet-namese to accept a U.S.-dictated peace.[6]

The United States was never able to construct a viable Quis-ling government or organize local forces capable of maintaining the U.S. creation against its Vietnamese enemies. As Richard West remarks, "when the Communists launched their attack in March 1975 they were still outnumbered by more than three to one in manpower and still more in equipment, in spite of the claims to the contrary issued from Saigon," but "the South"—

that is, the U.S. client regime and its supporters—had "simply lost the will to go on fighting." Historian Joseph Buttinger comments that its "swift and dramatic collapse...was not the result of an overwhelming attack by superior military forces" and "came about because of the degree of moral disintegration the South Vietnamese army had reached in 1975" which "in turn reflected the degree of moral and political decay to which South Vietnamese society had sunk after years of increasing political terror, mass misery and corruption"[7]—that is, after years of U.S. "nation-building" efforts. As seen by T.D. Allman, one of the most outstanding of the war correspondents for many years, the U.S. policy of refugee generation created

> what Senator Fulbright called "a society of prostitutes and mercenaries"—and the caricature of civilisation produced in South Vietnam by the American way of war is what now accounts for the collapse of a state that never had any economic, political or social basis except that provided by the Americans. The South Vietnamese soldiers fleeing an enemy which has not yet attacked and trying to push their motor bikes on to U.S. ships sum up the product of American "nation-building"—a militarist society with nothing worth fighting for; a consumer society that produces nothing; a nation of abandoned women conditioned to flee to the next handout of US surplus rice; of dispossessed gangs hitching rides on US planes to the next jerry-built urban slum.[8]

The speed and character of the collapse of the Saigon regime came as a surprise even to the usually well-informed leadership in Hanoi, and even more so to Washington, where it had been "optimistically" proclaimed not long before that the regime that the United States continued to support in violation of the scrap of paper signed in Paris in January, 1973 was successfully eliminating the parallel and equivalent authority in the South (the PRG) with which it was pledged to accommodate, and would be able to withstand any military response to its program of undermining the Paris Accords by force and violence.[9]

But the U.S. defeat was only partial. To understand events in postwar Vietnam it is important to recognize that the United States did in effect win the war in the South. It did not quite succeed in realizing the grim prediction of Bernard Fall that "Vietnam as a cultural and historic entity...is threatened with extinction" as "the countryside literally dies under the blows of the largest military machine ever unleashed on an area of this size."[10] But it came close. As the full power of the U.S. expeditionary force was let loose against the South in the following years, there was substantial success in "grinding the enemy down by sheer weight and mass" in the accurate words of pacification chief Robert ("Blowtorch") Komer.[11]

The southern-based indigenous resistance, which had called for the independence and neutrality of South Vietnam at a time when the U.S. client regime (and its sponsor) firmly rejected any such outcome, was virtually destroyed, as was the peasant society in which it had taken hold. Hence both the military and political phases of the struggle fell under the control of North Vietnam, viciously attacked, with a large part of its above-ground physical structures destroyed, but never crushed as a viable society. Frank Snepp, one of the top CIA analysts of Vietnamese affairs in the latter years of the war, writes: "At the time of the Communist victory the party apparatus in the south was in shambles, thanks in part to the depredations of the Phoenix Program. The [North Vietnamese] army thus remained the primary instrument of control."[12] This consequence of the U.S. war provided a propaganda victory for Western hypocrites, who could now maintain on the basis of the direct results of the U.S. assault that the United States was obviously now "defending South Vietnam from aggression from Hanoi."

The propaganda institutions have, needless to say, lost no time in exploiting their advantage. To select one of numerous examples, the *New York Times*, in an editorial concerned with what is "to be learned now from Indochina," writes: "In Vietnam, clearly, North has vanquished South. The National Liberation Front that we would not admit to political power has been destroyed more surely by Hanoi than Washington ever dreamed it could be."[13] A marvel of hypocrisy since, as we described earlier, Washington didn't merely "dream" but effectively killed the NLF "fish" by the deliberate process of "drying up the water" (i.e., destroying the peasant society of South Vietnam); but consistent with a long tradition of apologetics the *Times* editorial conveniently ignores the background of the alleged takeover.[14]

A second aspect of the partial U.S. victory in Vietnam is that most of the country, along with Laos and Cambodia, lies in ruins, so that a colossal task of reconstruction faces the survivors. The sight continues to amaze even experienced war correspondents. John Pilger, who reported for ten years from Vietnam, writes after a recent visit that "much of North Vietnam is a moonscape from which visible signs of life—houses, factories, schools, hospitals, pagodas, churches—have been obliterated. In some forests there are no longer birds and animals; and there are lorry drivers who will not respond to the hooting of a horn because they are deaf from the incessant sound of bombs." Vietnamese authorities report 30,000 cases of permanent deafness among children from the 1972 bombings alone, Pilger reports. He describes napalm, especially created for Vietnam, that "continues to smoulder under the skin's tissues through the lifetime of its victims"; areas bombed more heavily than Dresden; cities, such as Vinh, bombed so heavily that not even the foundations of buildings remain, and where now people live on the edge of famine, with rice rations lower than Bangladesh.[15] These consequences of the U.S. war are also regularly exploited by Western commentators who point to the extraordinary difficulties in reconstructing some kind of existence from the wreckage as proof of Communist iniquity.

These partial victories are important. To preserve the image of U.S. benevolence, always a crucial element in imperial ideology, it is necessary to preserve in the popular mind the Big Lie that the United States was indeed engaged in "defense against aggression," as was constantly proclaimed by Dean Rusk, Arthur Schlesinger, and other propagandists.[16] As noted, the dominant role of the North in the final stages of the war and after—a direct result of the U.S. success in demolishing the South—contributes to the preservation of this myth and is regularly exploited to this end by journalists and scholars.[17]

There was an equally important benefit flowing from the devastation. Internal documents reveal that a major concern of U.S. planners has always been the "demonstration effect" of potential Communist success, which might serve as a model for nationalist movements elsewhere in Western-dominated regions. The primary U.S. goal in the Third World is to ensure that it remains open to U.S. economic penetration and political control. Failing this the United States exerts every effort to ensure that societies that try to strike an independent course—specifically, those that are called "Communist" in contemporary political jargon—will suffer the harshest conditions that U.S. power can impose so as to keep "the rot from spreading" by "ideological successes," in the terminology employed by U.S. global planners.[18] Though the United States was unable to subdue the nationalist movements of Indochina, it has attained its secondary goal. In addition to the immense problems of underdevelopment that burden the former Western colonies, the countries of Indochina must somehow confront the task of overcoming the ravages of the U.S. war-without reparations or aid from the United States, and indeed in the face of continued U.S. opposition even to aid from elsewhere.[19]

Now that the countries of Indochina have been pounded to dust, Western ideologists are less fearful of the demonstration effect of successful Communism and exult in the current willingness of the Western satellites of ASEAN to engage in "peaceful competition." In the London Observer Gavin Young reports on

ASEAN's program of obliterating Communism "not with bombs but with prosperity," under the leadership of the smiling, humanitarian Marcos, Lee Kuan Yew, Suharto, Hussein Onn of Malaysia, and General Kriangsak of Thailand (with his "dark, puckish face, at once warm-hearted and mischievous"). These benevolent leaders understand the priorities ("slum clearance, rural poverty") and are now firmly setting out to eradicate the ills of their societies, as Young discovered when he interviewed them on their golf courses.[20] No one without access to the golf courses is interviewed, nor is there any discussion of the conditions under which most of the population of these potentially wealthy countries live, or why this situation persists, or concerning the past and ongoing atrocities conducted by the genial golfers and their ASEAN colleagues under the Western aegis. Imagine what the reaction would be in the West to a featured article in the press explaining how wondrous Asian communism is becoming, based exclusively on interviews with Kim Il-Sung, Pol Pot, etc. The comparison, once again, is informative as to the true character of the Free Press. Equally informative is the fact that it does not occur to the author or editors to note that this willingness to "see which system works best" followed many years of "working to obliterate communism" with bombs, with an impact on the victims that has conveniently been forgotten by the Free Press.

The U.S. government also suffered a defeat at home, but again, only a partial defeat. In the 1960s, a mass popular movement developed, unprecedented in scale and commitment, opposing the U.S. war in Vietnam. Contrary to common beliefs, the articulate intelligentsia remained largely loyal to the state propaganda system and, with some exceptions, only rarely approached even the periphery of this popular movement. Their opposition to the war, which developed at about the same time and for the same reasons as opposition in business circles, was

highly qualified and fundamentally unprincipled: the United
States simply could not get away with what it was doing at reasonable cost.[21]

Typical current assessments on the part of U.S. liberals run
along these lines:

> The American engagement in Vietnam continues to seem
> more bumbleheaded than evil; the progress of the war still
> appears to have been based upon a compendium of false anal-
> ogies, bad guesses and self-righteousness. Much of this was
> termed evil at the time, but the name callers often created
> their own faulty analogies and exhibited notably self-righteous
> qualities...This assessment is made without regard to the "mo-
> rality" of the American engagement...Johnson's policy was not
> repudiated by [left or right wing] critics, but by the traditional
> logic of pragmatism: it did not work. The Tet offensive...pro-
> vided the most dramatic evidence. No one could say for sure
> whether the Americans had won or lost at Tet, because no one
> was certain of the terms of victory and defeat. Such ambiguity
> sits poorly on the American psyche.[22]

Note the quotes around the word "morality." Only the acts of
enemies of the state are to be assessed in moral terms. Note also
the initial finding of an absence of "evil," and the later revelation
that "morality" is outside the terms of the discussion. Apart from
the inane reference to the "American psyche," Ross' conclusion
is accurate enough. "The logic of pragmatism" swayed not only
Johnson, but also most of the liberal critics of the war.

To cite another example, consider the Op-Ed by Charles
Peters, editor-in-chief of the liberal muckraking journal *Washington Monthly* in the *New York Times* (24 October 1977). He is
concerned to "heal the terrible wound that [the war] left with
us" by finding "some common ground" between the "left" and
the "right," both of whom must concede that they were in part
wrong. The error of the right was "that the massive escalation in
1965 was wrong and that the effort to bomb the North Vietnamese into submission was stupid"; "we began to go wrong in 1965

with our campaign of mass slaughter against the Vietnamese. And we were wrong when we forced draftees to fight and die in what could at best be described as a morally ambiguous situation." The slaughter of over 150,000 South Vietnamese by 1965, the U.S. bombing of villages, mass forced population removal, the institution and support for Diemist subfascist terror in an effort to overcome the "disaster" of the Geneva Accords, the earlier support for French imperialism against what was always understood to be the nationalist movement of Vietnam—all of this was before "we began to go wrong." Furthermore, "We weren't wrong to try to help the South [sic] with supplies and volunteers [sic], any more than the American left was wrong to give such help to the Loyalists during the Spanish Civil War."[23] This much is "common ground."

Where was the "left" wrong? In that it "surely...must concede... that there was in fact a substantial part of the population who did not want to live under Communism. The left needs to overcome its racist tendency to say that while Europeans should have democracy, Communism is just dandy for those yellow people."

A complete captive of the assumptions of the war propagandists, Peters is unable to comprehend that opponents of the war were insisting that Vietnam should be left to the Vietnamese, not to whatever fate is determined for them by the likes of Walt Rostow, Henry Kissinger, or the myriad sycophants of the Peters variety. To regard that commitment as "racist" reveals moral standards that are quite on a par with the intellectual level indicated by Peters' belief that opponents of the war must now "concede" that there were many anti-Communists in Vietnam, a great insight, no doubt. His implication that the United States was fighting for "democracy" for the yellow people in South Vietnam is ideological claptrap, refuted by the consistent U.S. support for terror regimes in South Vietnam (and indeed throughout the subfascist empire, as illustrated throughout Volume I).

We may compare Peters' plea for healing the wounds of war with that of William Colby, as illustrated in this item which we quote *in toto* from the *Boston Globe* (15 January 1977):

> Former CIA Director William Colby, who directed the 'paci-fication' program during the Vietnam war, said the United States and the Communist government of Vietnam should forget past animosities and build a relationship of respect and friendship. Both countries should 'agree to consign the mis-deeds of the past to the mists of history,' Colby said.

In keeping with the same desire for reconciliation, it is natural that Henry Kissinger, who bears heavy responsibility for the In-dochinese slaughter, should be honored with the Humanitarian Award of the National Conference of Christians and Jews (*Boston Globe*, 17 September 1977).

Other journalistic commentary is similar. At the war's end, the liberal *Washington Post* warned that debate over the war must be balanced:

> For if much of the actual conduct of Vietnam policy over the years was wrong and misguided—even tragic—it cannot be denied that some part of the purpose of that policy was right and defensible. Specifically, it was right to hope that the peo-ple of South Vietnam would be able to decide on their own form of government and social order. The American public is entitled, indeed obligated, to explore how good impulses came to be transmuted into bad policy, but we cannot afford to cast out all remembrance of that earlier impulse. For the fundamental "lesson" of Vietnam surely is...that we are capable of error—and on a gigantic scale. That is the spirit in which the post-mortems on Vietnam ought now to go forward. Not just the absence of recrimination, but also the presence of insight and honesty is required to bind up the nation's wounds.[24]

Note the typical assumption that "we" decided to under-take and pursue the Vietnam War. Note also the crucial words: "wrong," "misguided," "tragic," "error." That is as far as "insight and honesty" can carry us in reaching our judgment. The *Post*, incidentally, does not assign a date to that "early impulse" to help the people of South Vietnam "decide on their own form of government and social order," a wise oversight on their part.

Similarly, the most outspoken dove on the *New York Times* in the latter stages of the war, Anthony Lewis, sums up the history of the war as follows:

> The early American decisions on Indochina can be regarded as blundering efforts to do good. But by 1969 it was clear to most of the world—and most Americans—that the intervention had been a disastrous mistake.

Our nation-building effort was "a delusion" and "no amount of arms or dollars or blood could ever make it work." The lesson of Vietnam is that "deceit does not pay." We should avoid mistakes and lies, keep to policies that succeed and are accurately portrayed; that is the lesson of Vietnam.[25]

The regular commentator of the liberal *New Republic*, Richard Strout, also sees the war as "one of the greatest blunders of our history." "It was not wickedness; it was stupidity."[26] These conclusions he wrote from Paris, where he had been visiting monuments to Hitler's crimes. The emotional impact was overwhelming: "I hated the maniac Hitler crew; I could never forgive the Germans." But then he "thought of Vietnam," reaching the conclusions just cited. The "maniac Hitler crew" were presumably not guilty merely of "blunders" and "stupidity." Strout does not raise the question whether the cruelty of "maniacs" is more or less wicked than the cold-blooded decisions and rationally imposed terror of Washington politicians and military bureaucrats tabulating body counts and contracting for improved fragmentation bombs.

We wonder how Strout would react to looking at mile after mile of lunar craters, razed villages, and the graves of hundreds of thousands of permanently pacified peasants. The beauty of nationalism is that whatever the means your state employs, since the leadership always proclaims noble objectives, and a nationalist can swallow these, wickedness is ruled out and stupidity explains all despicable behavior. It is only for assorted enemies that we look closely at *real* objectives and apply the more serious observation that means are both important in themselves as measures of evil and are inseparably related to (and interactive with) ends.[27]

Bertrand Russell was one of the few who sought to bring some understanding of this chapter in imperial violence into the public arena, unfortunately to little effect. In 1964 he criticized the editorial stand of the U.S. social democratic journal *Dissent*, which opposed U.S. withdrawal from Vietnam as "something quite as inhumane" as the policy of "hopeless attrition of the Vietnamese people." Their reason was that withdrawal of U.S. forces would "almost certainly" be followed by "a slaughter in the South of all those who have fought against the Communists."[28] The editors seemed oblivious to the likely consequence of a U.S.-Saigon victory, though the record of Diem's murderous assault on the opposition (with U.S. backing) was well-known. Particularly revealing is the tacit assumption that the United States has the authority to intervene to impose its concept of humanity. As the war ended the *Dissent* editors commented that the position they had taken was correct, though one might question "nuances."[29] In particular, nothing in the intervening years led them to question the tacit assumption just noted. If the U.S. government is to be faulted, it is for the manner in which it has executed its mission. Russell's warning and analysis went unheeded. On these crucial issues, the "democratic socialists" of *Dissent* adopt the fundamental assumptions of spokesmen for the U.S. imperial state. In 1978 they proceeded to run a symposium asking whether in the light of events in postwar Cambodia, we should rethink "our opposition" to the Vietnam War[30]—we will not comment here on the astonishing assumptions that even permit that question to be raised.[31]

To cite one last example of a record that might extend to

a full book in itself, consider the criticism of Gloria Emerson's *Winners and Losers* by Homer Bigart, the highly-respected war correspondent of the *New York Times*, for her intolerance toward those who find Vietnam "less a moral crime than the thunderously stupid military blunder of throwing half a million ground troops into an unwinnable war."[32] Had the war been winnable or had there been less stupidity in fighting it, then the original U.S. aggression and the consequences for the victims would have been no "moral crime," according to this again quite typical reaction by someone who is generally regarded as a critic of the war.

Throughout the war U.S. liberalism kept pretty much within the limits of responsible thinking, as defined by the requirements of state propaganda. At one extreme, there was Joseph Alsop, who believed that we could win, and at the other, Arthur Schlesinger, who expressed his doubts while adding that "we all pray that Mr. Alsop will be right" and explaining that if, contrary to his expectations, U.S. policy succeeds, "we may all be saluting the wisdom and statesmanship of the American government" in conducting a war that was turning Vietnam into "a land of ruin and wreck."[33]

The popular movement of opposition to the war was doubly threatening to U.S. elites. In the first place, the movement developed out of the control of its "natural leaders," thus posing a grave threat to order and stability. What is more, the general passivity and obedience on the part of the population that is a basic requirement in a state committed to counterrevolutionary intervention was overcome in significant measure, and dangerous feelings of sympathy developed towards movements of national liberation in the Third World. It is an important task for the intelligentsia in the postwar period to reconstruct the ideological system and to reinstate the patterns of conformism that were shattered by the opposition and resistance to the U.S. war in Indochina.

The task is eased by the absence of an organized left in the United States, either as a mass movement or among the intelligentsia. As has long been noted, the United States is quite unusual among the industrial democracies in this regard. We cannot explore the causes here, but one should note that state repression is not an insignificant factor.[34]

1.3 Picking Up the Pieces: A Return to Counterrevolutionary Intervention

Despite domestic opposition and protest, the basic institutions of U.S. society survived the Indochina crisis undamaged and unchanged. Since the global interests of U.S.-based multinational corporations that have led the United States to militarization and world-wide counterrevolutionary intervention are completely intact, we must assume that the same forces will prevail in the future to produce both direct and indirect intervention when the need arises. Even before the Vietnam War had ended there appeared a spate of articles in the U.S. press and journals, some by opponents of the Vietnam War, urging U.S. military intervention in the Arab oil-producing states. In a secret memorandum leaked to the press in January, 1978, Secretary of Defense Harold Brown "ordered the armed services to plan a special highly mobile force of up to 100,000 troops backed by air and naval units for possible rapid intervention in the Persian Gulf and other areas outside of Europe."[35] Commentators across the narrow spectrum of articulate U.S. opinion, who reflect basic power forces in the United States, are restless and concerned that the "Vietnam hang-up" may pose obstacles to the use of force to protect "the national interest," a mystification favored by ideologues to refer to the interests of those small groups who dominate the domestic economy and play a major role in setting foreign policy.

The more general context is an attempt to heat up the cold war, which has served both superpowers so effectively as a cover for enlarging the military budget and creating the psychological environment for imperial intervention. President Carter, despite his sharp expansion of military outlays and general moves to restore an atmosphere of great power conflict, has been criticized by liberals as well as conservatives for failing to develop a consistently aggressive posture and to proceed forthrightly to develop such new weapon systems as the neutron bomb.[36]

In a typical lament, a *Wall Street Journal* editorial of July 12, 1978 observes sagely that "in the past few months, the Soviets have been toppling Third World nations like dominoes" in accord with "their assessment that this President and this administration can be successfully bullied, an assessment repeatedly borne out ever since their brutal rejection of the new administration's strategic arms proposals quickly brought forth a U.S. retreat in the negotiations." The strategic balance is shifting in favor of the USSR, while "on the psychological level, meanwhile, the U.S. has been wallowing in the wake of Vietnam, reducing defense spending and dismantling much of the CIA." "To prevent even harsher Soviet bullying in the future, the administration should forget about travel schedules and get about such business as reversing the decision postponing the neutron warhead, building a workable covert capability for the CIA and accelerating the development of the cruise missile." In short, back to the good old days.

One must at least admire the audacity of U.S. ideologists. Thus, only a few months after the war in Indochina ended, we find the respected political analyst Theodore Draper explaining that the Soviet Union has "had much more experience...than the Americans have had" in defining their interests "on a global basis" rather than on a solely continental basis, for "almost six decades." As evidence he cites two examples: Russian support for North Korea and North Vietnam.[37] Surely these examples amply demonstrate how Russian imperialism surpasses the timid and hesitant United States in its extent, its scale, and the vigor with which it pursues its global objectives. Such amazing commentary, not unusual among the intelligentsia, can easily be understood on the assumption that the United States is merely engaged in "blundering efforts to do good" when it bombs dams in North Korea in an effort to starve the population into submission or drives the peasants of South Vietnam into "protected areas," not to speak of earlier efforts in the Philippines and elsewhere.

Even as the Vietnam War was reaching its final stage, Kissinger directed the CIA to carry out subversion in Angola and to support a South African invasion and attacks from Zaire, setting off a Russian and Cuban counterreaction in support of the MPLA in Angola—which, predictably, is regularly offered by imperial apologists as proof of the decline of the West in the face of Russian aggression.[38]

While President Carter has not taken a sufficiently militant stance to satisfy the editorialists of the *New Republic* and the *Wall Street Journal,* nevertheless on occasion he has been gratifyingly belligerent. In his Wake Forest address of March, 1978, Carter proclaimed that "for many years the U.S. has been a truly global power. Our longstanding concerns encompass our own security interests and those of our allies and friends beyond this hemisphere and Europe...We have important responsibilities to enhance peace in East Asia, the Middle East, the Persian Gulf, and in our own hemisphere. We have the will, and we must also maintain the capacity, to honor our commitments and to protect our interests in these critical areas." He also announced that the Pentagon "is improving and will maintain quickly deployable forces—air, land, and sea—to defend our interests throughout the world," and defended his increase of the military budget in violation of campaign pledges,[39] and contrary to *Wall Street Journal* fantasies.

After a brief eclipse, the "defense intellectuals" are once again receiving a respectful hearing from liberal commentators

when they call for the use of force to "ensure access to vital resources or to protect embattled investments abroad."[40] "Pauker
deserves praise," the liberal analyst of the *Washington Post* explains, "for defining sharply one alternative to [sic] a wiser policy." Stephen S. Rosenfeld is impressed with Pauker's analysis
of the current North-South conflict, resulting from "the present
stage of the political mobilization of the Third World, following
several centuries of Western dominance" (Pauker). "Pauker is
dealing with elements of the real world that too few other people
are willing to look in the eye," Rosenfeld admiringly reports, even
though "one can argue with this or that assumption." "Whether
our frustration in coping with [the postwar world] leads, with
Pauker, to a reliance on force or to new forms of accommodation is the question of the age." History gives a good indication
of how this question will be resolved, and how the liberal intelligentsia will react, when it is resolved.

The close association of domestic liberalism and international militancy is a familiar phenomenon. The liberal intellectuals of the *New Republic* circle took credit for leading an unwilling
nation into World War I (victimized, as they failed to perceive,
by a most effective British campaign of atrocity fabrication; see
below, chapter 2, section 1). In more recent times, the liberal
intelligentsia have given crucial support to programs of counterrevolutionary violence, justified in terms of "containment" and
the other instruments of cold war rhetoric. The euphoria over
Kennedy's program of militarization, international subversion,
and brinksmanship is a familiar example. In fact, the liberal intelligentsia were as critical of Eisenhower for his insufficient militancy as many of them are now of Carter for his vacillation in
the face of threats to U.S. interests.[41]

In summary, there is every reason to suppose that the traditional U.S. government policies of international subversion and—
when circumstances warrant—overt aggression will continue so

as "to ensure access to vital resources or to protect embattled investments abroad" or the opportunity for future expansion of U.S.-based capital. The sources of these programs in domestic U.S. society have undergone no significant change. And the intelligentsia can be expected to resume their traditional role, somewhat eclipsed with the trauma of the war in Indochina, in support of state violence and terror. They will construct an appropriate version of history and an interpretation of the contemporary world that will enlist popular support for these programs, or at least ensure a requisite degree of passivity and unconcern. It is in this context that we must approach the investigation of how the propaganda system is coming to terms with developments in postwar Indochina.

2

Precedents

2.1 The Intelligentsia and the State

In considering the refraction of events in Indochina through the prism of Western ideology, it is useful to bear in mind some relevant precedents. The first class of precedents has to do with the ways in which influential segments of the intelligentsia have responded in the past to abuses of state power; the second, with the record of treatment of former enemies after revolutionary, civil or other military conflicts.

Consider first the typical relations of the intelligentsia to state power. Quite commonly, intellectuals have a strong moral attachment to some favored state—usually their own—and have devoted themselves to lauding its alleged achievements (sometimes real) and concealing its abuses and crimes. At times, the "herd of independent minds" (Harold Rosenberg's apt phrase) has succeeded in virtually stifling opposing views. One recalls, for example, the reaction to George Orwell's *Homage to Catalonia* at a time when Stalinist loyalties were influential—one may also imagine how he would have reacted to its rediscovery and conversion to a cold war document when fashions changed. Similarly today, when "support for Israel" has taken on some of the characteristics of the earlier Stalinism of the intellectuals, it has been difficult for studies critical of one or another aspect of Israeli policies to find a publisher, or if published to receive an honest appraisal, in the United States.[1]

When the herd stampedes in a different direction for one reason or another, and service to some favored foreign state no longer has its earlier appeal, we enter the "God that failed" phase, which at one time had a certain validity and integrity, but now has become, all too often, a pose for those who adopt the more typical stance of the intelligentsia, namely, service to the propaganda system of their own state. To this end, it is often convenient to manufacture past allegiance to the current enemies against which recriminations are directed.

The normal case of straight chauvinist bias is, of course, of central importance in shaping the responses and defining the role of mainstream intellectuals, in part for reasons we have already discussed in Volume I, chapter 1, section 16. A primary social role of the group that Isaiah Berlin called "the secular priesthood" is to speak positively of the institutions and objectives of the state and dominant power interests within it in order to help mobilize public commitment and loyalty.[2] The adaptability of intellectuals to quality variation in the social order for which devotion is sought has proven to be very great—the pre-Civil War southern intelligentsia even found the slave system worth cherishing despite its economic inefficiency ("slave labor can never be so cheap as what is called free labor") on the grounds of its sheer humanity and social beneficence ("what is lost to us [from inefficiency] is gained by humanity").[3]

A further traditional role of intellectuals is to disseminate propaganda concerning the evil practices, real or fabricated, of current enemies of the state. It is remarkable to see how susceptible intellectuals have been, over the years, to the machinations of the atrocity fabrication industry. A classic example is the success of the British propaganda agencies in whipping up hysteria in the United States over alleged "Hun atrocities" during World War I, particularly among intellectual circles committed to war after the 1916 presidential election, which Wilson had won on a pledge of peace. "It was in the group known as 'intellectuals,'" H.C. Peterson points out in his study of British efforts to induce Americans to support their cause, "that the best body of propagandists was enlisted." These efforts resulted in "the enlistment of most of the leaders of intellectual life in America...it was an imposing propaganda group." "Prominent men of America hastened to join a cause that was intellectually fashionable" and "College professors and school teachers repeated with a great show of wisdom the arguments which had originated" in the British and French propaganda services, whereas "in contradistinction to the easy surrender of American leaders was the stubborn pacifism of the great mass of the population."[4]

Particularly effective among the intellectuals was the Bryce Report, produced in 1915 by a committee of inquiry chaired by Viscount Bryce, "a venerable scholar"[5] and former ambassador to the United States, beyond suspicion of Germanophobia, as admitted even by German critics, because of his long association with German universities and receipt of highest honors from the Kaiser. His committee also included other distinguished intellectuals and jurists. Its report was widely circulated throughout the world and scored its greatest success in the United States where it was widely printed in full and had an "overwhelming effect on the American mind and heart" (*Daily Mail*). Lord Bryce was initially skeptical of atrocity propaganda and hoped that his committee would "reduce within a small compass the burden of the charge," according to an associate. But he was convinced by the "compelling mass of evidence" that had been gathered and became "an advocate of a fight to the finish" (Read).

The committee relied on some 1200 depositions, mostly by Belgian refugees in England, some by Belgian and British soldiers, as well as diaries of German soldiers, regarded as "the most weighty part of the evidence" in the report itself. The depositions were taken by twenty barristers. The committee was aware of the problems posed by refugee testimony and raised the case for skepticism in the introduction to the report:

> It is natural to ask whether much of the evidence given, especially by Belgian witnesses, may not be due to excitement and overstrained emotions, and whether, apart from deliberate falsehood people who mean to speak the truth may not in a more or less hysterical condition have been imagining themselves to have seen things which they said they saw.

But the committee was so careful in sifting and evaluating the material that they felt they had overcome this difficulty. The 1200 depositions, incidentally, have not been found.

The report cites innumerable atrocities of the most fiendish sort. However, a Belgian commission of inquiry in 1922, conducting its investigations at the scene of the alleged atrocities, failed to confirm these atrocious crimes and was in general far more restrained. Read himself concludes that "the refugees naturally desired to convince their English hosts that they had fled from monsters," and discounts the Bryce Report, which, in retrospect, contains little that is credible. According to Peterson,

> A large percentage of the events making up the report was based upon second and third hand information. Rumors and opinions were included uncritically. It is not impossible that many of the statements used were the product of leading questions. Incomplete versions of actual events were the basis of the report. In addition, this official report of the British government dignified a great many old wives' tales and considerable barrack-room gossip (pp. 53-54).

Of one story, Peterson notes, "This, of course, is but a rewrite of a standard wartime atrocity story. Senator Cullen of Nebraska used it in 1898" (p. 55). Of another, "This story is undoubtedly the work of someone's feverish imagination" (p. 55).

The Bryce Report is perhaps the most important example available of a careful analysis of refugee reports on the part of a group attempting to assess the crimes of an enemy state. It was compiled under near-optimal conditions, and should be carefully borne in mind in evaluating such reports (or alleged reports) under far more ambiguous circumstances, from much more dubious sources.[6]

While U.S. intellectuals assured one another that the nation had entered the war "under the influence of a moral verdict reached after the utmost deliberation by the more thoughtful members of the community,"[7] it is not unlikely that the British and French propagandists who were feeding them myths about babies with their hands hacked off by German barbarians, etc., were laughing up their sleeves. Very soon, U.S. scholars took their own initiatives, as when a group of historians engaged in what one called "historical engineering, explaining the issues of the war that we might the better win it," produced such material as *The German-Bolshevik Conspiracy,* a series of forged documents (as was suspected in Europe at the time) purporting to show that the Germans had materially assisted the Bolsheviks in coming to power and that Bolshevik leaders were paid agents of the German general staff.[8]

As intelligence services have become more sophisticated—or at least, better funded—they have learned to play upon the willingness of the more thoughtful members of the community to believe the worst about official enemies of the state to which they are devoted. One technique is to arrange for "scholarly studies," such as the book by Hoang Van Chi which had such remarkable success in establishing the mythology concerning the bloodbaths during the North Vietnamese land reform.[9] Another device is to plant stories in the foreign press, to be picked up by "witting" (or perhaps, witless) journalists and others. The CIA recognized long ago that foreign correspondents are particularly susceptible to such deception since they so often tend to rely on local contacts for their "insights." If these locals can be enlisted in the cause, the news can properly be arranged at the source. Some interesting examples of how it is done appear in the memoirs of Joseph Smith, a CIA agent who was impelled by the appearance of Philip Agee's exposure of the CIA to write in defense of the Agency.[10] He describes, for example, how he enlisted a local newsman in Singapore on whom "the big-name foreign correspondents...relied...for all their scoops and legwork." One of the useful contributions of this subordinate was to file a fake story, attributed to British defense officials, reporting that the Chinese were sending troops and supplies to the Viet Minh just prior to the 1954 Geneva conference; the purpose was to undermine the conception of the Viet Minh "as a purely indigenous Vietnamese group of national patriots" by identifying them "with the world Communist movement," thus strengthening the Western-backed groups at Geneva, Smith explains. Other CIA stations were alerted "to have their press assets ready to pick [the story] up and make sure [it] was used in as many newspapers as possible."

There is little doubt that such intelligence machinations have influenced scholarship.[11] One of the standard claims about the early stages of the U.S. involvement in Vietnam, faithfully repeated by John K. Fairbank, Edwin Reischauer and other leading Asian scholars, is that the U.S. intervention was grounded in a "tragic error," the false belief that Ho Chi Minh was a "frontline agent" for the international Communist conspiracy—had we not been so naive and uninformed, so unpracticed in the ways of imperialism, we would have perceived that Vietnamese communism was in reality a national movement and been spared the "American tragedy" of Vietnam.[12] This claim is thoroughly refuted by the documentary record, which reveals that from the beginning U.S. analysts understood perfectly well that the source of Viet Minh strength lay in its credentials as the leading force in Vietnamese nationalism, and that after the United States determined to intervene, for quite rational imperial motives that are carefully outlined in planning documents and just as carefully excluded from the scholarly record, efforts were set in motion to establish the preferred (but false) "facts" necessary to justify this intervention, namely, that the Viet Minh were really agents of Moscow or "Peiping."[13] Mainstream scholarship can be trusted to conform to the requisite mythology, just as in the true totalitarian societies.

Smith is not the only CIA source for information on news management. To cite only one further case, consider Snepp's account of the last days of the Saigon regime,[14] also presented from a standpoint quite favorable to the general goals of the CIA though critical of its errors. He points out, for example, that the U.S. embassy in Saigon organized "a noisy press campaign around recent reports that the Communists were torturing and mutilating recalcitrant civilians in newly captured areas," in the hope that this would generate sympathy for the "South Vietnamese,"[15] but the campaign had the unwanted effect of sparking "panic and chaos" among "the South Vietnamese population itself" (p. 297). Snepp also cites his notebook references to the

> atrocity stories...now imaginatively embroidered by Saigon radio, the local press and the Embassy. At the Ambassador's orders, Joe Bennett [the political counselor] is still zealously churning out his share of them, playing on thirdhand reports relayed out of Ban Me Thuot by a Buddhist monk. "They're tearing out women's fingernails up there and chopping up the town council," one of Bennett's younger staffers advised me gleefully this afternoon. "That should turn some heads in Congress."

The ambassador and CIA chief, Snepp reports, "apparently consider the latest crop too useful to risk putting them to any...test" of veracity; again, he notes, the stories terrorized the Vietnamese.[16]

Perhaps the most cynical example of atrocity management that Snepp cites was "Operation Baby-Lift," which "in a sense" was "a fraud from the start," in which children who "had been languishing for years in Saigon's orphanages and were in no immediate danger from the Communist offensive" were, in effect, kidnapped and flown out of the country to the United States in the hope, expressed by Ambassador Martin, "that the spectacle of hundreds of Vietnamese babies being taken under the American wing would generate sympathy for the South Vietnamese cause around the world." Not all of them made it; over 200 were killed in the crash of a C-5A air transport, somewhat diluting the intended propaganda effect, though the operation continued.[17]

It is predictable that the exposure of such tactics from the source, as in the past, will have little or no effect in diminishing the credulity of Western intellectuals with regard to the next batch of atrocity stories. We have discussed other examples of atrocities management in Volume I, chapter 5. The will to believe patriotic truths and a positive desire to aid the cause of one's own state are dominant forces, and those abiding by such principles may also anticipate corresponding rewards and privileges.

The general subservience of the articulate intelligentsia to the framework of state propaganda is not only unrecognized, it is strenuously denied by the propaganda system. The press and the intelligentsia in general are held to be fiercely independent, critical, antagonistic to the state, even suffused by a trendy anti-Americanism. It is quite true that controversy rages over government policies and the errors or even crimes of government officials and agencies. But the impression of internal dissidence is misleading. A more careful analysis shows that this controversy takes place, for the most part, within the narrow limits of a set of patriotic premises. Thus it is quite tolerable—indeed, a contribution to the propaganda system—for the Free Press to denounce the government for its "errors" in attempting "to defend South Vietnam from North Vietnamese aggression," since by so doing it helps to establish more firmly the basic myth: that the United States was not engaged in a savage attack on South Vietnam but was rather "defending" it. If even the hostile critics adopt these assumptions, then clearly they must be true.

The beauty of the democratic systems of thought control, as contrasted with their clumsy totalitarian counterparts, is that they operate by subtly establishing on a voluntary basis—aided by the force of nationalism and media control by substantial interests—presuppositions that set the limits of debate, rather than by imposing beliefs with a bludgeon. Then let the debate rage; the more lively and vigorous it is, the better the propaganda system is served, since the presuppositions (U.S. benevolence, lack of rational imperial goals, defensive posture, etc.) are more firmly established. Those who do not accept the fundamental principles of state propaganda are simply excluded from the debate (or if noticed, dismissed as "emotional," "irresponsible," etc.).

In a typical example, when the *New York Times* (5 April 1975) gave its retrospective assessment of the Vietnam tragedy, it referred to "the decade of fierce polemics" (to be resolved in due course by "Clio, the goddess of history") between the hawks who thought that the United States could win and the doves who were convinced that the U.S. objective was unattainable. Those who opposed the war in principle—specifically, the mainstream of the peace movement—were simply not part of the debate, as far as the *Times* was concerned. Their position need not be refuted; it does not exist.[18,19]

An excellent illustration of how the ideological institutions operate to buttress the state propaganda system by identifying the media as "hypercritical," so much so as to endanger "free institutions," is provided by a two-volume Freedom House study of the alleged bias and incompetence of the media in portraying the Tet Offensive as a defeat for the United States and thus contributing to the failure of U.S. arms by their excessive pessimism.[20] The name "Freedom House" should at once arouse a certain skepticism among people attuned to the machinations of modern propaganda systems, just as any good student of Orwell should have realized that a change in the name of the U.S. War Department to "Defense Department" in 1947 signalled that henceforth the state would be shifting from defense to aggressive war. In fact, "Freedom House" is no less of an Orwellian construction, as its record indicates.[21]

The study in question is in the Freedom House tradition. Contrary to its intentions and stated conclusions, any independent-minded reader should infer from its 1500 pages of text and documents that the media were remarkably loyal to the basic doctrines of the state and tended to view the events of the period strictly from the government's point of view. But these facts, though obvious from the documents cited, completely escaped the author and his Freedom House sponsors; naturally, since they take ordinary press subservience as a norm. What is most striking about the study, apart from its general ineptitude,[22] are the premises adopted without comment throughout: the press is unjustifiably "pessimistic" if it tends to believe that U.S. force may not prevail in "defending South Vietnam," and is "optimistic" if it expresses faith in the ultimate success of U.S. state violence. Pessimism is wrong even if based on fact and in conformity with the views of the Pentagon and CIA (as was often the case, specifically, in the instance in question). Since optimism is demanded irrespective of facts, the implication of this study is that "responsible" media must deliberately lie in order to serve the state in an undeviatingly propagandistic role.

To summarize the first class of precedents, the intelligentsia have been prone to various forms of state worship, the most striking and significant being subservience to the propaganda systems of their own government and social institutions. This subservience often takes the form of childish credulity that is effectively exploited by the organizations that are devoted to atrocity fabrication and other modes of ideological control. Sometimes the credulity is feigned, as the propagandist knowingly transmits a useful lie. All of this serves as a warning that should be borne in mind as we approach the issues at hand.

2.2 In the Light of History

We turn next to the second class of precedents, namely, the record of retribution following other wars. Here, one must be cautious with analogies. The U.S. war in Vietnam—later all of Indochina—reached levels of savagery and destructiveness that have rarely been paralleled, so that one might have anticipated that retribution by the victors would also pass well beyond normal levels. Nevertheless, it is useful to survey some of these "normal levels," as a suggestion of a "base line" for evaluation of the situation in postwar Indochina.

To begin with a recent example, consider the immediate aftermath of World War II—recalling that the United States was never attacked directly (Hawaii and the Philippines were colonies), so that the more primitive forms of vengeance were not to be expected. The U.S. army of occupation in Japan, according to Japanese sources, indulged in rape, pillage, and murder.[23] But that, perhaps, is to be expected of a conquering army, so let us consider the cooler and more considered behavior of the political leadership. In Japan, "some 5,700 Japanese were tried on conventional war crimes charges, and 920 of these men were executed" while "an administrative purge removed over 200,000 Japanese at least temporarily from political activity."[24] Some of the trials were sheer farce; for example, the trial and execution of General Yamashita for crimes committed by troops over which he had no control whatsoever.[25] The principles on which the prosecution was based were outlined by Justice Robert H. Jackson in these terms: "our test of what legally is crime gives recognition to those things which fundamentally outraged the conscience of the American people...I believe that those instincts of our people were right and they should guide us as the fundamental tests of criminality."[26] As Minnear comments, "Law so defined seems little different from the Nazi 'law' that had aroused so much antagonism among the Allies," specifically, the Nazi law of 1935 which held that "whoever commits an action which the law declares to be punishable or which is deserving of punishment according to the fundamental idea of a penal law and the sound perception of the people shall he punished."

"None of the defendants at Tokyo was accused of having personally committed an atrocity," Minnear writes, but only of having conspired to authorize such crimes or having failed to stop them, and no evidence was submitted that such crimes were government policy (66f.). One Japanese general was executed on the sole grounds that he had failed "to take adequate steps to secure the observance and prevent breaches of conventions and laws of war in respect of prisoners of war and civilian internees."[27] Consider the fate of the U.S. military and political leadership if such standards were applied in the case of Vietnam. The sentence, in this case, was based on a split decision with a majority of 6 of 11 Justices favoring the sentence of hanging that was administered. On the other executions, the Court was split 7 to 4. The U.S. Uniform Code of Military Justice requires unanimity of a court-martial for sentencing to death and a ¾ majority for confinement for more than ten years (Minnear, 91-2).

Keeping solely to the Tokyo Tribunal itself, of the 25 defendants, seven were condemned to death by hanging, two died during the trial, and six more died in prison (31, 172); Prime Minister Konoe committed suicide when he learned of his arrest (105). Of the many procedural inadequacies of the Tribunal, perhaps the most striking is that no neutral Justices were appointed (let alone Japanese), but only representatives of countries allied against Japan, including one Justice who was a survivor of the Bataan death march (76-82).

Acts committed by the anti-Japanese alliance were excluded

from consideration at the Tribunal. As Indian Justice Pal commented in his impressive dissent, "When the conduct of the nations is taken into account the law will perhaps be found to be *that only a lost war is a crime.*"[28] There was, for example, no reference to the atomic bombing of Hiroshima and Nagasaki—though as Pal correctly remarked, "Nothing like this could be traced to the credit of the present accused," and as Justice Röling of the Netherlands commented some years later: "From the Second World War above all two things are remembered: the German gas chambers and the American atomic bombings" (Minnear, 101).

Though it is difficult to assign a measure, nevertheless it seems likely that Western racism was a factor, over and above the general submissiveness to the state propaganda system, in permitting the atomic bombing to be so quickly forgotten, or more accurately, unheeded in the West. One of the leading statesmen of the era, Canadian Prime Minister Mackenzie King of the Liberal Party, made the following entry in his diary on August 6, 1945: "It is fortunate that the use of the bomb should have been upon the Japanese rather than upon the white races of Europe." Such sentiments are, of course, not to be publicly expressed. In fact, in *The Mackenzie King Record,* the 1968 biographical project of King's literary executors, the sentence is excised, though the diary was kept as a record to "recount and explain" the conduct of public affairs and is described in the official Canadian military history as "the most important single political document in twentieth-century Canadian history."[29] The same distinguished statesman also urged in 1944 that all "disloyal" Japanese-Canadians be deported "as soon as physically possible," while those adjudged "loyal" should be dispersed. Though civil libertarian pressures in Canada prevented the enactment of this proposal or other racist measures of the sort instituted against the local population of Japanese origin in the United States, nevertheless "over 4,000 persons, many of them Canadian since birth, were shipped to devastated Japan in 1946-1947."[30] Such vengeful and racist acts in a tolerant and wealthy Western country untouched by Japanese aggression are not recalled, needless to say, when the time comes to raise a chorus of protest—justified on libertarian and humanist grounds that are foreign to Western thought and practice—against expulsions and oppression in postwar Indochina.

The deep moral flaw of the Tokyo Tribunal, noted above, also undermines the moral basis for the Nuremberg Tribunal, which administered 12 death sentences to Nazi war criminals. The chief counsel for the prosecution at Nuremberg, Telford Taylor, has observed that "since both sides had played the terrible game of urban destruction—the Allies far more successfully—there was no basis for criminal charges against Germans and Japanese, and in fact no such charges were brought."[31] The Nuremberg Tribunal was empowered "to try and punish persons who, *acting in the interests of the European Axis countries*...committed any of the following crimes."[32] The operational definition of "war crime" is: criminal act committed by the defeated enemy and not (allegedly) by the victor. Only a lost war is a crime.

Apart from the major war crimes trial, the Allies conducted a "denazification" procedure in occupied Germany which was described by General Lucius Clay, who was responsible for the U.S. zone, as "perhaps, the most extensive legal procedure the world had ever witnessed." He reports that "in the U.S. zone alone more than 13 million persons had been involved, of whom three and two-thirds million were found chargeable, and of these some 800,000 persons were made subject to penalty for their party affiliations or actions."[33] This procedure was regarded as an indication of the deep moral principle of the victors.

The same is true of current reaction to the Allied treatment of captured POWs. In Britain, there were some 400,000 German POWs. By Autumn 1944 they were being used for forced labor as a form of "reparations." Repatriation began in September 1946 and continued until the summer of 1948, over three years after the German surrender. After the war, too, the POWs spent the harsh winter of 1945-1946 in tents in violation of the 1929 Geneva Convention. The POWs referred to themselves as "slave labour," with some justice. A "stereotype" was "heard among the POW that 'a venomous re-education drove back to National Socialism many a man who had honestly been seeking a new way of life.' The stereotype endured in varying measure for the whole of captivity and, as an expression of resentment, beyond it." The psychological state of the POWs changed "from the anxiety and hope of the first half of 1946 to the depression and nihilism of 1948," according to Henry Faulk.[34]

The British government, naturally, saw matters in a different light. The general aims of the "re-education" program, Faulk writes, were "to present the British Commonwealth of Nations as an example of a democratic community in action, while avoiding the projection of Britain as a model to be slavishly copied." Faulk does not explore the choice of representatives of this "democratic community" as "guest lecturers." Presumably they did not include, for example, Jawaharlal Nehru, who observed that the ideology of British rule in India "was that of the herrenvolk and the Master Race," an idea that is "inherent in imperialism" and "was proclaimed in unambiguous language by those in authority" and put into practice as "Indians as individuals were subjected to insult, humiliation, and contemptuous treatment."[35]

In the case of Britain, the abuse of German prisoners can be explained, if not justified, as revenge for the terror Britain suffered at their hands (residents of Hamburg and Dresden might have harbored similar thoughts). But no such justification can be brought to bear on the treatment of German POWs by the United States. Judith Gansberg, in a study based on recently declassified documents, provides an awed and admiring account of an "unusual plan to reeducate the 372,000 German prisoners."[36]

"The reeducation program," she notes, "adopted at the urging of Eleanor Roosevelt, was undoubtedly a violation of the spirit of the Geneva Convention's provisions against denationalization. It was a massive multimedia effort to bring about a democratic trend among the prisoners which would not only change their views but could also provide a vanguard for redirecting postwar Germany" and "to return the men to Christian practices"(2, 110-1). It was run by a "small group of talented and dedicated men" and was a "unique experiment in political reprogramming" (6). Only "the most incorrigible Nazis—less than 10 percent—never succumbed to any efforts to reeducate them"(99). There were some difficulties in reeducation; for example, some POWs were appalled by the treatment of Blacks in the United States. But in general it was regarded as a smashing success.

The general tone is conveyed in a commencement address to the prisoners by Professor Howard Mumford Jones of Harvard:

> It may seem odd to appeal to the spirit of a prison camp and of a military installation, but what is the idea behind Fort Kearney unless it is the notion of human dignity and of the brotherhood of man? When therefore I say to you it is my hope, as it is the hope of other members of this faculty, of officers of this post, and of your fellow prisoners...that the spirit of Fort Kearney may go with you wherever you are, I speak for these, your associates, as well as for myself, no less than for the American government which has sanctioned this amazing enterprise. May you be each one, a good Christian soldier in the campaign against hatred and ill will. (p. 84)

The first list of names of Fort Kearney prisoners to be repatriated was released in September, 1945 (prisoners remained in the United States until July, 1946). In September, 1944, it was decided that "reeducation" was an inappropriate term. An office memo states that "the terms 'reeducation' or 'reorientation' of prisoners of war will not be used in referring to the mission of this Branch. The term 'I.D. Program' (Intellectual Diversion) will be used whenever reference is made to the program" (p. 89).

Reeducation and intellectual diversion were not the only devices used to return the prisoners to Christian ways. A field intelligence officer "admitted having shot a German captive in the head to induce his comrades to talk. But that was only a first step..." The British beat prisoners to get information. "Many stories of brutality were true" in U.S. POW camps. Prisoners were starved into collapse, etc., but no official actions were taken to modify these practices. In July, 1945 a guard strafed POW tents, killing 8, among other atrocities.[37]

In the United States, as in Britain, prisoners were used for forced labor. Truman delayed repatriation for 60 days for POWs essential for the harvest. POWs performed 20 million man-days of work on army posts and 10 million for contract employers (farm work, lumber industry, etc.). Some were assigned to work at the Chemical Warfare Center at the Edgewood Arsenal in Maryland (pp. 34-7).

The "amazing enterprise" of "reeducation" (rather: Intellectual Diversion) has evoked much admiration in the United States. Reviewing Gansberg's book in the New York Times (1 February, 1978), Thomas Lask writes that "it was a startlingly original notion to work at converting German thinking, and no praise is too high for those United States Army men and educators who conceived and carried out the effort." He notes that the operation had to be carried out in secret—"the Army did not want American POW's in Germany to be subjected to the same treatment." The book has some flaws, Lask believes: it did not, for example, explore "American innocence" sufficiently. But in general, the reeducation program must be regarded as one of the marvels of American humanitarianism.

To appreciate the quite amazing hypocrisy of this reaction—indeed, of the book itself—it is necessary to turn to the flood of denunciations of the barbarity of the Vietnamese in conducting a program of "reeducation" (which includes rehabilitation of the hundreds of thousands of drug addicts, prostitutes, torturers, and other debris left by the U.S. war), during exactly the same period. Evidently, it all depends on whose ox is being gored.

The aftermath of World War II was not limited to the pleasures of military occupation—pillage, rape, and murder—judicial murder, "Intellectual Diversion," years of forced labor, occasional killings of POWs in prison camps, massive purges, and other such humane practices for the defeated; and massacres, union-busting by gangsters, and so on, for victors with the wrong politics as determined by their liberators. It also included direct retribution against collaborators with the Nazis on a scale that is not appreciated in the West, though it has been well-documented. French historian of the resistance Robert Aron is one of those who has honestly faced the grim task of determining the facts.[38] He cites police and other reports of murderous reprisals up to "ten months after the Liberation of practically the whole country," including collective massacres discovered many months after when mass graves were located. Many of the facts are unknown because "the families of the victims had often been terrorized and preferred to conceal their misfortunes rather than go to the authorities." Aron cites journalists' figures of 50,000 killed but notes, correctly, that such estimates must be disregarded as "figures adopted lightly in a climate of excitement by which armies in a campaign or frightened civilian populations crystallize their emotions." He also cites the study of Pleyber-Grandjean (one of the "victims of the Liberation"), "who made an effort to give an objective account of a number of atrocities in *Ecrits de Paris*. The facts he gives are for the most part exact, but he exaggerates the conclusions he draws from them." Pleyber-Grandjean estimated the number massacred at seven million—no doubt an exaggeration.

Aron undertook a careful study, basing himself in part on detailed information provided by the French gendarmerie. He concludes that the number killed in summary executions just prior to or after Liberation must be at a "minimum...between thirty and forty thousand"—"Approximately one Frenchman in a thousand was the victim to the excesses committed at the Liberation." Translating to South Vietnam, where the war was far more brutal and the aggressors and their collaborators exercised incomparably greater violence than the Nazis did in France, we would have some 20,000 murdered at the time of Liberation, or, if we accept the figures of "victims of the Liberation" with the credulity typical of Western commentators in the case of Indochina, about 3 million outright murders. Fortunately, the Vietnamese did not keep to the standards of Western humanism.

We might add that the massacres in France were carried out during a period when General Eisenhower, under a directive from President Roosevelt issued with Churchill's approval, exercised "supreme authority" in France, and the "ultimate determination of where, when and how civil administration...shall be exercised by French citizens." The Provisional Government of de Gaulle was not recognized until October, 1944.[39]

Imagine that Germany had survived the second World War unconquered, but driven from occupied Europe, still a major world power under the regime that had conducted the war. How would these events in liberated France have been perceived? One can easily guess. The figure of seven million dead would no doubt have become gospel truth—much as Americans and Frenchmen now circulate figures with wild abandon about Indochina, as we shall see—and there would be no limits to the indignation over the barbarism tolerated (or, the claim would be, encouraged) by the U.S. occupying forces that had conquered peaceful France, overthrowing its legitimate government virtually without French assistance. Similarly, we may imagine how an undefeated Japan might react to the spectacle of the annual reenactment of atomic bombing, e.g., at a Texas air show in

October, 1977 with a B-29 flown by Paul Tibbets, the retired Air Force general who dropped the atom bomb on Hiroshima, before an admiring audience of 20,000.[40] Perhaps the Germans, in our invented nightmare, would have proposed a reenactment of the second major atrocity that we recall from World War II, according to Justice Röling (cf. p. 37, above).

But Germany was defeated and occupied, so we are spared such venomous hypocrisy.

But even defeated Germany provides some precedents. The *Washington Post* (10 April, 1977) featured a report from Dachau, which "in its own way is reflective of West German attitudes toward the question of dealing with the Nazi era." There is, for example, "no mention of the participation of German industry in the use of slave-camp labor. 'It is a guilt never acknowledged here and rarely spoken about in our history books,' says Barbara Distel, the Dachau museum director...'The general attitude really is not to talk about it, to forget about it if possible,'" she adds, in reference to Dachau. But Germans, even those directly implicated, are quick to concede error, perhaps even "tragic error": "Under interrogation in captivity Goering said that the liquidation of the Jews was a vast political blunder; many would have made good nationalists and joined in the liquidation of the Communists. If only Hitler had not confused these two issues, he said."[41] And then there is the man known as the "hangman of Lyons," twice sentenced to death in absentia by French courts for war crimes and now residing in peace in Bolivia, who concedes that "the mass killings of Jews constituted a grave error. Many of us SS officers believed that the Jews could have been put to better use building roads to facilitate the advance of our troops" (*New York Times*, 18 May, 1975). Not all see error. For example, the chief legal officer of Lower Saxony, who resigned in March, 1978 after the disclosure that in a 1936 doctoral dissertation he had advocated that "only a racially valuable person has the right to exist within the community. Someone who is useless for the community because of his inferiority, or even harmful to it, is to be eliminated...The law as a whole must serve racial development." But he felt neither "morally, nor politically" obliged to quit (*New York Times*, 25 March, 1978).

We leave to the reader the choice of appropriate current parallels.

Like virtually all wars of imperial aggression, the war in Indochina was in part a civil war. Substantial Vietnamese forces fought with the French, and the U.S. invaders organized a large and well-equipped—though unwilling and demoralized—army, as well as a network of terror organizations to assist them in destroying local resistance and maintaining the U.S.-imposed civil regime. Civil wars tend to be unusual in the cruelty they evoke. As a final precedent, let us consider a civil war that played a significant role in U.S. and world history, namely, the American revolution, an example that was cited by Bernard Fall in reference to U.S. propaganda about "outside intervention" (by Vietnamese) in support of the South Vietnamese who were being massacred by the U.S. invaders in South Vietnam.[42]

The analogy is far from close. The American revolution was minuscule in comparison with the Vietnamese in the degree of force used by those opposed to the revolution, and in the level of internal military and social conflict that developed. "The willingness of both British and rebel leaders to accept, if not always enforce, the fairly humane conventions of eighteenth-century warfare served to mitigate some of the radical effects that civil wars often have on society" (Shy, 200), and obviously the force levels were of vastly different orders of magnitude. In addition, the relative affluence of the American colonies significantly eased the impact of the war, although there was much suffering. Shy writes: "Revolutionary America may have been a middle-class society, happier and more prosperous than any other in its time, but it contained a large and growing number of fairly poor people, and many of them did much of the actual fighting and suffering between 1775 and 1783: A very old story" (173). Furthermore, "one measurable effect of war might have been to widen the gap between richer and poorer Americans" (197).

It is important to recall that the war "remained a civil conflict in America after it had become a struggle between the United States and Great Britain"[43]—and between France and Great Britain. "In proportion to population almost as many Americans were engaged in fighting other Americans during the Revolution as did so during the Civil War" (Shy, 183). The fact has seldom been given prominence, in part because so many of the Loyalists simply fled, expecting, as one said, that if the rebels should gain independence "that unfortunate land would be a scene of bloody discord and desolation for ages."[44] "Palmer suggests that, unlike France, the American counterrevolutionary refugees never returned, creating an illusion of tranquility and unity in the post-war Republic."[45] Van Doren summarizes the exodus as follows:

> There are no accurate figures as to how many persons including women and children left the United States on account of loyalty to the British Empire, but it may have been as high as 100,000, of whom 35,000 may have gone from New York alone…The expulsion was so thorough that the next generation of Americans, with few former loyalists as reminders, almost forgot the civil aspects of the war and came to think of it as a war solely against England. The loyalists disappeared from American history, at least from ordinary knowledge of it [until the 20th century] (433).

Recall that the white population of the United States was then about two and a half million, and that "at least a fifth of the white population—a half-million people—behaved in ways that enable us to identify them as Loyalist."[46] Comparative figures for South Vietnam would be about 4 million supporters of the United States and 800,000 refugees fleeing the victors. Comparative figures for all of Vietnam would double these numbers, approximately.

During the war, thousands of Loyalists escaped with the British when they evacuated some area, most coming to live in New York "in swarming desperation" (Van Doren, 12-13). Later, tens of thousands fled with the British, including "ragged unpaid American soldiers drifting down the Hudson Valley to sign on as sailors in the ships which were evacuating British forces"(Shy, 17). "Genuine support for the war appears to have declined" from 1775, Shy writes, as people "grew weary of being bullied by local committees of safety, by corrupt deputy assistant commissaries of supply, and by bands of ragged strangers with guns in their hands calling themselves soldiers of the Revolution," and "got angry when British or Hessian or Tory troops misbehaved... The years from 1776 to 1782 might indeed be recounted as horror stories of terrorism, rapacity, mendacity, and cowardice, not to blame our ancestors for these things, but to remind us what a war fought by the weak must look like" (Shy, 13f.).

Both Loyalists and rebels "gave credit and currency to stories of inhuman deeds done by either to the other," and the Loyalists argued "that the American governments were more oppressive than the British had ever been" (Van Doren, 120). In particular, the British "had frequently upheld the rights of the Indians against encroaching American settlers" (*ibid.*, 120), one reason why many Indian tribes supported the British, as did many Blacks, recognizing what lay ahead for them if the rebels proved victorious.[47] In areas where the British "hardly appeared or not at all," "Tories either ran away, kept quiet, even serving in the rebel armies, or occasionally took a brave but hopeless stand against Revolutionary committees and their gunmen" (Shy, 178). Meanwhile, at home, the British government attempted "to justify a long expensive war to an unhappy public on the ground that the king had a solemn commitment to defend his numerous American supporters against a rebel bloodbath" (Shy, 185). How familiar it all sounds.

Some of the most graphic accounts of the nature of the civil conflict are found in the letters of General Nathanael Greene, who commanded the southern Continental Army from 1780 to 1783.[48] Greene wrote:

> ...the whigs and tories pursue one another with the most relentless fury killing and destroying each other whenever they meet. Indeed, a great part of this country is already laid waste and in the utmost danger of becoming a desert. The great bodies of militia that have been in service this year employed against the enemy and in quelling the tories have almost laid waste the country and so corrupted the principles of the people that they think of nothing but plundering one another...The country is full of little armed parties who follow their resentments with little less than savage fury...[the South is] still torn to pieces by little parties of disaffected who elude all search and conceal themselves in the thickets and swamps from the most diligent pursuit and issue forth from these hidden recesses committing the most horrid murders and plunder and lay waste the country (pp. 294-5).

Greene employed terrorism both to improve the morale of his supporters and to frighten the "disaffected." He told his subordinate, General Thomas Sumter, that partisans were "to strike terror into our enemies and give spirit to our friends" (308). An example was a successful raid that Greene described to Thomas Jefferson as follows:

> They made a dreadful carnage of them, upwards on one-hundred were killed and most of the rest cut to pieces. It has had a very happy effect on those disaffected persons of which there are too many in this country (p. 308).

But Greene also recognized that terror was a dubious tactic. In 1781 he outlined a new strategy to Sumter in the following terms:

> Don't spare any pains to take off the tories from the British interest for tho we have great reason to hate them and vengeance would dictate one universal slaughter yet when we

consider how many of our good people must fall a sacrifice in doing it we shall find it will be more for our interest to forgive than to persecute. This was always my opinion and if the war continues in this country, unless we can detach the people from the British interest we shall feel more inconveniences from them than from all the British army. Indeed we do now (p. 310).

Loyalist sympathies were sufficiently strong so that a British secret agent expressed his conviction that the British could raise a Provincial army strong enough to defeat Washington, whose troops were not, "as has been represented, a respectable body of yeomanry...but a contemptible band of vagrants, deserters, and thieves," mainly Irish (Van Doren, 110). The British did attempt "Americanization" of the war in the latter stages, in part because of the "unhappy public" at home (Shy, 185). The secret agent's judgment might have proven valid had it not been for the French intervention supporting the insurgency—what would now be called "terrorist bands." As it was, "New York alone furnished about 15,000 men to the British army and navy, and over 8,000 loyalist militia." With the contribution of the other colonies, "we may safely state that 50,000 soldiers, either regular or militia, were drawn into the service of Great Britain from her American sympathizers" (Van Tyne, 182-3).

During the war, the "persecuted tories had a sanctuary" in New York, to which they fled "from every colony...by boat, on foot, in carriage or on horse, ready to thank God when they had passed the British lines, and had left behind them the din of persecution," including tarring and feathering, "hoisting the victim upon a liberty pole," forced oaths of loyalty, jailing for long periods without trial, confiscation of lands, and other forms of oppression and terror. Many were prevented from fleeing, others driven out. "The records kept by the committees of safety prove, beyond the possibility of doubt, the Tory charges that committee rule was despotic and tyrannous," while "from the Tory pen we have a picture of an inexorable reign of terror" (Van Tyne, pp. 128, 61, 66, 230). While few were actually killed, many were tried and sentenced—Washington noted in a letter that "one or two have done what a great number ought to have done long ago, commit suicide"—referring to these "miserable set of beings," "these wretched creatures" who retained their loyalty to the crown (ibid., p. 57).[49]

Many fled abroad to await the outcome of the war, choosing to commit themselves "to the mercy of the waves at a tempestuous season rather than meet their offending countrymen," as one Tory wrote (Van Tyne, 57). The largest fleet ever seen in America, more than 170 sail, departed in March, "the most tempestuous month of the year on the American coast," fearing that "without a miracle the wretched fleet must be dispersed and lost...on their top-heavy decks were huddled a wretched throng of soldiers and refugees...It was impossible, thought one of them, that more events could concur to render their distress complete, and their ruin almost inevitable" (ibid., 58). "Sir Henry Clinton wrote that nothing distressed him so much as the applications he hourly received from great numbers of refugees who crowded to New York from every quarter of America. Many, he said, had been reduced from affluent circumstances to the utmost penury by their attachment to the king" (ibid., 254). As the British were withdrawn, more refugees fled, primarily to British American territories, including Nova Scotia, which one described as "the most inhospitable clime that ever mortal set foot on" (ibid., 294). There, "women, delicately reared, cared for their infants beneath canvas tents, rendered habitable only by the banks of snow which lay six feet deep" while "strong and proud men wept like children, and lay down in their snow-bound tents to die" (ibid., 305).

But the "boat people" were perhaps more fortunate than those who remained. In violation of the treaty with the British and in spite of the recommendation of Congress, after the war "confiscation still went on actively; governors of the states were urged to exchange lists of the proscribed persons, that no Tory might find a resting place in the United States; and in nearly every state they were disfranchised, while in many localities they were tarred and feathered, driven from town and warned never to return," or sometimes murdered (*ibid.*, 295).

One can imagine what a British Henry Kamm[50] would have made of all of this. We also note that these aspects of the Revolutionary War are not exactly centerpieces of school textbooks describing the struggle of "Americans" for freedom from onerous foreign rule.

We stress again that the analogy to Indochina, which will be obvious to any reader of the daily press, should not be drawn too closely. There are many crucial points of difference. The American rebels, as noted, were supported—indeed far outnumbered—by the military forces of France, while no foreign troops were engaged on the side of the Vietnamese. The force brought to bear by the British and their local allies was infinitesimal as compared with Westmoreland's killing machine, and in fact the civil conflict enflamed by foreign aggression from 1946 was also, naturally, far more fierce, given the nature of the intervention by France and the United States (and in the early stages, Britain, which prepared the way for the return of French imperialism). Vietnam is far poorer than the American colonies, which were already ranked high among the more affluent societies in the world, and its foreign enemy vastly richer and more powerful, as well as incomparably more savage. Nor is there in Indochina anything comparable to the exploitation of Blacks and persecution of native Americans. Despite these and other crucial differences, it is nevertheless interesting to recall this example of a civil conflict enmeshed in a struggle for national independence, and its consequences for the victims—Loyalists, Blacks and Native Americans.[51]

To conclude, we note that it is standard in later scholarly

work in American history to recount, in part at least, the torment
of Native Americans and Blacks at the hands of the victors in the
revolutionary struggle, though it is equally common to describe
this oppression, far from ended, as an unfortunate "exception" to
the general humanism of the American experience. In a review
of a book that is "rooted in the familiar nationalistic strains of
Daniel Boorstin's view of U.S. political history," Clarence Karier
makes the following apt comment:

> For the Irish who died building the railroads and canals in the
> East, the children who died in the coal mines of Pennsylvania,
> the women who died chained to their machines in factories,
> the Polish laborers burned to death in the steel mills of Gary,
> the Indians wasted by the Gatling gun in the West, or the
> slave who felt the white man's lash, Cremin enters the "caveat"
> that these were "inexcusable omissions." When, one might ask,
> do these "inexcusable omissions" cease to be "omissions" and
> when do they become an organic part of American history?[52]

This point might be borne in mind, along with the historical
background just recounted, when we turn to the question of
how the Indochinese peoples are facing their incomparably more
severe problems, unrelated to anything in the U.S. experience
not only because of the destructive impact of colonialism and
the absence of the immense natural advantages of the American
colonists, but also because they have been subjected to murderous destruction, the likes of which the world has rarely seen, on
the part of those who now feel no shame when they let the words
"human rights" fall from their lips.

Many other examples of a similar sort may be cited. The
historical record serves as a kind of "base line" against which
we may evaluate events in postwar Indochina. To repeat, while
Western propaganda attributes the suffering of the people of
Indochina—those who flee the war or its aftermath, those who
are persecuted within, and the vast majority who are attempting to reconstruct some sort of viable existence from the wreck-

age—to the evil effects of Communist ideology or the generally "uncivilized" character of the Third World, which has failed, to our dismay, to absorb Western humanism, an honest historical analysis would proceed quite differently. It would begin by establishing the common practice in comparable situations, then add an enormous increment attributable to the unusual barbarity of the U.S. attack with its legacy of destruction, bitterness and hatred. Atrocities and oppression that exceed this measure might reasonably be attributed to Indochinese communism.

Applying these standards to Vietnam, there seems little doubt that the aftermath of the revolutionary victory has been remarkably free of vengefulness. The same is true in Laos. No doubt Cambodia differs, even when one discounts for the stream of falsification in Western propaganda. Finally, in evaluating these painful and troubled issues, we must bear in mind the long record of atrocity fabrication and the traditional gullibility of the intelligentsia regarding the alleged evil practices of enemies of their own state.

3

Refugees: Indochina and Beyond

We now turn to the central topic of this volume, the nature of the evidence that has been presented in the West with regard to postwar Indochina, the uses to which such evidence is being put, and the significance of these facts.

One major focus of concern and outrage in the West has been the continuing flight of refugees from Indochina. In a review that is unusual in its honesty, the London *Economist* reports that:

> 16,000 boat people [from Vietnam] have landed in neighbouring south-east Asian countries so far this year; the monthly rate has increased from 980 in December to 6,000 in May. Partly because of the wide publicity these doughty seafarers have received, partly because refugees from Vietnam tend to have other advantages (gold bars, skills, relatives in America), a remarkable high proportion of the Vietnamese who have escaped since the spring of 1975 have been permanently resettled. Only 12,000 boat people (10,000 of them in Malaysia) and a few thousand other Vietnamese are currently waiting for a place to go...Thailand, by geographical ill-fortune, is still today the largest repository of unsettled Indochinese refugees, with 100,000 people registered in refugee camps. The great majority of these—83,500 Laotians and 14,000 Cambodians, who are mostly tribesmen and illiterate farmers—have little chance of moving on.[1]

The *Economist* is certainly correct in adding that "there is room for far more generosity" from the West with regard to these unfortunate victims.

What is unusual about the *Economist* report is that it is not limited to refugees from postwar Communism, as is the general practice. The *Economist* observes that "nearly 400,000 people have walked or sailed away from their home countries since the beginning of the year" in Asia[2] (far less than Africa, where the same report estimates the number of refugees at 2 million).[3] "The biggest single group," the report continues, are the Muslim Bengali people who have been fleeing from Burma to Bangladesh at the rate of about 2,000 a day. A June 24 report in the *Economist* estimates their number at 175,000. An earlier report of June 10 reports that they arrive in Bangladesh "bearing gruesome tales of atrocities committed by advancing waves of Burmese soldiers" and that they are being forced off their lands by Buddhist tribesmen.

We learn more about the refugees from Burma elsewhere in the foreign press. Richard Nations reports in the *Far Eastern Economic Review* (30 June 1978) that 200,000 refugees fled from Burmese terror in two months—a far higher rate than the 2,000 per day estimated by the *Economist*. During the initial phase of the flight, the rate was 8,000 per day according to "one United Nations veteran of relief operations throughout the world," who described the camps where they were kept "as absolute death traps—the worst I've ever seen," though there was improvement later. Nations continues: "Refugees tell of atrocities, rape, indiscriminate arrest, desecration of mosques and razing of villages by Burmese soldiers and local Mogh (Arakanese Buddhist) chauvinists," circumstances far worse than anything reported from Vietnam. William Mattern comments in the same journal that the fate of the "200,000 or more Burmese Muslim refugees now in Bangladesh" can be traced in part to a civil conflict that erupted during World War II, when the British organized the

Muslim community to fight the Japanese who were supported by the Burmese Buddhists in the Arakan mountains, leading to "one of the bloodiest communal riots in South Asian annals."[4] By the end of September, only about 250 of the refugees had returned home, according to unofficial reports in Rangoon, even though "in the squalor of the camps on the Bangladesh side, a return to their small farms and shops in Arakan—however impoverished—must have some attraction even for the downtrodden Muslims." Informed observers believe that "certainly, someone put fear into the hearts of the Muslims of Arakan—and is keeping it there."[5]

These 200,000 refugees of April-May 1978 were not totally ignored in the U.S. press. On May 1, the *New York Times* devoted 150 words on p. 13 to a report that 70,000 refugees had fled in three weeks, bringing "tales of torture, rape and robbery," including more than 18,000 in the preceding 24-hour period. They fled despite the efforts by Bangladesh forces to seal the borders and turn back illegal immigrants. "One refugee asserted that the [Burmese] army had launched an operation to clear the border area of the Moslem community that was not originally Burmese." Brief mention of this vast refugee flow also appears in subsequent stories. Humanitarians concerned with the suffering people of Asia, particularly the refugees from brutal atrocities and oppression, were clearly alerted to the existence of a major disaster, but the response was undetectable.

Returning to the London *Economist* report of June 17 on refugees, it points out further that 110,000 Chinese residents fled from Vietnam to China after the government cracked down on the black market and other illegal practices and nationalized businesses in the South; ethnic Chinese, the report notes, have been the most frequent "target of local hostility" in Asia, the most extreme example being the massacre in Indonesia in 1965-66.[6] Since the fall of Saigon and Phnom Penh, the report continues, more than 200,000 refugees have fled from Indochina to neighboring countries—a substantial number, though, as we have seen, small by such historical standards as the American revolution, both in proportion to the total population and relative to the character of the conflict. In addition, some 150,000 Cambodians, including 20,000 ethnic Chinese, have fled to Vietnam.

The *Economist* does not mention the refugees who fled from the Philippines to Sabah at an estimated rate of 400 a day, some 140,000 by mid-1977, constituting 14% of the population of the Sabah. The Malaysian government has agreed to allow 90,000 to remain.[7] Nor does it discuss the refugees fleeing from Indonesian terror in Timor—or according to the Western-approved version, fleeing from the fierce guerrillas who have "forced them" to live under their control—so that they can be "protected" by the Indonesians (see Volume I, chapter 3, section 4.4).

As for Vietnam, "Most of the refugees appear to come from middle-class backgrounds or better, and they believe, with some justification, that they have the most to lose under communism."[8] "Fear of being punished for past actions or associations seems to be a factor as well" and "officials who have questioned thousands of refugees say that nine out of 10 identify a desire for freedom as the major factor in the decision to abandon their homelands." Frederic Moritz comments that "the Vietnamese [in Thailand] are largely middle-class businessmen and former low-level employees of the Americans who say that they faced disruption, loss of freedom and income, and possible job discrimination if they had stayed behind. At the least, the Vietnamese refugees were former independent fishermen." "Vietnamese refugees say those who fail in escape attempts often are punished only mildly with short terms in 'reeducation camps' or other less severe measures," but the Laotian refugees, who "actively fought communist forces for more than a decade in collaboration with the U.S. Central Intelligence Agency," would presumably "expect far harsher treatment," long imprisonment or execution. The Cambodians still in camps—over 14,000—"are a mix of farmers, students, military men and minor government officials. Skilled Cambodians such as technicians and physicians or those with money have moved on to be resettled."[9]

A fuller account of refugees in Asia by mid-1978 would include the quarter of a million driven from their homes in West Asia by Israeli troops in March, 1978, after bombing of cities, villages and refugee camps with U.S. cluster bomb units[10] and heavy artillery, among other devices, in attacks reminiscent of Vietnam: "concentrated and heavy firepower and air strikes to blow away all before them—be they enemies or civilians—in order to hold down their own casualties," leaving "a broad path of death and wide-scale destruction" with "hardly a town...left undamaged" and some "all but totally flattened by air strikes and explosive shells"; "the scope and sweep of the damage here makes a mockery of Israeli claims to have staged surgical strikes against Palestinian bases and camps."[11] These quarter-million recall the 700,000 who fled (about half of them expelled, according to conservative estimates by such pro-Israeli scholars as Nadav Safran of Harvard) in 1948, the 400,000 who fled or were expelled in 1967, many of them long after hostilities ceased, the one and a half million driven out of the Suez region by Israeli bombing during the 1970 "war of attrition," and many others, including the former inhabitants of the Jordan Valley, cleared by force in 1969-70. Apart from those simply expelled by force, as in South Lebanon, there are the many who are escaping from the occupied West Bank, where the rate of emigration sharply increased to more than 17,000 in the past two years.[12]

By the latter part of 1978, we may add several hundred thousand Maronites driven from Lebanon by Syrian bombardment, added to the earlier Lebanese Muslim and Palestinian victims of Syrian force as Lebanon is further dismembered by civil strife and foreign invasion and intrigue too complex and remote from our focus here to receive a proper discussion. The *Economist* (7 October 1978) reports a Lebanese government estimate of 600,000 exiles, about half of them Maronite, in addition to hundreds of thousands of refugees within Lebanon.

The refugees in Asia and Africa by no means exhaust the grim story. In Volume I, we discussed the massive flight from U.S.-backed terror in Latin America: an estimated half million from Uruguay, perhaps 700,000 from Bolivia, many more from the other subfascist states. Keeping just to 1978, in September more than 16,000 refugees fled Somoza's terror to neighboring Honduras and Costa Rica, joining the 100,000 Nicaraguan exiles already living in Costa Rica, earlier victims of oppression in a country long favored with the benign attention of the United States.[13] These refugees have evoked no more interest in the United States than the hundreds of thousands fleeing Burma, the Philippines, Zaire, or other non-Communist states. Attention is reserved for refugees from Indochina. Editors and columnists plead for greater concern and aid for refugees and international condemnation of the repressive policies responsible for their flight, referring solely to the refugees from Indochina—and not calling for measures to alleviate the harsh conditions in Indochina that are surely a direct reason for the flight of refugees and also a factor in the institution of the repressive policies that so concern U.S. humanitarians. Discussion of the U.S. contribution to the plight of the refugees or of the vast flow of refugees elsewhere would simply not serve the needs of Western ideology at this moment. Consequently, these topics merit no comment or concern. The Social Democrats, USA, publish full-page advertisements in U.S. journals calling for "compassionate action" to help the Indochinese refugees, signed by a wide range of people including some of the most extreme and vocal apologists for U.S. aggression and terror in Indochina. Their compassion, however, is restricted to "Indochinese Refugees" and the statement makes no mention of any "compassionate action" to help overcome the consequences of the U.S. war.

By late 1978, the refugee flow from Indochina had reached quite substantial proportions. According to the UN High Commissioner on Refugees, over 71,000 had successfully escaped from Vietnam by sea since April 1975[14] and many more undoubtedly died in escape attempts, in addition to the ethnic Chinese who fled by land. In a speech before the Boston World Affairs Council, Richard Holbrooke of the State Department reported that in October 1978 "a record 10,000 'boat people' landed in Southeast Asian countries. In the first two weeks of November an additional 10,000 landed in Malaysia alone...fleeing unbearable conditions in their home countries." This "dramatic flow of refugees," most of them ethnic Chinese, "could be highly damaging to the emerging stability of Southeast Asia."[15] Apparently the flight of 200,000 Burmese Muslims to Bangladesh in April-June 1978, more than 18,000 in a single day, was not "dramatic" enough to have reached the attention of the Assistant Secretary of State for East Asian and Pacific Affairs, just as the flight of 140,000 Filipinos failed to reach this threshold. Among the refugees in Latin America there are also "boat people." For example, 1,000 refugees from Haiti who "voyaged 800 miles in flimsy sailboats to Florida, where they received harsh and discriminatory treatment by Immigration and State Department officials."[16] These refugees fled from oppression and torture in the subfascist U.S. client with the lowest living standards in the hemisphere.[17] "No rationale has been offered," Gollobin continues, for treating the Haitian "boat people" differently from the Vietnamese and Cubans "who have been given asylum as a group." The rationale, however, is obvious enough. As in the case of 140,000 refugees from the Philippines or a quarter of a million refugees from Southern Lebanon, the Haitians are not fleeing from "Communist tyranny," but rather from "unbearable conditions" in a client state, or the acts of a friendly ally, and therefore merit no special concern.

In addition to their unwise choice of oppressor, the Haitian boat people have another strike against them. The *New York Times* reports that there are some 15,000 Haitians in the Bahamas seeking refuge in Florida, which has "raised fears here that the poor on other islands in the Caribbean may also risk the dangers of the open sea to get a legal foothold in Florida." This is another reason why "only 26 Haitians have been granted asylum since 1972, the year when the rotting fishing boats made their first landings on Florida beaches."[18]

Fear of inundation by the poor and oppressed of the world can occasionally be relaxed, for example, when seasonal workers are needed in the Southwest or when some political capital can be gained by a demonstration of our humanitarian concern for victims of Communist tyranny—particularly when they are "orphans" (see chapter 2, note 17). But the Haitian boat people do not meet these conditions: "Now, as a signal to the rest of the world that just being poor is not enough reason to sneak into the U.S., federal officials are beginning a crackdown aimed at catching Haitians who have entered the U.S. illegally and sending them home" to the "poverty and repression" from which they have escaped.[19] Some 1,200 arrived from November 1977 to mid-1978, including "boat people" who spent weeks at sea in sinking craft and were arrested on their arrival—if they made it.[20] But the State Department denies that they will be in any danger if returned to Haiti, and a spokesman for the U.S. Immigration and Naturalization Services cited by Robert Press assures us that "the entire effort is being made with full regard to the administration policy of human rights"—which is true enough, though not exactly in the sense he was trying to convey.[21] Temporary work permits that had been granted for 3-4,000 Haitians are being revoked. Some officials and one church in Miami, Robert Press reports, "have charged the U.S. with 'racism' for turning its back on the needs of the Haitians—a black people." The fact that their oppressor is a U.S. client state is, however, sufficient to explain their treatment.

The ironies have not gone entirely unnoticed in the press. Karen DeYoung comments that "while the United States is acting to admit more Indochinese immigrants who wash ashore in Asia, it is attempting to deport other thousands of 'boat people' who have landed on southern Florida beaches from Haiti" (*Washington Post*, 22 December 1978). She notes that "the issue of the Haitian boat people has been simmering since 1972," though "it was not until a 1977 Supreme Court case, however, that the Justice Department recognized the rights of the Haitians to INS interviews to judge their political asylum claims." But the decision was virtually irrelevant. The INS Commissioner said in an interview that "practically none" of the 9,000 Haitians whose cases were being reviewed in Miami in December 1978 had been adjudged as meriting political asylum. Since the INS is no longer issuing work permits, "some Haitians are once again being thrown into jail while awaiting processing." A committee of civil rights lawyers charged that "the INS rarely bothers to find out if the refugees are likely to be persecuted if they are forced to return to Haiti" (and, of course, no questions are raised in the case of flight from a Communist state), and "deportation proceedings are initiated even before an interview is scheduled, under the 1977 Justice decision, to hear their claims for asylum." The group "charged that the INS, in response to the vast and unexpired numbers of poor illegal Haitians, decided to begin throwing them out—primarily to avoid setting an encouraging precedent for other Third World illegals." The London *Economist*, estimating the number of Haitians illegally in the United States at 30,000, most of them "boat people," added that "as many as

150 Haitians are being dealt with each day [by INS], with only one or two minutes for each case to be heard," while "spokesmen for the Haitian community in southern Florida wonder out loud why Haitians are not accorded the same treatment as thousands of Cubans and Vietnamese" (30 December, 1979).

The treatment of refugees in the mass media and by U.S. official action seems to depend, once again, on political-economic-ideological, rather than human rights considerations. The earlier classification of terror used in Volume I is fully applicable to the refugees as well: (1) benign (e.g., Burma, where no one cares); (2) constructive (e.g., Latin America, where the flow stems from actions serviceable to U.S. interests); (3) nefarious (Indochina, where the blame can be placed on the evils of Communism—overlooking the insignificant matter of the legacy of U.S. intervention). Refugees of the first and second categories can be shipped back to tyranny or left to rot in oblivion wherever they may land (as long as it is not here). But refugees of the third category call forth stirring cries of indignation, editorial denunciation, passionate speeches in the halls of Congress, outraged protest from spokesmen for human rights, and moving words— rarely deeds—of compassion in keeping with the lofty traditions of Western humanism.

In an editorial entitled "The Indochina Debt that Lingers," the *New York Times* writes:

> The case for American help to the refugees of Indochina continues to be self-evident. After our involvement in Southeast Asia, no debate over who owes whom how much can be allowed to obscure the worst horrors experienced by many of those in flight.

The *Times* recognizes no "case for American help" to the many hundreds of thousands of refugees elsewhere in Southeast Asia and beyond—indeed, one could hardly know of their existence from the pages of America's leading newspaper—and most remarkably, recognizes no debt to the victims of U.S. barbarism who remain in their ravaged lands and who vastly outnumber the refugees. For the editors of the *Times*, the efforts of the Indochinese governments to rebuild are the subject only for censure, because of the suffering their people endure—a sure proof of Communist iniquity. The remark in the editorial about "debate over who owes whom how much" is, perhaps, an oblique reference to one of the sayings of President Carter, who, in the midst of a sermon on human rights, was asked by a journalist about U.S. responsibility to the Vietnamese. We owe them no debt, the great humanitarian responded, because "the destruction was mutual," as a tour through the bombed out ruins of San Francisco and the Georgia countryside will reveal.[22] While this amazing statement was deemed worthy of no commentary in the Free Press, it is possible that it rankles a little at least.

We have already discussed the intellectual and moral standards by which the honesty of protest over human rights violations and concern for their victims should be judged.[23] Applying such standards, U.S. citizens concerned over the fate of refugees should distribute their efforts in accordance with the potential impact in relieving human misery. A refugee from Vietnam is no more or less worthy of concern, assistance, or admission to the United States than a refugee from Zaire, Burma, the Philippines, or Haiti. Articulate protest over the actions of U.S. clients such as Marcos or Suharto is far more significant in human terms— that is, in terms of potential benefit for victims—hence far more obligatory on grounds of moral principle than protest over acts or conditions in states beyond the reach of U.S. power. What we find, however, is that articulate opinion—at least, that part that is able to reach more than a tiny segment of the public—is focused almost exclusively on victims of Communist oppression, a concept that includes the rigors of life amidst the ruins, and is careful to evade the question of actions that would alleviate the conditions that are a primary cause for the flight of the refugees.

The *New York Times* has assigned one correspondent, Henry Kamm, to virtually full time coverage of the misery of postwar Indochina, though others too report frequently on this topic. No comparable concern is shown outside of Indochina. "The Pulitzer Prize for international reporting was won by Henry Kamm, chief Asian diplomatic correspondent for the *New York Times*, for his articles on the plight of the so-called 'boat-people,' war refugees from Indo-China."[24] No such prize is, or will be offered for studies of the misery of refugees (or those not lucky enough to escape) from U.S. client states, or from countries such as Burma that have not been so ignoble as to defend themselves successfully from U.S. invasion. In fact, the Pulitzer Prize jury had recommended Les Payne of *Newsday* for the prize in international reporting for a series of articles on conditions in South Africa, but "the winner chosen by the [advisory] board was Henry Kamm of the *New York Times*, whose articles on Vietnamese refugees had been the jury's fourth choice," we learn in a brief AP report carried by the *New York Times* on April 22.[25] The Pulitzer Prize advisory board is, evidently, more finely tuned to the needs of contemporary ideology than the professional jurors.

In sum, the United States *ought* to have a real concern for the peoples of Indochina, victims of a long and agonizing U.S.-sponsored cataclysm. But as this concern has been selectively exhibited in the postwar period, the cruelties and hypocrisies of the entire Vietnam war intervention display themselves in new form. The main victims, the bulk of the rural population who remain in Indochina, are ignored, and the concern for refugees is so intertwined with ideological warfare and a rewriting of history that the humanitarianism is once again shown to be hopelessly compromised by political interests. The ghastly episode of the Vietnamese "orphans," discovered at the last moment and spirited out in a brazen effort to gain public support for the war, was, regrettably, a microcosm of the continuing U.S. response to the war victims. The lack of any comparable concern for the vast flow of refugees from terror within the U.S. sphere of influence, or the victims of benign terror, also tells us a great deal about the power of political economy to twist human rights into such shape that its humanistic component is hard to locate.

4

Vietnam

In the preceding chapter, we discussed the highly selective concern over the plight of refugees, many of whom are first or second order victims of Western intervention ("modernization" or pacification). Deep concern is also voiced for those unfortunates who have not yet succeeded in fleeing from the rigors of Communism. True, things are perhaps a shade better than was predicted by those who invoked the near certainty of a massive bloodbath as justification for their support for continued U.S. intervention;[1] and now that we have looked briefly at a few moments of Western history, under circumstances incomparably more mild and favorable and with much less cause for revenge, one can perhaps begin to perceive the basis for such expectations.

One of those who confidently predicted a mass slaughter in Vietnam was the noted expert Patrick Honey, friend and adviser of Diem, former Reuters Saigon correspondent and Foreign Editor of the *Economist,* author of a book on North Vietnam published by the Center for International Studies at MIT, and a respected commentator on Vietnamese affairs—also a self-styled "pacifist" who urged such measures as bombing the dikes in North Vietnam as early as 1965. One of his more perspicuous insights was that after a Communist victory

> All believed to pose a threat, real or potential, to the Communist regime will be killed at once, and some of the remainder

may be permitted to postpone execution as long as they continue to work as unpaid slave labourers. Calculated on the basis of past Communist deeds, and given the size of South Vietnam's population, the minimum number of those to be butchered will exceed one million and could rise to several times that figure.[2]

In fact, the predictions of Honey and other comparable experts have not been fulfilled. There has been no credible evidence of mass executions in Vietnam, certainly nothing similar to what happened in France or perhaps even Japan after World War II, to cite two examples discussed above where the provocation was far less. But some of the measures enacted by the victors have nevertheless been invoked to demonstrate both Communist perfidy and the "double standards" of those who opposed the war. One example which provides a good insight into the practices of the Free Press is a front-page story in the *New York Times* by their Asia specialist Fox Butterfield, which includes the following "information."

> The Communists say they have also forced 260,000 Montagnards, the nomadic hill tribesmen in the south, to settle down in the last three years. Similar efforts by South Vietnamese regimes before 1975 drew angry protests from Americans opposed to the war.[3]

Since it seemed to us unlikely that the Communists would say that they had "forced" montagnards to resettle, and since we recall no "angry protests" over earlier resettlement of montagnards, we wrote Mr. Butterfield to inquire as to the source of his information. He was kind enough to respond (which is unusual; most efforts to track down the source of what appears in the press are unavailing). In a letter of 12 June 1978 from Hong Kong, Butterfield cites as his source a 19 March report by the Vietnam News Agency which he quotes as follows:

> 300,000 former nomads in the central highlands provinces of Gia Lai—Cong Tum, Dac Lac and Lam Dong have now settled and together with soldiers and pioneers from the plains,

cleared hundreds of thousands of acres of virgin lands and built hundreds of new economic zones.

He also cites "a Tass dispatch on 25 January giving figures for both north and south, with the specific figures of 260,000 for the south."[4] Note the way this information has been transmuted into a "forced" resettlement as it becomes a feature story in the *New York Times*.[5]

With regard to the protests by Americans, Butterfield writes: "I can only tell you that during more than two years as a correspondent in Vietnam, I often received letters from American friends suggesting I write articles detailing U.S. and South Vietnamese measures to compel the montagnards to settle down... In fairness, if such a standard was applied to [the actions of the Diem, Khanh, Ky and Thieu governments], it should be maintained now for a communist regime."

This response gives an interesting indication of the kind of thinking that informs the news columns—not to speak of the editorials—in the Free Press. First, we may ask whether letters from friends are correctly described as "angry protests from Americans opposed to the war" and provide a sufficient evidentiary basis for characterizing and defaming a mass popular movement. Second, note the assumption—based on no cited evidence—that the Communists have *compelled* the montagnards to resettle. Note finally the belief that fairness requires that "Americans opposed to the war" now direct "angry protests" against the Vietnamese Communists.

Even if Butterfield had some factual basis for his assertions, consider the standards he invokes in his news column. The Vietnamese have resettled 300,000 montagnards by means that he does not know. In comparison, the U.S.-imposed government claimed to have moved no less than one third of its population to "strategic hamlets" by the summer of 1962 to "protect" them from the Communists, who, according to U.S. officials, had the support of about half the population while the U.S.-imposed regime could claim only minimal popular support. This was undoubtedly a forced relocation, as contemporary reports and later studies make very clear.[6] The montagnards were particularly hard hit by the forced relocation programs. Dennis Duncanson of the British Advisory Mission, a passionate supporter of the U.S. intervention and now a widely respected commentator on Indochina, reports without critical comment that the policy of random bombardment of villages in "open zones" was the "principal cause of a huge migration of tribesmen in the summer of 1962," citing estimates from 125,000 to 300,000.[7] The *Pentagon Papers* cite intelligence reports on "indiscriminate bombing in the countryside" which is "forcing innocent or wavering peasants toward the Viet Cong" and on the flight of 100,000 montagnards from Viet-Cong controlled areas "due principally to Viet Cong excesses and the general intensification of the fighting in the highlands," noting again "the extensive use of artillery and aerial bombardment and other apparently excessive and indiscriminate measures by GVN military and security forces..."—a more plausible cause for the flight than "Viet Cong excesses," a phrase that was very possibly added as a reflex in the typical ideological style of intelligence reports. A CIA report of July, 1962 mentions "extensive relocation Montagnards" allegedly resulting from fear of Viet Cong "and new found respect for power GVN has manifested bombing attacks and use helicopters."[8] Recall that U.S. pilots were flying some 30% of bombing missions by 1962 and that all the equipment of course was supplied by the United States to the forces it trained and organized.

The impact of these murderous programs on the montagnards then and in subsequent years was severe. Gerald Hickey, who worked with montagnards in close association with U.S. government agencies for many years, wrote in 1973 that "in the past decade at least 85 per cent of these [montagnard] villages

for one reason or another have been relocated, and whole ethnic groups have been moved out of their traditional territories."
While he is a bit coy about the reasons, other sources, such as
those just mentioned, make them clear enough. He reports, that
according to Saigon officials in the Ministry of Ethnic Minorities, 200,000 of 900,000 montagnards perished during this grim
decade. And at least 120,000 "are crammed into dreary and
inadequate refugee centers" where they are shattered and demoralized. Most of their territories were then under NLF-NVA
control "and the South Vietnamese out of fear of losing control
of population prefer that relocated montagnards remain where
they are," in the refugee centers. Hickey concludes that "there
may be a glint of hope in reports that in some of the Communist
controlled areas montagnard refugees are being returned to their
former sites to rebuild villages. If this is so it could mean the
salvation of the montagnard way of life, particularly a restoration
of their self-sufficiency and with it their dignity."[9]

Other Americans have also observed their fate. Earl Martin
describes the situation of hundreds of montagnards swept up
along with 7,000 Vietnamese farmers in OPERATION MAL-
HEUR, sent to a camp where "camp life for the tribal people
looked less like integration than genocide." In fact, "gradually
they started to die off," pleading in vain to be permitted to return
to their hills, even though these areas were being subjected to
constant U.S. bombardment.[10]

Contrary to the statement of the *Times* correspondent, there
were, regrettably, few if any "angry protests" at the time of these
programs by Americans opposed to the war.[11] During the early
programs, which were among the most savage, there was no visible peace movement at all. But even if there had been angry
protests, as the facts certainly demanded, would it be proper to
accuse such protestors of a double standard for failing to protest
the current relocation of montagnards? Does fairness require

that when a Vietnamese government relocates 300,000 montagnards (by means that are unknown), U.S. citizens must protest exactly as they did (rather, should have done) when the U.S. government and a regime that it forcefully imposed, armed and trained, bombed hundreds of thousands of montagnards into "protected areas" or drove a third of the population of South Vietnam into virtual concentration camps, surrounded with barbed wire and controlled by police? That is an odd standard of fairness. By honest and moral standards, protest by U.S. citizens would be directed primarily against the United States and its clients, even if there were some remote degree of parity in the measures undertaken, for reasons that we have already discussed (cf. Volume I, chapter 1, section 16).

In fact, there is a clear case of "double standards" illustrated here, quite apart from the falsification of evidence in the *Times* story. The *Times* did not protest, either editorially or in its constant editorializing in news reports, when the United States and its client regime drove hundreds of thousands of montagnards from their homes by "random bombardment" or conducted the forced resettlement programs of 1962-1963, or even when it later carried out its massive programs of "forced draft urbanization" by bombs and artillery. Occasionally the *Times* would complain that the programs were not efficacious or well-designed, but we recall no *principled* protest over this or other aspects of U.S. aggression in Indochina. And as we have seen, at the war's end not only the *Times* editorial writers but also their most outspoken doves saw the war only as a blunder. In his news report and the attitudes that lie behind it, Butterfield exemplifies once again the typical hypocrisy of the media, raising a moral issue which takes the form of a criticism of alleged double standards on the part of others, but quite incapable of perceiving the real double standard to which the *Times* consistently adheres; or better, the single standard of service to the basic principles of the state propaganda system.

In the same news story Butterfield reports that Vietnam plans to resettle 10 million people, one-fifth of the population, in the next 20 years. "In its scope and severity, Hanoi's plan dwarfs the forced evacuation of refugees during the Vietnam war." He criticizes a Vietnamese spokesman for having "made no reference to the cost in human terms of moving 10 million people from one part of the country to another and from their accustomed lives in the city to uncleared land in the countryside."

Assuming that in this case the *Times* has some evidence for what it reports, consider the judgments expressed in this news story. Would the resettlement of 10 million people in 20 years dwarf in scope and severity the U.S. program of *bombing* approximately the same number of people into U.S.-controlled urban concentrations during the 1960s? It is quite important to recall that contrary to much current propaganda, these programs of forced relocation, which in fact displaced some 10 million people in the South according to the representative of the U.N. High Commissioner for Refugees (see below, p. 82), were consciously designed to drive the rural population to the U.S.-controlled cities, a fact obvious enough from their predictable effect, and in fact were explicitly recommended for this purpose.[12] Furthermore, as we have already noted, all competent authorities agree that a program of resettlement is an absolute necessity if the country is to survive, a point to which we will return. What evidence does Butterfield adduce, or have, that the specific program to which he objects is an improper one, given the clear necessity for massive resettlement? The comparison to violent relocation by a foreign invader in an effort to undercut the social base of a popular resistance movement is truly astonishing.

What of the failure to refer to "the cost in human terms" of moving people from "their accustomed lives in the city" to "uncleared land in the countryside"? Butterfield evidently wants us to assume that the Communists, with their customary cruelty, are simply dismantling the cities where people live in comfort and sending them to uncleared land (in preference to the cleared land that otherwise awaits them?). He himself acknowledges factors that make this utter nonsense.[13] The "accustomed lives in the city" were sheer hell for vast numbers of victims of U.S. savagery, while those more favored could hardly maintain their "accustomed lives" after the collapse of the totally artificial foreign-based economy and must turn to productive work, unless there is to be mass starvation. That much is elementary. Nor is there any reason to suppose that the Vietnamese are purposely sending urban residents to "uncleared land" out of some peculiar form of malice. Such evidence as exists, quite apart from mere common sense, suggests that they will attempt to create a viable economy self-sufficient in agriculture. All of this is obvious, except to correspondent-editorialists in the U.S. propaganda institutions.[14]

It is interesting to compare the *Times* analysis with that of Nayan Chanda (see footnote 4), based on long familiarity with the region and a recent visit. Like the *New York Times,* Chanda discusses the 50,000 "functionaries and political personalities of the former regime, civil and military" in reeducation camps,[15] the sometimes troubled accommodation of the bitterly anti-Communist Catholics to the new regime and the conflicts between certain segments of the Buddhist community and the Communist authorities, the discontent and suffering of urban residents of the South who blame the Communists for the radical decline in living standards for the bourgeoisie when the U.S.-based economy collapsed with the U.S. withdrawal, and the problems of corruption and bureaucratic inefficiency. As distinct from the *Times* and other U.S. media, he also outlines the background and context of what is happening in Vietnam and discusses in some detail the careful and "progressive" measures that are being taken by the regime to try to deal with the awesome problems of "reconstructing the socio-economic structures ravaged by two decades of separation and war."

In the South, Chanda writes, the security situation is "much improved" over 1976, with no armed military patrols in Saigon and no military in evidence on the road leading to the Mekong Delta or on bridges. Nevertheless, armed resistance reportedly continues in parts of the country, and he finds plausible the official explanation that "the principal reason" for detaining elements of the U.S.-backed regime "corresponds to the imperatives of security, the government wishing to assure itself, before freeing them, that those detained will have no opportunity to cause harm."[16] He reports the testimony of a recently released Thieu government functionary who says that most of his detention was spent farming or in political discussions after a three month study of "the history of the revolution and the causes of the American defeat." The liberation of those with a "serious criminal past" will be delayed beyond the expected three years, Chanda believes, while bureaucratic inefficiency may delay the release of others.

There are 1.5 million unemployed in the South, according to officials whom Chanda quotes, including 300,000 in Saigon, most of whom had enjoyed, "thanks to the massive influx of American dollars, an easy life and a standard of living absolutely without relation to the level of economic development of the country." According to a confidential report of the World Bank, the worst threat of famine in the South was overcome by imports from the North and external assistance. Far from draining the South of resources, as the editors of the *New York Times* have claimed (see chapter 1, footnote 13), the Vietnamese authorities appear "concerned to avoid the collapse of normal living standards in Saigon" and continue to divert essential products to the South, including even gasoline for thousands of private vehicles, "to the degree that the standard of living in [Saigon] is higher than anywhere else in Vietnam."

Chanda gives a sympathetic account of the efforts to resettle residents of overcrowded urban areas to "new economic zones," prepared for settlement by army units, groups of young villagers, volunteer students, and members of the Young Communist League. There were admitted errors in the early stages of the settling of Saigonese in inadequately prepared new economic zones, leading to rumors of "new Siberias," but these appear to have been overcome, Chanda reports. He describes the significant improvements in a region that he had visited in 1976, then "an arid plain without trees" and now a flourishing state farm, with schools, nurseries, tractors, and bulldozers. The cited World Bank report praises the new economic zones and urges international aid, while the U.S. press, in contrast, prefers to deplore the cruel evacuation of the Saigonese from their "accustomed lives in the city to uncleared land in the countryside."

Chanda also describes the slow and careful moves that the government is making to encourage cooperation among the individualistic peasants of the Mekong Delta and to increase food production, the introduction of double harvests, and "impressive projects" to improve the land as well as efforts to develop small-scale industry to offer needed goods to the peasants so that they will agree to send the agricultural surplus to the cities. As for the corruption, described with much glee by Western journals,[17] he writes that it is "in a way an inevitable phenomenon after thirty years of sacrifice and privations," particularly in Saigon where substantial quantities of imported consumer goods are still to be found, though the government, which has quite openly discussed the problem, is taking measures to overcome it not overlooking the severe temptations for a soldier who has been fighting in the jungle for ten years and would now like to send a small present to his wife at home.

This description, while not sparing in criticism, is radically different in character from the bulk of what is presented in the U.S. press in an effort to demonstrate Communist depravity. It even suggests that the United States might have some lessons to learn—lessons that might be applied in its Latin American domains for example—from people who entirely lack the resources of the world's richest country and who are facing problems immeasurably more severe than those in the U.S. satellites.[18] Or perhaps the lessons might be applied in the outright U.S. colonies such as Guam, where, according to a report by Butterfield, Asian workers "have been systematically underpaid, physically abused and intimidated by threats of deportation if they complain—often, apparently, with the complicity of United States government officials"—the situation is "like slavery in the South before the Civil War," says a Department of Labor official who adds that his life was threatened when he was sent here to investigate the situation.[19]

One might even be so naive, perhaps, as to imagine that the facts that Chanda reports might lead the *New York Times* editors, who are presumably aware of them, to reconsider their high-minded belief that "our Vietnam duty is not over," referring solely to the "horror" of the refugees,[20] and to conceive of this lingering debt as encompassing also a response to the appeal of the Comsymps in the World Bank for international assistance for the resettlement projects within Vietnam.

The World Bank is not alone in recommending resettlement. "A vast resettlement of Vietnamese, away from the cities and back to the countryside, is likely to get under way soon—probably aided by United Nations-sponsored funds."[21] A UN report describes such mass population movement as a "top priority" if Vietnamese agricultural production is to recover. The head of the UN aid mission that visited Vietnam for a month in March, 1976 told a news conference at the UN in New York that "I am satisfied in light of my experience that coercion is not exercised." He also expressed his opinion that those who crowded into the cities of the South during the war did not want to stay in the cities. In the North, he observed, "some villages have been totally erased from

the earth—you have some cities without a house left standing."
He added that the Vietnamese had shown a "very friendly, constructive attitude" towards the UN mission and permitted them
to travel freely. He urged an international aid program, to which
Sweden and some other Western countries have already begun to
contribute—but those who erased the villages from the earth have
banned aid to the victims, or even trade.

The representative of the UN High Commissioner for Refugees, Alexander Casella, now a senior associate of the Carnegie
Endowment, gave his impressions of 18 months in postwar Vietnam in Foreign Policy, Spring 1978. This detailed report is rather
similar in tone to Chanda's, and again radically different from the
stream of invective in the nation's press. Casella concludes that
"if one considers the material problems the country faces and the
hatreds accumulated by 30 years of war, the potential for a major
economic and human catastrophe [after the war] was enormous.
The least credit that the leadership deserves is for having averted
that catastrophe." When the war ended, there was an "administrative vacuum" in the South, and "northern officials had to be rushed
to the south" along with "doctors, technicians, medical supplies,
and fuel." The reason for the administrative vacuum is simple:
"The Saigon administration had dissolved, and the PRG did not
have the manpower to take over." In the early 1960s about half of
the party members were in the South; by 1976, the proportion was
less than one in six. Why had the proportion changed?

> A major reason for the imbalance is the Phoenix program—the
> American euphemism for the system of assassinating South
> Vietnamese Communists—which, according to official Viet-
> namese sources, had about 100,000 victims. They were not
> merely party members, but in most cases experienced function-
> aries. In other words, the local administrative structure of the
> PRG was for all practical purposes eradicated, and in the last
> years of the war the operating life-expectancy of a Communist
> party cell leader in Saigon was not more than four months.[22]

The Western press generally prefers a different interpretation of the northern takeover, as we have seen: "As soon as the war was over the NLF was discarded," Martin Woollacott explains.[23] "In retrospect, it is clear that the NLF was never a true coalition of Communist and non-Communist forces, nor was it ever an independent southern entity." His evidence is that the Communist Party revealed in internal documents that it hoped to control the Front, and the judgment of "most authorities" that "by 1966 the majority of key cadres were northerners" (that is, after ten years of savage repression, 4 years of U.S. bombing, and a year of full-scale military invasion with its awesome concomitants). Without a word on the methods that were used to destroy the NLF and the peasant society it had organized, Woollacott observes that the "revolutionary theory" of the NLF "in the end turned out to be wrong": there was no general uprising or "negotiated coalition government" (which is true, given the U.S. refusal to implement the 1973 agreements; see chapter 1, section 1) but rather the war ended "by a massive conventional military campaign" (in response to U.S.-Saigon military actions, as is noted by every reputable observer) and now the Front "has been ceremonially laid to rest in Saigon" (having been decimated by U.S. terror). The omissions, here parenthesized, are revealing.

Casella goes on to describe the "shattered economy" of the South, an artificial U.S. creation, as well as "an exhausted North Vietnam, whose economy was just marginally self-supporting" having been reduced to the production level of 1955, and "now required to divert some of its functionaries to help govern the south, and to prop it up economically as well. The south, or what was left of it, had little to offer the north."

Discussing the impact of the war, Casella writes that "between 1965 and 1975, some 10 million people were at one time or another displaced" in South Vietnam. By the summer of 1975, he writes, "it was clear that there was no economic alternative but to return to the countryside for the five million displaced persons who had sought refuge in the cities and were now mostly unemployed." Of these, two million were fortunate enough to be able to return to their original villages; "of the other three million, many had seen their villages destroyed and the land wasted." These "would have to be resettled in 'new economic zones' (NEZs)." As for the resettlement program, "both for individuals and for the nation, there is no alternative."

Early efforts at resettlement in NEZs were ill-prepared: "Hence, the NEZs unjustly acquired the reputation of an Asian Gulag, especially among the petty bourgeoisie from Saigon, who had always looked down on manual labor." By the fall of 1975, he writes, the situation had been reassessed and a "pattern of resettlement established," news of which had not reached the *New York Times* desk in Hong Kong, whereby the army corps of engineers first clears land, disposes of mines, builds access roads, some simple housing, and health facilities before settlers are brought in. Casella then describes some successful examples in extremely poor areas.

Is there coercion involved? "If forcing means at gun point, then the answer is an emphatic no. But it would also be incorrect to say that there is no pressure on the unemployed people of Saigon to leave for the countryside." Explaining these pressures, he describes what Butterfield calls "the accustomed lives in the city" for the poor, who rarely arouse the compassion that beats so strongly in the hearts of Western commentators for middle and upper class collaborators with the imperial venture. Saigon's fourth precinct "is one of the poorest areas in the city, one into which few foreigners ever ventured." Situated in a swamp, "it is a maze of alleys in a jungle of dilapidated shacks made of corrugated iron and the leftovers from plywood packing cases." Its population rose from 60,000 in 1960 to 200,000 by the war's end, about half unemployed. "Resettlement of the displaced per-

sons in the fourth precinct was given priority, and by the summer
of 1977, 60,000 had already been moved to new economic zones
in Long An[24] and Tay Ninh, the areas most had come from."
He quotes a member of "the people's committee of the fourth
precinct and a survivor of seven years in prison on Con Son island," who claims "that we have more people who volunteered
for resettlement than we can handle."

The problem of resettlement also exists in the North, where
"most of the populated areas along Route One [south from
Thanh Hoa to the 17th parallel] looked like a lunar landscape,
pitted with bomb craters for mile after mile;" some 2 million
people were displaced in the North, he estimates, mostly from
regions that were among the poorest in Vietnam.[25]

The food crisis is severe because of the war. The land area
under cultivation declined by almost two-and-a-half million
acres "due to the exodus of the population" from 1965 to 1975.
Furthermore, "Cratering also had a long-lasting effect on agriculture," since the explosion compresses the earth so that the
huge craters left have no excess soil for fill on the perimeter.
As U.S.-financed fertilizer imports abruptly ended, new strains
of "miracle rice" could no longer be used, leading to "a drop in
productivity"—generally attributed in the U.S. press to Communist mismanagement and peasant discontent. Unusually severe weather has further hampered plans to achieve agricultural
self-sufficiency by 1980, although the area under cultivation in
the South has increased. Since Casella wrote, the worst floods
in many decades have caused further devastation and misery.

Casella also discusses the "re-education camps," which are
"obviously not vacation spots" though "it has yet to be proved
that they are as bad as the old prisons of the Saigon regime." As
for the men now returning from them, "considering the length
of the war and the bitterness it engendered, they could hardly
have hoped for better." The incompetent U.S. evacuation effort,

described in detail by CIA analyst Frank Snepp,[26] failed to evacuate "endangered Vietnamese" to the United States, "a solution that both they and the Communists would surely have found less burdensome." The Hanoi leadership, Casella writes, "concluded that retribution *per se* carried no redeeming value" for the 1.5 million members of the Saigon army and civilians of the Saigon regime. For the rank and file, "re-education...usually meant only one or two days of lectures," though "problems arose with what had been the hard core of the Saigon regime—the officer corps, police officials, and the like;" for example, those engaged in the U.S.-sponsored assassination campaigns, whose names were no doubt known to the victors because of the failure to destroy U.S. intelligence files (see Snepp). "For the former ruling elite, re-education became a far more complex and time-consuming process." While trials "have a certain appeal to the Western mind, anyone familiar with Vietnam instinctively realizes that the last thing the individuals concerned would have wanted was a trial, which would have narrowed down responsibility and probably led to far heavier sentences" as opposed to the three to five year detention (approximately) specified by "official decrees." It is likely that since Casella wrote, a combination of natural disasters and serious international complications involving China and Cambodia, and perhaps other factors, have seriously aggravated the internal situation.

Despite the rigors of the war, the regime "did manage to attain some significant, tangible achievements." "Illiteracy was practically wiped out, and North Vietnam today probably has the most comprehensive primary education system and rural health program in continental Asia,"[27] as well as "one of the most decentralized of the Communist economies, one in which considerable leeway is left to local authorities." The current trend "is to try to duplicate this pattern at the level of industrial management," with involvement of trade union and party representatives in a "search for an original type of Socialist management." It will take a full decade, he believes, before Vietnam reaches "a point from which an economic take-off appears feasible" and the material and social damage of the war is repaired. "A full assessment of where Vietnam stands will have to wait until that day"—a day that could be advanced were the United States not bent on retribution.

Casella's account, like Chanda's, is supported by much direct evidence provided by Western visitors and analysts who have spent long periods in Vietnam, including postwar Vietnam in some cases; for example, the detailed and ignored study by Jean and Simonne Lacouture in 1976.[28] The most extensive and by far the most serious report of a visit by a U.S. reporter, Richard Dudman's ten-part series in the *St. Louis Post-Dispatch*, reaches quite similar conclusions: "After 30 years of war and only 2½ years of peace, Vietnam appears to have made a remarkable start at tackling the problems of peace." He confirms that "the South appears to be a burden rather than a prize for Hanoi" and reports the view of "some of the best informed Western diplomats in Hanoi" that the shortage of Communist cadres as a result of Operation Phoenix and other U.S. terrorist programs remains a major problem in the South. Western diplomats report a net rice transfer from North to South in 1975 and 1976, but probably not 1977. The new Ho Chi Minh City (Saigon) "probably is better for many factory employees and others now known as 'workers,'" but "worse, at least economically, for much of the middle class and for many of the self-employed"—which is not very surprising, given the collapse of the artificial economy that was based on a foreign dole. For the time being, "South Vietnam has something of the feel of an occupied country," Dudman writes. Unlike most U.S. journalists, Dudman describes the social and economic development programs undertaken to overcome the effects of the war and reports interviews with Ngo Cong Duc and other well-known non-Communist intellectuals who support the new regime, and are therefore blanked out of the U.S. press (see below). All in all, his report, with its professional character and integrity, stands in striking contrast to the exclusive search for negatives that is labelled "news about Indochina" in the nation's press.[29]

The liberal weekly *Newsweek* depicts events in postwar Vietnam in its issue of May 23, 1977. In the index we read:

> Two years after the fall of Saigon, the unified Socialist Republic of Vietnam is still no worker's paradise. Nearly 100,000 former South Vietnamese soldiers and officials are suffering in 'reeducation camps' from which many of them may never emerge. With the economy in bad shape, hordes of city folk have been moved to 'new economic zones' in the countryside, which lack nearly all the comforts of home.

—such as the comforts of the fourth precinct in Saigon or the villages that have been erased from the map in the war always supported (sometimes with timid reservations) by *Newsweek* editors. The accompanying article gives no insight into why the economy is in bad shape; nor has *Newsweek* been noted for its sarcasm about the "workers' paradise" in, say, the Philippines, South Korea, Guam, or much of Latin America, to mention a few cases where U.S. influence and control extends beyond two years and where instead of B-52 treatment the United States is supposedly *aiding* the population (see Volume I, chapter 4, however, for a discussion of the *de facto* impact of this "aid").

The journal than presents a discussion of "Life in the New Vietnam," revealing that two years after the Communist victory, there are still beggars, prostitutes, and black marketeers in Saigon; sure proof of Communist iniquity as compared with the benevolent humanitarianism of the United States, which would never tolerate such a scene in Saigon, Manila, Guam, or Santo Domingo—or Harlem. "Western intelligence reports and the tales told by refugees and foreign travelers paint a dreary picture of life in Vietnam." They quote a Frenchman returning from Vietnam who reports the feeling in the country that "two years after the war is really too long for this sort of thing to go on," referring to the reeducation camps but failing to offer a comparison to the warm and sympathetic treatment of collaborators by the French, or the British and U.S. reeducation camps and forced labor for POWs up to three years after the German defeat. (See chapter 2, section 2.)

Newsweek also describes the new economic zones to which city dwellers have been removed, deprived of "all the comforts of home": "Many of these zones have already become rural slums of shabby huts inhabited by dispirited city people trying to coax crops out of marginal farm land. In many cases, the government has failed to provide the new farmers with seeds and tools." In its sole reference to the war, *Newsweek* writes that "the war has left Vietnam's economy in a dreadful state." "The North Vietnamese, some residents of Saigon believe, are intent on leveling the economy of the once-prosperous south 'to punish us'"—which is true; some residents of Saigon do believe this, in defiance of the facts cited above that are nowhere mentioned by *Newsweek*. Nor is there mention of the fact that the "once-prosperous south" (needless to say, the fourth precinct and its counterparts throughout the country deserve no mention) "was an entirely external, artificially induced phenomenon" (Casella) created as a service economy (complete with hundreds of thousands of prostitutes, drug addicts, beggars and servants) for the benefit of the U.S. invaders and their local clients, which disappeared when "the economic crutch that had supported South Vietnam for the previous 15 years collapsed" in April, 1975 (Casella). The article also discusses Hanoi's admission of serious managerial errors, corruption, black marketeering, and resistance. There is no mitigating word, not a mention of the past or continuing U.S. role.

Three accompanying pictures enliven the account. One is captioned "Lecture at a 're-education camp.' Two years after the fall of Saigon, routine scores are still being settled" (so different from the U.S. practice, discussed in chapter 2, section 2). A second is captioned "Camp officers relax: Don't spare the rod" (no rod is visible). The third picture shows rather well-dressed children holding agricultural implements under a red flag—for all we know, it might be a picnic. The caption reads: "'New economic zone': Hardship post for city folk."

Small wonder that the same issue of *Newsweek* contains a letter from a reader defending Nixon, with the following comment: "We forgave the British, the Germans, and the Japanese, and are currently in the process of forgiving the Vietnamese. Doesn't Richard Nixon deserve the same consideration?" Nothing could reveal the power of the U.S. propaganda system more persuasively than the fact that readers who gain their picture of reality from *Newsweek* and similar specimens of the Free Press can speak of our "forgiving the Vietnamese" for their sins against us. Perhaps there are also enlightened Germans who are in the process of forgiving the Jews.[30]

A few weeks earlier the *New York Times* presented its lengthy feature analysis of the "painful problems of peace" in Vietnam, once again by Fox Butterfield.[31] While "some progress has been made by the new Communist leaders in improving the lot of the 50 million Vietnamese," nevertheless the general picture is one of unrelieved dreariness and oppression. "Northern soldiers and officials in Saigon have bought up or confiscated vast amounts of desirable goods and shipped them home," one indication of how "the northern Vietnamese have tended to treat the formerly more prosperous South like conquered territory." Another indication is that Hanoi has sent tens of thousands of teachers and officials to the South and has assigned a "virtual monopoly on key policy-making posts in the unified government" to northerners.[32] No mention is made of the reasons for the shortage of skilled personnel from the resistance forces of the South, though it has long been obvious that these consequences followed directly from the success of the Phoenix mass murder program and Westmoreland's killing-machine.[33] Nor does Butterfield take note of the efforts of the North to divert scarce and precious resources to the South to maintain the artificial living standards of those Saigonese who benefited materially from their association with the U.S. invaders.

The careful reader, however, will notice that something is amiss in Butterfield's account of how the North is treating "the formerly more prosperous South like conquered territory." An accompanying AP dispatch from Saigon reporting "a recent 1,000 mile trip from Hanoi to Saigon by road and air disclosed a still-spartan way of life in the North and a relatively affluent one in the South." From Hanoi southward down Highway 1 "the scene is one of furious activity" as "men and women work until after dark, bringing in produce or laboring in construction gangs building canals and dikes" or repairing roads and bridges ("Every bridge along the way was destroyed by United States bombing"):

> In the North, where factories and brick kilns work around the clock, effort seems concentrated on industrial construction. In the South the real business is in the cities; Saigon, in particular, appears to be almost as active as it was before the Communist victory two years ago. While the bicycle prevails in Hanoi, which seems in some ways like a country town, motor scooters and cars still buzz through Saigon which still boasts bars and hotels as well as freewheeling markets...The people of Hanoi still live in a do-it-yourself society where nothing seems to be wasted, least of all time.[34]

Returning to Butterfield's survey, he next turns to the "new economic zones" and the population transfers. Curiously, in this May 1977 article he gives exactly the same figures and projections (700,000 Saigonese relocated and 10 million to be transferred in the coming years, including montagnards) that inspired him to such denunciation and scorn in his May, 1978 article, discussed above. He writes that "700,000 people from Saigon, many born there, have been moved to 'new economic zones' to clear scrub jungle or uncultivated land." Compare the accounts by Chanda, the World Bank and UN officials, cited above. Butterfield states that "the Communists have defended the population transfers as natural and necessary since Saigon and other southern cities, in their view, were always artificial products of American military spending and aid." He fails to add that this was not only the Communist view, but the universal view among people with the slightest familiarity with the situation—and surely is his view too—nor does he note that Saigon and other cities were not just artificial products of "American military spending and aid," but also of programs of "urbanization" by massive bombardment and destructive ground sweeps designed to force refugees to urban areas, a fact worth mentioning in this connection, one might think. He cites Communist sources who claim that "almost everyone in...[Saigon]... was in an unproductive service industry," again failing to note that this is not simply a pretense of Communist officials, but an unquestioned fact. Casella estimates that "70 per cent of the economic activity in Saigon was service-oriented and only 7 per cent industrial"—he is presumably not including the hundreds of thousands of prostitutes in South Vietnam, another product of "American military spending and aid," nor those engaged in the drug traffic which had devastating effects in South Vietnam as a direct consequence of the U.S. intervention (by all accounts the drug problem was extremely limited before).

Butterfield goes on to say that "the Communists defend the sharp drop in Saigon's standard of living as a progressive development, bringing its residents back to earth after a decadent flirtation with the luxuries of American consumer society." Recall the facts: there was a sharp drop in standard of living for some Saigonese. Hardly all, but as Casella notes, U.S. reporters rarely entered the massive urban slums of South Vietnam where refugees and others lived in swamps and tin huts. The drop was hardly a matter of Communist "choice." Rather, it was an immediate consequence of the withdrawal of the U.S. crutch that had created an artificial economy in the South at the same time that U.S. force was inexorably destroying its agriculture and village life. Unless the U.S. taxpayer decides to continue flooding Saigon "with the luxuries of American consumer society," a possibility that Butterfield does not explore and that has yet to be advocated editorially in the *Times*, it is a matter of dire necessity, as all serious observers recognize, to resettle the "urbanized" population on the land and turn them to productive effort. But of this there is no word in the *Times* retrospective analysis of "conditions in Indochina two years after the end of the war there." Rather, all of the problems are the result of Communist policy.

Butterfield was a *Times* war correspondent in Vietnam and is certainly aware, as are the editors of the *Times*, that something more than Communist decision is involved in causing a situation in which "many Southerners feel a sense of hardship." In an article of some 2,500 words, Butterfield scatters a phrase here and there that might recall to the reader some of the other factors. He speaks of the "substantial tracts of land made fallow by the war"—a phrase that would have made Orwell gasp. He reminds us that 80% of the population are farmers, which may stir some memories about U.S. programs undertaken to defeat the rural-based insurgency by eliminating its base, "urbanizing" the rural population. He notes that "large numbers of urban residents" are being resettled in the countryside, permitting a person familiar with elementary school arithmetic to conclude that large numbers of former farmers are being returned (or perhaps, perish the thought, allowed to return) to farms—to their own villages, where these still exist.

Butterfield informs us that "Saigonese, with a few exceptions, did not support the Communists during the long war." Surely Butterfield knows virtually nothing about the attitudes of most Saigonese; for example, those driven into Saigon by U.S. military action from neighboring Long An province, where, as Jeffrey Race's study shows, the Communists had gained the support of the mass of the population by 1965. As we have noted, U.S. officials in the early 1960s estimated that about half the population of the South supported the NLF. A substantial part of that population was driven to Saigon and other urban areas. Did they still support the NLF? Is the estimate of U.S. officials, which we would expect to be on the low side, an accurate one? To answer these questions one would have to pay some attention to Vietnamese who were not associated with the U.S. effort. This, reporters generally failed to do,[35] though again there were noteworthy exceptions. The real source for Butterfield's judgment is suggested by the accompanying analysis, where he illustrates the attitudes of the "Saigonese" with a single example: the family of a colonel in the Saigon army, one of whose sons had been a major in the army medical corps and another a lawyer in Saigon, and whose daughter had been a "low-ranking employee in the Ministry of the Interior." It is perhaps less than obvious that an account of this "family's woes" serves adequately to illustrate the attitudes of "Saigonese," though it is not untypical of the Western concept of "Saigonese."

Butterfield notes the problems of writing about Vietnam, given the limited sources of information. Thus "there is little verifiable information on the new economic zones—no full-time American correspondents have been admitted since the war."[36] His conclusions about the "problems of peace" are therefore based on reports by "diplomats, refugees and letters from Vietnam." The same complaint appears in a more exaggerated form in an article a few months later by the *Times'* Pulitzer Prize winner Henry Kamm, who writes that "southern Vietnam has become virtually impenetrable by foreigners and only the Hanoi Government's picture of life in the reunited country is presented to the world" so that refugees "are the principal source of critical first-hand information."[37] While the pretense is useful for *Times* ideologues, it is far from true. As the editors could have informed their correspondents, the *New York Times* requested a report on a trip to Vietnam from the distinguished U.S. historian Gabriel Kolko, but refused to print it, and indeed refused to permit *Asahi* (Tokyo) to print it, presumably on grounds of its ideological inadequacies from their point of view.[38] Furthermore, while sources of information are no doubt restricted, there has been plenty of first-hand material in the public record since the end of the war. For example, there is the book by Jean and Simonne Lacouture, already cited, which appeared in 1976, and much else to which we return.[39] If *Times* correspondents choose to limit themselves to reports by refugees and selected diplomats, they merely reveal again their ideological bias, not the factual contingencies.

A look at the book by the Lacoutures (which, as noted, is far from uncritical) explains why they have been consigned to oblivion—on this matter; not in reference to Cambodia, as we shall see in chapter 6. They report that "the capitalist economy of the South was unable to solve the [agricultural] problems that socialist planning, with many more natural handicaps, has just about overcome in the North," and they provide information and insight into the partially successful efforts made to change the society that was called "irremediably miserable" by the French specialist Pierre Gourou.[40] They also describe what Butterfield calls "the tracts of land made fallow by the war"—to be more accurate, in their words, the land with "its bridges destroyed, its trees mutilated, its leprous earth, its vegetation rendered anemic by defoliants, it is the antechamber of desolation," deprived of its population "fleeing combat or forced by the Americans to abandon the countryside to be regrouped in strategic hamlets or the vicinity of the cities" (95, 195). Like all other competent observers, but unlike the U.S. journalists who enlighten the public here, the Lacoutures point out that "it was absolutely urgent to reinstall the peasants on their land," referring to an estimated 8 million displaced by the war in the South (197). They visited several villages in new economic zones and spoke to inhabitants, for example, in the region of Cu Chi, "scalped by the war," where "it is for the most part the former peasants who have returned" (200). Their conclusions are relatively optimistic: "the method seems progressive, based on voluntarism, taking account of the ravages provoked by malaria" (202). True, they are not "full-time American correspondents," but it is unclear why their direct testimony lies beyond the pale, given Jean Lacouture's long experience and distinguished record as a historian and journalist in Vietnam—or rather, it is quite clear.

The refusal to concede the existence of direct eye-witness reports from Vietnam enabled the *New York Times* and its colleagues to evade the question of the consequences of the U.S. war and the problems of reconstruction that face the survivors. It enabled them to avoid the thoughts aroused by such passages as the following:

> The traveller returning to the South a year after liberation cannot fail to be surprised at the transformation of the countryside. The thousands of young volunteers and peasants who are busy constructing dikes in the villages of Song-My (where the My Lai massacre took place) to the sound of revolutionary music from loudspeakers, well symbolize the new epoch.[41]

Though one can imagine how brainwashed U.S. reporters would convey this scene, even if they were to concede its existence.

On the rare occasions when the devastating consequences of the war are noted, care is taken to sanitize the reports so as to eliminate the U.S. role. The *New York Times*, for example, carried an AP report from Manila (21 March 1976) on a World Health Organization study, describing South Vietnam as "a land of widespread malaria, bubonic plague, leprosy, tuberculosis, venereal disease and 300,000 prostitutes...one of the few places on earth where leprosy was spreading and bubonic plague was still taking lives." The WHO report states that "if the bomb-shattered fields are to be made fertile again, and the socio-economic conditions of the people improved, freedom from malaria will have to be first insured," while in the North the main health problem is to reconstruct the 533 community health centers, 94 district hospitals, 28 provincial hospitals and 24 research institutes and specialized hospitals that "were destroyed during the war"—by some unknown hand. The sole mention of the United States in this grisly report is the statement that the United States has been invited to a meeting "to consider helping the two countries"—the "two countries" being North and South Vietnam; while the *Times* recognized the integration of East Timor into Indonesia in 1976 it had not yet recognized the unification of the "two countries" of Vietnam.

Since we owe the Vietnamese "no debt" because "the destruction was mutual," as Mr. Human Rights has explained to his admiring audience,[42] no help will be forthcoming from the United States to reconstruct the hospitals so mysteriously destroyed or to deal with the half-million drug addicts, the 80,000 to 160,000 cases of leprosy in the South, the estimated 5,000 cases of bubonic plague annually, or the rampant epidemics of tuberculosis and venereal disease reported by the W.H.Q.[43] Congress, as noted, has banned aid to Vietnam for its "human rights violations," which so offend the U.S. conscience.[44] The United States was the only country out of 141 that refused to endorse a UN resolution urging "priority economic assistance" to Vietnam.[45] A request from Vietnam to the Asian Development Bank for assistance might take "quite a long time" to consider, according to the Bank's President Taroichi Yoshida, representative of another country well-known for its "blundering efforts to do good" (see chapter 1, p. 17) in Southeast Asia. "Observers believed that Mr. Yoshida's caution stemmed, in major part, from the reluctance of the United States to extend economic assistance to Vietnam until the political relationship between the two countries has been put on a normal peacetime footing"[46]—a process allegedly impeded by Vietnamese cruelty in refusing to settle the problem of MIAs, the sole outstanding issue between the two countries.[47]

So stern is U.S. moralism that even recipients of U.S. "Food for Peace" aid must refrain from assisting the errant Vietnamese. The government of India wanted to send 100 buffaloes to Vietnam to help replenish the herds decimated by the same mysterious hand that destroyed the hospitals, left the land "fallow," and made Vietnam into a land of widespread disease and suffering, but it was compelled to channel the gift through the Indian Red Cross to avoid U.S. retribution, since Food for Peace (Public Law 480) prohibits assistance to "any exporter which is engaging in, or in the six months immediately preceding the application for such financing has engaged in, any sales, trade or commerce with North Vietnam or with any resident thereof ..." while another clause bars "any nation which sells or furnishes or permits ships or aircraft under its registry to transport to or from Cuba and North Vietnam any equipment, materials, or commodities so long as they are governed by a communist regime."[48]

Returning to the pretense of the *New York Times* specialists that "southern Vietnam has become virtually impenetrable by foreigners and only the Hanoi Government's picture of life in the reunited country is presented to the world," there had been many other unnoticed observers who had visited Vietnam, beyond those already mentioned. For example, in an account of a visit by Inder Malhotra of the independent *Times of India*,[49] he notes that his plane to Hanoi was "packed with travelers of many nationalities—from Cuban to Japanese," including one U.S. citizen leading a delegation sent to Vietnam by the UN Food and Agriculture Organization, and a number of Dutch journalists. But a look at Malhotra's report of his visit quickly explains why it too, like those of the Lacoutures and others, must be consigned to oblivion. Malhotra emphasizes "the whore-like, parasitic mentality that the American years bred even among those South Vietnamese who had nothing whatever to do with the prostitutes and their pimps" (of whom there still remain "a staggering number," though the Communists, he reports, are making impressive efforts to rehabilitate them and to cure the many dope addicts, preponderantly young boys and girls). "Most Saigonese would rather 'make money' than earn it. To them work is a dirty word; they would rather 'do business.'" He reports that "the new regime, very sensibly, has decided not to use the big stick to combat this mentality." Saigonese men and women who openly announce their opposition to the new regime also "confirm, on cross-examination, that despite their known dislike for the regime no one is hounding them out of the city." He also contrasts the spartan existence in the North (where "there are no pavement dwellers... and no beggars" and there is general tranquility—"Late at night it is not unusual to see a lone girl or several reading under a street lamp in front of darkened houses," just like New York) with the imported and artificial affluence of Saigon: "the contrast between the lifestyle of Hanoi and Saigon is so great that to go from the Northern metropolis to the Southern one is like leaving a monastery and plunging headlong into Hamburg's red light district." He also reports the ravages of the U.S. war.

Better, no doubt, to pretend that no foreigners can enter Vietnam.

The same considerations explain the nonexistence of Hugues Tertrais, who reported on his stay in Saigon where he was working "as a 'cooperant,' (a sort of French Peace Corps worker)."[50] Like all other direct observers, he discusses what he calls "the war's most crippling legacy," the artificial consumer-oriented "urban society based on 'services' and consisting largely of shanty towns," which must be radically transformed and returned to productivity if the society is to survive. He reports that there is "complete religious freedom" and discusses the efforts to reconstruct the stagnated economy and the resettlement in new economic zones ("the system now seems to be running smoothly, in spite of a slight sluggishness resulting from the nonauthoritarian nature of the operation"), where "young volunteers accompany the migrants to give them a hand with the preliminary work, and the people's army often makes lodgings available." He quotes Mme. Ngo Ba Thanh, a courageous U.S.-educated non-Communist dissident who was well-known to Americans in Saigon, who explains the effort "to promote 'revolution in production relationships,' 'ideological and cultural revolution,' and 'scientific and technical revolution,' which has a key role to play."

Among others who have escaped the keen and inquiring eyes of the analysts of the *New York Times*, searching for every scrap of evidence about Vietnam, are several Canadian Vietnamese who have visited their native country. Father Tran Tam Tinh and Professor Tran Dinh Khuong of Laval University (Quebec), both officials of *Fraternité Vietnam*, reported on their visit to Vietnam in the summer of 1976 in *Le Soleil* (Quebec), January 7, 1977.[51] Their impressions are rather like those of other direct observers, though in some respects more detailed. They describe the functioning of "solidarity cells" (social welfare groups in their view, though regularly described as agencies of state surveillance and coercion by the U.S. press); "solidarity workshops" organized by Catholic and Buddhist intellectuals in such regions as the "Iron Triangle," devastated by U.S. terrorists, who say that they are volunteers; schools that engage the youth in communal activism and cultural events (which they witnessed); and so on. *Fraternité Vietnam* has also circulated a detailed report by Professor Tran Dinh Khuong on his seven-week tour, which included visits to industrial and artisans cooperatives, schools, hospitals, Catholic journals directed by priests and lay Catholics, churches,[52] etc., in both North and South Vietnam, where he spoke with many functionaries, doctors, journalists, and so on. The major concern of his visit was to prepare for humanitarian assistance from abroad, and he ends his report by saying that "we will be happy to furnish additional information and explanations to aid organizations that would like to participate in these programs." Presumably he would also be pleased to offer further information to U.S. journalists concerned with fact rather than service to the state propaganda system, but the opportunity has evidently not arisen.

In a letter published in the Toronto *Globe and Mail* (5 April 1977), the two Canadian Vietnamese visitors report that they were "each living with our own families" and "we wandered through the streets of Ho Chi Minh City (formerly Saigon) and met with people of all social categories," engaging in "discussion with many average and ordinary Vietnamese." The fact is significant, given allegations featured in the Free Press to which we return.

Actually, even the careful reader of the *New York Times* will be able to ascertain that other sources of information do exist beyond those to which the *Times* analysts choose to restrict themselves,[53] and that they often give a picture that differs substantially from the dreary and dismal scene of oppression and misery that the *Times* specialists construct from their carefully selected sources. Kathleen Teltsch reported from the UN in New York that "Westerners who visited Vietnam almost two years after the end of the war report that agricultural recovery is progressing although rice rationing continues in both North and South," referring to "separate groups of Mennonites and Quakers," UN officials, and "a World Bank mission that spent four weeks assessing the economic situation."[54] In paragraph 12, five lines are devoted to the report by the UN coordinator for rehabilitation assistance to Vietnam who "has said that significant progress has already been made but that reconstruction requirements remain vast." In paragraph 7, Max Ediger, "a Mennonite social worker from Kansas who lived in Vietnam from 1971 to 1976," is reported as saying that on his return to Vietnam "he was struck by the greening of the country-side, with areas once burned to the ground already turned into crop land." The reader who may be interested in further details will not find them in the *New York Times*.

More attention is given to the failure of these Western observ-ers to ask to see reeducation centers where "it has been alleged, the authorities have interned tens of thousands, including soldiers and supporters of the American backed Government," posing a "human-rights issue" which "could loom large in President Car-ter's consideration of relations with Hanoi," the latter comment, typical Western cynicism. The response of the Quaker group to this charge is taken up under the heading: "Issue of Repression By-passed." The sole contents, under this heading, is a series of com-ments by Wallace Collett, a businessman who headed the Quaker mission. He reports that after travelling widely and "talking freely with Roman Catholic and Buddhist leaders, with intellectuals and with Vietnamese 'known over the years as people whose accounts were reliable,'" his group was convinced that accusations of wide-spread repression are untrue, though, as he said, "the Vietnamese make no apologies for holding some [former officers or officials of the Thieu government] and tell us they do so for offenses we'd consider treason." Though the *Times* does not mention the fact, the group contained Vietnamese-speaking members who had lived and worked in Vietnam and met with non-Communist Vietnamese who had long been known for principled resistance to oppression.

It is interesting that this denial of repression by a group that specifically investigated it,[55] apparently relying on sources that seem reasonable enough, should appear under the heading "Issue of Repression Bypassed." The explanation for this anomaly, surely, is that the conclusions reached by the visitors did not conform to the doctrinal assumptions that guide "news reporting" in the Free Press. Consequently, the editors simply lied about the contents of the story in the subheading and reporters made no further effort to determine to whom the delegation spoke and what these informants said—a matter of some interest, as we shall see—just as their account of general conditions has had no impact on reporting and analysis in the press and receives no more than passing mention in a context that suggests that it can be dismissed, in contrast to material that *Times* ideologues find more to their taste.

Since the United States is a Free Society, it is possible for the assiduous investigator to determine what the Mennonite and Quaker visitors discovered on their visit. Max Ediger of the Mennonite Central Committee, who worked in Vietnam for 5 years and remained for 13 months after the war, reported on his two-week visit in January, 1977 at a February 9 private conference that included members of the Senate and House.[56] Since the war's end, this was the third Mennonite delegation to visit Vietnam, where the Mennonites had worked for 23 years. Ediger discussed the vast improvement in the educational system, in which he had been involved during his years in Vietnam, the efforts to find employment for urban refugees and their return "to their old villages in the countryside," where "they continue to face many hardships." It is not the "human cost" of the return to the land, which so preoccupies *New York Times* analysts, that Ediger reports, but rather the fact that "unexploded mines and other munitions litter their fields. Well trained military units first sweep the fields to try to clean them, but the farmers are still being killed." In a letter of May 11, 1977 to *Worldview* magazine, Ediger reports that "an elderly member of a small congregation I occasionally attended returned to his farm after many years of living as a refugee" and "was instantly killed" when "he had only begun to turn over the fallow soil...[and]...his hoe hit an M79 grenade." Ediger heard many reports of similar deaths, and asks, reasonably it would seem: "If we produced the munitions, and put them there, do we not have a moral responsibility to take them out so the farmers can live?" The editors of the *New York Times* have yet to recognize such a responsibility, when they remind us that "Our Vietnam Duty is Not Over."[57]

Another problem that Ediger discusses in his testimony is "the vast destruction of soil and facilities inflicted by the past war," a problem aggravated by the termination of U.S. aid (particularly fertilizers) and the necessity to do all work by hand. The church, he reports, "continues to function freely and normally," and the government "has helped the Protestant church rebuild five of their structures destroyed by bombing in Da Nang. "Saigon is still suffering from major over-population and other war-related problems," but "one can sense a certain feeling of relaxation among the people which was not there during the war."

In his letter to *Worldview* Ediger adds further information. He visited a Buddhist seminary that had recently opened in Hanoi to train monks "for service in the numerous pagodas throughout the country," where Buddhist scriptures were being translated from Sanskrit to Vietnamese "so that it will be available to all Vietnamese." He also "met several old friends who, because they were officers in the old army, spent nine months in re-education camps. They made no mention of torture and mistreatment" but "rather talked about learning how to work with their hands" and said that they had learned "about the new economic and social system they were living under. One young doctor, after completing his reeducation course, was made director of a drug rehabilitation center near Saigon." A Protestant church rebuilt with the assistance of the government was dedicated on Christmas day; it had "received a direct hit from an American bomber in 1971 which resulted in the death of 80 Christians who had taken refuge there." He also visited badly-needed development projects in the countryside and "programs set up to help former prostitutes and drug addicts receive training so that they could re-enter society as productive members of that society rather than as outcasts."

Ediger does not doubt that there are serious human rights violations in Vietnam, and is aware that his tour undoubtedly was restricted. But he rather gently makes some important points: "Unless we accept the fact that we too are violating rights in Vietnam, and strive to correct that, we lose our basis for speaking about others' possible violation of human rights...Is it not the right of a human being to be able to return to his/her farm and till the soil without the threat of being blown to bits by an M79 grenade or a claymore mine?...If we helped destroy [hospitals and schools], are we not violating the rights of the Vietnamese people if we refuse to help them rebuild those structures?" These questions are foreign to moralists in the Free Press.

Beneficiaries of the Freedom of the Press can also learn about the Quaker visit that was so quickly dismissed by the *Times* (see p. 100 above), which included two members fluent in Vietnamese, Louis Kubicka (on the staff at AFSC's Quang Ngai Rehabilitation Center from 1967-1971 and then AFSC representative in Laos) and Sophie Quinn-Judge (AFSC Saigon Representative for 1973-1975 and then co-director of the Southeast Asia Seminar Program).[58] The Quaker group travelled by road from Da Nang to Ho Chi Minh City (Saigon). The "most ambitious single reconstruction effort" they visited was a dam and dike near Quang Ngai, destroyed by the United States in an area that was later subjected to some of the most brutal operations in the war.[59] In Hanoi they met Jean-Pierre Debris, a Frenchman who had spent two years in Saigon's Chi Hoa prison (his effort to reach the U.S. public in a subsequent tour here was virtually blanked out by the press) and now works with Catherine Debris at the Foreign Languages Publishing House in Hanoi. In the South they had discussions with many of the best-known leaders of the non-Communist opposition under the U.S.-backed regimes and renewed acquaintances with staff at the AFSC Quang Ngai clinic. Their account of a country rebuilding under the miserable conditions left by the United States is similar in tone and content to other eyewitness reports that we have discussed, so we will not proceed to review it.

Recall that the *Times* did report that the Quaker delegation had met well-known non-Communists in the South who had denied reports of widespread repression, but made no effort to discover the contents of these discussions; nor did other mainstream journalists to our knowledge, despite (or more accurately because of) the obvious significance of this material for anyone concerned with the facts. Ly Chanh Trung, who had been a leading spokesman for the non-Communist opposition under the Thieu regime, took pains to deny reports of repression, asking the Quaker delegation to convey a personal message to antiwar activists whom he knew in the United States:

> We here are among the people who have been struggling for human rights in Saigon. If a violation of human rights occurs, we ourselves will raise our voices. We will not wait for our friends from abroad to raise theirs. When we were struggling for human rights here we saw that all the so-called human rights related to basic rights—not personal rights, but national rights: independence and freedom of the nation. If you don't have these rights, you don't have any rights whatsoever...Socialism can guarantee the most basic of human rights, and guarantee them for everyone. These are the right to live, the right to have work to do, the right of health protection service, the right to education, the right to build a better future, not for myself alone, but for all the people. These rights are not guaranteed by a capitalist society.

He went on to deny that the reeducation camps "have the purpose of revenging or killing [officers or high-ranking servants of the old regime] gradually." Both he and Ngo Cong Duc emphasized that there was much bitterness after 30 years of war and that "now the problem is how to have people live with one another, be reconciled to one another, and to understand one another."[61]

It is conceivable that these courageous human rights activists, non-Communists who were well-known to Americans in Saigon (the press included) and who struggled and suffered for many years, are now so ignorant or so terrorized by the new regime that their reaction can be dismissed. Or it may be that their voice is as important now as it was under the regime of U.S.-imposed subfascism. A free and honest press would present the evidence, permitting readers to come to their own conclusions. But the U.S. press reacts quite differently. There is no mention of the views of the leading non-Communist oppositionists, and even a passing reference to the fact that they had been in contact with Americans who had known them in the past appears only under the heading "Issue of Repression Bypassed."

The Third Force leader who was best-known in the West was Mme. Ngo Ba Thanh, who had attended Columbia Law School and was the founder of the Women's Movement for the Right to Life, was imprisoned and tortured by Thieu for her courageous opposition to his despotism and released only after a widespread international protest, and is now a Member of Parliament. She met with a Swedish delegation led by Birgitta Dahl, a Social Democrat MP, on February 15, 1977.[62] In this statement she reiterates that "I am *not* a communist" (her emphasis) and recalls the brutality and repression under the U.S.-imposed regime, which had jailed her four times for a period of about 5 years. She too strongly denies the charges of violation of human rights and "the attacks coming from the U.S. imperialists through the naive actions of good people," referring to a petition signed by former antiwar activists that was featured in the *New York Times*.[63]

She asserts that:

The great majority of the people who were forced to serve the puppet regime are considered by the revolutionary government only as victims. But if these people are to live in peace and true democracy, we could not tolerate traitors who committed monstrous crimes and still continue to be the instruments of imperialism—and we give this small minority no opportunity whatsoever to sabotage the wise policy of reconciliation and the huge task of reconstruction after so many years of a war we never wanted.

She calls upon people who have protested human rights violations in Vietnam to recognize that U.S. leaders "need to invent all kinds of stories to destroy trust" and "to support our post-war struggle, for our legitimate right to be a member of the United Nations, to take up the new challenge of our times."

Again, her reaction would seem to be of some significance in the light of her long and courageous struggle as a leader of the non-Communist opposition to the client regime imposed by U.S. force. Perhaps she too has been intimidated or deluded. Readers of the U.S. press might judge for themselves, given the opportunity.

To be precise, Mme. Ngo Ba Thanh has received some press coverage. A report by George McArthur, formerly a war correspondent in South Vietnam, was devoted to an article of hers that was carried by Hanoi Radio in March, 1977.[64] The topic of the report is the scope of imprisonment in re-education camps. "The strongest hint about the numbers of South Vietnamese in camps indicated a minimum figure of about 110,000," McArthur writes, adding that "in the view of refugees coming from the South, this estimate is ridiculously low." How does McArthur arrive at this figure? His source is the article by Ngo Ba Thanh, who, he writes, was "the most persuasive spokeman advanced by North Vietnam" in their response to criticism from the United States (in which they follow "the Moscow line in attacking Carter's internationalist approach to human rights," which this correspondent, like most of his colleagues, does not perceive as something less than "internationalist"). She was, he adds, "in the forefront of antigovernment demonstrations in the South" and is now "one of the few Southerners who have attained or maintained influence with the Communist regime since Saigon's fall." In her article, she "extolled Hanoi's lenient attitudes and went on to say,

> Before returning to normal life, prolonged reeducation will be necessary for some 5 percent of utterly degraded former members of the puppet army and administration, such as members of the Green Berets, the Rangers, the paratroopers, marines, policemen, prison guards, district officials, village chiefs, and secret agents who were trained by the United States."

McArthur interprets the alleged comments as implying that 5 percent of the 1.1 million man army and police forces and the 100,000 civil servants will "be held for a 'prolonged period'"—namely 110,000 people. (We take no responsibility for the arithmetic.)

The Quakers, Mennonites, reporters from the international press, Canadian Vietnamese Catholics, relief workers, UN officials, and others cited are not the only people who have been able to penetrate the "virtually impenetrable" barriers placed by the Hanoi government around southern Vietnam, compelling the *New York Times* to restrict itself to reports of refugees and selected diplomats. Well before Henry Kamm's complaints, an extensive report was published of a visit by a Friendshipment delegation concerned with humanitarian aid to the South,[65] again reporting meetings with Ngo Ba Thanh and other Third Force leaders, and focusing primarily on economic and social reconstruction. Granted that these issues do not appeal to the U.S. press, still their report might have been noted for the record.

A moderately enterprising reporter could have discovered numerous other sources. Consider for example James Klassen, who was engaged in relief and social services for the Mennonite Central Committee from October, 1972 until April, 1976, and who speaks, reads and writes Vietnamese fluently.[66] A devout

Christian, he comments that "while not involved with business interests like so many French missionaries before them, American Protestant missionaries—except for a precious few—generally supported the U.S. political and military involvement in Vietnam."[67] Klassen taught Bible classes throughout 1975. Contrary to many fears, he writes, "The government in Vietnam adopted a policy of religious tolerance and based on my experience I do not feel that there was any systematic repression of religion by the government." Some churches are "dynamic and growing"; "The Evangical Church of Vietnam (Protestant) continues to offer Bible correspondence courses and in fact advertised them in the *Tin Sang* newspaper," a "rather independent daily newspaper" with the Catholic Ngo Cong Duc as head of its editorial staff. Former Mennonite schools continue to operate as before with basically the same personnel and the government now paying salaries that were formerly contributed by North American Mennonites. "Although the government in Vietnam has adopted a tolerant policy toward religion, there has been a de-centralization of power so that people down at the local level have quite a bit of control, more like the typical structure used to be," so there may be considerable variation from place to place. Church attendance is high and religious books are widely available. A Buddhist nun and a (relatively conservative) Catholic priest were elected to represent Saigon in the National Assembly. Religious training centers maintain high enrollment. "Young people in Vietnam are typically full of idealism and enthusiasm, and now on their days off this is being channeled into constructive projects to help build their homeland, including digging canals and working alongside the farmers so that the country's economy can be based solidly on agriculture once again." Vietnamese Christians are coming to recognize that if the church is to survive, "we've got to make our religion attractive by the way we live" (a Vietnamese pastor in Saigon). A young Vietnamese-Protestant medical doctor, addressing "the young people who packed the large Tran Cao Van Church in Saigon" in February, 1976 as part of the lunar New Year festivities said that "Christians need to support and participate in the worthwhile programs of the government—building a new society, rebuilding our country, helping our people ..."[68]

Or consider an Italian missionary priest, now in Hong Kong, who circulated privately an account of his 15 months after liberation in Vietnam where he lived in a small village in the suburbs of Saigon with a small group of Christians called "the Missionaries of Vietnam."[69] He felt "that what I was witnessing was the last stage of a real revolution, a long revolution that has freed the country first from the French and then from the Americans. This revolution was liberating the Vietnamese people from the control of foreigners and from all the problems they had brought along to Vietnam." He explains why, with considerable personal detail. As for refugees, he expresses sympathy and compassion:

> one must admit that those who are unwilling to live in a certain system have the right to be welcomed in other countries, of a type more suited to their taste. It is, nevertheless, terribly dishonest to make these refugees say, in the countries that have received them, those things that the welcoming countries strongly wish to hear.

A warning that is supported by the historical record; see the discussion of the Bryce Report, chapter 2, section 1. It is still more dishonest to proclaim that there is no information apart from the reports of refugees.

Many more examples may be added.[70] It is quite true that information regarding Vietnam is limited, and that much of what is available (apart from refugees), though by no means all, is derived from "guided tours." But the limitations on the press are to a significant extent self-imposed, reflecting ideological constraints rather than the exigencies of reporting under difficult conditions.

The professional literature has also succeeded in escaping the unfortunate limitations on evidence that are bewailed in the press. For example, in the Canadian journal *Pacific Affairs*, Professor William S. Turley of Southern Illinois University, one of the small group of U.S. academic specialists on Vietnam,[71] contributed a study of postwar Vietnam in which he made use of Vietnamese sources among others.[72] The victors faced numerous problems, among them, "a near famine condition among the poor," the collapse of the economy, and urban over-population. The war, he writes, "grossly enlarged the service sector of the economy, encouraged private consumption without corresponding develop-ment of productive capacity, exacerbated inequalities, and eroded social discipline." He compares PRG and postwar programs with those attempted by the Thieu regime, concluding that the former have been far more successful and that "progress already made under the new regime must be considered all the more remark-able and the ultimate goal, if reached, an astonishing achieve-ment." He comments on the "even handed pragmatism" of the PRG and current programs, the "massive extension of popular participation, and maximum feasible reliance on voluntary com-pliance to bring about major social and demographic changes" including campaigns to assist the poor and in general ensure that "social values henceforth would be redistributed downward" through the efforts of popular organizations "under the guidance of party cadres," which he describes in some detail. Prominent anti-Thieu non-Communists, such as Mme. Ngo Ba Thanh, have appeared in a leadership role in these efforts:

> The principal reasons for so quickly developing these forms of popular participation were to build a social base where the revolution had had only latent or secret support, to gain access to the urban population in order to instruct it in the values and perspectives of the new order, to obtain popular assistance in the implementation of certain practical measures, and to iso-late close associates or unrepentant supporters of the previous regime by organizing those who had been ignored or disen-

franchised by it. In this mobilization of the urban population, the PRG has been successful to a degree that its predecessor, whose leaders assumed the cities were 'secure,' had never attempted to achieve. RVN governments had been preoccupied with the military conflict in rural areas and had neglected the cities, while the elitist and fractious opposition groups seldom engaged in urban ward-heeling. Ironically, many city-dwellers, probably the vast majority, now have experienced political participation and have been called upon to show active support for their government for the first time in their lives.[73]

The urgently needed redistribution of population has achieved "notable results" though difficulties remain. "The primary candidates for resettlement were people who had been forced to evacuate their homes by US-RVN military strategy." Turley stresses the voluntarism of the program that is "urbanizing the countryside as it decongests the cities," a program "best understood *not* as a reversal of war-time flow of peasants to the cities (though this is one element) but as a movement of poor and unemployed city dwellers, some semi-urbanized peasants, from the city to the country," escaping the "wretched living conditions" of many urban areas ("less prevalent in Saigon," where "the proportion of war-time growth accounted for by in-migration was smaller than in other cities"). Interpretations such as this rarely find their way to a general audience.

What the press wants to hear, and hence publicizes widely, is such testimony as that of Nguyen Cong Hoan, to whom one full session of the June-July, 1977 congressional hearings (see note 70) was devoted. Hoan was a member of the National Assembly representing a South Vietnamese province before his escape in March, 1977, and is described in the hearings as a former member of the Saigon Assembly who "was known for his opposition to Thieu's government."[74] He gives a grisly account of "the suffering of millions of my countrymen," and says that "given the new rule, many like myself come to better appreciate the U.S.

involvement in Vietnam." "All the basic rights are suppressed," he reports. Specifically, all religions "are under intense persecution... There is almost no religious life left in the country...most of the churches have been destroyed or requisitioned by the state and the few that are still standing are attended on Sunday by only a few older people...In the South the training to become monk or priest is expressly forbidden...Every religious library has been confiscated and the contents burned...All religious mass organizations are proclaimed to be illegal and forbidden to meet or carry out activities... the Protestants in Vietnam also are persecuted and all the pastors are considered CIA agents."

Furthermore, "individuals and political parties once involved in the preservation of democratic liberties in South Vietnam, even those closely allied with the National Liberation Front and the Provisional Revolutionary Government are behind bars." A few "former so-called Third Force elements were voted into the National Assembly, for instance, Mrs. Ngo Ba Thanh or Professor Ly Chanh Trung, but these were elected more to deceive world opinion rather than anything else" and "they are totally helpless." Similarly, Tran Quoc Buu, former head of the Vietnamese Federation of Labor, is considered by the Communists to be "one of the CIA bosses in Saigon"; whereas "formerly, all the [union] leaders were elected by the workers," now the union "is totally created by the Communists."

"No Vietnamese dares to talk to a foreigner unless he is given permission to do so." Furthermore, "eliminations and killings have occurred on a widespread scale and under many forms, some so subtle that no outside observers can possibly detect," including some 700 killed in his own province (see p. 118 below). Some people were buried alive or "eliminated after extremely atrocious tortures" while others "died in concentration camps." The number of political prisoners is 200,000 at a minimum.[75]

As for the New Economic Zones, they "are no better than

prison camps...lands of exile that no one in his right mind would choose to go unless forced to do so." They are far worse than the "agrovilles" or "New Life Hamlets" of Presidents Diem and Thieu ("people were never afraid to go there even during the war where there was still a good measure of insecurity involved").

Hoan escaped when "I realized that their main policy was for the impoverishment of everybody so that they can use a Communist leverage on the people and try to dominate their thinking." The government also plans "to exterminate land owners" either by "physical elimination" or imprisonment.[76]

In the North, suffering is even worse than in the South. "Through my contacts with the people of North Vietnam I realized that they are also very dissatisfied with the Communist regime...many people in the North are trying now to flee to the South so that they can live under not so much fear in a society which is freer than in the North." He urges that the United States "refrain from giving aid"—all kinds—to Vietnam. Thus, no food, no medical assistance, etc.

Turning to foreign policy, Hoan alleges that North Vietnam is supporting Communist insurgents in Thailand and Malaysia and "Vietnam also sells arms worth some $2 billion to other nations."[77]

Some of what Hoan reports is no doubt accurate, particularly concerning severe restrictions on personal freedom, including freedom of expression and travel. How credible is his testimony in general? His account of religious persecution is expressly contradicted by direct observation of Westerners and Vietnamese who lived in or visited Vietnam, including those already cited.[78] Either we must assume that the visitors who report having attended church services and observed ongoing religious activities are all lying and that the religious leaders they spoke to (including those who travelled in Europe) are also Communist agents or are too intimidated to speak, or we must conclude that Hoan is hardly a reliable observer, on these grounds alone.

The same is true of his reference to the Third Force activists, who expressly reject his account of their situation and activities, though one could not know this from the U.S. press. As for Tran Quoc Buu, he is not simply considered by the Communists to have been "one of the CIA bosses in Saigon"; he was one. Frank Snepp refers to him as a "CIA client," "the noted labor leader who had long been a CIA collaborator." He was the "pride of the Station [CIA] in the fall of 1972," having been turned into a "collaborator" a year earlier and since used by the CIA "quite profitably, as an instrument for keeping the unions loyal to Thieu and for channeling pro-government propaganda to labor organizations around the world." He was even suggested by the CIA chief as "a token opposition candidate" so as to avoid "the embarrassment of a one-man contest" for Thieu.[79] No doubt unions are now agencies of the state, but it is far from clear that workers have less of a role in them than hitherto.[80]

Hoan's account of the New Economic Zones does not conform to that of direct observers, including those cited above (he reports no direct experience). It seems hardly more credible than his reference to the forced resettlement programs under Diem[81] or the Thieu programs.[82] It is difficult to see why the leadership in Hanoi, which has certainly been dedicated to economic development (whatever one may think of its politics), should try to resettle the population in "prison camps" or dedicate itself to general impoverishment as Hoan asserts without evidence. Hoan's claim that no one dares to talk to foreigners without permission is difficult to reconcile with what is reported by visitors with long experience in Vietnam, e.g., visiting Vietnamese who lived with their families, the Mennonite and Quaker visitors or Don Luce, all of whom report personal meetings with friends and former associates, or with reports of relief workers who stayed in Vietnam for a long period after the end of the war.[83] Either the many visitors and Westerners living in Vietnam who expressly contradict his claims are, once again, lying, or a charade of astonishing proportions is being enacted—or, more plausibly, Hoan is simply not a reliable commentator.

Hoan's plea that no aid, even humanitarian, be offered to Vietnam contrasts strikingly with the recommendation of the Pope, for example, in his meeting with visiting church dignitaries from Vietnam (see note 68), and again might cause some raised eyebrows, along with his report of northerners fleeing to the South or Vietnam's foreign involvements.[84]

In short, a reporter of any integrity would be quite cautious in relying on Hoan's testimony, though it would be a mistake to disregard it.

In dramatic contrast to the authentic leaders of the non-Communist opposition to the U.S.-imposed regimes (see, e.g., those listed in note 74), who have vainly attempted to reach a U.S. audience through the medium of the many visitors whose existence is ignored or denied by the Free Press, Hoan has been granted considerable publicity and no questions have been raised about the reliability of what he has reported, despite the substantial evidence that contradicts it. On his arrival in Tokyo, he was interviewed by representatives of the international press. The London *Economist* (7 May 1977) reported Hoan's statement that there is extensive food rationing, "not because of shortages but as a 'communist ruse to break down all possible resistance'" (the *Economist* added that "there are *also* genuine shortages" because of bad weather; our emphasis), and that Bishop Nguyen Van Thuan is rumored to have been killed.[85] Hoan and two other South Vietnamese politicians who escaped with him said, according to the *Economist*, "that, in retrospect, they believe the American intervention in the Vietnam war was right." The *Economist* speculates that "the government may be clamping down on the remnants of the 'third force.'" It does not report, and to our knowledge has never reported, what well-known Third Force leaders have told to visitors.

Hoan's charges were also reported by David Tharp from Tokyo.[86] Tharp describes him as "an anti-American leader of the 'peace bloc' under the regime of President Nguyen Van Thieu," which is untrue so far as we can determine, but adds some spice to the story. Hoan "described the lack of food not as a matter of shortages but as a means of breaking down resistance." "Ordinary Vietnamese" who meet journalists are required to "speak through an official interpreter, even though the Vietnamese may be fluent in the language used by the newsman, said Mr. Hoan."[87] "Mr. Hoan said he now thinks many Vietnamese are prepared to accept another war to sweep out the Communists." He is quoted as saying: "The American intervention was right. Just the manner was wrong. They supported a weak government." He also requested "weapons, food, and medical supplies for anti-Communist guerrilla bands."

Henry Kamm also reported from Japan on an interview with Hoan,[88] repeating similar charges. Hoan and his fellow-escapees "said that their disenchantment with Communist rule was shared by all the prominent persons from the old anti-Government organization still in Vietnam, from its best known leaders to the few who still hold public positions." Like his colleagues, Kamm has never reported the views expressed by these former Third Force leaders and does not inquire into the credibility of Hoan's report of their views, contradicting their own repeated expression of support for the regime to visitors and friends. Finally, Kamm reports that "so far, the Japanese Government has effectively confined them [Hoan and his fellow-escapees] to this fishing town about 100 miles from Tokyo, where their access to the world public is limited." He does not compare the "limited access" of Hoan to the U.S. and world press with that of people who actually were courageous leaders of the non-Communist opposition.[89]

Kamm returned to the same theme a few weeks later.[90] Hoan

and his friends from "what used to be the pro-peace opposition in the Saigon parliament" now "find themselves prevented from giving their testimony or the world unwilling to listen." "People are indifferent," Hoan told him, "not only the Japanese but even the Vietnamese who have been here for a longer time." It is quite true that members of the pro-peace opposition to the Thieu regime have been prevented from giving their testimony; Henry Kamm is a well-placed example of those who have refused to allow such testimony to be heard. But Hoan is the only former member of this group who has succeeded in gaining an international audience, despite his insignificant role. The pretense by those who dominate the press that they cannot get their message through is a common device that has often proven useful for propaganda purposes. It is a constant complaint of businessmen, for example. We return to other examples of this useful gambit, which nicely supplements the constant lament that the media are "anti-government" and "fiercely independent." We have already discussed the ways in which Kamm and his colleagues in the Free Press dealt with the defection of a highly-placed collaborator with the Indonesian government in Timor (see Volume I, chapter 3, section 4.4, note 208 and text), contrasting their silence in that case with the publicity afforded to Hoan, coupled, typically, with the pretense that Hoan is being silenced.

Theodore Jacqueney, who worked with USAID in Vietnam until 1971 when he resigned in disagreement with U.S. support for Thieu and has since become a leading and very well-publicized critic of human rights violations in Vietnam, reported on Hoan's congressional testimony in the pro-war AFL-CIO *Free Trade Union News,* claiming that it confirms "steady refugee reports of Vietnam's Gulag Archipelago."[91] He describes Hoan as "a radical Buddhist peace advocate in South Vietnam's legislature," a judgment that may well reflect the assessment of Jacqueney's U.S. government associates at the time, who commonly interpreted even the mildest dissent as "radical." Jacqueney then reports on a series of interviews with Hoan in which he elaborated on his congressional testimony. Hoan's information about 500 people allegedly executed in his native province derives from a dismissed Communist province chief. Jacqueney reports Hoan's account of what this man told him as follows:

> He explained that during the first days after the war they had to eliminate dangerous elements to provide an example and to satisfy desires for revenge. Some people killed were police officials under Thieu who had imprisoned and tortured revolutionaries. Some were simply civilian officials, or just members of political parties. Even ordinary people were killed for personal revenge.

As we have noted before, only by humanitarian standards that are completely foreign to the history and culture of the industrial democracies is it an atrocity to take revenge on torturers. Yet such standards are selectively invoked in the West in the case of a country that has recently freed itself from a century of Western oppression culminating in an explosion of unprecedented barbarism. They are invoked by someone who loyally served those responsible for the rule of the torturers through the worst and most vicious period of their attack on victims who are now denounced for their violation of human rights, in the journal of an organization that not only supported this endeavor but has a long record of support for policies that involve hideous atrocities elsewhere in U.S. domains. Quite apart from these not entirely irrelevant facts, note that if Jacqueney's account of this second-hand report from a highly unreliable source concerning revenge against torturers or even personal revenge against completely innocent people demonstrates that Hanoi has imposed a "Gulag Archipelago," then we will need some new and as yet uninvented phrase, expressing vastly greater levels of horror and indignation, to describe the period of U.S. civil-military administration in France or the behavior of U.S. military and civilian

authorities in Asia after World War II, not to speak of the reality
of life under the U.S. aegis in Guatemala, Uruguay, and a long
list of other subfascist states. But such elementary observations
as these have no place in the current phase of Western ideology.

Continuing with Jacqueney's article, he writes that according to Hoan, the worst treatment in the prisons "was reserved
for members of political parties who opposed the Communists,
even if they also opposed Saigon dictatorships." Jacqueney then
proceeds to report some authentic cases of political repression
(e.g., the imprisonment of Tran Van Tuyen, who died in confinement), and others that are more questionable, for example, the
arrest of Father Tran Huu Thanh whom Jacqueney describes as
"a popular Catholic priest who led mammoth demonstrations
against Thieu regime repression and corruption...[preaching]...a
vivid gospel of social justice comparable to that of Martin Luther
King, Jr." Father Thanh was arrested after the quelling of the
armed rebellion centered in the Vinh Son Church (see note 68).
In fact, he was a psychological warfare specialist who trained
ARVN officers at the Central School of Psychological Warfare.
Before that, he had been an adviser to Diem, and came to oppose Thieu as ineffective in the war against Communism. He
described himself in December, 1974 as belonging to the First
Force (with Thieu): "So from the beginning we thought only of
replacing the leader and maintaining everything in the structure
of the regime." His anti-Thieu movement called for "clean government" so that the Communists "have to accept to come and
live with us as a minority," the standard U.S. government line
at the time. Authentic opponents of the U.S.-imposed regime
suspected him of operating with U.S. assistance, and there is
supporting evidence. In short, hardly a Martin Luther King.[92]

As this review indicates, the exposure that the press offers
to non-Communist dissidents in Vietnam is not a function of
their prominence, their demonstrated courage and reliability, or

the credibility of what they have to say as compared with the direct testimony of others. Rather, it is determined by a simple principle: the more negative their report, the more prominently it is featured. This principle, while occasionally violated, serves rather well as a first approximation and falls under the general theory of the Free Press as an agency of the state propaganda system, which, as we have seen throughout these two volumes, is quite well confirmed.

The same principle applies in the case of Western visitors or residents in Vietnam. As we have noted, there have been many, and quite a few of them have excellent credentials for reliability and long experience in the country; in some cases, in postwar Vietnam. But their reports, often critical though sympathetic, have been almost entirely ignored by the Free Press. There has, however, been a glaring exception to the general disregard for testimony by Westerners who remained in Vietnam for a considerable period after the war's end, or who have returned to the country where they worked and lived; namely, the case of Father André Gelinas, a Canadian Jesuit who spent 15 months in Vietnam after the war's end. An interview he gave to the Paris L'Express (amplified by a telephone interview) was reported in the New York Times (16 December 1976), in an AP report from Paris. The L'Express article was translated in the New York Review of Books (17 March 1977) and excerpted in the Washington Post (13 March 1977), and was the subject of editorials in the New York Times (21 March 1977) and the Wall Street Journal (21 April 1977). A similar article appeared in the Sunday Telegraph (London) and was reprinted in the Globe and Mail (Toronto, 23-24 March 1977). It has also appeared and been the subject of comment elsewhere in the English-language press. This exposure contrasts strikingly with that afforded to reports of others who had spent roughly the same period in Vietnam, or, for example, to the book by the Lacoutures, which, as we have noted, was unable to find an

American publisher and was not reviewed in the United States, to our knowledge.[93]

Not coincidentally, Gelinas's account is the most harshly critical among eyewitness reports by Westerners with comparable experience.

Though Gelinas had spent many years in Vietnam,[94] he was quite unknown in the West prior to the fall of 1976, and appears to have made no public statement during his 13, or 19, or 28 years in Vietnam concerning the U.S. war—of which, as we shall see, he was and remains a firm supporter.

The initial reaction to Gelinas was tinged with skepticism, for good reasons. The report in the *Times* (December 16), headed "Priest, Back from Saigon Speaks of Mass Suicides," dealt only with Gelinas's most sensational charge, namely, his claim that "15,000 to 20,000 Vietnamese have committed suicide rather than live under Communism." How did Gelinas find out this alleged fact? He is quoted as saying that his estimate was "based on conversations with hospital officials and some of the would-be suicides themselves." In the original AP dispatch, not included in the *Times* account, he is reported to have said that he calculated the estimate of suicides "from figures he got from dozens of hospital officials."[95] Further information about the alleged wave of suicides appears in the *L'Express-New York Review* article.[96] Here he provides a date: the "epidemic of suicides" in which "thousands of ruined and desperate Vietnamese put an end to themselves" followed a September 1975 announcement that each family had the right to only about 1,000 French francs. "Entire families killed themselves with revolvers," including a police officer who shot his ten children, wife and mother-in-law and then himself and a father who distributed poisoned soup to his family. "A young woman told me that she had awakened in a hospital corridor piled with hundreds of bodies. Those who were still living had their stomachs pumped out. Group suicides went on for several weeks."

So, in summary, Gelinas is claiming that in September-October, following the announcement of currency reform, 15-20,000 Vietnamese committed suicide, as he learned from discussions with hospital officials, would-be suicides, figures provided by dozens of hospital officials, and other sources.

In his congressional testimony of June 16, 1977 (see note 70), Gelinas did not repeat the story of mass suicides, which was featured in the earlier news report and article and which had originally brought him to public notice in the United States. Two likely reasons for this curious omission come to mind. The first is that one of the witnesses in the same session was Julia B. Forsythe of the AFSC, who lived two blocks from the Alexandre-de-Rhodes Center through October, 1975, and would therefore have been in a position to know something about such a wave of suicides.[97] A second reason is the unfortunate experience that Gelinas had had with these charges. The December, 1976 AP dispatch, citing his charges of mass suicides, reports that "there was no independent confirmation of the estimate...Western diplomatic sources said, 'we cannot verify these rather startling figures.'"[98] The *Times* article of December 16, 1976, after reporting Gelinas's headlined charges, turns to a denial of these claims by Richard Hughes, "head of the Shoeshine Boy Foundation, which sheltered and nurtured homeless children in Vietnam," who remained in Vietnam until a month after Gelinas's departure, living and working with poor Vietnamese (see note 83). Hughes denied the report, saying "Absolutely impossible that I wouldn't have heard about it. I was out in the neighborhoods and there were all kinds of people in contact with me, not only from the city, but coming from Da Nang and Hue and the delta. If 40 people in one place had committed suicide it would not have gotten past me."

Shortly after the sensational charge which introduced Gelinas to the U.S. (in fact Western) public, the following incident took place:

Two or three days later [after the December 16 *New York Times* story], Amy Hirsch, producer of the "Good Morning, America" show on ABC called Father Gelinas for a possible interview on the air. She sat him down with Dick Hughes and listened to the two argue and discuss for over two hours. She decided there was not enough to his story to even put Gelinas on the air. "He wouldn't name the hospitals...he was very sweet, but he just hadn't seen very much. There wasn't enough substance to put him on." During their conversation in the studio, confirmed by both Hirsch and Hughes, Fr. Gelinas explained the "15-20,000 suicides." He told the story of a young woman, an attempted suicide, who woke up in a hospital corridor surrounded by "hundreds of bodies." As it turned out, according to his source, these were attempted suicides, too, though it was unclear why she claimed the bodies were "piled." In any case, Gelinas explained, "From that, I took the number of hospitals in Saigon...I multiplied it times the number of hospitals..." Thus, the mass suicides in Vietnam turn out to be, after all, an extrapolation of *attempted suicides* from a single source in a hospital that Fr. Gelinas would not name.[99]

Gone are the figures provided by dozens of hospital officials, the entire families that killed themselves with revolvers, etc. This extrapolation merits comparison with that of Hoang Van Chi, for years the primary source on alleged North Vietnamese atrocities of the 1950s.[100]

Hughes has provided us with a detailed report of his several hours of conversation with Gelinas (to which we return), which reveals many more examples of his apparent ignorance of events in South Vietnam and his willingness to frame the most implausible charges against the new regime (see note 106). Hughes, who was known to U.S. reporters and others as a very reliable observer with intimate knowledge—rare among Americans—of the life of the impoverished mass of the population, sent a letter to the *New York Times* (31 March 1977) commenting on the *Times* editorial of March 21 on Gelinas. In this letter he discusses his "probing, three-hour conversation with Father Gelinas" and his failure to unearth any direct evidence for his charges, which appear to illustrate how "second-hand information fed rumor, and bitterness bias" for a foreigner who was one of the many who "could spend literally decades in Indochina and still remain within a small, isolated world," not an unusual phenomenon in colonial history—one recalls how commonly Western settlers, slave owners, and the like have been shocked to discover the feelings of their charges when insurrection and dissidence arise. The *Times* editorial, Hughes wrote, was "a tragic disservice to both the American and Vietnamese peoples, and to the healing process which has only just begun"—and has since aborted, thanks in part to the dissemination of Gelinas's charges in the *New York Review* and *Washington Post,* which appear to have been influential among liberal Congressmen[101] and certainly were so in the press and among the public. In contrast, the responses to Gelinas have been generally ignored.

Recall that the events of December, 1976 took place well before Gelinas received substantial publicity in the national media. Hirsch's scruples in investigating the "startling" charges by an unknown commentator, unverifiable by Western diplomatic sources and contradicted by others present in Vietnam at the time to which they refer, were not observed by many of her colleagues.[102]

While Gelinas appears to have abandoned the story about the mass suicides, his other comments do not exactly heighten his credibility. He is quoted as saying that the Vietnamese expelled him because "they do not want embarrassing witnesses"[103]—which is curious, since many other witnesses who could prove no less "embarrassing" have since been admitted—adding that "I was not treated badly for the regime had strict orders from Moscow not to make martyrs."[104] How could Gelinas have known about these "strict orders"? The question too does not seem to have been raised by the journals that printed this or other "information" provided by Gelinas without inquiry or comment.

In an interview in the *Montreal Star*, Gelinas said:

> People in South Vietnam today are praying for war...the way peo-
> ple in France were praying for it in 1942. They want to be invad-
> ed...I could hardly believe it when I heard people talking about
> war. They'd been at war for 20 years [sic]. But I actually had
> people say to me, "why don't the Americans send us the atomic
> bomb? It's the only way we'll get rid of the Communists."[105]

Some skepticism is perhaps in order when we read that South Vietnamese are praying for an invasion and plead for atomic bombing,
even apart from the direct testimony of many Western visitors and
residents who have received a rather different impression.

Gelinas goes on to say that "the new cadres (North Vietnamese officials) lived like kings. They were almost the only
fat people in Saigon and their children were driven to school
in limousines (usually Chevrolets captured from the Americans)." Again, this claim is in dramatic contrast to the reports
of Western observers about the general behavior of the North
Vietnamese, apart from cases of corruption that have been
discussed by the Vietnamese themselves. Braid notes that this
claim is rejected by Father Tran Tam Tinh, who "denies that
the cadres live rich lives" and says: "I've visited them where
they live and they live in poverty, like the rest of the people."
But, Braid continues, "Father Gelinas does not seem troubled
by such criticism. He says his critics are repeating what the
government has told them to say..."—knowledge derived from
the same source, perhaps, as the "fact" that he was well-treated
by orders from Moscow. Presumably those under government
orders include also the journalists, visitors and long-time Western residents who have reported the poverty and dedication of
the cadres, as well as his many critics.

Gelinas's widely publicized interview in the *New York Review*
elicited a response, dated March 16, 1977, from Earl Martin,
who worked with the Mennonite Central Committee from 1966

through 1969 and again from 1973 until the end of the war. It contains a response to Gelinas's major charges, based on eyewitness testimony, which is so detailed and specific that it seems unnecessary to review the charges and their refutation here.[106] Martin's response appeared on May 12, 1977, with no accompanying response from Gelinas, contrary to standard (virtually invariable) practice. The long delay and the lack of response suggests that the *New York Review* was unable to obtain a response to Martin's point-by-point refutation of Gelinas's charges.

Gelinas's further claims, which are hardly plausible in themselves, are entirely inconsistent with eyewitness reports by journalists and others cited above: e.g., his claim that "the official line that the girls [prostitutes] have been sent away for 're-education' is simply propaganda," that "one of the first aims of the Vietnamese Communists was to empty the cities," or that "the economy is also impoverished by the exactions of the North," etc.[107] Gelinas offers no evidence beyond what he claims to have seen and heard. Anyone who reads through his series of charges and contrasts them with other sources, and who compares the reliability of Gelinas and those who have explicitly denied his claims or others who have presented substantial evidence to the contrary, can scarcely fail to agree with Earl Martin's conclusion that "André Gelinas has seriously eroded any basis he might have had for serving as a credible witness."

Nevertheless, it is Gelinas's story that has remained "the truth" for the Free Press. In an editorial,[108] the *Times* conveys without any question "the picture that Father Gelinas paints of South Vietnam"—overlooking, for example, the doubts raised in their own news report of December 16, 1976. This is entirely appropriate—since Gelinas's account is very critical of an official enemy, its truthfulness is irrelevant and no further analysis is required. There is no need, for example, to assess his reliability, to weigh the testimony of other witnesses with a different view, or to consider the evidence of his critics. The *Times* editorial focuses on the "bitter and inescapable ironies" contained in Father Gelinas's report "for those who opposed the war."

Suppose, contrary to fact, that Gelinas's report was credible. In what respect would it then pose "bitter and inescapable ironies" for people who are opposed in principle to aggression and massacre? That question the *Times* editors do not discuss, and undoubtedly could not comprehend, so mired are they in official ideology, which does not permit this principle to be expressed with reference to the United States. Rather, in the official version to which the *Times* is committed, questions of principle do not arise: one may either support the policies of the United States or back its enemies, "look[ing] to the Communists as saviors of that unhappy land." The latter phrase is the standard *Times* straw man concerning those who opposed U.S. aggression in Vietnam on grounds of principle instead of inefficacy; recall that such views do not enter the spectrum of debate, as defined by *Times* ideologists.[109] The *Times* argues that "the Vietnam experience was always more complex than ideologues of either side could allow. America may have played a villain's role there, but the heroes of that tragedy were never easy to discern." The "heroes" of the German war against the Jews would be equally hard for mildly critical ex-Nazis to discern, and one can imagine a German super-patriot pointing to Israeli abuse of the Palestinians as somehow relevant to evaluating the "complexities" of the "final solution." Incapable of conceiving of the possibility that its own state was guilty of unprovoked aggression and massacre of innocents that could be condemned in and of itself, the *Times* is compelled to suppose that attitudes towards the war were restricted to its own chauvinism or to comparable blind loyalty to some other regime.

Referring to that "minority, small but vehement, that looked to the Communists as saviors of that unhappy land," the editorial continues:

> One organ of this celebration was *The New York Review of Books*, and so it comes as a surprise—a welcome one—to find reprinted in a recent issue an article from the French journal *L'Express* by André Gelinas, a French-Canadian Catholic priest and Chinese scholar who settled in Vietnam in 1948 and was expelled in July, 1976.[110]

This extends further the *Times'* false portrayal of opponents of the war; the reader can easily determine, by turning back to the articles on the war that appeared in the *New York Review of Books*, that it never was an "organ of celebration" for the Communists as "saviors" of Vietnam, although it did publish articles documenting the atrocities and outrages that the *Times* supported, with its occasional whispers of complaint about blunders and failures and its suppression of evidence on many of the worst of these atrocities. What is more, the *Times* editors surely know that while the *New York Review* was unusual in that it was open to the peace movement and the U.S. left for several years (though hardly restricted to such circles), that tendency had come to an end years before, as the *Review* rejoined the mainstream of American liberalism. But for the state propaganda institutions that masquerade as the "independent press," the pretense is a useful one, as is the further pretense that Gelinas's picture is utterly definitive and beyond question.

The *Wall Street Journal*, as might be anticipated, took up the same theme.[111] Like their colleagues on the *Times*, the *Journal* editors describe the "national debate" over the war between those who supported the U.S. effort and those who claimed that President Johnson's "picture of Communism was a paranoid fiction" and argued that Communism could hardly be "worse than the repressive South Vietnamese regime that the Americans were already supporting." It is incomprehensible to the editors of the *Wall Street Journal*, as to other true believers in the state religion, that people might oppose U.S. aggression on grounds of principle, while holding quite a range of views (including total condemnation) or simply taking no stand on the merits of the Vietnamese resistance *per se* or relative to the elements placed in power by U.S. force, but rather guided by the odd notion that the Vietnamese should be allowed to solve their problems in their own way without the benefit of U.S. tutelage by bombs, artillery, murderous search-and-destroy missions, assassination teams, "population control," or subversion.

Returning to the "national debate," the editors observe that "for better or for worse, history has given us the opportunity to judge the debate"—we now see that "Mr. Johnson's prediction was not so paranoid after all." As proof, they refer to the interview with Andre Gelin [sic][112] who "had lived and worked there for 28 years," reprinted "without editorial comment" in the *New York Review of Books,* a most "remarkable" fact since this journal "had printed some of the most violent of the opposition to the American anti-Communist effort in Vietnam." They recount without editorial comment "Gelin's" picture of life in South Vietnam—since it accords with the doctrines of their faith, it must be true, regardless of the facts, so that any serious check on its contents is beside the point—and they demonstrate no awareness of the actual nature of the criticism of the U.S. war that appeared in the *New York Review* during the years when it was open to the peace movement and American left.

The "embarrassment" of former antiwar protestors, the *Wall Street Journal* continues, "is richly deserved." Anyone who was acquainted with the history of Communism could not "have trusted this experience and at the same time reviled America and American motives in Vietnam as the antiwar movement came to do." If the editors were not propagandists quite uninterested in fact, they would know that the criticisms of the U.S. war in Vietnam that appeared in the *New York Review* were written for the most part by people who were long-time anti-Communists.

Furthermore, if the editors were capable of rationality on these matters, they might understand that criticism of acts and "motives" of the U.S. government is logically quite independent of one's attitude toward Communism, exactly as one may "revile Russia and Russian motives in Eastern Europe" without thereby committing oneself to "trust the experience" of the exercise of U.S. power. But these points, however obvious, are of little concern to editors whose ideological commitment is total.

Father Gelinas has also been welcomed by the more fanatical wing of British scholarship. Patrick Honey, the pacifist advocate of dike bombing (see above, p. 69) who (with Dennis Duncanson of the British mission to Vietnam) had long been one of the more passionate advocates of U.S. aggression, chaired a meeting Gelinas at the School for Oriental and African Studies in November, 1976.[113] One can see why. Imagine a man of the cloth who was able to live for 13 (or 19, or 28) years in Vietnam through the worst barbarism of the U.S. war, never raising a peep of protest so far as is known, then inventing mass suicides and North Vietnamese coups to order for an admiring international audience.

Gelinas's description of the U.S. involvement in Vietnam and the regime it imposed would have sufficed for anyone with a minimal acquaintance with the history of the past years to reveal that he is hardly to be trusted, a fact that appears to have been of no concern to those who published his reports or commented editorially on them.[114] In the widely-cited interview that made his fame, he writes that the North Vietnamese troops who conquered the South[115] "discovered a country with freedoms, and a rich one, a real Ali Baba's cave." It takes either supreme cynicism or the kind of classical colonialist ignorance that comes from hobnobbing solely with the rich to depict South Vietnam simply as a land of freedom and wealth. Gelinas evidently did not know or care about the rotting urban slums to which the peasants had been driven by U.S. bombardment, or the lunar landscapes of central Vietnam, or the beggars, prostitutes, drug addicts, wounded and tortured prisoners of the Ali Baba's cave in Saigon; and he seems unable to comprehend the nature of the riches of the South and their relation to the colonialist enterprise of which he was a willing part.[116] The most that he can bring himself to say about the Western contribution is that "the old regime and the Westerners also did great harm and made many errors"—and even this criticism is more than he was able to bring himself to express in public during the years when an honest witness might have mattered. He insists, in his congressional testimony, that "this people is now in a terrible state, not because of American presence in the past, for my conviction, but because of the oppressive rule of the government" (43)—a statement that is truly shocking in its cynicism, even if we were to believe every word of his claims about the postwar period, or worse. The United States, he continues, "has done so much, spent so much, and given so much of its blood for Vietnam," which is "not just any other country" but rather "a country that has been fighting alongside this country [the U.S.]" (45). Vietnam has been fighting alongside the United States; the United States has done so much for Vietnam. No wonder that such a man can tell us that Vietnamese pray to be invaded with atom bombs so that they can regain their past freedom and wealth, to the applause of his Western admirers.

The most severe condemnation of the regime in Vietnam yet to appear from a serious source is that of R.-P. Paringaux of *Le Monde* (5 October 1978). Paringaux writes from Ho Chi Minh City (Saigon) that the new regime has come to resemble its predecessor, the U.S. client regime in Saigon, with "systematic recourse to repression, preventive arrest on simple suspicion, denunciation, making informing on others a duty and allowing all those who do not conform to the new model to stagnate in camps, aggravating their hatred and hopelessness." He cites figures of 80,000 former collaborators still under detention, noting that refugee sources in Paris give figures ten times that high supported by documentary evidence. Few have been released, Paringaux maintains, apart from doctors, technicians and teachers whose services are needed. He quotes official sources which claim that 95% of the prisoners have been released. Paringaux writes that "known [non-Communist] activists who were courageously devoted to defense of political prisoners under the former regime have now become silent." He indicates that the former prisons are once again full, perhaps even more than before. He does not suggest that the current regime, however repressive, is practicing the hideous tortures characteristic of its U.S.-imposed predecessor.

Shortly after Paringaux and other French reporters wrote their critical reports about Vietnam, after their 10-day visit, John Fraser of the Toronto *Globe and Mail* spent four weeks travelling through the country with, he writes, "more access and freedom to roam independently throughout Vietnam (seven provinces and the two principal cities) than any western journalist since 1975." He was specifically interested in verifying the observations and conclusions of the French journalists. Fraser is very critical of the regime for slowly compelling the bourgeoisie to become farmers (though he appreciates the economic motives) and for its repression of critics and opposition. But he came to the conclusion that the reports of the French journalists were vastly exaggerated. He explains why in considerable detail, relating his own much more extensive experiences, including many discussions with Vietnamese who were highly critical of the regime, and considering the social and economic conditions of the country as well as official policy.[117] A detailed analysis of the report by Paringaux in *Vietnam South East Asia International* (Oct.-Dec. 1978), also points out that the source of the 800,000 figure that Paringaux cites, and that has been uncritically repeated in the Western media, is a document by a group of Indochinese emigres in Paris which includes in the figure for prisoners "not only those alleged to be in detention but also those who have left the cities for new economic zones, for which a figure of 750,000 was given in early 1978." Thus the 800,000 figure is consistent "for security reasons." As we have noted, independent observers do not confirm the allegation that those who have been moved to the New Economic Zones were forcibly deported to a form of "imprisonment;" and these observers generally agree that such a move to the countryside was essential for Vietnam's survival.

Paringaux's report and the accompanying editorial condemnation ("Crimes de paix") in *Le Monde* received immediate attention in the national media in the United States. They were reported the same day on radio, television and the press.[118] It is entirely appropriate for the national media in the United States to feature this report from a respected foreign journal.[119] One's admiration for the professionalism of the U.S. media is quickly dissipated, however, by their virtual disregard of Fraser's different view and their uncritical acceptance of "worst view" interpretations of matters such as the New Economic Zones. We may also recall media behavior on other occasions when *Le Monde* published far more sensational reports, which are, furthermore, incomparably more significant in the United States. For example, in July 1968, the distinguished Southeast Asia correspondent for *Le Monde*, Jacques Decornoy, published eyewitness reports of the devastating American "secret bombing" of northern Laos.[120] Over a year later, the *New York Times* finally became willing to publish the fact that, as Decornoy had reported, the U.S. Air Force was trying to destroy "the rebel economy and social fabric" (with no editorial comment on the significance of this fact).[121] In the interim, considerable efforts were made to convince the *New York Times, Time-Life,* and other major journals in the United States merely to report the facts, which were not in doubt. They refused. To take another case, the Latin American correspondent of *Le Monde*, Marcel Niedergang, reported in January, 1968 that the vice president of Guatemala stated in a public speech that "American planes based in Panama take part in military operations in Guatemala" in which "napalm is frequently used in zones suspected of serving as refuge for the rebels."[122] The same speech was cited in the British press by Hugh O'Shaughnessy, who went on to say that "similar things are happening in Nicaragua, which is virtually a U.S. colony and where guerrilla warfare broke out this year."[123] Whether the official Guatemalan claim was true or not, the very fact that a high official of a client state announces that U.S. planes are carrying out bombing raids with napalm in "zones suspected of serving as refuge for the rebels" (zones of civilian settlement, presumably) is quite sensational news, or would be, in a country with a free press. But this information too was suppressed by the Free Press, though in this case as well, it was repeatedly brought to their attention.[124]

Reports of U.S. bombing of the economy and social fabric of countries with which the United States is not at war are incomparably more significant than the report on Vietnam that was so quickly publicized by the national media in the United States in October, 1978. Not only are the atrocities far more severe, but they are also more important to know about in the United States, for the obvious reason that public opinion might be effective in bringing them to a halt, which is, plainly, not the case in Vietnam, whatever the situation may be there. We see once again how remarkably analogous the Free Press is in its behavior to the media that operate under state control in totalitarian societies. It would come as no surprise at all to discover that *Pravda* quickly discovers and features *Le Monde* stories on U.S. atrocities (perhaps describing *Le Monde* as the "rightwing French journal"),[125] though we would be surprised indeed to see a *Le Monde* report in

Pravda on the invasion of Hungary or Czechoslovakia.

In this discussion we have not attempted to give a systematic portrayal of the nature of the Communist regime in Vietnam or to portray the society that is arising from the wreckage of the U.S. war. Rather, our concern has been to show how the Free Press selects evidence from what is available to paint a picture that conforms to the requirements of state propaganda in the post-Vietnam War era. The media have not been entirely uniform in this respect, as we have noted, and ideologists still must face the problem of dealing with the fact that many millions of Americans participated actively in a popular movement to bring the war to an end. Though this opposition is being quickly written out of history by contemporary ideologues, memories remain and the brain-washing process still has a long way to go before it is successful. But successful it will be, in the absence of any continuing mass movement that creates its own organs of expression outside of the conformist media, and its own modes of organization and action to constrain the violence of the state and to change the social structures that engender and support it.

5

Laos

The U.S. war in Laos is typically called a "secret war," and with reason. During the period of the most ferocious bombing of the civilian society of northern Laos, which even the U.S. government conceded was unrelated to military operations in Vietnam or Cambodia, the press consciously suppressed eyewitness testimony by well-known noncommunist Western reporters. Earlier, fabricated tales of "Communist aggression" in Laos had been widely circulated by a number of influential correspondents.[1] In the elections of 1958, which the U.S. government vainly attempted to manipulate, the Pathet Lao emerged victorious, but U.S. subversion succeeded in undermining the political settlement. At one point the United States backed a right-wing Thai-based military attack against the government recognized by the United States. All of this barely entered public awareness. The same was true of the CIA-sponsored subversion that played a significant role in undermining the 1962 agreements, a settlement which, if allowed to prevail, might well have isolated Laos from the grim effects of the war in Southeast Asia.

The hill tribesmen recruited by the CIA (as they had been by the French) to hold back the social revolution in Laos, were decimated, then abandoned when their services were no longer needed. Again, the press was unconcerned. When John Everingham, a Lao-speaking Australian reporter, travelled in 1970

137

"through dying village after dying village" among the Hmong who had been "naive enough to trust the CIA" and were now being offered "a one-way 'copter ride to death'" in the CIA clandestine army, no U.S. journal (apart from the tiny pacifist press) was interested enough to cover the story, though by that time even the *New York Times* was permitting an occasional report on the incredible bombing that had "turned more than half the total area of Laos to a land of charred ruins where people fear the sky" so that "nothing be left standing or alive for the communists to inherit" (Everingham). The Hmong tribesmen cannot flee to the Pathet Lao zones or they too will be subjected to the merciless bombardment, he wrote: "Like desperate dogs they are trapped, and the CIA holds the leash, and is not about to let it go as long as the Meo [Hmong] army can hold back the Pathet Lao a little longer, giving the Americans and their allies a little more security 100 miles south at the Thailand border."

It is only after the war's end, when the miserable remnants of the Hmong can be put on display as "victims of Communism," that American sensibilities have been aroused, and the press features stories that bewail their plight.[2]

Extensive analysis of refugee reports was conducted at the time by a few young Americans associated with International Voluntary Services in Laos. In scale and care, these studies exceed by a considerable measure the subsequent studies of refugees from Cambodia that have received massive publicity in the West, and the story is every bit as gruesome. But the press was rarely interested and published materials, which appeared primarily outside the mainstream media, were virtually ignored and quickly forgotten.[3] As in the case of Timor, the agency of terrorism made the facts incompatible with the purposes of the propaganda system. The press, and scholarship as well, much preferred government tales of "North Vietnamese aggression," and continued to engage in flights of fancy based on the flimsiest evidence while ignoring the substantial factual material that undermined these claims.[4]

With the expulsion of John Everingham of the *Far Eastern Economic Review* from Laos by the new regime, no full-time Western journalists remain in Laos so that direct reporting is sparse and most of what appears in the press derives from Bangkok. Such testimony must be regarded with even more than the usual care.[5] Direct reporting by Westerners from Laos can still be found, however, by those who have learned over the years not to rely on the established press for "news." For example, two representatives of the Mennonite Central Committee, Linda and Murray Hiebert, left Vientiane at the end of January, 1978, after five years of volunteer service in Laos and Vietnam, and wrote several articles "prepared on the basis of research in Laos, including visits to a wide variety of places and projects, interviews with government officials and ordinary people, and evaluation of data collected by United Nations and Lao government agencies."[6] We will return later to their eyewitness accounts and those of others who also bring perspectives that render them unusable by the Free Press.

The media have often feigned a touching regard for "lovely little Laos" and its "gentle folk," even while they were suppressing the abundant evidence on the murderous U.S. attack on the land and its people. When the war ended, Harry Reasoner, the commentator for ABC News, offered a fairly typical reaction, which was considered sufficiently profound to merit reprinting in the press.[7] He expressed his "guess" that the Laotians, with their "innate disbelief and disinterest in these bloody games" played "by more activist powers like Russia and China and the United States and North Vietnam"—these are the "activist powers" that share responsibility for the turmoil in Indochina—will show that "there is some alternative for small, old places to becoming either Chile or Albania." So Laos may preserve its "elephants, eroticism, and phallic symbols"—and presumably, though he does not mention it, its average life expectancy of 40 years, its infant mortality rate of over 120 per thousand births (one of the highest in the world) and the rate of child deaths which will kill 240,000 of 850,000 infants before their first birthday in the next five years.[8]

Reasoner continues: "I hope the benign royalty which has presided over the clowning of the CIA and the vicious invasion of the North Vietnamese will be able to absorb and disregard a native communist hierarchy." The "invasion of the North Vietnamese" was largely a fabrication of U.S. propagandists duly transmitted by the press and scholarship[9] and the "clowning of the CIA" included those merry games that virtually destroyed those Hmong naive enough to trust them, while massacring defenseless peasant communities and converting much of Laos to a moonscape, still littered with unexploded ordnance.

The *New York Times* presented a historical analysis of the war as it came to an end.[10] "Some 350,000 men, women and children have been killed, it is estimated, and a tenth of the population of three million uprooted" in this "fratricidal strife that was increased to tragic proportions by warring outsiders." In actuality, as in the case of Vietnam, it appears unlikely that there would have been any extended "fratricidal strife" had it not been for outsiders, of whom the United States was decisively important. The "history" is very well-sanitized, as befits America's "newspaper of record." The U.S. role is completely ignored apart from a few marginal and misleading references.[11] As late as 1975, the *New York Times* is still pretending that the U.S. bombers were striking only North Vietnamese supply trails—Saxon mentions no other bombing—although the ferocious aerial warfare waged against the civilian society of northern Laos was by then well-known, and had even been reported occasionally in the *Times*.[12] Ideologically based misrepresentations of history pervade the article, e.g., in the reference to the 1954 Geneva conference which "left Laos with an ineffective International Control Commission and enough ambiguities for the Pathet Lao to retain its stronghold." The ICC was indeed ineffective in preventing U.S. subversion in subsequent years, as the United States attempted to exploit "ambiguities" it perceived or invented in international agreements that permitted Pathet Lao control of the areas in question and laid the basis for their integration into the national political system in 1958, with consequences already noted.

When the war ended in 1975, the victorious Pathet Lao appear to have made some efforts to achieve a reconciliation with the mountain tribesmen who had been organized in the CIA clandestine army. One of the leaders of the Hmong ("who are best known to the outside world by the pejorative name 'Meo'"), Lyteck Lynhiavu, held the position of director of administration in the Ministry of the Interior in the coalition government. He was the leader of a small group of Hmong who had refused to join the CIA-Yang Pao operation. Lyteck tried to stem the flight of Hmong tribesmen (who "had reason to be fearful because it was they who had done much of the hardest fighting against the Pathet Lao and their North Vietnamese supporters") to Thailand, but in vain. Lyteck "alleged that the U.S. had flown leaflets to Long Cheng [the base of the CIA army] and that these caused the Hmong people there to fear for their lives." U.S. officials denied the charge; "other sources said that the leaflets were in circulation long before Gen. Yang Pao left Laos and that they had been produced for propaganda purposes by an officer who had worked for the general," who was commander of the CIA clandestine army.[13] "Whatever their origin, the leaflets appeared to be a fabrication. They were written in a complicated style that would have been difficult for many of the Hmong to understand."[14]

Lewis M. Simons, another correspondent with a record of serious reporting, gave a detailed account of Pathet Lao "reeducation" programs shortly after.[15] He interviewed people who had participated in Pathet Lao-organized "seminars" where "to the surprise of even some of the more skeptical, a lot of what they are taught seems to make sense to them." One office clerk reported: "The Pathet Lao are genuine patriots. They want to teach us pride in ourselves and our country, something we never had under the old regime." A graduate student expressed admiration for what he called the "scientific" approach the Pathet Lao took at the seminars, which he said were "tailored to the educational level of the people attending" and included persuasive arguments, though the authoritarian character of the system that was being introduced was evident enough: "There's no doubt in my mind that they're sincerely interested in improving the lives of the common people. That's more than you could ever have said for the previous government."

How common such reactions may be is an open question. Norman Peagam, a Lao-speaking correspondent of demonstrated integrity, wrote a long and critical report from Vientiane in the *New York Times* a year and a half later.[16] "Little of the surface of life seems to have changed in Vientiane two years after the Communists' gradual and bloodless seizure of power," though the economy is run down "partly as a result of the halt in United States aid in 1975 and the blockade imposed by neighboring Thailand," which controls Laos's access to the outside world. But there have been changes: "Crime, drug addiction and prostitution have been largely suppressed" and "everyone is expected to work hard and take part in communal rice and vegetable projects in the evening and on weekends." Most of the professional and commercial elite are among the 100,000 people who have fled (the great majority of whom, however, were hill tribesmen), and some farmers and urban workers have also escaped despite the border guards who often shoot at refugees. Many others "want to leave but lack the money, the connections or the courage," while "there are many others who support the new Government or at least accept it despite all the difficulties," and hundreds have returned from France and other Western countries.[17] Outside of Vientiane, "it seems likely that the Communists have a solid political base in the two-thirds of Laos that they effectively controlled during the recurrent conflicts that began in the 1950s. In the fertile populated Mekong Valley, where they are still relative newcomers, their power is largely maintained through apathy and the threat of armed force." Western diplomats estimate the number in reeducation centers at 30,000. "They are being kept in centers ranging from picturesque islands for juvenile delinquents, drug addicts and prostitutes[18] to remote labor camps barred to outsiders from which only a handful of people have so far returned." "Western diplomats list firm political will, honesty, patriotism and discipline as the new rulers' main strengths. But, they maintain, the priority of ideological over technical considerations, the Communists' deep suspicion of Westerners and intolerance of dissent and their poor managerial skills seriously hamper efforts to develop the country." Another "factor hampering development has been the activities of rebels"; "it seems apparent that Thai officials give them support." Another problem is corruption and the "new elite" of government and party officials who "enjoy numerous privileges not available to others," creating cynicism and leading to exploitation of peasants "partly to feed this unproductive class."

As in the case of Vietnam, one can find little discussion in the U.S. press of the Lao programs of reconstruction and social and economic development, or the problems that confront them. Repression and resistance, in contrast, are major themes of the scanty reporting. A brief report from Thailand describes "harsh concentration camps and a network of labor farms holding tens of thousands of political prisoners...Informed Western sources estimate that 60,000 persons, many with little hope of rehabilitation, are in about 50 camps."[19] Henry Kamm cast his baleful eye on

Laos in March, 1978,[20] reporting the continued flow of "Meo hill tribesmen of Laos who fought for the United States in the Indochina war,"[21] some still carrying "their American-issued rifles." The refugees report "a major military campaign by Laotian and Vietnamese forces"—U.S.-style, with "long-range artillery shelling, which was followed by aerial rocketing, bombing and strafing," burning villages and food supplies, driving villagers into the forests (March 28). And again on the following day: "The Communists are bombing and rocketing Meo villages, presumably causing civilian casualties." "Resistance groups of various sizes, operating independently and without central direction or foreign assistance, are active throughout Laos, according to self-described resistance fighters, other recent refugees and diplomatic sources."

That the resistance forces are operating without U.S. or Thai assistance seems dubious (cf. Peagam, above, and notes 17 and 24), in the light of the long history of U.S. intervention in Laos based in Thailand, always the "focal point" for U.S. terror and subversion in Southeast Asia.[22] And the record of U.S. journalism with regard to Laos is in general so abysmal that even if there is an American hand, if a long tradition prevails, the reader of the *New York Times* will be unlikely to hear about it—though an exposé may come years later when the dirty work is long finished and the CIA is once again being reformed, in keeping with traditional U.S. commitments to justice, democracy, and freedom.

The guerrilla groups, Kamm claims, are "led mainly by former officers of the Laotian regular and irregular armies"—the latter term being the euphemism for the forces organized and directed by the CIA—"and are said to include significant numbers of defectors from the Pathet Lao, the Communist guerrilla organization [who, incidentally, constitute the present government, recognized by the United States], who are unhappy about the growing Vietnamese influence in their country."[23] Kamm's "picture of the Meo's situation in Laos" conveniently omits any discussion of the U.S. program to organize them to fight for the United States, trapping them like desperate dogs and throwing away the leash when they lost their usefulness. Other problems and developments in Laos are not on the beat of the *Times* Pulitzer prize winner.[24]

The continued resistance of the Hmong serves as an inspiration to the editors of the *Christian Science Monitor*, who write (5 April 1978) that "one can only marvel at the human spirit and the tenacious longing of men for independence," sentiments that they never expressed when Laotian peasants were struggling to survive in the face of a ferocious U.S. attack that vastly exceeds in scale anything that the Communists are capable of mounting. "The fighting serves to remind the world—a long five years after the Indo-China war—that the communists have not won the hearts and minds of the people. They have victimized them." Note that for these representatives of the Free Press, "the people"—a term that rarely appears in U.S. journalism—are the hill tribesmen, who, as Kamm correctly reports, "fought for the United States in the Indochina war."

The *Monitor* editorialists are as oblivious as Henry Kamm to the past record of U.S. involvement with the hill tribesmen (nor do they seem aware of their own news reports; see above, p. 140). But they do know that Laos was bombed, though they do not seem to recall by whom: "Mercilessly bombed during the war, today Laos is hounded with problems, including a terrible food shortage (it was once self-sufficient in food), a disrupted economy, an exodus of skilled technicians, and of course political domination by the Vietnamese"—of course. "Little Laos is in fact tragically caught between the anvil and the hammer: a pawn of the Vietnamese as the frontline of defense against Thailand and a client of the Soviet Union in its big-power competition with China."

In the light of the well-known historical facts, it is no less than amazing that a major U.S. newspaper, one of the few that attends seriously to international affairs, and one that exudes moralism in its editorial commentary, can fail to make any mention whatsoever of the U.S. role, past and present, in creating these "problems," presented as if they were entirely the fault of the Communists. Once again, we see the remarkable similarities between the Free Press and its counterparts in the totalitarian states.

But, the *Monitor* informs us, "some signs of hope for the long-suffering Laotian people are emerging." In particular, "if they [the Laotian Communists] were to resolve the issue of the MIAs, they would also be able to improve relations with the United States." At this point, words fail.

And then these final thoughts:

> In the final analysis, it will all depend on Hanoi. The question is how soon the Vietnamese want to establish normal links with the West and derive the benefits that come from being responsible members of the international community. As the men in Hanoi ponder their strategy, the people of Laos go on enduring.

If only Hanoi would choose to become a "responsible member of the international community," joining the country that pounded Laos to dust while the *Monitor* looked the other way, then the long-suffering people of Laos might see a ray of hope. Hanoi is responsible for their tragedy, not the murderers and their accomplices in the press.[25]

The *New York Times* did run an Op-Ed describing the scandalous refusal of the Carter Administration to respond to the appeal of the Laotian government for international assistance "to stave off the impending disaster" of starvation after a terrible drought.[26] This Op-Ed cites the two Mennonite relief workers who had just returned from Laos[27] who report "that irrigation networks have collapsed and that paddy fields are pockmarked with bomb craters."[28] Others have estimated that so many buffalo were killed during the war that farmers "have to harness themselves to plows to till fields" while "unexploded bombs buried in the ground hamper food production." But the U.S. Administration, fearing "that it will appear to be pro-Communist, thereby jeopardizing the canal treaties," has refused to send any of its rice surplus (the world's largest) to Laos, despite impending starvation.[29] The problem is compounded by the fact that "last year the Congress specifically forbade direct aid to Laos," though the "Food for Peace law" permits an exception. "Any more delay in Washington would simply compound the barbarity that the United States has already brought to that region"—and specifically, to Laos, though one could hardly learn that fact from current reports in the Free Press.[30] For an indication of the impact of this statement, see the *Monitor* editorial (just cited), three weeks later.

While in the United States, it is axiomatic that "of course" the Vietnamese dominate little Laos, caught between the Vietnamese hammer and the Russian anvil, others, who suffer the disadvantage of familiarity and concern with fact, express some doubts. Nayan Chanda writes from Vientiane that:

> Diplomats here dismiss some of the sensational Bangkok press stories about ministries crawling with Vietnamese advisers, but they believe that a sizable number of Vietnamese—soldiers and engineers—are building roads and bridges in eastern and central Laos. Although old colonial routes 7, 8 and 9 are dirt tracks unusable during the monsoons, they helped bring essential supplies from Vietnam in the dark days of 1975 when Thailand closed its borders. The Vietnamese now working to repair these routes are thus helping to reduce Lao dependence on Thailand.[31]

Lao dependence on U.S.-backed Thailand has been a crucial element in its postwar distress—a fact which escaped the attention of the *Monitor* in its ode to the human spirit—alongside of U.S. cruelty in withholding aid, which likewise escaped notice. "Both Lao and Vietnamese officials privately admit," Nayan Chanda reports, "that Thailand is going to be Vientiane's lifeline to the world for years to come."[32] The heavily-bombed roads to

Vietnam and Cambodia "need large-scale repairs before being put to commercial use" and problems in Vietnamese ports make it doubtful that this construction will be of much help to Laos in the short term. Meanwhile, Thailand is controlling the lifeline effectively: "A *de facto* blockade by Thailand has virtually halted the trickle of foreign aid and Laos' own drive to earn foreign currency through exports." The Lao government reported that the blockade "has been asphyxiating the economy," and foreign missions complain of "harassment by Thai customs."[33]

Quite apart from food and supplies, Thailand had refused to ship medicines ordered and paid for by the International Red Cross. Meanwhile in Laos malaria has been raging since the United States cut off its malaria prevention program in 1975, "killing adults and children indiscriminately, infecting pregnant women, and weakening many people so that they cannot work"—it is "having a 'devastating effect' on the Lao population," according to foreign doctors, along with intestinal and respiratory illnesses, typhoid and malnutrition. When the oxygen-producing plant broke down and surgical operations had to be suspended, Thailand refused to allow emergency deliveries of oxygen, according to Laotian officials.[34]

Warnings of imminent starvation as a result of the recent severe drought and other causes have been repeatedly voiced by UN officials, foreign journalists, and others.[35]

In addition to the problems caused by the consequences of the U.S. air war, the drought, and the Thai blockade that had virtually halted the trickle of foreign aid as well as Lao exports, Laos faces structural problems that are a legacy of French and U.S. imperialism.[36] The economy inherited by the Pathet Lao was "totally artificial," with its "crippling dependence" on dollar aid, and "the nature of the outside influence brought serious distortion to a subsistence economy," Chanda observes.[37] He cites a confidential World Bank report of 1975 which pointed out that in the Vientiane zone industrial production (almost entirely comprising brewing and soft-drink manufacture), and the structure of urban services in general, were "heavily influenced by the demand of expatriates and a tiny, wealthy fraction of the Laotian population." The main "production" of towns like Vientiane was administration, services for the administration and foreign personnel attached to it, and, of much less importance, production and services for the rest of the urban population—and, finally, for the country at large.

It is "the structural imbalance and artificial economy inherited from the old regime" that lie "at the root of the present crisis," though "a series of blunders by the new Government worsened the situation." The same World Bank report "warned that termination of the [foreign, largely U.S. aid] programme 'would cause the collapse of organised administration, and much of urban life.'" The aid was terminated, even vital food, malaria control and medical supplies. Without large aid commitments from West or East, and lacking export earnings, "harsh economy measures are inevitable" and "the exodus of refugees seeking a better life abroad continues," stirring the compassion of Westerners who deplore Communist depravity as Laos groans between the Vietnamese hammer and the Russian anvil.

Like other beneficiaries of Western tutelage and benevolence for many years, the Lao often do not find it easy to comprehend the profound humanitarian commitments of the West—recall their "deep suspicion of Westerners"—thus leading them to mistake as well the meaning of the noble Human Rights Crusade now being led, once again, by the United States:

> Asked how he viewed the opposition of the American Congress to direct or indirect aid to the countries of Indochina, [Lao Vice-Foreign Minister Khamphay Boupha] referred to his recent meeting with Frederick Brown (the officer in charge of Laos, Cambodia and Vietnam affairs at the U.S. State Department) during the latter's visit to Vientiane. "I told him that the US talks a lot about human rights, but what would they do in the face of a situation like ours?

"The US has dropped 3 million tons of bombs—one ton per head—forced 700,000 peasants to abandon their fields; thousands of people were killed and maimed, and unexploded ordnance continues to take its toll. Surely the US does not show humanitarian concern by refusing to help heal the wounds of war." Khamphay revealed that Brown had asked them to wait for a period—and in the meanwhile, he wryly added, "they have forced Thailand to close the border."[38]

Meanwhile the people of Laos die from malnutrition, disease, and unexploded ordnance, arousing no sympathy in the country that bears a substantial responsibility for their plight with its "clowning of the CIA," and now coldly withholds aid because, as the press sees it, Hanoi refuses to join the community of "responsible nations." The 240,000 of 850,000 infants who will die before their first birthday in the next five years (see page 140), and the many others who will expire with them, may be added to the accounts of imperial savagery, quickly forgotten by Western humanitarians.

But the efforts to rebuild continue:

The problem is the shortage of essential tools, draught animals and the costly legacy of war—unexploded ammunition. One official of the UN High Commissioner for Refugees who recently visited newly-resettled areas on the Plain of Jars described efforts to grow food in small patches of land in a dusty bomb-cratered landscape.

The official gave the example of Muong Pek, with a population of 33,000, out of which 25,000 were displaced persons who returned to their villages after the war. Before the war, the population of the district owned 83,000 buffaloes to provide draught power and meat. When peace came there were only 250 buffaloes.

Although the number has since gone up to 2,000, it is still inadequate for ploughing the hardened soil abandoned for years. In some places, men have to strap themselves to a plough to turn the earth. Last year, not surprisingly, the peasants in the area produced only enough rice for between two and four months. In one commune in the district with a population of 3,500, 15 people were killed by ammunition left after the war.[39]

A few months later Chanda visited the Plain of Jars, "the scene of some of the heaviest bombing during the Indochina War," where "people are making a start on reviving what was once a prosperous rural society."[40] From the air, the Plain of Jars "resembles a lunar landscape, pockmarked as it is with bomb craters that are a stark testimony to the years of war that denuded the area of people and buildings," a consequence of "six years of 'secret' bombing" by U.S. aircraft.[41] "At ground level, the signs of death and destruction are even more ubiquitous." The province capital was "completely razed." "But the once-flourishing rural society of the plain is slowly coming back to life, raising bamboo-and-mud houses on the ruins of the old, reclaiming abandoned rice paddies, turning bomb craters into fish ponds, and weeding out the deadly debris of war that litters the area." Thousands are now returning from refugee camps and "many have emerged from their forest shelters and caves in the surrounding mountains" to villages where sometimes "not even a broken wall is to be seen." The peasants of one village have to work in rice fields 15 kilometers away because "heavy bombing in the nearby mountains brought hundreds of tons of mud hurtling down into the river that once irrigated" their paddy fields. A peasant who joined the Pathet Lao, recruited by U.S. bombs, recalls the day when a U.S. jet "scored a direct rocket hit on a cave in which 137 women and children of the village, including his own, were hiding. The cave was so hot from the explosion, he says, that for more than a day he could not go near it." Today, "death still lurks in every corner of the plain" in the form of such "war debris" as "golf-ball size bombs containing explosives and steel bits released from a large canister" and other products of American ingenuity that killed thousands during the war, and continue to exact their deadly toll.[42]

There are Vietnamese present, Chanda observes; namely "Vietnamese workers and soldiers" who are "building schools and hospitals, improving the road network...repairing roads and bridges," and "were never seen carrying guns." "If any Soviet experts were in the area, they were well hidden," and there were few "visible items of Soviet assistance." There are slow efforts to introduce cooperative stores and cooperative farming, facilitated by "the economic dislocation caused by the US in its attempt to defeat communism" which makes it easy to persuade "villagers to pool their resources" in construction and farming. "Despite moves towards a Marxist-Leninist order, socialism in Laos remains a typically soft, Lao variety which does not conform to the rigid dialectical materialism of European Marxists." Traditional ceremonies are preserved—at least that should please Harry Reasoner.

Louis and Eryl Kubicka visited the Plain of Jars on the same trip. They quote Chit Kham, whose wife and three daughters were among the 137 people killed when an F105 jet bomber "succeeded in hitting the cave entrance with three out of four rockets it fired, according to an eyewitness with whom we spoke...whose job it was to monitor the bombing from a tree-top perch." Asked what the United States might do "to regain the respect of the people here," Chit Kham answered: "Of course we want aid, but they have killed us, so many lives were lost...we want back those lives that were lost."[43] Kubicka also describes the vast destruction, the unexploded ordnance (his wife "found a CBU bomblet [by nearly stepping on it]"), the "billions of pieces of shrapnel scattered over" the province, "the lack of pulling power" because of the killing of buffaloes. He left believing "that few Americans could personally visit here and see what we saw with the quiet amicable people who hosted us, without feeling a sense of basic human sympathy, or without being ready to lend a helping hand."

Earlier, Kubicka had published a report from Vientiane on the U.S. program of bombing the peasant society of northern Laos and the Lao efforts to reconstruct. He quotes a UN official who had returned from the Plain of Jars, where some refugees had already been resettled: "I've seen a lot of refugee situations in my time throughout the world, but this is the best organization I've ever seen. If this is what Laos is going to be like in the future, we're going to see some significant development here." But of course assistance will be needed: "Conspicuously absent from the list of those proffering assistance is the United States," Kubicka comments, adding that "every other major nation represented diplomatically in Vientiane is currently providing Laos with some aid."[44]

The November 1977 visit was the first by journalists to the Plain of Jars, an area which, for people who have freed themselves from the Western system of indoctrination, has come to symbolize the terror that can be visited by an advanced industrial society on defenseless peasants. To our knowledge, no word about it appeared in the mainstream media, which continue to guard their secrets.

The Hieberts described this visit to the Plain of Jars on their return to the United States from Vientiane in January, 1978 (see note 6). They too describe in detail the ravages of U.S. bombing and the efforts to reconstruct, with the assistance of Vietnamese workers who are, according to Vietnamese diplomats, "fulfilling their two years of national service by working in Laos." The Hieberts, who were engaged in relief work in Laos, also describe the attempts of the new regime to undertake rehabilitation of the human debris of war—orphans, drug addicts, and others—and to bring health services to the countryside, and the problems caused by severe drought, the withdrawal of U.S. aid from the artificial economy it had created, and the "on and off blockade by Thailand," which in September, 1977, blocked fuel imports from Singapore, Swedish road-building supplies, 2,000 tons of rice donated by the UN for refugees, $100,000 worth of medicines, and drought-related equipment and supplies.

No U.S. government aid had to be obstructed.

Cambodia

The third victim of U.S. aggression and savagery in Indochina, Cambodia, falls into a different category than postwar Vietnam and Laos.[1] While the Western propaganda system has selected and modified information about Vietnam to convey the required image of a country suffering under Communist tyranny—the sole source of its current problems—it has been unable to conjure up the bloodbath that was confidently predicted (Laos, as usual, is rarely noticed at all). In fact, by historical standards, the treatment of collaborators in postwar Vietnam has been relatively mild, as the precedents reviewed indicate, though the provocation for merciless revenge was incomparably greater than in the instances we surveyed. But in the case of Cambodia, there is no difficulty in documenting major atrocities and oppression, primarily from the reports of refugees, since Cambodia has been almost entirely closed to the West since the war's end.

One might imagine that in the United States, which bears a major responsibility for what François Ponchaud calls "the calvary of a people,"[2] reporting and discussion would be tinged with guilt and regret. That has rarely been the case, however. The U.S. role and responsibility have been quickly forgotten or even explicitly denied as the mills of the propaganda machine grind away. From the spectrum of informed opinion, only the most extreme condemnations have been selected, magnified, distorted,

155

and hammered into popular consciousness through endless repetition. Questions that are obviously crucial even apart from the legacy of the war—for example, the sources of the policies of the postwar Cambodian regime in historical experience, traditional culture, Khmer nationalism, or internal social conflict—have been passed by in silence as the propaganda machine gravitates to the evils of a competitive socioeconomic system so as to establish its basic principle: that "liberation" by "Marxists" is the worst fate that can befall any people under Western dominance.

The record of atrocities in Cambodia is substantial and often gruesome, but it has by no means satisfied the requirements of Western propagandists, who must labor to shift the blame for the torment of Indochina to the victims of France and the United States. Consequently, there has been extensive fabrication of evidence, a tide that is not stemmed even by repeated exposure. Furthermore, more tempered and cautious assessments are given little notice, as is evidence that runs contrary to the chorus of denunciation that has dominated the Western media. The coverage of real and fabricated atrocities in Cambodia also stands in dramatic contrast to the silence with regard to atrocities comparable in scale within U.S. domains—Timor, for example. This coverage has conferred on that land of much suffering the distinction of being perhaps the most extensively reported Third World country in U.S. journalism. At the same time, propagandists in the press and elsewhere, recognizing a good thing when they see it, like to pretend that their lone and courageous voice of protest can barely be heard, or alternatively, that controversy is raging about events in postwar Cambodia.[3]

Critics of U.S. violence find themselves in a curious position in this connection. Generally ignored by the press, they find that in this case their comment is eagerly sought out in the hope that they will deny atrocity reports, so that this denial can be featured as "proof" that inveterate apologists for Communism will never learn and never cease their sleazy efforts, which create such problems for the honorable seekers after truth who must somehow penetrate the barriers erected by those who "defend Cambodia."[4] When no real examples can be found, the Free Press resorts to the familiar device of invention; the alleged views of critics of the propaganda barrage who do exist are known primarily through ritual denunciation rather than direct exposure. Or there are somber references to unnamed people who "make use of the deaths of millions of Khmers to defend [their] own theories or projects for society."[5]

Another common device is to thunder that the doves "had better explain" why there has been a bloodbath,[6] or "concede" that their "support for the Communists"—the standard term for opposition to U.S. subversion and aggression—was wrong; it is the critics who must, it is claimed, shoulder the responsibility for the consequences of U.S. intervention, not those who organized and supported it or concealed the facts concerning it for many years, and still do.

It is, surely, not in doubt that it was U.S. intervention that inflamed a simmering civil struggle and brought the horrors of modern warfare to relatively peaceful Cambodia, at the same time arousing violent hatreds and a thirst for revenge in the demolished villages where the Khmer Rouge were recruited by the bombardment of the U.S. and its local clients. Matters have reached such a point that a social democratic journal can organize a symposium on the quite astounding question of whether opposition to the U.S. war in Indochina should be reassessed, given its consequences in Cambodia.[7] Others claim that the scale of the atrocities in Cambodia or their nature—peasant revenge or systematic state-organized murder—does not really matter; it is enough that atrocities have occurred, a stance that would be rejected with amazement and contempt if adopted with regard to benign or constructive bloodbaths.

Predictably, the vast outcry against alleged genocide in Cambodia led to calls for military intervention in the U.S. Congress; we will comment no further on the fact that such a proposal can be voiced in the Congress of the United States or what the fact implies in the light of recent history. A look at some of these proposals reveals how effectively any concern for mere fact has been submerged in the tide of propaganda.

Representative Stephen J. Solarz raised the question "of some kind of international police action under the auspices of the United Nations."[8] This proposal was advanced during the testimony of Gareth Porter, who had exposed earlier bloodbath lies and also raised doubts about the evidence offered in connection with Cambodia.[9] As evidence for the genocidal nature of the Cambodian regime, Solarz cited "Khieu Samphan's interview with Oriana Fallaci" in which he allegedly acknowledged "that somewhere in the vicinity of 1 million had been killed since the war." As Porter commented in response, the interview was not with Oriana Fallaci, contained no such "acknowledgement," and is at best of very dubious origin and authenticity, as we discuss below. Undeterred, Solarz raised the question of international intervention.

In congressional hearings a year later, Senator George McGovern gained wide—and unaccustomed—publicity when he suggested military intervention during the testimony of Douglas Pike, who is described in the press as a "State Department Indochina specialist."[10] According to an AP report, McGovern "called yesterday for international military intervention in Cambodia to stop what he called 'a clear case of genocide,'" citing "estimates that as many as 2.5 million of Cambodia's 7 million people have died of starvation, disease and execution since the Communist takeover three years ago." He is quoted as follows:

> This is the most extreme I've ever heard of...Based on the percentage of the population that appears to have died, this makes Hitler's operation look tame...Is any thought being

given...of sending in a force to knock this government out of power? I'm talking about an international peacekeeping force, not the United States going in with the Marine Corps.[11]

McGovern went on to speak of the "crime when an estimated two million innocent Cambodians are systematically slaughtered or starved by their own rulers," a case of "genocidal conduct" that cannot be ignored by "the United States, as a leading proponent of human rights."[12] On CBS television the same day he said that "here you have a situation where in a country of seven million people, possibly as many as a third of them have been systematically slaughtered by their own government," that is, "by a band of murderers that's taken over that government."[13] He returned to the same theme a few days later, informing the Congress that "a band of murderous thugs has been systematically killing their fellow citizens. Two million Cambodians are said to have been destroyed."[14]

If 2-2½ million people, about 1/3 of the population, have been systematically slaughtered by a band of murderous thugs who have taken over the government, then McGovern is willing to consider international military intervention. We presume that he would not have made this proposal if the figure of those killed were, say, less by a factor of 100—that is 25,000 people—though this would be bad enough.[15] Nor would he have been likely to propose this extreme measure if the deaths in Cambodia were not the result of systematic slaughter and starvation organized by the state but rather attributable in large measure to peasant revenge, undisciplined military units out of government control, starvation and disease that are direct consequences of the U.S. war, or other such factors. Nor has McGovern, or anyone else, called for military intervention to cut short the apparent massacre of something like one-sixth of the population of East Timor in the course of the Indonesian invasion, though in this case a mere show of displeasure by the government that provides the military equipment and the diplomatic and economic support for these atrocities might well suffice to bring the murderous attack to a halt.

Assuming then that facts do matter, we naturally ask what McGovern's basis may have been for the specific allegations that he put forth. An inquiry to his office in Washington elicited no source for these charges or documentary evidence to substantiate them. It is interesting that McGovern's call for intervention, widely discussed in the press (occasionally, with some derision because of his record as a dove), has not been criticized on grounds that he seems to have had no serious basis for his charges. Nor did any journalist, to our knowledge, report an inquiry to McGovern to determine what evidence, if any, lay behind the specific factual claims that he put forth in calling for military intervention. (At our urging, one TV newsman has made such an inquiry, and was informed by the staff that his source may have been Lon Nol! For the sake of McGovern's reputation, we would prefer to believe that the numbers were invented).[16]

On the assumption that facts do matter, we will inquire into the reporting of postwar Cambodia in the Western (primarily U.S.) media. We concede at once that for those who "know the truth" irrespective of the facts, this inquiry will appear to be of little moment. As in the other cases discussed, our primary concern here is not to establish the facts with regard to postwar Indochina, but rather to investigate their refraction through the prism of Western ideology, a very different task. We will consider the kinds of evidence used by the media and those naive enough to place their faith in them, and the selection of evidence from what is available. We will see that the general theory of the Free Press, well-supported by what we have already reviewed, is once again dramatically confirmed: the more severe the allegations of crimes committed by an enemy, the greater (in general) the attention they receive. Exposure of falsehoods is considered largely irrelevant. The situation is rather different from the manufacture of Hun atrocities during World War I, to take an example already discussed, since at that time the falsehoods were exposed only years after—in this case, they continue to surface though refuted at once. The U.S. responsibility is largely ignored, though critics such as Jean Lacouture are not guilty of this incredible moral lapse,[17] and virtually no effort is made to consider postwar Cambodia, or the credibility of evidence concerning it, in the light of historical experience such as that reviewed in chapter 2.

Ponchaud comments that there is a *prima facie* case in support of atrocity allegations: "the exodus of over one hundred thousand persons is a fact, and a bulky one, that raises enough questions in itself."[18] We would add that by parity of argument, the same considerations apply elsewhere; the exodus of approximately one hundred thousand persons fleeing from the victors of the American revolution also raises questions, particularly when we recall that the white population was about 2½ million as compared with 7-8 million Cambodians and that this was after a war that was far less bitterly fought and lacked any comparable atrocities by foreign powers.[19]

Most of the well-publicized information concerning postwar Cambodia derives from reports of refugees—or to be more precise, from accounts by journalists and others of what refugees are alleged to have said. On the basis of such reports, these observers draw conclusions about the scale and character of atrocities committed in Cambodia, conclusions which are then circulated (often modified) in the press or the halls of Congress. For example, Barron-Paul present some examples of what they claim to have heard from refugees and then conclude that the government of Cambodia is bent on genocide, a conclusion which is then presented in various forms by commentators. Similarly Ponchaud cites examples of refugee reports and concludes that the government is engaged in "the assassination of a people," giving estimates of the numbers executed or otherwise victims of centralized government policies. Reviewers and other commentators then inform the public that Ponchaud has shown that the Cambodian government, with its policies of autogenocide, is on a par with the Nazis, perhaps worse. With each link in the chain of transmission, the charges tend to escalate, as we shall see.

Evidently, a serious inquiry into the facts and the way they are depicted should deal with several issues: (1) the nature of the refugee testimony; (2) the media selection from the evidence available; (3) the credibility of those who transmit their version of refugee reports and draw conclusions from them; (4) the further interpretations offered by commentators on the basis of what evidence they select and present. We will concentrate on the third and fourth issues. But a few observations are in order about the first and second.

It is a truism, obvious to anyone who has ever dealt with refugees or considers the historical record or simply uses common sense, that "the accounts of refugees are indeed to be used with great care."[20] It is a truism commonly ignored. For example, the *New York Times* Pulitzer prize-winning specialist on refugees from Communism interviewed Cambodian refugees in Thailand "in a cage 8 feet square and 10 feet high in the police station of this provincial capital," where "9 men are huddled on the bare floor" rarely speaking and staring "into the narrow space before them with dulled eyes."[21] It does not occur to him, here or elsewhere, to treat the accounts offered under such circumstances with the "great care" that Ponchaud properly recommends. The media favorite, Barron-Paul, is based largely on visits to refugee camps arranged in part by a representative of the Thai Ministry of the Interior, whose "knowledge and advice additionally provided us with invaluable guidance."[22] In the camps to which they gained access with the help of this Thai official, who is responsible for internal security matters including anti-Communist police and propaganda operations, they "approached the camp leader elected by the Cambodians and from his knowledge of his people compiled a list of refugees who seemed to be promising subjects"[23]—one can easily imagine which "subjects" would seem "promising" to these earnest seekers after truth, to whom we return. Citing this comment,[24] Porter points out that "the Khmer camp chief works closely with and in subordination to Thai officials who run the camps and with the Thai government-supported anti-Communist Cambodian organization carrying out harassment and intelligence operations in Cambodia." The camps and their leaders are effectively under Thai control and the refugees who eke out a miserable existence there are subject to the whims of the passionately anti-Communist Thai authorities, a point that should be obvious to journalists and should suggest some caution, but is entirely ignored by Barron-Paul, as well as by many others. The story is just too useful to be treated with the requisite care.

Ponchaud, who is more serious, describes the treatment of the refugees in Thailand: they spend a week or more in prison before being sent to camps where they are "fed increasingly short rations" and "have to offer some token of gratitude to the camp guards for letting them out to look for work." He continues:

> There is little hope for them. They live with their memories, constantly reliving the horrors they have witnessed. Each one recounts what he saw or heard, his imagination and homesickness tending to exaggerate and distort the facts.[25]

Essentially the same point is made by Charles Twining, whom the State Department regards as "really the best expert [on Cambodian refugees]...that exists in the world today."[26] Stating that executions continue, he says that "we hear about executions from refugees who have just come out. You must talk to a refugee as soon as he comes out or the story may become exaggerated."[27] How exaggerated it may become by the time it reaches Barron-Paul or Kamm, the reader may try to estimate. The issue does not concern them, judging by their reports. Nor has it concerned those who rely on and draw firm conclusions from these reports.

Access to refugees is generally controlled by Thai authorities or their subordinates (to speak of "election," as Barron-Paul do without qualification, is odd indeed under these circumstances). The translators also presumably fall in this category, or are believed to by the refugees who depend for survival on the grace of their supervisors. Clearly, these are unpromising circumstances for obtaining a meaningful record—compare in contrast, the circumstances of the Bryce report with its record of apparent fabrications.[28] Ponchaud is unusual in making the obvious point that great care must be exercised. Clearly, the reports of refugees should be carefully heeded, but the potential for abuse is great, and those who want to use them with propagandistic intent can do so without serious constraint.

Not surprisingly, there are many internal contradictions in refugee reports. In the *May Hearings* Porter cites the case of Chou Try, who told a CBS reporter that he had witnessed the beating to death of five students by Khmer Rouge soldiers. In October 1976, he told Patrice de Beer of *Le Monde* that he had witnessed no executions though he had heard rumors of them.[29] Porter notes that he was "chosen to be the Khmer chief" of the refugee camp at Aranyaphrathet, where a great many of the interviews have taken place. There are many similar examples. As Porter and Retbøll both insist, refugee reports should certainly not be disregarded, but some care is in order. Evidently, interviews arranged under the circumstances described by Kamm or Barron-Paul are of limited credibility.

One refugee who became both well-known and influential in the United States is Pin Yathai. At a press conference held under the auspices of the American Security Council, Yathai, described as "one of his country's top civil engineers and a leading member of the government" who escaped to Thailand in June of 1977, testified that people were reduced to cannibalism under Khmer Rouge rule:[30] "A teacher ate the flesh of her own sister" and was later caught and beaten to death as an example, he alleged, citing also another case of cannibalism in a hospital and other stories of starvation, brutality, and disease.[31] He was interviewed by Jack Anderson on ABC television,[32] and his stories were also featured in the mass circulation *TV Guide* in "an article on the paucity of media coverage of the Cambodian holocaust by Patrick Buchanan," one of Nixon's speechwriters.[33] Later, they became the basis for a substantial right wing attack on the *Washington Post* for its failure to cover Pin Yathai's news conference, and in general, to give what these groups regard as adequate coverage to Cambodian atrocities. *Le Monde* also published two articles based on Pin Yathai's allegations as well as a letter from another Cambodian attacking his credibility and accusing him of having been a member of the "Special Committee" of the Lon Nol government that was engaged in counterespionage, assassinations, perhaps the drug traffic, and was believed to have been funded by the CIA.[34]

The right wing *Bangkok Post* did report the press conference in which Pin Yathai presented his account of cannibalism and other horrors.[35] The *Bangkok Post* story observed that "Cambodian refugees in Thailand yesterday discounted reports that cannibalism is frequent in Cambodia and even doubted if it has occurred at all." It also quoted "another Cambodian civil engineer who had long talks with Pin Yathai while he was in Bangkok" and who told AFP: "No more than 40 per cent of the statement Pin Yathai made in the United States is true. He never went so far while talking to fellow refugees in his own language." This information was not circulated by Accuracy in Media in its attacks on the *Washington Post* nor has it been presented by others who gave wide publicity to Pin Yathai's accounts.

Not all refugees are welcomed so eagerly as Pin Yathai. Consider, for example, a story in the *London Times* on a Vietnamese refugee who escaped from Vietnam through Cambodia to Thailand, which he entered in April 1976.[36] He walked 350 miles through Cambodia over a two-month period.[37] A civil engineer "with high qualifications" who speaks French, Thai, Khmer and Lao in addition to English, this refugee with his unique experience in postwar Cambodia, where "because of his fluency in Khmer and local knowledge he was taken everywhere for a Cambodian," seems a prime candidate for interviews in the press. But, in fact, he never made it to the *New York Times, Time, TV Guide*, or other U.S. media. His lack of qualifications are revealed by his comments when he arrived in Thailand, where he heard stories of massacres in Cambodia:

> I could not believe it. Walking across the country for two months I saw no sign of killing or mass extermination and nobody I spoke to told me of it. I still don't believe it happened.

Note that the observations of this man, a middle-class refugee from Vietnam with the appropriate anti-Communist credentials, do not contradict the stories of brutal atrocities told in profusion by refugees. Rather, they are consistent with the remarks by State Department Cambodia watchers and other specialists on the geographical limitations of the worst atrocity stories, and suggest that there may be a good deal of local variation rather than the coordinated campaign of state-directed genocide that the media and their main sources prefer. But this very fact suffices to consign this report to oblivion in the United States, despite its undoubted significance as a rare window on inner Cambodia from what appears to be a fairly credible source. We will return to other examples, merely noting here the striking contrast between the media exposure in this case and in the case of Pin Yathai.

In fact, even the witnesses who are specifically selected to recount atrocity stories often add significant qualifications. For example, one of the witnesses at the Oslo Hearings on Human

Rights Violations in Cambodia held in April 1978, was Lim Pech Kuon, who said that he "well understood" the Khmer Rouge policy. He asserted, "that he had never heard the Khmer Rouge indicate that they intended to kill all classes except the workers and poor peasants":

> It was perhaps more correct to say that, in the Khmer Rouge interpretations, the relics of the classes would be abolished—not eradicated. He also said that he had never seen an execution with his own eyes. When he arrived in Phnom Penh after the Khmer Rouge victory he had seen a number of corpses in the streets, but the corpses were covered, and so he could not see whether they were soldiers or civilians. He made it clear that it was the lack of freedom which made him flee by heliocopter.[38]

While the media give the impression that refugees have uniformly recounted stories of horrible atrocities, journalists have occasionally noticed that the reports are actually more varied. John Fraser of the *Toronto Globe and Mail*, whose reports from Vietnam we discussed briefly in chapter 4, also visited a Cambodian refugee camp in Vietnam, "fully prepared for a host of atrocity stories about mass executions, bloody beheadings and savage Khmer Rouge brutality," particularly since the camp was only 50 miles from the border where there had been "deadly combat":

> To my surprise I got lots of tales of hardship, but no atrocities save for a second-hand account of an execution of two men. The accounts of life in Cambodia were grim enough and the atrocity stories too well authenticated to doubt, but still no one at that camp was able to tell me one. I finally had to ask if there was anyone who knew of an execution and after some time I got the second-hand story. I offer no conclusions on this singular fact, except that it was strange with so many refugees not to be able to get more information, particularly since it would have been useful for Vietnamese propaganda.[39]

We know of only one Khmer-speaking Westerner who is an academic specialist on Cambodia and has visited refugee camps in Thailand without the supervision of authorities, namely, Michael Vickery, who reports as follows on his August 1976 visit:

> Since I speak Khmer I was something of a curiosity for them and it was easy to gather a crowd around and listen to what they said whether in response to questions or to unorganized conversation. It was soon clear that there was much disagreement among the refugees about conditions in Cambodia. Some pushed the brutality line, others denied it, or emphasized that killings were rare and due to the cruelty of a few individual leaders. Thus many of the refugees admitted that they had left because they disliked the rigorous working life under the new regime, not because they were themselves threatened with death or brutality. So much, though, was already apparent from a close reading of newspaper accounts. What I found more intriguing was that once when alone with one of the men he called attention to the lack of agreement and added that it was never noticed by outsiders because they didn't understand Khmer. According to him, camp authorities had organized French and English speaking refugees as informants to give the official line to journalists who came to visit.[40]

We return to Vickery's published and private comments, which are valuable and very much to the point.

Not everyone who is interested in analyzing refugee accounts is permitted the kind of access offered by the Thai Ministry of Interior to Barron and Paul. Cornell University Cambodian specialist Stephen Heder, who was a journalist in Phnom Penh, speaks and reads Khmer, is the author of articles on contemporary Cambodia—and has been notably skeptical about the standard conclusions drawn by journalists after guided tours through refugee camps—received funding from the Social Science Research Council and the Fulbright-Hays Program to do a systematic study of postwar Cambodia based on refugee testimony and Phnom Penh Radio broadcasts. He was informed by the Secretary-General of the National Research Council of Thailand that "the present political situations [sic] in Thailand do not favour us to consider this type of research. Therefore, if you still have an intention to do a research works [sic] in Thailand, please be advised to change your topic." One way to give the impression that refugee stories consistently and without exception report atrocities is to prevent competent researchers fluent in Khmer, who do not need the guidance of Thai ministers or "elected camp commanders," from examining the evidence for themselves. We have no doubt that when Heder publishes on contemporary Cambodia, his work will be criticized by those who do not approve of his conclusions on the grounds that he "ignores refugee data."

To summarize, several points are worth noting. Refugee reports are to be taken seriously, but with care. In their eagerness to obtain "evidence" that could be used to defame the regime in Cambodia, such reporters as Barron and Paul or Henry Kamm, as their own testimony indicates, failed to observe the most obvious and elementary cautions that should be second nature to any serious journalist and that are specifically emphasized by Ponchaud, Twining, and others. The media, furthermore, have their own criteria for deciding which reports to emphasize and which to ignore. To evaluate refugee reports it is necessary to take into account extreme bias both in selection of stories and treatment of them. The apparent uniformity of refugee testimony is in part at least an artifact reflecting media bias. In particular, it would be difficult to construct an argument in support of the thesis of central direction and planning of atrocities on the basis of alleged uniformity of refugee reports, since in fact there appears to be considerable variety; to sustain such a thesis other evidence is required, for example, documentary evidence. The unwillingness of the Thai authorities to permit independent scholarly study also raises questions, given the obvious interest of the Thai—shared by Western media and governments—in presenting the worst possible picture of postwar Cambodia. We will consider these questions in more detail below, but even a brief look at the handling of refugee reports suggests that a degree of caution is in order.

Refugee reports constitute one essential category of information about a society as closed to the outside as postwar Cambodia has been. The second link in the chain of transmission of information, which in this case is subject to some independent check for credibility, is the reporters and others who transmit their stories. To inquire into their credibility is surely a crucial matter in evaluating the material that reaches the public. People who have expressed skepticism about the press barrage are commonly accused of refusing to believe the accounts of miserable refugees, a line that is much easier to peddle than the truth: that they are primarily raising questions about the credibility of those who report—and perhaps exploit—the suffering of the refugees and what they are alleged to have said.[41] When refugee stories are transmitted by reporters of demonstrated integrity,[42] they merit more serious attention than when the account is given by someone who is otherwise unknown or has an obvious axe to grind. When a reporter from *Pravda* describes the horrors of U.S. bombing in Northern Laos, a rational observer will be more skeptical than when similar eyewitness reports are provided by Jacques Decornay of *Le Monde*.[43] Similarly, when Leo Cherne, chairman of the International Rescue Committee, discusses the barbarism of the Khmer Rouge,[44] a rational reader will recall the previous history of this longtime apologist for U.S. violence and oppression who attempts to disguise this miserable display under a humanitarian cloak—for example, his supremely cynical description of the victims of U.S. bombings in South Vietnam: "There are more than 700,000 additional refugees who have recently fled the countryside dominated by the Vietcong and with their act of flight have chosen the meager sanctuary provided by the government of South Vietnam."[45]

To determine the credibility of those who transmit reports is a critical matter for anyone concerned to discover the truth, either about Cambodia or about the current phase of imperial ideology. There is only one way to investigate this question: namely, to pay careful attention to the use of quotes and evidence. Such an inquiry may seem pointless or irrelevant, or even cruel, to people who are quite certain that they already know the truth. Lacouture expresses feelings that are not uncommon in his "Corrections":

> Faced with an enterprise as monstrous as the new Cambodian government, should we see the main problem as one of deciding exactly which person uttered an inhuman phrase, and whether the regime has murdered thousands or hundreds of thousands of wretched people? Is it of crucial historical importance to know whether the victims of Dachau numbered 100,000 or 500,000. Or if Stalin had 1,000 or 10,000 Poles shot at Katyn?[46]

Or perhaps, we may add, whether the victims of My Lai numbered in the hundreds, as reported, or tens of thousands, or whether the civilians murdered in Operation SPEEDY EXPRESS numbered 5,000 or 500,000, if a factor of 100 is relatively insignificant?[47] If facts are so unimportant, then why bother to present alleged facts at all?

If, indeed, the Cambodian regime was, as Lacouture believes, as monstrous as the Nazis at their worst, then his comment might be comprehensible, though it is worth noting that he has produced no evidence to support this judgment.[48] But if a more appropriate comparison is, say, to France after liberation, where a minimum of 30-40,000 people were massacred within a few months with far less motive for revenge and under far less rigorous conditions than those left by the U.S. war in Cambodia, then perhaps a rather different judgment is in order.[49] As we shall see, there is a considerable range of opinion on this score among qualified observers, though the press has favored Lacouture's conclusion, generally ignoring mere questions of fact.

We disagree with Lacouture's judgment on the importance of accuracy on this question, particularly in the present historical context, when allegations of genocide are being used to whitewash Western imperialism, to distract attention from the "institutionalized violence" of the expanding system of subfascism and to lay the ideological basis for further intervention and oppression. We have seen how effectively the Western propaganda system creates, embroiders, plays up, distorts, and suppresses evidence according to imperial needs. Western domination of world communications adds to the importance of closely evaluating evidence that so conveniently meets pressing ideological requirements. In this context, it becomes a question of some interest whether in Cambodia, for example, a gang of Marxist murderers are systematically engaged in what Lacouture calls "autogenocide"—"the suicide of a people in the name of revolution; worse, in the name of socialism"[50]—or whether the worst atrocities have taken place at the hands of a peasant army, recruited and driven out of their devastated villages by U.S. bombs and then taking revenge against the urban civilization that they regarded, not without reason, as a collaborator in their destruction and their long history of oppression. Future victims of imperial savagery will not thank us for assisting in the campaign to restore the public to apathy and conformism so that the subjugation of the weak can continue without annoying domestic impediments. Especially in such countries as France and the United States—to mention only two international gangsters whose post-World War II depredations are not dismissed so quickly by past and potential victims as they are at home—it is a crucially important matter to be quite scrupulous with regard to fact, to pay careful attention to past history and to subject to critical analysis whatever information is available about the current situation.[51]

Attention to fact was a particularly significant matter under the conditions of 1975-78, when extreme and unsupported allegations could be used to support military intervention, not a small consideration as we see from McGovern's statements already discussed or—more significantly, as recent history shows—from the context of the Vietnamese invasion discussed in the preface to this volume.

Quite apart from these considerations, which seem to us rather important, it is surely worthwhile, if one is going to discuss Cambodia at all, to try to comprehend what has in fact taken place there, which is quite impossible if critical standards are abandoned and "facts" are contrived even out of honest anger or distress.

The inquiry to which we now turn will appear to be a pointless exegetical exercise to people who share Lacouture's judgment or for whom facts are simply an irrelevant nuisance, like the editors of the *Wall Street Journal*. While the latter reaction merits no comment, Lacouture's is not so quickly dismissed, though we feel that it is deeply wrong in the case of an investigation of postwar Cambodia, and entirely untenable if one is concerned—as we are here—with the workings of the Western propaganda system.

There is a related methodological point that merits comment, if only because it is so commonly misunderstood. Plainly, we may divide the evidence available into two categories: (1) evidence subject to some independent verification; (2) evidence that must be taken on faith. A person who is at all serious will concentrate on category (1) in trying to determine how much trust to place in unverifiable reports of category (2).[52] If it turns out that some source is quite untrustworthy when claims can be checked, then naturally one will view with corresponding skepticism reports from this source that are subject to no such check. But in the sources that raise the charge of genocide, the overwhelming bulk of the evidence is of category (2). Therefore it is easy to be misled into thinking that even if the evidence of category (1) does not withstand critical analysis, the matter is of no serious import since it is of such a minor nature as compared with the far more serious (and unverifiable) charges. A moment's thought should suffice to show that this conclusion is entirely untenable; nevertheless, as we shall see, it is not at all uncommon.

Let us return now to McGovern's call for intervention and the press reaction to it. McGovern provided no source for his estimate of 2-2½ million systematically killed by thugs who had taken over the government of Cambodia, though such charges have been bandied about widely in the press since immediately after the Khmer Rouge victory.[53] Nor did McGovern attempt to sort out the relative proportions of those who were killed by government plan or edict or in random acts of violence (evidently, rather different categories) as compared with those who died from malnutrition and disease.

McGovern's remarks, as well as much of the press commentary concerning them, amount to the claim that the population is suffering in misery under a savage oppressor bent on genocide. Mere common sense, even apart from special knowledge, should raise at least some doubts about this picture. In the first place, is it proper to attribute deaths from malnutrition and disease to the Cambodian authorities? Compare, for example, the case of Laos already discussed, where relief workers speak of hundreds of thousands of deaths from malnutrition and disease as a legacy of colonialism and more specifically, the U.S. attack on a defenseless society, while the United States withholds desperately needed aid. It surely should occur to a journalist or the reader to ask how many of the deaths in Cambodia fall to the U.S. account. There is evidence on this matter, but it is systematically excluded from the press. Or, one might wonder, how can it be that a population so oppressed by a handful of fanatics does not rise up to overthrow them? In fact, even in the hearings where McGovern reported the estimates of 2½ million deaths attributable to the Khmer Rouge and "called for international military intervention," the State Department response should have aroused some questions in the mind of a moderately serious reporter. Douglas Pike, responding to McGovern, said that "the notion of a quick, surgical takeout of the government of Cambodia probably is not possible":

> He pointed to Cambodia's unique government consisting of a ruling group of nine men at the center and communal government 'in the style of the 14th century' in the villages, with no regional or provincial governments in between..."To take over Cambodia you're going to have to take over the villages—all of them," he said.[54]

Evidently there must be at least some support for the group of nine men at the center if it will be necessary to take over every village to overthrow their rule. The quandary has been expressed by other State Department experts. Charles Twining, who says that he was "sent to Bangkok [by the State Department] as the Indochina watcher with responsibility primarily for finding out what is happening in Cambodia and Vietnam," made the following remark in response to Rep. Solarz's query as to "how people at the top manage to establish their authority over these young soldiers out in the villages who are carrying out this policy of extermination":

> It is a difficult question. We know the levels of administration in Cambodia; it goes from the central to the region to the sector to the district to the commune to the village. Presumably, then, there are loyal people at all of these levels. What really binds together these largely Paris-educated fanatics at the top with almost purposefully ignorant farm boys at the bottom who are the ones with the guns carrying out their orders—I really don't know what it is that keeps them together and I wonder in the future how long something like this can continue, how long that glue can hold.[55]

It is, indeed, "a difficult question."

Similar doubts were raised by experts close to the U.S. government during the earlier *May Hearings*. In response to Rep. Solarz's remarks about possible intervention, Peter A. Poole, formerly a Foreign Service Officer in Cambodia and now a professor of international relations at American University, said that "I think that an international police force would be one of the worst possible things we could do." On the evacuation of Phnom Penh, he said: "They obviously overdid it. They obviously did it very badly. But the general thrust of moving people out of the city was something that practically any regime would have contemplated and done at some stage in that year, getting the people back on the land and producing rice." The Khmer Rouge, he added, "took over at a time when society was in ruins, so that there were no normal means of government...in a state of social, political, and economic chaos" and ran the country with "an ignorant peasant teen-age army, a rather large, very obedient army, well-armed and totally flexible, totally obedient to orders" who might respond to a command to march the people down the road by shooting those who do not obey. As to how the Khmer Rouge were able "to establish that sense of total discipline in the ranks of the army," Poole answered: "I don't know the answer to that question."[56]

Another former Foreign Service Officer in Phnom Penh, David P. Chandler, now a senior lecturer at Monash University in Australia, added some further comments which had little impact on the subsequent proceedings:

> What drove the Cambodians to kill? Paying off old scores or imaginary ones played a part, but, to a large extent, I think, American actions are to blame. From 1969 to 1973, after all, we dropped more than 500,000 tons of bombs on the Cambodian countryside. Nearly half of this tonnage fell in 1973... In those few months, we may have driven thousands of people out of their minds. We certainly accelerated the course of the revolution. According to several accounts, the leadership hardened its ideology and got rid of wavering factions during 1973 and 1974...We bombed Cambodia without knowing why, without taking note of the people we destroyed...it is ironic, to use a colorless word, for us to accuse the Cambodians of being indifferent to life when, for so many years, Cambodian lives made so little difference to us.[57]

Chandler's comment was rejected by Rep. William F. Goodling on the following grounds:

> Our bombs didn't single out certain segments or certain peoples in Cambodia. Our bombs hit them all [sic]. And whether you thought it was right or I thought it was right, the military at that particular time thought it was right.[58]

The comment is a fitting one from a leading apologist for the U.S.-backed Indonesian atrocities in Timor.[59]

Twining's "difficult question" is addressed in an article by Kenneth Quinn of the National Security Council Staff,[60] one of the three leading U.S. government experts on Cambodia.[61] Basing himself primarily on refugees who fled Cambodia in 1973-1974, Quinn reviews Khmer Rouge programs in an effort to explain "how a small but dedicated force was able to impose a revolution on a society without widespread participation of the peasantry" and indeed in the face of strong peasant opposition. He does not remark that since his evidence derives primarily "from the in-depth interviewing of selected refugees," it will obviously be negative; those who might approve of these programs are excluded from his sample. But ignoring this trivial point, Quinn states that "the evidence overwhelmingly demonstrates that the peasantry was opposed to almost all of the [Khmer Rouge] programs." Quinn discusses programs which included land reform, establishment of cooperatives, ensuring "that all citizens have roughly the same degree of wealth," obliterating class lines by confiscating property from the wealthy and compelling university students to plant and harvest rice, distributing excess crops "to feed other groups whose harvest was insufficient," etc. He notes that "as a result [of collectivization], production has outstripped previous individual efforts" and that "political-psychological [Khmer Rouge] efforts" seem to "have achieved significant results...according to all accounts" among the youth, who "were passionate in their loyalty to the state and party," "rejected the mystical aspects of religion," and "stopped working on their family plot of land and instead worked directly for the youth association on its land." He also comments that the Khmer Rouge "success is all the more amazing when it is realized that they had few, if any, cadres at the village or hamlet level...In most cases, there was no separate party existence nor were there political cadres at the village level or at any level below," though there were small, apparently locally recruited military units (in the midst of the civil war), as well as "interfamily groups" of a sort that "have existed in other Southeast Asian countries for years" and were used by the Khmer Rouge "for forcing the population to carry out a whole series of radically new programs."

Quinn then asks the "difficult question": "How did such a small group of people carry out such a varied and all-encompassing effort?" His answer is that "they cowed people and suppressed dissent and opposition through harsh and brutal punishments; and they constructed a governmental apparatus at the village and hamlet level which allowed them to exercise tight control over every family in the area." The possibility that some of the programs he reviewed might appeal to poor peasants is nowhere considered; it is excluded on doctrinal grounds.

Quinn claims that in 1973 the Khmer Rouge programs became extremely harsh as new cadres took over, described as "fanatics," who were "austere" and "did not take anything for themselves and seemed willing to live a frugal life" but instituted widespread terror. Other sources, as we have seen, confirm that the Khmer Rouge programs became harsh in 1973—as the United States stepped up its murderous program of saturation bombing, a possible causal factor that Quinn is careful never to mention.

There are other aspects to the "difficult question" that properly troubled government specialists. How indeed do the Khmer Rouge manage to maintain control? Here, the refugee reports evoke some questions. For example, R.-P. Paringaux reported interviews with two high functionaries of the Lon Nol regime who had escaped to Thailand.[62] They report that armed surveillance was "almost nonexistent" in the village to which they were sent. "In case there are problems, the village chief can call upon a militia group of 12 Khmers Rouges who maintain order in the ten villages of the sector." One of these functionaries comments that the "old people"—those who were with the Khmer Rouge during the war—offer more support to the new regime: "they are peasants, who have always been used to hard work and to be content with little.[63] It would seem not unlikely that part of the answer to the difficult question, and a reason why a dozen militiamen can maintain order in ten villages, is that the regime has a modicum of support among the peasants.

Other questions arise. If 1/3 of the population has been killed by a murderous band that has taken over the government—which somehow manages to control every village—or have died as a result of their genocidal policies, then surely one would expect if not a rebellion then at least unwillingness to fight for the Paris-educated fanatics at the top. But the confused and obscure record of the border conflicts with Thailand and Vietnam would appear to indicate that there are a substantial number of "purposefully ignorant farm boys" who have not exactly been awaiting liberation from their oppressors.[64] As Pike observed in response to McGovern's call for intervention, the Vietnamese tried a "quick judo chop" against the Cambodian regime with 60,000 troops but "failed abysmally."[65] Basing herself on Pike's testimony, Susan Spencer of CBS raised the question to McGovern in a TV interview.[66] When McGovern referred to Cambodia as "an underdeveloped country that has gotten out of control and is systematically slaughtering its own citizens," Spencer make the following comment:

> You mentioned that we should apply pressure. It seems, though, that the Vietnamese, who periodically are at war with

Cambodia, have found that the Cambodian citizens, at least the villagers, seem to support the government. What lever do we have to break in—to break that?

Spencer's question is a bit odd to begin with. If the villagers of this largely peasant society support the government, as Spencer assumes, then exactly what right do we have to find a "lever" to "break that"? And how does that alleged support square with the charge of genocide? These questions did not arise, however. McGovern simply replied that "the evidence is that about nine men are controlling that government in Cambodia" without a "loyal infrastructure out across the country" and it is "hard to believe that there's mass support for the Cambodian government."

The problem is implicit, though rarely discussed in these terms, in other reports concerning Cambodia. Robert Shaplen, who has been the Far Eastern correspondent for *The New Yorker* for many years, observes that in the border war with Vietnam, "the Cambodians have proved to be tough, ruthless and relentless fighters."[67] The Southeast Asia correspondent for the *Christian Science Monitor* comments that "despite Vietnam's superior size, economy, and military power, Cambodia appears to have emerged the technical 'victor' after the Vietnamese invasion that ended with a military withdrawal in January...In fact, Cambodian attacks across Vietnam's borders currently are described by one analyst as 'heavier than ever'...Vietnam appears to have underestimated the strength of Cambodian resistance, several analysts note."[68] The continuing conflict with Thailand brings out similar anomalies. Whatever the facts may be—and they are far from clear—it seems that Cambodian forces held their own, so much so that U.S. analysts "voice skepticism about Hanoi's ability to crush Cambodia" despite its overwhelming military advantages, because of "factors such as the apparently excellent morale of Cambodia's ground forces."[69]

Various explanations have been offered for these facts, which at the very least raise questions about the allegations that the population is groaning under the heels of the conquerer.[70]

William Buckley explains the difficulty away with resort to the mysterious Asian mind: nationalism carried to such lengths "is utterly alien to the western experience."[71] Ponchaud argues that "the old Hindu core, which regarded authority as a divine incarnation, was still strong in the Khmers...The Cambodian sticks to the rule'; The Khmer people still respect authority with a respect that to us is tinged with fatalism, even passivity, but that eminates an underlying confidence in the abilities of those in power...The underlying ideology [of the revolution] may come from somewhere else, but the methods employed show every mark of the Cambodian character," and Khmer culture makes it possible for the authorities to rule "the countryside with terror and lies," though "under Marxist influence, perhaps the Khmer will suddenly open a critical eye." "Another cause of the radicality of the Khmer revolution lies in the Khmer way of reasoning, which is bewildering to Cartesian minds. The Khmer thinks by accretions or juxtapositions, but adheres strictly to the rules of his own internal logic," apparently incapable of "Cartesian" logic.[72]

The non-specialist may wonder about the cogency of these explanations of the "difficult question" that government specialists rightly find troubling. It is noteworthy that in the varied attempts to find a solution to this most difficult question, one conceivable hypothesis does not seem to have been considered, even to be rejected: that there was a significant degree of peasant support for the Khmer Rouge and the measures that they had instituted in the countryside.

As we begin to inquire a little further, other difficult questions arise. Consider the numbers game. What is the source of the figures invoked by the press? We shall see that the sources are obscure or misrepresented, though when corrected, they continue to surface. Furthermore, there is considerably more controversy among knowledgeable observers than the standard line of the press would indicate. For example, Lewis M. Simons, the outstanding *Washington Post* correspondent, reported from Bangkok that "disease and malnutrition combined with a dropping birthrate are taking a greater toll of Cambodia's population than Communist executions, according to some of the latest analyses made here." There is a

> major reversal in Western judgments of what had gone on inside Democratic Kampuchea...Most Westerners who make an occupation of observing Cambodia from Thailand are talking in terms of several hundred thousand deaths from all causes. This is a marked shift from the estimates of just six months ago, when it was popular to say that anywhere between 800,000 and 1.4 million Cambodians had been executed by vengeful Communist rulers.[73]

He also noted that "few Cambodia-watchers believe that

> "The Organization" [*Angkar*, the governing group] is organized well enough to control much of the country. It is generally accepted that local military commanders, operating from jungle bases, conduct their own small-scale border rations [sic] and impose summary justice.

There are two noteworthy points in this report by Lewis Simons—which was accepted with one irrelevant qualification as "excellent" by the State Department's leading Cambodia watcher. First, the number of deaths is estimated by "most Westerners" who are close observers as in the several hundred thousand range, most of them from disease and malnutrition. Second, most Cambodia watchers doubt that the "summary justice" is centrally organized, believing rather that it is the responsibility of local commanders. Again we are left with some doubts, to put it conservatively, as regards the standard media picture: a centrally-controlled genocidal policy of mass execution.

Note also that the numbers killed were estimated by the leading government expert as in the "thousands or hundreds of thousands."

(Twining, who adds that "very honestly, I think we can't accurately estimate a figure.") His superior, Richard Holbrooke, offered an estimate of "tens if not hundreds of thousands" for "deaths" from all causes.[74] He offered his "guess" that "for every person executed several people have died of disease, malnutrition, or other factors ..." (which he claims were "avoidable," though he does not indicate how).[75] Twining's colleague Timothy Carney—the second of the State Department's leading Cambodia watchers—estimated the number of deaths from "brutal, rapid change" (not "mass genocide") as in the hundreds of thousands.[76] What about deaths from causes other than killing? A major source of death, Simons reports:

> appears to be failure of the 1976 rice crop. The government averted famine in mid-1975 by evacuating Phnom Penh and other cities and forcing almost every ablebodied person to work the land. But food production fell badly last year.

If this "excellent" analysis is correct, as Twining indicates, the evacuation of Phnom Penh, widely denounced at the time and since for its undoubted brutality, may actually have saved many lives.[77] It is striking that the crucial facts rarely appear in the chorus of condemnations. At the time of the evacuation, AFP reported from Bangkok that:

> Recent aerial photographs by American reconnaissance planes are said to have shown that only 12 percent of the rice paddies have been planted. The monsoon, which marks the beginning of the planting season, came a month early this year. There was also the problem of the acute shortage of rice in the capital when the Communists took over on April 17. According to Long Boret, the old Government's last premier, Phnom Penh had only eight days' worth of rice on hand on the eve of the surrender.[78]

In a New York Times Op-Ed, William Goodfellow, who left Cambodia with the final U.S. evacuation in April, 1975 wrote that "A.I.D. officials reported that stockpiles of rice in Phnom Penh could last for six days." Commenting on the "death march" from

Phnom Penh, he writes that "in fact, it was a journey *away* from certain death by starvation...[which]...was already a reality in the urban centers." The director of the U.S. aid program "estimated that in Phnom Penh alone 1.2 million people were in 'desperate need' of United States food, although at the time only 640,000 people were actually receiving some form of United States food support" and "starvation was widely reported."[80] Goodfellow also correctly assigns the responsibility for the impending famine: it was caused primarily by the U.S. bombing campaign which "shattered" the agrarian economy—an unquestionable fact that has since been quietly forgotten.

The situation in Phnom Penh resulting from the U.S. war is graphically described in a carefully-documented study by Hildebrand and Porter that has been almost totally ignored by the press.[81] By early 1974 the World Health Organization estimated that half the children of Phnom Penh, which was swollen to almost 5 times its normal size by the U.S. bombardment and the ravages of the war directly caused by U.S. intervention, were suffering from malnutrition. A Congressional study mission reported "severe nutritional damage." Studies in late 1974 and early 1975 revealed "a disastrous decline in nutritional status," indicating "a caloric intake during a year or longer of less than 60 percent of the minimum required to maintain body weight." A Department of State study of February 1975 reported that these statistics "confirmed the universal medical impression given us by those involved in Cambodia health and nutrition that children are starving to death." Starvation also lowered resistance to infection and disease. There were reports that cholera was spreading rapidly in Phnom Penh. The medical director for Catholic Relief Services declared in March, 1975, that "hundreds are dying of malnutrition every day." Red Cross and other observers reported thousands of small children dying from hunger and disease. Note that all of this refers to the period before the Khmer Rouge victory.

As Hildebrand and Porter remark, "those children who did not die from starvation will suffer permanent damage to their bodies and minds due to the severe malnutrition." They quote Dr. Penelope Key of the World Vision Organization, working in Phnom Penh:

> This generation is going to be a lost generation of children. Malnutrition is going to affect their numbers and their mental capacities. So, as well as knocking off a generation of young men, the war is knocking off a generation of children.

Porter added relevant information in his Congressional testimony:

> It must be noted that the same official sources who were claiming [a postwar death toll of 800,000-1.4 million] had been saying in June 1975 that a million people were certain to die of starvation in the next year because there were simply no food stocks available in Cambodia to provide for them.[82]

Porter drew the conclusion that the postwar death tolls were exaggerated by officials who "had an obvious vested interest [in] not admitting their failure to understand the capacity of the new regime to feed its people." Alternatively, suppose that their postwar estimates are correct. Since the situation at the war's end is squarely the responsibility of the United States, so are the million or so deaths that were predicted as a direct result of that situation.[83]

The horrendous situation in Phnom Penh (as elsewhere in Cambodia) as the war drew to an end was a direct and immediate consequence of the U.S. assault—prior to the U.S. actions that drew Cambodia into the Indochina war, the situation was far from ideal, contrary to colonialist myths about happy peasants, but it was nothing like the accounts just reviewed by Congressional study missions and health and relief workers. The same is true of the vast destruction of agricultural lands and draught animals, peasant villages and communications, not to speak of the legacy of hatred and revenge. The United States bears primary responsibility for these consequences of its intervention.

All of this is forgotten when sole responsibility is assigned to the Khmer Rouge for deaths from malnutrition and disease. It is as if some Nazi apologist were to condemn the allies for postwar deaths from starvation and disease in DP camps, though the analogy is unfair to the Nazis, since the allies at least had the resources to try to deal with the Nazi legacy.

Consider again what lies behind the call for military intervention in Cambodia. The leading State Department specialist estimated killings in the "thousands or hundreds of thousands," and attributed a still larger number of deaths to disease and malnutrition—in significant and perhaps overwhelming measure, a consequence of U.S. terror. Furthermore, a news report that the State Department specialist regards as "excellent" notes that "it is generally accepted" by Cambodia watchers that "summary justice" is not centrally-directed. Another government expert insists that it would be necessary to conquer every village to subdue the Khmer Rouge. But when a leading senatorial dove calls for military intervention, the *Wall Street Journal*, which backed the U.S. aggression and massacre through the worst atrocities, has the gall to make the following editorial comment:

> Now, having finished the task of destroying [the U.S. presence in Indochina, American liberals] are shocked and dismayed by the news of the grim and brutal world that resulted. One of the few good things to come out of the sordid end of our Indochina campaign was a period of relative silence from the people who took us through all its painful contortions. They should have the grace to maintain their quiet for at least a while longer.[84]

About postwar Cambodia, they have only this to say: the "present Communist rulers have starved, worked, shot, beaten and hacked to death upwards of a million of the country's citizens." Not a word about the U.S. role or continuing responsibility for death and suffering, let alone an effort to evaluate the evidence or to face the "difficult questions" that arise.

It would take a volume to record the material of this sort that dominates the U.S., indeed the Western press. Before turning to the nature of the evidence adduced concerning the scale and character of postwar atrocities in Cambodia, we will cite only one more example selected out of the mass of comparable instances, along with an example of journalistic integrity that is another of the rare exceptions.

On July 31, 1978, *Time* magazine published a "Time Essay" entitled: "Cambodia: An Experiment in Genocide," by David Aikman. The essay is short on documentation but not sparing in its outrage. The sole documentation offered is the "interview" with Khieu Samphan already cited—an example that was specifically pointed out in advance to a *Time* reporter preparing background for this article as a probable fabrication—and a statement on Radio Phnom Penh that "more than 2,000 years of Cambodian history have virtually ended," which Aikman presents as a "boast of this atrocity," though other interpretations easily come to mind.

According to *Time*, "the lowest estimate of the bloodbath to date—by execution, starvation, and disease—is in the hundreds of thousands. The highest exceeds 1 million, and that in a country that once numbered no more than 7 million." Figures apart, what is striking about this claim is that nowhere in the article is there any reference to any U.S. role or responsibility, no indication that deaths from starvation and disease may be something other than a "bloodbath" by the Khmer Rouge.

A major theme of the *Time* essay is that "somehow the enormity of the Cambodian tragedy—even leaving aside the grim question of how many or how few actually died in Angka Loeu's experiment in genocide—has failed to evoke an appropriate response of outrage in the West," and even worse, "some political theorists have defended it, as George Bernard Shaw and other Western intellectuals defended the brutal social engineering in the Soviet Union during the 1930s"; "there are intellectuals in the West so committed to the twin Molochs of our day—'liberation' and 'revolution'—that they can actually defend what has happened in Cambodia." In fact, the Western press since 1975 has poured forth reams of denunciations of Cambodia in the most strident tones, repeating the most extreme denunciations often on flimsy evidence, in striking contrast to its behavior in the case of massacres elsewhere, as in Timor; the U.S. press is particularly notable for a marked double standard in this regard, though it is hardly alone. And there is good reason why Aikman fails to mention the names of those "political theorists" who have defended "the Cambodian tragedy"—as this would require differentiating those who have exposed media distortions and tried to discover the facts, instead of joining the bandwagon of uncritical abuse, from those who say that no serious atrocities have occurred (a small or non-existent set that *Time* has searched for, apparently without success).[85] Specificity also might require publicizing the views of critics of the current propaganda barrage, which would make it difficult to avoid discussion of the crucial U.S. role in postwar suffering and deaths in Cambodia or of the actual nature of what *Time* regards as "evidence." For *Time* ideologists, a defender of the "Cambodian tragedy" is one who fails to place all the blame for postwar suffering on the Khmer Rouge and who otherwise contests the patriotic truths handed down by the *Reader's Digest* and similar sources.

For the ideologists of *Time*, the Cambodian tragedy is the "logical conclusion" of "bloodbath sociology" associated with socialism and Marxism. The "moral relativism" of the West makes it difficult to see that the Cambodian experience "is the deadly logical consequence of an atheistic, man-centered system of values, enforced by fallible human beings with total power, who believe, with Marx, that morality is whatever the powerful define it to be and, with Mao, that power grows from gun barrels." Unlike the more "humane Marxist societies in Europe today," the

Cambodians do not "permit the dilution of their doctrine by what Solzhenitsyn has called 'the great reserves of mercy and sacrifice' from a Christian tradition." As for the significance of the Christian tradition for the Third World—not to speak of the European experience—*Time* has no more to say than it does about the great reserves of mercy and sacrifice shown by the U.S. leaders who sent their angels of mercy to flatten the villages of Indochina while the editors of *Time* lauded this noble enterprise.[86] And it is fitting indeed that they should cite Solzhenitsyn, the profound thinker who denounced the West for failing to carry this enterprise to a successful conclusion, in the spirit of Christian humanism.

To show in contrast that honest journalism remains possible, consider a report by Richard Dudman just after the fall of Phnom Penh.[87] Dudman was captured in Cambodia while serving as a U.S. war correspondent in Southeast Asia, and wrote an important book on his experiences with the Khmer Rouge.[88] Dudman writes that "the constant indiscriminate bombing, an estimated 450,000 dead and wounded civilians to say nothing of military casualties, and the estimated 4,000,000 refugees were almost inevitable results of the short U.S. invasion of Cambodia and the subsequent proxy war that ended in defeat for the United States as well as for its client regime in Phnom Penh." Relying in part on his personal experience in captivity, he adds that "the U.S. invasion spread the Communist-led guerrillas through most of Cambodia" and drove the Vietnamese Communists and the Cambodian population "into an alliance as comrades in arms against a common enemy—American tanks and bombs," which were a "catalyst": "we [the Khmer Rouge prisoners] could see Cambodian peasants turning to a friend in need in the form of the military forces of the Vietnamese Communists."

To ignore these basic facts in reporting postwar Cambodia is as disgraceful as to attribute the U.S. legacy of starvation, disease, and bitter hatreds simply to atheistic Communism carried to its "logical conclusion."

Let us now turn to an evaluation of the evidence that is used by the media as support for their denunciations. Simons examined this question in an analysis after his return from several years as *Post* correspondent in Bangkok.[89] Accompanying the article is a photograph showing workers under military guard with the following caption: "Photo from smuggled film purports to show forced labor in Cambodian countryside." Simons comments that "a number of journals, including the *Washington Post, Newsweek, Time* and *Paris Match,* have published several photographs purporting to show atrocities in Cambodia." But he continues:

> Several U.S. and other experts believe that these pictures were posed in Thailand. "They're fakes," commented a State Department officer who has followed Cambodian affairs closely since before the end of the war.

As we shall see there is more to the story: the photographs continued to be published long after they were exposed as frauds, and corrections were refused by the journals that published them.

Simons next turns to the interview in which Khieu Samphan is alleged to have conceded that the Khmer Rouge are responsible for a million deaths, which he writes, was "subsequently referred to in the *New York Times Magazine.*" He adds that the very occurrence of that interview is denied by François Ponchaud. Again, as we shall see, there is more to the story.

Simons then makes the following interesting observation:

> Oddly, those few Western governments which have diplomatic relations with Cambodia generally refuse to accept the genocide allegation. "We'd need a lot more evidence before we'd be ready to believe such a serious charge," said an ambassador from a Scandinavian country. Representatives of his government have visited Phnom Penh several times since the war ended.

This lead too deserves to be explored. It is indeed "odd" that

Western visitors to Phnom Penh refused to join the chorus. At the very least, a rational person might well heed Simons' observation that "reports about Cambodia should be treated with skepticism."

Simons offers other reasons for skepticism. Noting that "just one member of the U.S. embassy staff in Thailand [presumably, Twining] is assigned to monitoring Cambodian affairs," Simons comments:

> Most information gathered by this official and by journalists in Southeast Asia comes from interviewing Cambodian refugees who have fled to Thailand. Almost all of these refugees come from the northwestern part of Cambodia, an area which was never well controlled by the Communists and where reprisals by long-embittered guerrillas were fierce in the months immediately following the Communist victory. From this bare-bones intelligence gathering, nationwide projections have been drawn. It is these projections that have led to the conclusion that Cambodian leaders are genocidal monsters and that the torment of this once-gentle land has no parallel in modern history.

Again, what Simons reports has been emphasized by specialists to whom we return.[90] The State Department's Cambodia watcher, Charles Twining, comments that "our information is just inadequate. Most of it is from northwestern Cambodia and we have virtually nothing from northeastern Cambodia, so it is awfully hard to put together a significant figure and I think none of us want to give an estimate [of deaths]."[91]

Simons cites Gareth Porter's comment that the forced evacuation of urban centers "was well-advised, though 'heavy-handed.'"[92] He quotes Porter as follows:

> The fact is that the evacuation and the regime's concentration on rice production have averted mass starvation. If you look at the three Indochinese countries today, you'll find that Cambodia undoubtedly is in the best food position.

Simons continues: "This claim is more or less supported by State Department officials," who say "people are probably eating better" and note reports of rice exports. We will return to reports by visitors that confirm these conclusions, contrary to the standard picture presented by the media of mass starvation or even systematic policies of starvation undertaken by the leadership, as Lacouture and others contend. It is particularly worthy of note that visitors in late 1978 found food supplies to be more than adequate. The severe floods of the preceding months had a devastating effect on agricultural production throughout the region, causing a very serious shortage of food in neighboring countries. Some reports indicate that Cambodia may have been the hardest hit of all the countries of the region,[93] but it seems that the extensive development of dikes and dams in the postwar period, which has consistently impressed visitors, sufficed, despite some damage, to overcome the worst effects and to afford the population an ample supply of food, even including a surplus for export, according to the regime; an achievement that U.S. specialists describe as "spectacular" if true.[94]

Simons takes note of the U.S. attack on Cambodia and gives an accurate account of doubts raised by critics of the Western propaganda system, whom he misleadingly describes as "supporters of the Cambodian regime" (or "defenders," or "friends," of the regime); concern for factual accuracy carries no such implication. He asks why the most extreme conclusions about Cambodia have been "widely accepted" despite their often flimsy basis, and suggests two reasons: "First, while figures may be subject to doubt, what's the difference between whether tens of thousands or a million people have been killed?"[95] Second, the refusal of the government to permit outside observers itself suggests that they are attempting "to hide some horrible secret." Simons argues that these points "have acceptable moral bases" but "sidestep key issues." Reprisals have been common after other wars, and while the Cambodian government's policy towards foreigners "may be judged extreme xenophobia, it does not prove that genocide is being carried out behind the bamboo curtain." We are more skeptical about the moral basis for these points, for reasons already discussed. We wonder, for example, whether the reaction would be the same if some critic of the United States were to charge that U.S. troops had killed 40,000 civilians at My Lai, then responding to a correction by asking what's the difference—just a factor of a hundred. Recall further that it is the more sensational claims that have been endlessly repeated by the media and have led to a call for military intervention in Cambodia. As for Cambodian "xenophobia," it is worth considering just what the experience of Cambodian peasants has been with the West, not only under French colonialism but also in the few years of the war.[96] Does the term "xenophobia" accurately convey their reaction?

This report, by one of the few serious U.S. correspondents who have recently worked in Southeast Asia, stands alone in the U.S. mass media, to our knowledge, in its fairness and accuracy in presenting the views of critics of the media barrage and its concern for the quality of available evidence, though Simons's skepticism, like that of many other close observers, has been drowned in the deluge.

Let us now consider in detail the several points that Simons raised. To begin with, consider the photograph that appeared along with Simons's article. This is one of several that have, as he notes, been widely circulated in the press as sure proof of Communist barbarism.

On April 8, 1977, the *Washington Post* devoted half a page to "photographs believed to be the first of actual forced labor conditions in the countryside of Cambodia [to] have reached the West." The pictures show armed soldiers guarding people pulling plows, others working fields, and one bound man ("It is not known if this man was killed," the caption reads). Quite a sensational testimonial to Communist atrocities. But there is a slight problem. The *Post* account of how they were smuggled out by a relative of the photographer who died in the escape attempt is entirely fanciful. Furthermore, the photos had appeared a year earlier in France, Germany, and Australia, as well as in the *Bangkok Post* (19 April 1976), where they appeared under the caption "True or False?" This strongly anti-Communist journal turned down an attempt by a Thai trader to sell them the photos "because the origin and authenticity of the photos were in doubt." The photos appeared in a Thai-language newspaper two days before the April 4th election. The *Bangkok Post* then published them, explaining that "Khmer watchers were dubious about the clothes and manner of the people depicted, and quoting "other observers" who "pointed to the possibility that the series of pictures could have been taken in Thailand with the prime objective of destroying the image of the Socialist parties" before the election. This speculation seems eminently reasonable. Westerners in Southeast Asia have reported that the Thai press, including the *Bangkok Post*, was exploiting "horror stories" from Cambodia to undermine the Socialist parties in Thailand.[97]

The facts were reported in the *U.S./Indochina Report* of the Washington-based Indochina Resource Center in July, 1976, along with the additional information that a Thai intelligence officer later admitted that the photos were indeed posed inside Thailand: "'Only the photographer and I were supposed to know,' he confided to a Thai journalist." The full details were again given in the *International Bulletin* (circulation 6,000).[98] A letter of April 20 to the *Washington Post* correcting its story was not printed, though "the *Post* published a short item acknowledging the doubts, but pointing out that the pictures had been published elsewhere."[99] The "freedom of the press" assures that readers of the *International Bulletin* could learn the true facts of the matter concealed by the mass media.

We reviewed the story thus far shortly thereafter.[100] But it continued to evolve. The major newsweeklies did not want to miss the opportunity to offer their readers visual evidence of Khmer Rouge tyranny, and could not be deterred merely because the evidence was faked—repeated exposure has rarely dimmed the lustre of other familiar propaganda tales, such as the North Vietnamese land reform bloodbath of the 1950s, discussed in Volume I. On November 21, 1977, *Time* magazine ran the photo of the bound man. While the *Washington Post* had withheld judgment on whether the victim was killed in the staged photo, doubts had now been eliminated and *Time* assured the reader that he was executed. Several letters were sent to *Time* reporting the facts just reviewed and also noting that their fakery went beyond that of the *Washington Post*. Those who had wasted their efforts alerting *Time* to the facts were rewarded by the following response:

> TIME printed that photograph of a Khmer Rouge execution (if indeed that is what it is) in good faith. We were assured of its authenticity by the Sygma agency who provided us with it: they say they obtained it from a Cambodian refugee now living in Paris, whose name did not appear in the credit for fear of endangering his family in Cambodia. We note that the authenticity of the photograph has been questioned, but it seems to us that there is no way of proving it one way or the other. However, we do thank you for alerting us to the problem.

Not to be outdone, *Newsweek* leaped into the fray in its issue of January 23, 1978. The executioner and his victim appear on the cover of the international edition, and two other faked photos appear within, one with the caption "The executioners: For the condemned, a swift, primitive and brutal death," and the other, "Life under the Khmer Rouge: Armed guards supervise forced labor in the fields."

In a February 16, 1978, story filed by the Pacific News Service, Douglas Foster added some further details. He cites a State

Department intelligence source who labels the photos a fake and said in an interview that he was "appalled" and "shocked" to see the photographs in the press. Foster also interviewed the director of the Sygma agency which had been distributing these intelligence fabrications to eager customers. She claims to have alerted *Time* to the possibility that the photos were propaganda plants, but held that the photographs were useful anyway, regardless of their authenticity, on the following grounds: "...As the people at *Newsweek* told me, if the photograph hasn't been absolutely proved false, (the questions) don't matter. Besides that, the Khmer Rouge do these things, like blowing people's heads off. So the photos are like drawings ..."

Foster notes that the photos have appeared widely in the U.S. and Western Europe (also in Australia), and comments: "No Western publisher who has used the photos has yet alerted readers that the pictures may well be bogus."[101]

The reaction of the *Washington Post, Time, Newsweek,* the Sygma agency, and others who have been engaged in this little exercise of atrocity fabrication,[102] recalls some of George Orwell's remarks on the Stalinist press:

> When one considers the elaborate forgeries that have been committed in order to show that Trotsky did not play a valuable part in the Russian civil war, it is difficult to feel that the people responsible are merely lying. More probably, they feel that their own version *was* what happened in the sight of God, and that one is justified in rearranging the records accordingly.[103]

Putting aside the manifest dishonesty, suppose that the photographs had been authentic. We might then ask why people should be pulling plows in Cambodia, as one of the faked photographs claims to show. The reason is clear, though unmentioned in this propaganda exercise. The savage U.S. assault on Cambodia did not spare the animal population. The Cambodian government reports that the attack on rural Cambodia led to the destruction of 50-60% of livestock in some areas, 30-40% in others.[104] One can learn from the reports of refugees that "they had to pull the plows themselves because there were no oxen."[105] Some died from the exhausting work of pulling plows. Who is responsible for these deaths? The U.S. press did not have to resort to propaganda plants to depict the facts. A hundred-word item buried in the *New York Times* cites an official U.N. report that teams of "human buffaloes" pull plows in Laos in areas where the buffalo herds, along with everything else, were decimated (by the U.S. bombing, although this goes unmentioned in the *Times* in accordance with postwar taboo).[106] Much the same is true in Vietnam, as already noted. Quite possibly the U.N. or the Laotian Government could supply photographic evidence, but this would not satisfy the needs of current propaganda.

Let us now turn to the second example that Simons cites, namely, the interview in which Cambodian premier Khieu Samphan is alleged to have conceded a million deaths at the hands of the Khmer Rouge. This is the most widely-circulated "crucial evidence" offered of the barbarity of the regime—we have already given several examples—and is regularly cited by academic specialists, intelligence analysts, and Cambodia watchers. Frank Snepp, one of the top CIA analysts for Indochina, writes the following, with regard to the atrocities of the Khmer Rouge—which typically, he claims have been ignored in the West:

> Khieu Samphan himself has provided perhaps the most reliable estimate of the casualties. During a conference of non-aligned countries in Colombo in August 1976 he admitted to an Italian journalist that the population of Cambodia had dropped by a million since the end of the war. When asked what had happened to all these people, he replied, "It's incredible how concerned you westerners are about war criminals."[107]

Similarly, Timothy Carney, a State Department specialist

on Cambodia,[108] testified before Congress, without qualifications, that "in a 1976 interview with an Italian magazine, Khieu Samphan said that there were 5 million people in Cambodia."[109] Given roughly 1 million killed or wounded during the war (a "close" estimate, according to Carney), and a prewar population on the order of 7-8 million, we have over a million postwar deaths (i.e., victims of the Khmer Rouge, with a little further sleight-of-hand). As Carney notes, the alleged estimate of 5 million by Khieu Samphan contradicts the estimate by the Cambodian government that the population is 7.7 million, but he offers no explanation for the discrepancy.

Simons reports that the alleged interview was "supposedly given by head of state Khieu Samphan to an obscure Italian Catholic journal, *Famiglia Cristiana,* in September, 1976, and subsequently referred to in the *New York Times Magazine,"* though its authenticity is denied by Ponchaud, "a French Catholic priest who is a bitter opponent of the Cambodian Communists," who wrote in August, 1977 that he knows "for certain" that the interview never took place. These statements are correct, but are only part of the story. To add some further detail, in the *New York Times Magazine,*[110] Robert Moss (extreme right-wing editor of a dubious offshoot of Britain's *Economist* called "Foreign Report," which specializes in sensational rumors from the world's intelligence agencies) asserts that "Cambodia's pursuit of total revolution has resulted, by the official admission of its Head of State, Khieu Samphan, in the slaughter of a million people." Moss offered no source for this "official admission." We speculated that his source was probably the *Reader's Digest,* that noteworthy journal of cool and dispassionate political analysis, and Moss informed us in a personal letter that that suspicion was correct. Turning back to Moss's source, we read in the Barron-Paul book, expanding their *Reader's Digest* article:

> Khieu Samphan, as Cambodian chief of state, attended the

Colombo Conference of nonaligned nations in August 1976
and while there was interviewed by the Italian weekly magazine
Famiglia Cristiana. "Those traitors that remained have been executed," the magazine quoted him as saying. It further quoted
him: "In five years of warfare, more than one million Cambodians died. The current population of Cambodia is five million.
Before the war, the population numbered seven million."[111]

Barron and Paul then write that in response to a query as to the
fate of the missing one million people, Khieu Samphan replied:
"It is incredible how concerned you Westerners are about war
criminals." They conclude that "if quoted accurately, Khieu Samphan indicated that between April 17, 1975, and the time of the
interview in August 1976 roughly a million Cambodians died."

Note that even if Khieu Samphan had "indicated" that a million Cambodians had died, that is not quite the same as an "official
admission...[of]...the slaughter of a million people" as a "result" of
Khmer Rouge policy, as in Moss's rendition, which he saw no need
to correct when the discrepancy was pointed out to him.

Ponchaud's denial of the authenticity of the interview was in
a letter of August, 1977.[112] The denial is particularly pertinent because Ponchaud is cited as the sole independent (nongovernmental) expert source in Barron and Paul's book. Furthermore, both
Barron and Paul refer to their close association with Ponchaud.[113]

In the light of these facts, we have repeatedly asked Ponchaud in personal letters to present publicly the details of this
matter, in view of his expressed devotion to the "search for truth
about the events in Cambodia"[114] and the fact that the alleged
interview is not only widely circulated and used as a basis for
conclusions about Cambodian atrocities, but had even been offered as grounds for military intervention.[115] In response to these
requests, Ponchaud sent a letter to John Barron stating what he
knew of the facts. Unfortunately, he has refused permission to
quote from this five-page French letter unless it is quoted in its
entirety, a requirement that in effect keeps it from the public

domain. We are therefore unable to offer his information about the alleged "interview" or other relevant matters.

The matter is taken up by William Shawcross in a review of Barron-Paul.[116] He points out that journalists who were present at Colombo, the site of the alleged interview with Paola Brianti, "say that none of them was ever able to get anywhere near Khieu Samphan...Two reporters have asserted flatly that she could not have gotten the interview and that it is a fake," though "she sticks by her story."

Note that in their book Barron and Paul qualify their comment by saying "if quoted correctly ..." The qualification is certainly in order, if only because they misquote the *Famiglia Cristiana* interview (it was the interviewer, not Khieu Samphan, who is alleged to have offered the 7 million figure). Furthermore, as they and others fail to note, Khieu Samphan explicitly denied the massacre reports in the "interview." There is every reason to be skeptical as to whether there was such an interview, or if there was, whether the "quotes" are anywhere near accurate.

It is doubtful that the journalists and others who have referred to Khieu Samphan's "admission" of a million deaths (or a million "slaughtered") have ever seen the original article in *Famiglia Cristiana*, which is hardly a well-known source on international affairs. In fact, not a single copy of this journal is to be found in a library in the United States. The journal is a weekly published by the Pauline sisters and is primarily found in churches. It has apparently not occurred to the journalists, scholars, Cambodia specialists, intelligence analysts and congressmen who have quoted or misquoted this "interview" to wonder why Khieu Samphan, at a time when the Cambodian government was not making extraordinary efforts to reach out to the Western World, should have chosen Paola Brianti and *Famiglia Cristiana* as the medium for approaching Western public opinion. Nor has it occurred to them to be skeptical about a chain of transmission that proceeds from

Famiglia Cristiana to the *Reader's Digest* and then to the international community, or to wonder why Khieu Samphan should have offered a figure of 5 million Cambodians when his government was estimating the population at about 7.7 million.[117]

The *Famiglia Cristiana* "interview" has not only been picked up by the U.S. press, congressmen, and intelligence analysts, but also by the foreign press and the scholarly literature.[118] For example, the *Economist* gives the following version:

> When the Khmer Rouge leader, Khieu Samphan, was confronted by these stark statistics last summer—a 7m population in 1970, an estimated 1m killed during the war, a presumed 5m people left in 1976—he replied blandly, "It's incredible how concerned you westerners are about war criminals." What is incredible is how little foreign outrage these figures provoke.[119]

What is perhaps incredible is that the *Economist* should place such reliance on this "interview."

No less incredible is the review of the Barron-Paul book in the *Far Eastern Economic Review* by Donald Wise,[120] which begins as follows:

> *Scene:* The Non-Aligned Nations Conference, Colombo, August 1976.

Then comes the Barron-Paul mistranslation of the probably fabricated *Famiglia Cristiana* interview, plus the inevitable comment that the world "is *not* concerned about the genocide in Cambodia" (his emphasis).

Turning to the scholarly literature, Kenneth M. Quinn writes that the figure of 7.7 million offered by the Cambodian government "was revised downward to five million by Khieu Samphan in an interview he gave to the Italian magazine *Famiglia Christiana* [sic]."[121] Again, no qualifications and no question about the source. The Quinn account is perhaps independent of Barron-Paul, given the dates and the fact that it does not offer the standard mistranslation by Barron-Paul, contenting itself with misspelling and misrepresentation of the contents. Quinn, who is described in *Asian Survey* as a State Department representative on the National Security Council Staff, is one of the experts who Barron and Paul cite as having made data available to them and having "guided us to other sources,"[122] including, perhaps, this one.

A year later, Professor Karl D. Jackson surveyed the situation in Cambodia once again for *Asian Survey*.[123] Attempting to reconcile apparently conflicting claims about the grain problem, he suggests as one possibility that although food production has still not reached prewar levels, it may suffice "to feed a substantially reduced population, i.e., the five million people cited by Khieu Samphan in 1976, rather than the eight million cited by various officials including Pol Pot." His reference for Khieu Samphan's "estimate" is Donald Wise's review in the *Far Eastern Economic Review* which begins by citing the Barron-Paul mistranslation of the alleged *Famiglia Cristiana* interview, which, to compound the absurdity, had already been cited in *Asian Survey* a year earlier by a State Department analyst who may well have been the source for Barron-Paul. No doubt the next reference to Khieu Samphan's "admission" will appear in an article by Quinn citing Jackson.

A few months after Khieu Samphan's now famous "admission" that his regime was responsible for the deaths of about one-sixth of the population of Cambodia, Indonesian Prime Minister Adam Malik admitted that 50-80,000 people, close to the same percentage of the population, had been killed in East Timor in the course of what the Indonesian propaganda ministry and the *New York Times* call the "civil war"—that is, the U.S.-backed Indonesian invasion and massacre—though one could not have discovered this fact from the U.S. media.[124] While Khieu Samphan's "admission" was concocted by the media and scholarship on the basis of a fanciful interpretation of remarks that quite possibly were never made, Malik's admission, by contrast, was clear and explicit. A comparison of media reaction to the actual admission by Malik and the concocted "admission" by Khieu Samphan gives some insight into what lies behind the machinations of the Free Press.

These examples, far from exhaustive, reveal how desperate Western commentators have been to find "evidence" that could be used in the international propaganda campaign concerning Cambodia. The credible reports of atrocities—and there were many—did not suffice for these purposes, and it was necessary to seek out the most dubious evidence. It hardly needs emphasis that journals of the quality and renown of *Famiglia Cristiana* (or, for that matter, the *Reader's Digest*) in the enemy camp would be regarded with the utmost skepticism, if not dismissed outright, were they to offer comparable "evidence" about Western atrocities.[125]

In this case, the *Famiglia Cristiana* "interview" bears all the earmarks of an intelligence fabrication of the type that the CIA is known to have indulged in repeatedly.[126]

Before turning to the next example cited by Simons, let us consider further the Wise review of Barron-Paul in the *Far Eastern Economic Review*, cited above. To conclude the review which began with the Barron-Paul mistranslation of the probably fabricated interview, Wise offers the following quote from a Cambodian official transmitted by Barron and Paul:

> ...to rebuild a new Cambodia, 1 million men is enough. *Prisoners of war (people expelled from the cities and villages controlled by the Government on April 17) are no longer needed, and local chiefs are free to dispose of them as they please.*

Surely this is a damning indictment of the Khmer Rouge, on a par with Khieu Samphan's "admission." So let us therefore examine it, to determine whether it has any more credibility than the "interview" that has been so widely exploited to prove Communist iniquity, by Wise among others. As we pursue the trail, we enter into a curious comedy of errors.

Wise's quote is from Barron-Paul:

Francois Ponchaud, the noted French authority on Cambodia, reports that on January 26 an *Angka* official in the Mongkol Borei district declared: "To build a democratic Cambodia by renewing everything on a new basis; to do away with every reminder of colonial and imperialist culture, whether visible or tangible or in a person's mind; to rebuild our new Cambodia, one million men is enough. *Prisoners of war [people expelled from the cities and villages controlled by the government on April 17] are no longer needed, and local chiefs are free to dispose of them as they please.*"[127]

Apart from an insignificant error, Wise reproduces Barron-Paul correctly. Barron-Paul give no source, but the source must be an article by Ponchaud in *Le Monde*[128] where he asserts that a Khmer Rouge military chief made this statement in a directive to local authorities of the district on January 26, 1976. The accuracy of the translation has been challenged, but we will ignore this matter, since far more serious doubts arise.[129]

Before turning to these, let us look into the identification of "prisoners of war." Barron-Paul quote the interpolated remark accurately from Ponchaud. In an article in *Le Monde* on the preceding day Ponchaud makes the same point. He says that refugees distinguish two categories of people: "the 'old people' from the regions liberated before 1975, and the 'new people' liberated on April 17, 1975. These 'new people' are always considered as 'prisoners of war' and have no rights." The allegation appears in a somewhat different form in Ponchaud's subsequent book. Here he writes that Khmer Rouge soldiers had "more than enough to eat and refused themselves nothing; they had rice, meat, and fish in plenty," but they were withholding food from workers who "were literally dying of hunger"[130]: "Their reasoning was simple enough: 'You are prisoners of war. We went hungry for five years. Now it's your turn!'"[131] No source is given for the latter quote, and no evidence is cited suggesting its general applicability. As we shall see, Ponchaud uses the device of quotation with considerable abandon, so that skepticism is in order about this particular case.

Turning now to the quote given by Wise from Barron-Paul, who cite Ponchaud, note that they say Ponchaud attributes it to "an *Angka* official" on January 26, 1976. In fact, he attributes it to a Khmer Rouge military chief who issued a directive to local authorities on January 26. In his subsequent book, which one would expect to be more careful and considered than a newspaper article, Ponchaud does not give the quote at all. The sentiment surfaces only in the following quote: "Il suffit de 1 ou 2 millions de jeunes pour faire le Kampuchéa nouveau,"[132]—literally: "One or two million young people are enough to build the new Cambodia." Not only have the numbers changed—from one million men to 1-2 million young people—but so has the source. The quote is now attributed not to a Khmer Rouge military commander on January 26, 1976, but is rather given (still in quotes) as "the formidable boast" of the Khmer Rouge. The full context is this: "The Khmers Rouges are coldly realizing their formidable boast: '...'" ("Les Khmers Rouges réalisent froidement leur redoutable boutade: '...'"). This statement closes the chapter entitled "The Calvary of a People."

Ponchaud's statement in the book plainly implies that the Khmer Rouge are in the process of eliminating all but one or two million young people—that is, a total of some 5-7 million people, including all who are not young, out of a population that he estimates at 8 million in 1970. A few lines earlier Ponchaud gives estimates of war deaths (600-800,000) and "peace deaths" (note: not killings but deaths) ranging from 800,000 to 1,400,000, the higher estimates allegedly from U.S. sources. The difference between approximately *a million deaths* and the *elimination in process of some 5-7 million* people a few lines later would seem significant. It is typical of the way that Ponchaud and others use numbers and their care with the distinction between killing and dying (e.g., from disease and malnutrition caused by the war); recall the prediction from U.S. government sources that the numbers who would die from such causes would be on the order of one million.[133]

Elsewhere, Ponchaud gives the alleged quote as follows. After stating that the number of postwar dead "certainly exceeds a million," he writes: "In the view of the revolutionaries, such a slaughter is no catastrophe: 'one or two million resolute young people are enough to reconstruct Cambodia,' is a boast [boutade] frequently used by cadres during meetings."[134] Here again the implication is that the revolutionaries would not be overly concerned with the massacre of many millions of people, the overwhelming mass of the population. In another publication from the same period, Ponchaud gives still another version of what appears to be the same "quote." He writes: "A Khmer Rouge stated: 'If there should remain in Cambodia only 20,000 young people, we will build the new Cambodia with these 20,000.'"[135] The numbers have changed once again, this time substantially, and there is no specific source. In this case, Ponchaud does not imply that the revolutionaries are in the process of eliminating all but 20,000 young people.

We now have a number of versions of the alleged quote, which Ponchaud evidently regarded as of some significance, given its prominence in his writings in 1976-1977, and the conclusions he drew from it. In only one of these sources (Le Monde) is the quote specifically attributed: to a Khmer Rouge military commander issuing a specific directive on a specific date, who says that "one million" are enough—the rest can be "disposed of" (the Barron-Paul translation, which Paul claims was approved by Ponchaud). Ponchaud gives the entire "quote" from this commander in italics in a separate paragraph in this Le Monde article, emphasizing its significance. The context, as well as the Barron-Paul rendition, suggest that he must have had some text or other document. In other articles written at the same time and in Ponchaud's subsequent book, the context and the quote disappear. There is no reference to the alleged directive. Rather, a "formidable boast" of the Khmer Rouge is given without attribution but in quotes: "one or two million young people" will be enough to build the new society. Nothing is said about disposing of the remainder, but it is implied that the Khmer Rouge are eliminating them.

In his review of the book, Lacouture gives still a different version: "When men who talk of Marxism are able to say, as one quoted by Ponchaud does, that only 1.5 or 2 million young Cambodians, out of 6 million, will be enough to rebuild a pure society, one can no longer speak of barbarism" but only "madness."[136]

We mentioned the discrepancy between the *Le Monde* account and the book in the review-article cited in note 100, adding that "this is one of the rare examples of a quote that can be checked. The results are not impressive."

In his letter commenting on this article,[137] Ponchaud explained that the original *Le Monde* reference was based not on any text but rather on a report by a refugee who said that he had heard this remark from the chief of the Northwest region of Cambodia at a meeting; in our view, it would have been a good idea to state the source accurately in the original article. Ponchaud writes that he subsequently heard similar reports from refugees with numbers ranging from 100,000 to 2 million, and "in a spirit of truth," gave a more qualified account in his book, without a specific source. Ponchaud interprets the alleged statements:

> not as a firm wish to reduce...Cambodia to 1 million people, but as expressing a resolution to purify Cambodia without taking into account people's lives. It is therefore more a "redoutable boutade" [a formidable boast] than an explicit affirmation of intention.

We wonder whether under this interpretation, it is still proper to imply, as Ponchaud clearly did in his book, that the Khmer Rouge are in the process of eliminating 5-7 million people in accordance with this "formidable boast." We continue to be unimpressed. This seems to us a curious way to use the device of quotation. Recall that this is one of the very few cases where an alleged quote can be checked, because in this instance it was reported in at least two separate sources (we will see that other quotes that are subject to verification fare no better, on inquiry). To our minds, it raises serious questions about the authenticity of the quotations that are offered in what is, we again emphasize, the most serious of the critical work on postwar Cambodia. The reader will observe how this rather vague report of what someone is alleged to have said, subject to a qualified interpretation, has been transmuted into a firm declaration of genocidal policy in its long voyage from refugees, to Ponchaud, to Barron-Paul, Lacouture and Wise.

Apparently Ponchaud has since had still further thoughts about the reference. It is deleted entirely from the American edition of his book, the one from which we have been quoting.[138] But the long and dubious chain of transmission has left it as part of "history."

We mention specifically here the "American translation" because, curiously, the quote remains intact in the simultaneous British translation, where the last paragraph of chapter 4, "The Calvary of a People," reads as follows:

> A large part of the deported population appears to have been sacrificed. Its role in the history of Democratic Kampuchea will thus have been to build up the country's economic infrastructure with its own flesh and blood.[139] *Now a country of the pure should arise. 'One or two million young people are enough to make the new Kampuchea!' was the blood-chilling boast of the Khmers Rouges, which they are now grimly turning into a reality.*[140]

The two sentences that we have italicized are omitted in the American edition. The British translation is, perhaps, a bit free, but both the French original and the British translation do clearly imply that the Khmer Rouge are in the process of cold-bloodedly eliminating something on the order of 5-7 million people.

In the British Penguin edition, a slightly different version of Lacouture's misstatement of this "quote," or "boast," or whatever it may be, attributing it to "men who talk of Marxism" and concluding that it goes beyond barbarism, appears on the book's cover. In the American translation, it is entirely deleted from the book, along with the claim that some 5-7 million people (including all but the young) are being eliminated to build "a country of the pure." We leave it to the reader to decide what to make of all of this.[141]

Some further skepticism about this "quote" or "boast" is aroused by the Congressional testimony of State Department expert Charles Twining:

> The Khmer Rouge sometimes on a local level will tell villagers that, "we can afford to lose 1 million or even 2 million people." You hear this story often enough from enough places to make you think it has been handed down from on high.
> We can lose 1 million or 2 million if we must to create the new Cambodia...[142]

The reference is suspiciously familiar. In this case, the 1-2 million are not those who will be left (the others cold-bloodedly eliminated by the Khmer Rouge, according to Ponchaud's rather fanciful construction which he has withdrawn), but rather those who may be "lost." And the quote is not attributed; rather Twining surmises that it has been "handed down from on high." It is a reasonable suspicion that this is a residue of the same alleged "boast." At this point, one must really belong to the faithful to believe that there is anything at all to the whole story. And our trust in those who transmit it without qualification in various forms correspondingly diminishes.

Yet another source for this garbled report is suggested by a Phnom Penh radio broadcast on military problems in which it is explained how Cambodia can defeat the Vietnamese even though much outnumbered:

> Using these figures, 1 Kampuchean soldier is equal to 30 Viet-
> namese soldiers...If we have 2 million troops, there should be
> 60 million Vietnamese. For this reason, 2 million troops should
> be more than enough to fight the Vietnamese, because Viet-
> nam only has 50 million inhabitants. We do not need 8 million
> people. We need only 2 million troops to crush the 50 million
> Vietnamese; and we still would have 6 million people left.[143]

Again the statement is suspiciously familiar. It may well be
that if there is any source at all for these various accounts, it is
some sort of patriotic slogan, formulated with various rhetorical
flourishes.

Wise is clearly much enamoured of this "quote." In the same
issue of the *Far Eastern Economic Review* in which he reviewed
Barron-Paul,[144] Wise has an article on Cambodia in which he explains that "the new regime is too harsh for the formerly fun-loving, easy-going Cambodians."[145] As evidence for the harshness, he
writes that "a senior Khmer Rouge official was quoted as saying
that Cambodia needs no more than 1 million people to get started
on its new course and all prisoners—that is, people from zones
unoccupied by the Khmer Rouge at the April 1975 ceasefire—are
no longer required and may be disposed of as local commanders
think fit." In a review of the English (British) translation of Ponchaud's book, he cites it once again, in the following context:

> Nobody can suggest a reliable figure for the "peace-dead," says
> Ponchaud, "but it certainly exceeds a million." Yet the Khmers
> Rouges boasted: "One or two million young people are enough
> to make the new Kampuchea."[146]

The implication is that the "peace-dead" are victims of the Khmer
Rouge who "boast" of this massacre because one or two million
people are all that are needed. Notice again how the facts, if
any, have been skillfully transmuted in their passage through the
Western propaganda system. In the first place, there is a serious

question as to how many of the "peace-dead" fall to the Western account, rather than that of the Khmer Rouge. There is the further question whether the victims for whom the West does not bear direct responsibility are the victims of peasant revenge or a coordinated policy of massacre. Finally what of the "boast" of the Khmer Rouge—which stands in dramatic contrast to their persistent denial of massacres and expressed commitment to building up the population to 15-20 million? This "boast" is Wise's version of Ponchaud's version of a variously-attributed remark that has dissolved upon inquiry. Note again that it is a central element of his review of both Barron-Paul and Ponchaud, and that he also cited it in a separate article. It apparently never occurred to him to wonder why the "quote" he repeats is given and attributed differently in these two sources, or to inquire further into its authenticity on these grounds. In such ways as these the Western system of indoctrination spins its web of deceit.[147]

Recall Lacouture's question whether it is important to decide "exactly which person uttered an inhuman phrase." The example just mentioned was one of the cases under consideration—in other cases to which we return the distortion was still more flagrant. It is also one of the examples that Lacouture did not rectify in his "Corrections," and that he continues to use long after Ponchaud had recognized that it had no basis.[148] Lacouture used the "quote" to show that men who talk of Marxism are going "beyond barbarism." In fact, it turns out that there was no quote but only a remembered "boast" of dubious import, variously presented by Ponchaud and sufficiently questionable to have been eliminated from the American (though not British) edition of his book after inquiry, and suspiciously similar to a remembered slogan of quite different import attributed to many refugees by the State Department's leading expert. The example is perhaps not particularly important in itself, but gains significance in the light of the publicity accorded it and the fact that it is one of the rare cases of a "quote" for which independent verification is even possible.

It is also worth mentioning that these "quotes," which have a curious habit of disappearing on analysis, form the most substantial part of the evidence behind one crucial element in the thesis to which the propaganda machine is committed: that the Khmer Rouge leadership was committed to systematic massacre and starvation of the population it held in its grip, that is, to "autogenocide." It would be of little use to contemporary Western ideology it if were to be shown that peasant revenge, undisciplined troops and similar factors (still worse, the legacy of the U.S. attack) were responsible for deaths and killings in Cambodia. It is crucial to establish in the public consciousness, whatever the facts may be, that a centralized and carefully-planned program lay behind the atrocities. As we have seen, one cannot appeal to the refugee reports for this purpose. Therefore "quotes," "boasts," "slogans," "interviews," and similar documentation are of vital significance, as demonstrations of intent and recognition. It is therefore interesting to see how flimsy is the basis on which such elaborate constructions are founded, again, a useful insight into the mechanism and goals of current Western propaganda.

The examples just discussed, which are among the most widely diffused in the Western media and the springboard for many impassioned accusations, are by no means atypical. Let us turn now to the next observation by Simons, namely, that Western governments that have maintained direct contacts with Cambodia and have sent visiting delegations "generally refuse to accept the genocide allegation." One would think that with the intense concern over the internal affairs of Cambodia, evident from the extensive press coverage and denunciations despite repeated laments to the contrary, and the difficulty of obtaining information from a country virtually closed to the outside world, the reports of Western visitors would have received considerable notice. Such visitors would have been interviewed in

depth, one might suppose, and their writings eagerly perused
and circulated. That has not quite been the case, however. Their
trips were sometimes reported, though just barely, and there
was little effort to follow up beyond the first news conference.
And Simons's interesting observation, which should have immediately sparked some doubts among journalists with a modicum
of skepticism, occasioned no further inquiry.

By late 1978, the regime was beginning to open its doors
more widely to foreign visitors. UN Secretary-General Kurt
Waldheim was invited in October,[149] and two U.S. reporters—
Richard Dudman and Elizabeth Becker—visited in December,
along with the British specialist on Southeast Asia Malcolm
Caldwell, who was assassinated on the final day of their visit.
Another group of visitors from the United States (including one
member, Stephen Heder, a specialist on Cambodia, who had
lived in Phnom Penh and is fluent in Khmer) had reached Peking
when the Vietnamese invasion closed off access to the country
in January 1979, and other invitations had been issued. As we
noted in the preface to this volume, some observers regard the
improvement in the international image of the regime as perhaps the major factor in the timing of the Vietnamese invasion.
With large parts of the country under military occupation, there
will be no further opportunity to observe at first-hand the social
order that had been constructed or to evaluate the picture presented in the West on the basis of refugee reports, selected and
transmitted in the manner we have been discussing. Therefore,
it is a matter of some interest to review the material that could
have been exploited, the leads that could have been followed up
by journalists and others concerned to establish the truth about
postwar Cambodia. It is obvious that visitors on guided tours,
like refugees selected on guided tours to refugee camps, can only
present a partial and perhaps misleading picture, but their reports certainly offer a view of the social reality that would have

been carefully investigated by anyone seriously concerned with the truth. We will divide this review into two sections, considering first the visitors who preceded the two U.S. reporters, then turning to their reports.

The Swedish Ambassador to Peking, Kaj Bjork, led a delegation on a two-week visit to Cambodia in February-March, 1976. The visit was quite newsworthy, for one reason, because it coincided with an apparent bombing in Cambodia of disputed origin. (Cambodia claimed that the United States was responsible, a charge dismissed in the West but apparently not in the Third World).[150] Ambassador Bjork was taken to the site of the bombing. His account of his trip received some notice, including a front-page story in the *New York Times*.[151] Ambassador Bjork, the *Times* reported, "described Cambodia as a nation under tight military control and led by nationalistic Marxist intellectuals whose goals are more revolutionary than those of the leaders of China." He found no private ownership, no money or wages, no private shops. "Mr. Bjork said that he saw no signs of starvation[152] and attributed this to the controversial decision of Cambodia's leaders to force people out of the cities to work in the rice fields"—a conclusion that is, as we have seen, apparently consistent with the judgment of State Department experts and others. He was struck by the emptiness of Phnom Penh, where he was not permitted to walk freely, though he noticed more activity in the outskirts. In the countryside he saw "total mobilization" to construct water control and irrigation systems and develop agriculture, the basis for all other progress.

As for popular attitudes, Ambassador Bjork said that "around Phnom Penh you could see youngsters marching, all of them with a hoe and a spade, some of them also carrying a gun. I got the very strong impression that the regime has active support from this kind of young person." The leadership are men who returned from study in Europe with "a great deal of knowledge, a good deal of Marxist theory, and came back to Cambodia and reacted very strongly to existing social conditions. They have very strong collectivist and egalitarian ideas with a very strong overtone of nationalism." Khieu Samphan, in particular, "gives the impression of being an intellectual of quality"—compare the contemptuous and disparaging account in the best-seller on Cambodia by Barron and Paul of the *Reader's Digest*.

It might have been interesting to hear more about the impressions of this Swedish delegation, but the press was not interested. Scholars and reporters so assiduous as to discover *Famiglia Cristiana* might have learned something more, with a little enterprise. The Swedish journal *Vietnam Bulletinen* carried an interview with Jan Lundvik, who accompanied the Swedish Ambassador.[153] His eyewitness report is quite different in character from the picture that dominates the media. Lundvik described the massive efforts to reconstruct the agricultural and irrigation systems, all by hand because there is no equipment. He reports two "lasting impressions" from his visit. The first is "the very strong patriotism" in a population that had been colonized and had not enjoyed complete independence for centuries, patriotism that "expresses itself in a very strong drive for independence—in all domains." The second lasting impression is the incredible destruction: "One can barely imagine how destroyed are the agricultural areas. Phnom Penh is like an island in a land destroyed by bombing." Virtually everything seen on a trip from Phnom Penh to Kompong Tham was destroyed.[154] In Phnom Penh there were 100-200,000 people, he reports.[155] The evacuation of the cities in April 1975, he believes, was not "as noteworthy for the Kampuchean people as had been represented in the West," because Cambodia is an agricultural country; he also cites historical precedents. The revolution represents "the victory of the countryside over the city," in a country that is overwhelmingly agrarian—or was, prior to the forced urbanization caused by the U.S. bombing.

Lundvik reports schooling until age 12—at which time children join in production—and severe shortages of medical supplies. He speaks of a great effort to increase the population from the present 8 million to 15 million. He then adds the following comment:

> In this connection I want to point out that the articles that are being written about a "bloodbath" in Kampuchea rely on assumptions that have been misunderstood or falsely interpreted. When the Kampucheans say that they can make do with 1 million inhabitants, they mean that they can achieve every task no matter how few they are, not that one is about to liquidate the remainder. The lack of labor power is a problem, and on this account they are trying to achieve a high birthrate.

Quite possibly, Lundvik has in mind here the Ponchaud "quote" in *Le Monde* which we have just discussed. Lundvik's comment supports Ponchaud's more qualified observations in personal correspondence, cited above, though not the various and mutually inconsistent published accounts. It is evident not only from these comments but from his observations on what he saw that Lundvik gives little credence to the stories, then already circulating widely, on genocide.[156]

In general, Lundvik's description of popular commitment and patriotism in a land ravaged by war and passionately committed to independence and development is positive and strikingly different in tone from the reports that were designed for a mass audience in the West. It is relevant to the "difficult question" that troubled Twining and others. It is noteworthy that a Swedish visitor does not feel compelled to evade what seems to be a plausible answer to this question: that the regime had support among the peasants.

The Swedish ambassador to Thailand, Jean-Christopher Oberg, visited Cambodia in December, 1977. He said "that he saw no sign of oppression or cruelty...[and]...discounted refugee reports that about one million people had died or been killed since the takeover." He also "said he saw very few armed Cambodians"—in fact, he saw four, "including one girl"—and "saw nothing to corroborate reports that the Cambodians were working under armed threats."[157]

Ambassadors from Sweden, Finland, and Denmark visited Cambodia again in January, 1978. A Reuters report from Peking on their trip appeared in the *Washington Post* and in an abbreviated version in the *New York Times*,[158] with a second-hand account of what they are said to have told "Nordic correspondents" on their return to Peking. There seems to have been no effort to pursue the matter further. This single second-hand report is uninformative. The Danish Ambassador is quoted as saying that Phnom Penh resembled a "ghost town" (a comment since widely circulated) and the Swedish Ambassador as having said that more land was under cultivation than in 1976 and that "traces of the 1970-1975 war were still considerable" though they have decreased. "There were no signs of starvation." Little else was reported.

Inquiries to the Swedish Embassy in Washington in an effort to obtain further information about the latest trip have been rebuffed on grounds that the ambassador's report is not available to the public. What the explanation for this curious response may be, we do not know, and apparently no journalist has been sufficiently intrigued to pursue the matter further.

The Foreign Minister of Thailand spent four days in Phnom Penh in early 1978. The fifth paragraph of Henry Kamm's story in the *New York Times*, which we quote in its entirety, gives this account of what he saw:

> Reporters at the airport were struck by Mr. Uppadit's effort to say nothing unkind about Cambodia. He volunteered a comment that reports about conditions in Cambodia since the Communist victory might have been exaggerated. Asked about his impressions of life in Phnom Penh, Mr. Uppadit said it had seemed like a normal city. Scandinavian ambassadors who visited the Cambodian capital last month described it as a "ghost city."[159]

The Thai government, of course, is extremely right-wing and passionately anti-Communist, but Uppadit's comments might be
treated with skepticism on grounds that he had returned from
an attempt to improve relations with Cambodia.

In April 1976, a Japanese newsman, Naoki Mabuchi, who
had remained in Phnom Penh until May 1975, reentered the
country and was held in detention in the border town of Poipet
for a week. "While in detention, he said, he was free to watch
activities in Poipet from the balcony of his room and even to
wander outside the building, although he did not stray far." He
"says he speaks the Khmer language well enough to carry on
casual conversation." Mabuchi said that "the people he saw all
appeared to be well-fed and in good health. He said his observations convinced him that reports in the Western press 'placed too
much stress on the dark side' of life in Cambodia under Khmer
Rouge rule." The Bangkok press reported that as he crossed into
Cambodia he was beaten, later tortured, by Khmer Rouge soldiers. On his return to Thailand, he denied these reports: "I was
not beaten or tortured. I was treated by the Cambodian officials
very nicely. They gave me the same food they had, and I think I
gained some weight."[160]

Michael Vickery adds an interesting personal observation
based on the story of the Japanese newsman, which has some
relevance to the kind of reporting offered concerning Cambodia.
He visited the border in Aranyaprathet shortly after the Japanese reporter had crossed into Cambodia. During the next two
days that he spent in that town, he heard repeated "eye-witness"
reports that the newsman had been "beaten with rifle butts,"
"probably killed," and then "definitely killed," the last being the
accepted account when he left the town. A few months later,
Vickery discussed the incident with a member of the U.S. Embassy in Bangkok, with a special interest in Cambodia, who
claimed that the Japanese newsman had obviously lied and had

indeed been badly beaten. Why did he lie? To protect future Khmer-Japanese relations or in hopes that he would be invited back, Vickery was informed. The evidence that he had lied was "eyewitness reports." But what of the eyewitness reports of his death? "Shrug of shoulders." The U.S. official further admitted that he had not tried to meet the reporter or to judge the credibility of his report. Vickery comments:

> No, his possibly true story was of no interest, although, obviously, the rumours of his mistreatment or death were highly interesting. I think this is characteristic of an irresponsible attitude among those who are directly concerned with the manufacture of many of the stories about Cambodia which have been circulated.[161]

Vickery emphasizes correctly that whatever the facts might have been about the experience of the Japanese newsman, they would tell us little about contemporary Cambodia. It is, nonetheless, interesting to trace the fate of the story.

Four Yugoslav journalists visited Cambodia in March 1978, and reported on their visit in the Belgrade press. U.S. readers could find a translation of excerpts in the radical-pacifist journal *Seven Days.*[162] They estimated the population of Phnom Penh at no more than 20,000, contrary to official estimates of 200,000. Money had been eliminated and the basis of social life was a system of cooperatives, one of which they visited. There they were told that work-related payment had been abolished and "complete equality prevails." "We didn't get the impression that the Kampuchean countryside is suffering any food shortages." They described newly constructed buildings, workers "bustl[ing] past the wavy palms" in Phnom Penh, some "carelessly" carrying arms (the same was true throughout Cambodia, they report, "probably a carryover from the revolutionary days"; there were some armed supervisors of work groups, "although that was not a striking phenomenon"). They visited schools and "huge" construction projects which they found "impressive," where construction crews work an 8½ hour day with three free days a month devoted to lectures and discussion of work problems. Among the workers, primarily young, were small children, former Buddhist monks and "students from the now-suspended high schools and universities who, carried away by enthusiasm for their work, were forgetting their French but acquiring other skills." They report an interview with Prime Minister Pol Pot,[163] who expressed the hope that the population (which they report to be 7-8 million) will quickly grow to 15-20 million. They were struck by the absence of civil government or other organizations ("with the exception of unions on the factory and enterprise level") and "the absence, even in mild form, of political indoctrination." The most striking features of the society were its "egalitarianism," "fundamentalist radicalism in interpreting the concept of relying on one's own resources," and "the very evident sense of national pride" which "is reminiscent of the behavior of a quiet and introverted person whose opinions were hardly ever taken into account earlier, but who now speaks out, unexpectedly, but invariably passionately."

More extensive excerpts appear in the BBC summary of world broadcasts, from a six-part report by Slavko Stanic.[164] The former residents of the cities, Stanic reports, are now "mainly members of mobile brigades, which go from one building site to another to build new earth dams or construct artificial lakes," or they live in cooperatives. He reports a 9-hour work day and writes that "we had the opportunity to convince ourselves that there is definitely no longer any hunger in Cambodia." He describes a school for skilled electricians in a Phnom Penh suburb where "the lecturers were former workers who had passed through the 'school of the revolution,'" and an agricultural school where the lecturers "were skillfully applying science to the production of seeds for new varieties of rice." "The hospitals seemed to be in the hands of the old renowned Phnom Penh doctors." Stanic reports that there are great differences among the cooperatives. "In the rich Province of Battambang and wherever there were villages before, private plots around the houses are much bigger, the peasants have cows and pigs and other livestock in private ownership," and "there are not many of the pre-fabricated barracks which serve as common canteens in which all members of the co-operatives and their families eat." In the "newly established economic zones where the former inhabitants of the cities live" conditions are harsher, and "thousands of families live in dwellings on stilts or in improvised barracks," while it is planned that by the end of 1979 every family should have a house. "The chief concern of the new authorities in Phnom Penh is the construction and rehabilitation of the villages, an increase in the standard of living of the peasants and the growth of the population." The suburbs of Phnom Penh, he was told, have about 220,000 people. He believes the current "policy of empty towns is a part of the strategy of the country's defence." New economic installations (e.g., a shipyard) are being installed in the vicinity of towns and their workers housed in the towns, which Stanic assumed would be slowly resettled.

Stanic also comments on the attitude of the regime towards Buddhism. He quotes Yun Yat, the Minister of Culture, Information, and Propaganda: "She told us that 'Buddhism is incompatible with the revolution,' because it was an instrument of exploitation...Buddhism was dead, and the ground had been cleared for the laying of the foundations of a new revolutionary culture." Stanic also reports that at Angkor Wat, "some of the members of our escort hurried as a sign of respect to touch images of Buddha carved in stone. Some high ranking Party cadres also greeted us in the Buddhist manner when they met us, and one of the Buddhist priests who has replaced the robe with the revolutionary uniform disagreed with Minister Yun Yat. He told us that Buddhism and communism had the same humane goals, and that there was no great antagonism between them."

Reports of the Yugoslav visit appeared in the U.S. press. Michael Dobbs, in a report from Belgrade,[165] emphasized the abandonment of Phnom Penh and the "new order...based on the village ..." and on the cooperative and mobile brigade. "The Yugoslavs do not appear to have raised the controversial question of the hundreds of thousands of people believed to have been killed by the Khmer Rouge shortly after their victory," Dobbs writes in a typical reference to what "is believed"; "The only allusion to such massacres was made by the *Politika* correspondent, Ranchic, who said: 'We were inclined to believe the statement of our guides that the class enemy has been relatively quickly eliminated in Cambodia.'" The more favorable impressions that appear in the actual report are ignored or underplayed.

Citing the Yugoslav visit, AP reported that "Cambodia is training boys and girls as young as 12 to replace the industrial working class that was swept away after the Communist takeover three years ago."[166] The reference to the "industrial working class that was swept away" by the Communists and is now being "replaced" is an embellishment of the Yugoslav report by AP. In fact, the "industrial working class" was very small and there is no indication in the Yugoslav report that it was "swept away." Refugees from the Battambang area, for example, report that in general workers remained in their jobs in a jute processing plant outside Battambang after the war.[167] Perhaps AP has confused its dates and the agent of destruction; it is true that some of the few Cambodian industrial installations, and presumably workers and their families as well, were "swept away" by U.S. bombers, without noticeable indignation in the media. Programs of vocational training for 12-year-olds are, furthermore, not generally regarded as an atrocity in a poor peasant society. The anti-Communist Sihanouk regime, for example, took pride in its programs of technical and vocational training in "model primary schools" and featured pictures of young children working with industrial machinery in its information publications, noting that the youth must not "take refuge in administrative careers" but must "have the ideal of productive labor."[168] We do not recall protests in the West over such savagery.

The AP report also describes work-study programs and a nine-hour work day with evenings "set aside for alternating classes of political indoctrination and technical education." Again, a nine-hour work day hardly seems a major atrocity in a country of the economic status of contemporary Cambodia, and the Yugoslav report actually noted "the absence, even in mild form, of political indoctrination," as we have seen.

The *New York Times* carried a report of the Yugoslav visit by David A. Andelman from Belgrade.[169] He repeats Ranchic's comment, cited above, and the report of the abandonment of Phnom Penh (he reports the Yugoslav journalists as writing that the population was about 200,000, "though most seem to live in the surrounding area and only about 10,000 downtown"). He also reports their account of work brigades with the comment that "it was clear that they were impressed labor," without explaining how this was clear. He too downplays or ignores the more favorable impressions conveyed, for the most part. Henry Kamm cited the Yugoslav visit in a column devoted to refugee reports.[170] He tells us that one of the Yugoslav journalists "reported that they were appalled by much of what they saw, although, restricted by the conventions of Communist fraternalism, they said so only implicitly in their dispatches."[171] As evidence, he cites their report of "child labor in rigorous agricultural tasks" which the Cambodians urged them to film despite the alleged statement of a Yugoslav TV reporter that this "would make a bad impression on the outside world."[172] Kamm claims that the Yugoslav reports bear out the refugee accounts of "continuing bloodletting, even among factions of the ruling party, and starvation, nationwide forced labor and regimentation," with a work day beginning at 4 a.m. and lasting often until 10 p.m. How he derived these conclusions from published accounts or the reports concerning them in the U.S. press he does not say.

François Rigaux of the Center for International Law of the Catholic University of Louvain was a member of a delegation of the Association Belgique-Kampuchea who spent two weeks in Cambodia in mid-1978, covering 2,000 km. in several regions of the country and engaging in discussion with representatives of regional and municipal administrations, cooperatives, factories, workers groups, schools, hospitals and government. He has written a very detailed factual and analytic report of his experiences, which presumably would be available to journalists and others interested in his impressions of what he found.[173]

Initially struck by the apparent emptiness of Phnom Penh, Rigaux discovered after a few days that quite a few sections were settled and that people appeared to be engaged in normal urban existence. The surrounding industrial sections were more densely settled, and again, life seemed quite normal. The most striking feature of the cities was the complete absence of commerce.

In the countryside, people appeared to be well-fed, quick to enter into conversation, jokes and laughter, and in general engaged in normal activities with good-will, as far as he could determine. Rigaux was struck by the extreme decentralization and the progress in agricultural development. Schools combined study with light work (raising animals, cultivating fruits and vegetables, etc.), and the same was true in a secondary school that he visited. In a Phnom Penh factory, too, he found that workers were raising their own pigs, poultry, and vegetables. Cadres and administrative personnel participated in productive labor as well as taking responsibility for cleaning offices and so on.

Like other visitors, Rigaux was taken to the Ang Tassom collective. He reports that the work force was divided into three categories: people under 35 were responsible for heavy work, and those who were unmarried were assigned work in more remote areas; those in the 35-55 age bracket and young mothers carried out lighter work near their homes; and such activities as weaving and basketwork were reserved for people over 55. The cooperative had a medical center and primary school with four hours of instruction a day for children and some adult education. Each family had its own house with an adjoining area for raising tobacco, fruit, etc.

In the area of family life, his own professional specialty, Rigaux reports that he found a picture not unlike that of Western European villages before the industrial revolution, with a strong emphasis on family life. Children over a year of age had collective care during the work day, and he reports efforts to arrange for married couples and families to share related occupations where possible. With the extreme decentralization and local arrangements for personal affairs, bureaucracy appeared to be reduced to a minimum.

Rigaux takes the "political objective" to have been "to place the entire population under the conditions of life and work of the poorest, the peasants." What there was, was shared equally. Children of 15 years of age were expected to devote themselves to productive labor, a situation that should, he writes, be "compared to the fate of a great number of children of third world countries of the same age who are beggars or prostitutes [or, we may add, the 52 million child laborers, including 29 million in South Asia, whose fate evokes no outrage], rather than to the privileged condition of well-educated adolescents of the industrialized societies." Similarly, medical care is not concentrated in the cities and reserved for the elite but is distributed through the most backward regions with an emphasis on preventive medicine and hygiene.

"The best propaganda for the new regime," Rigaux writes, was the attitudes and behavior of the older peasants whom he came upon by chance during his travels. To Rigaux, they appeared to have acquired dignity, serenity, and security after a lifetime of oppression and violence.

Rigaux also reports on the discussion meetings for arranging work schedules and other tasks at various levels and the methods for selecting administrative personnel. He believes that factories, schools, cooperatives, and other organizations permitted a substantial degree of free exchange of opinion and popular decision-making. He notes the absence of the rights taken for granted in Western industrial societies, but points out that not only is the level of economic development incomparable, but also there were, he believes, elements of control over work and supervisors that are foreign to the industrial democracies.

Rigaux remains unconvinced by the explanations offered by the regime with regard to repressive policies after liberation, including severe punishment and execution. He notes, however, that the conditions described with horror by many of the refugees (which he believes have "considerably improved") are "those of the majority of the Khmer peasants, conditions of which [the refugees] were unaware during the period when their privilege permitted them to keep at a distance" from the lives of the poor.

Rigaux believes that "relative to what it was before liberation, or compared to that of the peasants of Bangladesh, India or Iran..., the condition of the Khmer peasant has improved notably." For urban or Western elites, the results are "shocking," in part because of the deliberate insistence on equality, which requires that all share in "the conditions of work to which the immense majority of the world's population have been subjected for millenia." Now everyone faces "the exalting task of cooperating in the progressive improvement of the conditions of life of the entire population." "Conceived in a very poor country ravaged by war, the economic and political system of Cambodia does not pretend to be a model for an advanced industrial society, but it would be foolish to judge it in accordance with the needs and experiences" of such societies.

No doubt Rigaux, like other visitors, was shown what the regime wanted him to see. The picture he presents in his detailed observations should be worth some attention, one might imagine, and in fact might help explain both the apparent commitment of significant parts of the population to the new regime and the horror and indignation of others at its practices. As he notes, he had no opportunity to assess the veracity of the many stories of massacre and cruel oppression, but again, we note that there is no direct inconsistency between these stories and the quite different impression obtained by visitors in a country that is, by all accounts, highly decentralized and perhaps quite varied from place to place.

There were many other visitors to Cambodia from the Scandinavian countries, some from Communist groups, some non-Communists from "friendship associations," some journalists. Their reports appeared in the mainstream press and journals in Sweden and Denmark, but have yet to be mentioned in the United States, though the sources are hardly obscure and some of the visitors (e.g., Jan Myrdal) are quite well-known in the United States. We will not review their reports, which are in general quite favorable though often qualified by the observation that while they personally witnessed scenes throughout the country of people engaged in productive work with apparent contentment and enthusiasm (working a 9-hour day, but according to Gunnar Bergstrom, at a slower pace than is typical in Europe), they do not speak Khmer and cannot comment on what they were not shown. These visitors too report no indications of starvation or malnutrition.

A Japanese delegation from the Peking embassy visiting in the fall of 1978, reported that the regime was stable and "the people did not seem undernourished" ("there were plenty of vegetables and fruit, and the peasants' diet could be supplemented by pork"). An economist who had been in Cambodia during the Lon Nol regime "observed that rice production and irrigation are now better organised." Phnom Penh "is a desolate city by day" but "a delegation member said he saw large numbers of people returning to the city in the evening from small-scale industries located outside."[174] U.S. readers, deluged with reports about Cambodian horrors at exactly this period (as before), were thoughtfully spared any exposure to the reports of the Japanese embassy delegation.

To our knowledge, that exhausts the accounts on the part of visitors who might, conceivably, be taken seriously in the West, prior to the visit of the two U.S. reporters in December 1978.[175] There were others. A visit by a group led by an "editor of a Chicago-based Marxist weekly" received a 38-line notice in the *New York Times*[176] reporting only that they "painted a glowing picture of life under the Communists" and denied atrocity claims. Daniel Burstein, editor of the Communist Party Marxist-Leninist newspaper *The Call* (Chicago) was interviewed on the *MacNeil/Lehrer Report* (see note 53), where, again, he denied these claims on the basis of interviews with "average people" in the cities and countryside. Their account will naturally be given little credence in the West, since it is taken for granted that this Maoist group, with their ideological preconceptions, will report favorably on their visit. Skepticism is no doubt in order, though for accuracy, we should add that exactly the same is true in the case of reports by John Barron and Anthony Paul in the *Reader's Digest* of stories allegedly told them by "promising subjects," to whom they were "guided" by Thai officials, or reports by Henry Kamm of what he claims to have heard from a Cambodian in a cage in a Thai police station. If refugee reports transmitted by these highly dubious sources are given any attention, there could be no good reason to ignore the eyewitness reports of the only U.S. citizens to have visited Cambodia prior to December 1978. It should come as no surprise, however, that the accounts of the U.S. Marxist-Leninists were ignored or ridiculed in the press, while journalists and scholars greeted Barron-Paul, Kamm, et al., as unbiased seekers after the truth. There is more to the Burstein story. Given the uniqueness of his visit, major media enterprises had offered to publish photographs and text to be provided by Burstein. Specifically, he received payment for submitted material from *Time, Newsweek,* ABC television, and the *Washington Post.* Many months later, the first three stalwarts of the Free Press had definitely rejected the text artd photographs (refusing suggestions to rewrite, etc.), while the fourth was still mulling the question over. It is noteworthy that *Time, Newsweek,* and the *Washington Post*[171] all had featured the faked photographs discussed earlier long after the fabrication was exposed, refusing to publish letters stating the unquestioned facts or to print retractions.

Visitors and refugees transmit quite different pictures. Refugees were brutalized, oppressed or discontented; otherwise they would not be refugees. Visitors are offered only a partial view, and they were for the most part initially sympathetic. We should anticipate, then, that visitors' accounts will be more favorable than those of refugees—though, as we have noted, and will see again, refugee accounts are not so uniform as the media barrage depicts. Note again that when we correct for the factors mentioned, conflicts between the refugee and visitor accounts need not be taken as indicating that one or the other must be dismissed; all might be accurate, in a country that presents a mixed picture with considerable local variation. That, in fact, would appear to be a fair conclusion from the full range of evidence so far available.

The media, however, pursue a different course. A highly selected version of what refugees have reported under quite unfavorable conditions was transmitted by observers of evident bias and low credibility, and given massive publicity as unquestionable fact. Reports of visitors were ignored or distorted. This was not an absolutely uniform picture, but it was a fairly general one. We have given a number of examples in the course of the exposition. A look at the material featured in the press in the fall of 1978, at the end of the period under review, confirms this picture.

The *New York Times Magazine* carried a major story by Henry Kamm in November entitled "The Agony of Cambodia."[178] We have already investigated examples of Kamm's reporting on Timor and Vietnam, noting his extreme bias and unreliability.[179] We have also seen how he distorted the account by the Yugoslav reporters. In the case of Vietnam, as we saw in chapter 4, Kamm pretended for a long period that there was no source of information apart from refugee reports, an obvious falsehood. By November 1978, Kamm evidently recognized that the pretense must also be dropped in the case of Cambodia. By that time U.S. journalists and other non-Communist observers had received invitations, and there were many reports available (outside of the Free Press) such as those we have surveyed. Kamm therefore describes the sources available as follows:

> With the country almost hermetically sealed off from the world, except for rare and carefully guided tours for carefully selected visitors, refugees who cross the heavily mined and closely guarded borders to Thailand and Vietnam are the only reliable source of information about life in Cambodia since the Khmer Rouge troops strode into Phnom Penh on April 17, 1975.

In short, we can continue to dismiss the reports of visitors—as Kamm proceeds to do—and rely solely on what Kamm claims to have heard from the refugees he interviewed under the circumstances already described, or reports transmitted from Vietnam, which is at war with Cambodia. These reports are "reliable"; others are not.

Kamm then proceeds to outline what he says he heard from refugees. Much of it is inconsistent with what visitors have reported, from their own direct experience. But this fact deserves no comment, since the visitors have already been dismissed as unreliable. Thus, Kamm says that the Phnom Penh radio "is not listened to by the people of Cambodia, who have no radios." In contrast, Gunnar Bergstrom of the Swedish-Kampuchea Friendship Association (non-Communist, but sympathetic to the regime) reports that peasants had radios in the cooperatives he visited and listened to the radio regularly.[180] Kamm also claims that the refugee reports are "told with striking similarity of detail in hundreds of refugee interviews." As we have seen, and will again see below, the reports vary considerably, as attested by qualified and independent observers. Kamm does not comment on the conditions of his interviews—though once again he describes an interview in a Thai police station—or what these conditions imply. He describes a regular work day of 13 hours with a half-hour break, again without reference to reports of visitors that explicitly contradict this account. His major conclusion is that "Cambodia's people labor to exhaustion, but they do not eat the rice they grow." "In a country once abundant with food, where hunger was the one human misery almost unknown, Cambodians go hungry all the time." This he describes as a "mystery." There seems to be adequate rice production, and little is exported, but the people are starving. He concludes that "rational explanations have perhaps never been the surest guide to understanding" Cambodia. Rational explanation is indeed difficult when dubious premises and preconceived conclusions must be reconciled with recalcitrant facts, a problem familiar to propagandists everywhere. Kamm does not tell us whether rational explanations are a surer guide to understanding the behavior of a superpower that pounded Cambodia to dust, or the practice of journalists who try to conceal the long-term impact of that not insignificant fact, perhaps because he knows that rational explanations do suffice in this case, unfortunately.

Kamm's belief that hunger was "almost unknown" in prewar Cambodia is in flat contradiction to analyses of the peasant society by specialists, who conclude that hunger and even starvation were common. His report that the people are now starving is in flat contradiction to the eyewitness testimony of non-Communist visitors, including the Swedish and Japanese embassy delegations as well as others. A possible resolution of his "mystery" is that the accounts he claims to have gathered in Thai police stations or under similar conditions of surveillance and coercion are inaccurate, and that even accurate refugee accounts give only a partial indication of a more complex reality. Even if we grant that Kamm is transmitting accurately what he heard, that would seem a plausible solution, but it is one that he is incapable of considering on ideological grounds, leaving him no alternative but to conclude that "what happens to the rice of Cambodia is one of the many mysteries enveloping the country."

Kamm's account is presented in the New York Times as "fact," not as the reactions of a highly biased observer of limited credibility. And it is taken as simple fact by others who have been trained to rely on the press without critical standards. Thus Mary McGrory, a liberal syndicated columnist who was strongly opposed to the U.S. war in Indochina, writes that "except for a Yugoslav television crew that was admitted by the government, the People's Republic of Kampuchea, as it is now called, has been cut off from the outside world. The ghastly accounts of its existence come from refugees all of whom tell the story...,"one of unrelieved misery and massacre: "In a recent article in the New York Times, Henry Kamm pointed out that while rice production is up, the Cambodians are on near-starvation rations."[181]

On the same day that the New York Times published Kamm's article on Cambodia, the Boston Globe published a front-page feature story with a headline running across the entire top of the front page: "Cambodia now a 'slaughterhouse,' say refugees."[182] The report, by Michael Parks, is reprinted from the *Baltimore Sun*, and was also given front-page coverage elsewhere.[183] It is unclear why this story, which repeats material that has been presented in abundance in the press, adding nothing new or particularly topical, merits a screaming front-page headline. Parks relies almost entirely on refugee accounts; he does not indicate whether he heard these accounts himself or is transmitting them from some other source. These accounts, he writes, "vary little" and provide a "uniform catalogue of horrors that verges on genocide." He repeats examples of the sort that have been widely publicized in the West since mid-1975.

Parks also refers to Japanese visitors to Cambodia, whom he does not identify, including "a Japanese correspondent" and "sympathetic visitors." He states that their description of cooperatives was "almost as grim" as the refugee stories of virtual genocide. This description he presents as follows: "With 5,000 persons, it had just brought rice production up to 1975 levels. The first efforts were just being made to build simple houses; a reopened elementary school had 190 children." Since he does not identify his source, we cannot judge whether his reference to "1975 levels" is correct; "prewar levels" seems more likely, considering what is known of 1975 levels, and Parks is silent on why it was necessary to try to achieve earlier levels of rice production. It is, perhaps, less than obvious that the description just quoted is "almost as grim" as a story of virtual genocide. This comment gives some insight into the way he evaluates the data available to him, however.

Parks also quotes the unidentified Japanese correspondent who writes ("nonetheless"): "We received the impression that these people [in the cooperative] had adjusted well to their new environment. In many ways the leisurely relaxed atmosphere peculiar to rural areas in the tropics had survived the political changes" (perhaps it is this remark that is "almost as grim" as a description of virtual genocide). Parks notes that the Japanese visitors asserted "that the peasants were well fed," but claims that they calculated the average diet at the cooperative as only 7 or 8 ounces of rice a day, far below other estimates; lacking any reference, his claim cannot be checked.

Parks is outraged by the report he attributes to the Japanese visitors that "Khmer Rouge leaders in Phnom Penh were living in luxury." Henry Kamm, in his story on the same day, also observes scornfully that government leaders "look remarkably well-fed, in splendid health and at ease in comfortable surroundings," while the population, he claims, is starving. Note again that visitors have reported that the population seems well fed, while at least some refugees and the leading U.S. government specialists have denied that Khmer Rouge cadres receive privileged treatment.[184] But let us suppose that Park and Kamm are correct. If so, then Cambodia is similar in this respect to the other countries on their regular beat, where a minority lives in fabulous luxury while the peasants and urban slum dwellers subsist in misery. This fact, however, elicits no outrage beyond Indochina (the one region where there is reason to believe it is untrue).[185]

We mentioned earlier William Shawcross's lengthy article on Cambodia in *New Times,* in which he expresses great concern over child labor—in Cambodia.[186] Shawcross observes that Cambodia has been visited by Yugoslav journalists, "delegates from friendly Maoist parties in the West and trade groups from various Southeast Asian countries." He too states that in Cambodia "before the war, there was (in Southeast Asian terms) little hunger and no famine" and "the way of life was indolent"; so it may have appeared from a visit to Phnom Penh. He gives what appears to be a paraphrase of the Yugoslav report, but with a marked difference in tone. The Cambodians, he writes, "have developed the concept of the mobile Gulag," referring to the fact reported by Stanic and others that work teams move to wherever their labor is required. Furthermore, "Quite apart from shortages of food, life in the new cooperatives is hard. Work begins at 5 A.M. and lasts for at least nine hours," and there is often another shift at night. He does not explain how he knows that the work teams are a "mobile Gulag" rather than an attempt to rebuild a country destroyed by war. Nor does he comment on the apparent success of these efforts in overcoming the devastating effects of the U.S. war, which he describes, including the destruction of the agricultural system. He also fails to explain why he is so offended by a 9-hour work day in an impoverished peasant country. If indeed the cooperatives have managed to reduce working hours to a 9-hour day with occasional extra shifts, that would seem to be a considerable accomplishment. Such a work schedule was not at all unusual, for example, in Israeli kibbutzim a few years ago, to take an example from a far richer country receiving enormous aid from abroad, where such efforts were not denounced as evidence of the extraordinary harshness of the regime. For some Western journalists, a 9-hour work day may seem a major atrocity. Peasants, or for that matter farmers and workers in advanced countries, might have a rather different view.

Shawcross also states that "an estimated two million people, nearly one quarter of the population, have been killed in war and in internal purges." Since less than a million were reportedly killed in the war, Shawcross is asserting that over a million have been killed "in internal purges" since, a figure about ten times as high as the estimates by Barron-Paul or Ponchaud. He cites no source for this "estimate." But this is again typical of the numbers game in the case of Cambodia.

Shawcross observes that the numbers are less important than the question "whether or not the government has used murder and terror as deliberate acts of policy." He writes: "The evidence is overwhelming that it has done so. Madness of this nature defies rationalization." He does not, here or elsewhere, present evidence that the use of terror is systematic and deliberate policy, though he does relay reports of refugees who have recounted gruesome tales of terror. Presumably, he concludes from these reports that the policy of the regime was one of deliberate murder and terror. Perhaps his conclusion is correct, despite his failure to construct a case.[187] Again, it is noteworthy that neither the quality of his evidence, its selection, the demonstrated lack of credibility of his major sources (of which he was by then aware, at least in part), or the vast gap between his evidence and his conclusions seems to him to require any discussion.

Here as elsewhere Shawcross is quite careful to discuss the effects of U.S. military and diplomatic intervention. Others are less scrupulous in this regard. Thus Jack Anderson, interviewing Lon Nol ("a sad symbol of the serene little country of Cambodia, which he once ruled") presents the pre-1975 history as follows:

> The Cambodians are a gentle if emotional people. They wanted only to live in peace in their lush kingdom, with its rich alluvial soil, washed by the pelting rains. But with the collapse of U.S. power in Southeast Asia, Lon Nol gave way to a fanatic regime that has brutalized the populace. Hundreds of thousands have been murdered by their new rulers, and other thousands have fled in terror.[188]

Anderson is one of the country's major liberal syndicated columnists, who has devoted many columns to Cambodian atrocities, beginning with a report on June 4, 1975, alleging that the Khmer Rouge "may be guilty of genocide against their own people."[189] He has ample staff and resources, and surely knows that it was not simply "the collapse of U.S. power in Southeast Asia" that is responsible for starvation, disease, destruction, and revenge in Cambodia. But it is appropriate, in the current phase of imperial ideology, to excise from history other major factors with which he is quite familiar (as well as others that he may know nothing of, such as the realities of peasant existence), and to speak of Cambodia as a "serene little country" of "gentle people" plunged into disaster and misery by the "collapse of U.S. power."

In discussing Sihanouk's characterization of Communist Cambodia in the preface to this volume, we pointed out that he presented a dual picture, with aspects that were, from his point of view, both positive and negative. The reports of visitors tend to substantiate the picture he presented on the basis of the very limited evidence available to him. But their reports were either ignored, or else generally reinterpreted in the Free Press to conform to the required negative image. The two U.S. reporters who visited in December 1978, Richard Dudman and Elizabeth Becker, were able to reach an unusually large audience with their own words.[190]

The New York Times dismissed their visit in a line. Bernard Weinraub, in the 11th paragraph of a 13-paragraph story on reported purges in Cambodia, remarked that their visit "produced no substantial surprises since the visitors saw only what the government wanted them to see."[191] It is true enough that their visit produced no substantial surprises, at least for people who were not restricted to the Free Press for their information. In fact, what Dudman and Becker observed was not very different from what had been reported by earlier visitors. But it was markedly different from what the New York Times and other journals had been offering as standard fare, as we see at once when we compare their eyewitness reports with the version of postwar Cambodia that had been offered by the Reader's Digest, the New York Times, the New York Review of Books and other mainstream Western sources.

Richard Dudman, an experienced foreign correspondent with excellent credentials, commented that although "the visit amounted to a conducted tour...there was plenty of opportunity for observation in tours of 11 of the 19 provinces." His conclusions conform to the dual picture that emerges from consideration of the range of evidence previously available:

> It seemed evident throughout this reporter's visit to Cambo-
> dia before the recent Vietnamese attack that the new Cam-
> bodia's version of Communism had no place in it for anyone
> who wanted to read, write, or even think independently, or
> for anyone who wanted to own more than a bare minimum of
> personal property.
>
> At the same time, the physical conditions of life may well
> have improved for many peasants and former urban dwellers—
> possibly for the vast majority of the population, as the regime
> claimed.

Apart from the "austere standard of hard manual labor" and
restrictions on "the freedoms accepted or at least professed by
most of the rest of the world" that Dudman observed, his inability to make contact with former urban residents tended to confirm the dark picture of repression and atrocities conveyed by
the refugee accounts that have been publicized. "The new Communist Cambodia," Dudman wrote, "became one huge work
camp, but its people were clearly not being worked to death and
starved to death as foreign critics often charged":

> What I have found in two weeks of touring Pol Pot's Cambo-
> dia—under strict government supervision but with a good op-
> portunity for observation—was a regimented life of hard work
> for most Cambodians, leavened, however, by much improved
> housing, regular issuance of clothing, and an assurance of appar-
> ently adequate food. I did not find the grim picture painted by
> the thousands of refugees who couldn't take the new order and
> fled to Thailand or Vietnam. In this lull between wars, those who
> remain appeared to be reasonably relaxed at the height of the
> busy harvest season. They sometimes leaned on their hoes like
> farm workers everywhere. And they often stared and then smiled
> and waved at the rare sight of Western faces. Workers usually
> appeared to be operating under their own direction. There were
> no signs of government cadres giving orders or armed guards en-
> forcing the working hours, although individuals seemed to know
> what was expected.

The work day, Dudman found, lasted from about 6 a.m. to 11 a.m. and again from 1 p.m. to 5 p.m. Dudman found the housing program ("one of the world's great housing programs") particularly impressive, "a sudden mass upgrading of the individual family homes from the standard that has existed for centuries," which "probably meant better living, too, for the hundreds of thousands of country people who were driven into the cities by the five year war ..." as well as for the peasants who remained on the land. Until the Vietnamese invasion, prospects for economic development "appeared bright." Cambodia was feeding itself and had resumed rice exports, and the crucial water-control programs of the postwar years appeared to have been generally a success. He saw no evidence of starvation, contrary to standard claims in the U.S. media, and found the country "to be flourishing and potentially prosperous—at least until the Vietnamese invaders moved in." U.S. specialists, Dudman wrote, "have acknowledged that the Cambodian claim of reviving rice production to the point of resuming exports would, if true, be a spectacular achievement." It may well have been true.

Dudman also describes "a wide range of industrial growth—concentrated more in tiny and primitive cottage industries such as brick-making, silk spinning, and local blacksmith shops, but including also a fairly sophisticated rubber factory..." Development was decentralized and aimed for a high degree of local self-sufficiency. He describes "a progressive industrial growth plan" that seemed not unrealistic, judging by the account that he and earlier visitors have given. He also gives a brief account of the organization of the cooperatives.

Recognizing that the peasant population probably did not regard the "austere standard of hard manual labor" (specifically, a nine-hour work day) as an onerous imposition of the regime, and may not have been overly concerned that privileged urban sectors were compelled to share the hard but improving life of the poorer peasants, one might reach the conclusion that much of the population may well have supported the regime, particularly if it is true, as Dudman was informed but could not establish, that "decisions were taken collectively" in the cooperatives and even the army.

Elizabeth Becker's six-part series in the *Washington Post* covers much the same ground in less depth, and is in some ways more revealing about the character of U.S. journalism than it is about Cambodia. She found the development program generally incomprehensible: "no one seems able to offer a coherent philosophical basis for the extreme upheaval that has taken place." She does not go into how this alleged failure compares, say, with the "philosophical basis" for the developments in far more favored Thailand discussed in the preface to this volume, or comparable phenomena in other regions where a dependency model has been imposed. She writes that she is "forced to conclude" that the economic system "seems to be working," revealing plainly the initial bias that colored all of her observations. It is also remarkable to see how uncritically she accepted Cambodian charges which, she claims, supported U.S. positions during the Vietnam war. She writes that she was given "a remarkable new document"—namely the Cambodian government *Livre Noir* of September 1978,[192] which had in fact been on sale in New York well before she left for Cambodia—which "confirms" U.S. claims and "discloses" that there were 200,000 to 300,000 Vietcong in the northeast region of Cambodia, including the Central Committee of the Vietnamese Party (COSVN), when Nixon ordered the 1970 invasion. It estimates the total number of Vietcong in Cambodia in 1970 at 1.5-2 million.[193] The *Livre Noir*, which is a bitter attack on the Vietnamese Communists, is certainly worth reading, but surely no serious commentator would accept uncritically a propaganda document produced in the midst of an ongoing war. U.S. reporters have rarely paid attention to material from comparable sources "confirming" or "disclosing" alleged facts that contradict positions taken by the U.S. government.[194]

We have already noted the *New York Times* dismissal of the Dudman-Becker visit. *Newsweek* ran an uninformative article by Becker[195] and *Time* reviewed their visit in an article that simply repeated its familiar rhetoric about "the shroud of terror and darkness" of a regime that was attempting to "counteract its worldwide image as a merciless, anonymous and genocidal regime," systematically avoiding the direct observations that Dudman (and, in part, Becker) had reported, in particular, those that were positive.[196]

Malcolm Caldwell was assassinated on the final day of the visit, in Phnom Penh. According to Dudman, "Caldwell expressed general sympathy with the Cambodian brand of Communism prior to the Vietnamese invasion" and "the report that he was experiencing a change in views was not true," as Dudman knew from conversations throughout the two-week trip "up to a few hours of his death." In these conversations, "Caldwell remained sympathetic to the Cambodian revolution, without blinding himself to its faults," likening it to early stages of the industrial revolution in England. It "seems out of the question," Dudman writes, that the Cambodian government, which "had everything to lose from the incident," could have had anything to do with the assassination, contrary to speculations that have been rife. Dudman's conclusion seems well-founded. The true story will probably never be known, but the consequences of the assassination are clear enough. It is most unlikely that Caldwell's account of what he had seen would have reached any segment of international opinion apart from the left. And for the left, judging by what he had written in personal letters and articles before his trip and by the fact that "he remained fully sympathetic to the Cambodian revolution" (Dudman), his message would have tended to support the Pol Pot regime and to undermine the justification for the Vietnamese invasion that was being presented in the Western and Soviet bloc press.[197]

As we have seen, refugee accounts are not as uniform as accounts in the press suggest. A further look bears out the conclusion. The most extensive published report of a refugee interview, to our knowledge, is a study based on conversations with Peang Sophi, who escaped from Cambodia in January, 1976, and arrived in Australia three months later.[198] "His account of life under the revolutionary regime," Chandler comments,

> differs in two important ways from others readily available in the West. Firstly, he spent over six months working actively— and rather happily—under revolutionary guidance; unlike many refugees, he was not punished by the regime for having roots in the "old society." Secondly, from about September onwards, he enjoyed considerable responsibility, as the "economic" foreman of an 800-man rural work team.

Chandler also observes that his experiences may not be typical. He lived in a province with "a unique (but recent) revolutionary tradition" and unusual prosperity, where "revolutionary cadre... may have been especially vengeful and undisciplined, too; certainly most tales of atrocities told by refugees refer to events in Battambang" [Sophi's province].[199] Sophi reports that the Khmer Rouge cadre were "thin and pale," mostly young peasants. They admitted that in the early stages of liberation "they were subject to 'uncontrollable hatred'" and that "in this mood" conducted executions of Lon Nol officials and destroyed military equipment. They were "real country people, from *far* away" (Sophi's emphasis), illiterate, unfamiliar with urban amenities and frightened even of tin cans. "One speaker allegedly said: 'We were so angry when we came out of the forest that we didn't want to spare even a baby in its cradle.'" But Sophi reports that the executions were ordered halted shortly after. The cadres had no special privileges and were friendly in their relations with villagers and workers.

Their program was successful because it seemed attractive, with a special appeal to youth. "Although he remained unconvinced by the totality of Khmer Rouge teaching, Sophi was impressed by the integrity and morale of many cadre, and by the ideology embodied in official directives and revolutionary songs." Their goals were a vast increase in the population, distribution of power and responsibility to people with poor peasant background,[200] hard work (though working conditions, he says, were not particularly severe, hours were flexible, and rations usually sufficient), "the moral value of collective labour," and true independence based on self-reliance. Differences in status were obliterated, along with "begging and arrogance," and there was a consistent "puritanical strain" in regulations. Obviously unhappy with the new society, Sophi nevertheless offers an account that is not unsympathetic—and that has yet to be reported in the mass media, to our knowledge. His account also suggests an answer to the "difficult question," though one too unwelcome to be reported.

Chandler elaborated on these observations in an article in *Commonweal*.[201] Here he stressed again how one-sided is the information available from refugees—by definition, those disaffected with the regime. Again he points out that the worst reports are from the Northwest, "where radical politics before liberation were weak, rural class differences especially pronounced, and agricultural production higher than elsewhere in the country. For these reasons the liberating forces there seem to have been especially vengeful and undisciplined." He then adds the qualification already cited in note 199.

Chandler makes some important and generally forgotten historical observations. Peasants, he writes, "have been 'outside history' for many years":

> we know very little, in a quantitative or political terms, about the mass of Cambodian society, many of whom, for most of their history, appear to have been slaves of one sort or

another. The frequency of locally-led rebellions in the nineteenth century—against the Thai, the Vietnamese, the French and local officials—suggests that Cambodian peasants were not as peaceable as their own mythology, reinforced by the French, would lead us to believe.

The French were not concerned with the peasantry, "preferring to reconstruct Cambodia's ancient temples, nurture a small elite, and modernize the economy to provide surpluses of rice and rubber." Little is known of what actually went on in earlier history, the colonial period, or the "early independence period" (1953-1970).[202]

Lack of familiarity with the historical experience of the Khmer peasants makes it difficult to comprehend what lies behind the violence of the post-revolutionary period, though the atrocities of the civil war were reported at the time,[203] along with the impact of the U.S. war.[204] Citing Sophi, Chandler speaks of the "uncontrollable hatred" that led to early postwar atrocities in Battambang. He discusses the revolutionary ideology in terms similar to those already outlined. Continuing, Chandler comments:

> Collective self-reliance or autarky, as preached by the regime, contrasts sharply with what might be called the slave mentality that suffused pre-revolutionary Cambodia and made it so "peaceful" and "charming" to the elite and to most outsiders—for perhaps two thousand years...In the Cambodian case, in 1976, autarky makes sense, both in terms of recent experience—American intervention, and what is seen as the Western-induced corruption of previous regimes—and in terms of Cambodia's long history of conflict with Vietnam...Self-reliance also explains turning away from Cambodia's past to make a society where there are "no rich and no poor, no exploiters and no exploited."[205]

Chandler asks: "Is the price for liberation, in human terms, too high?" On this question, he says, "we Americans with our squalid record in Cambodia should be 'cautiously optimistic' about the new regime, 'or else shut up'" (citing a friend), though he adds that the closed character of the regime (not to speak of refugee reports) raises serious doubts about such cautious optimism.

It would be incorrect to say that such relatively positive, though tempered comments on the revolutionary regime do not appear in the critical literature concerning Cambodia. It would be correct to say, however, that where they did appear, they were ignored as the story filtered through to a mass audience. Ponchaud, for example, describes the brutality of the civil war and the destructiveness of the U.S. attack, and a major theme of his book—though one could hardly know this from reviews and press comment—is his discussion of the "genuine egalitarian revolution" in Cambodia, where there is a new "spirit of responsibility" and "inventiveness" that "represents a revolution in the traditional mentality": with their vast construction projects, "the people of Kampuchea are now making a thousand-year-old dream come true" and both men and women find new pride in driving trucks and other constructive work.[206] Where this important theme of his book is mentioned at all, it is offered as evidence of "destruction of a culture." Ponchaud, clearly, feels that the price was far too high, and perhaps he is right; but it is important to stress that contrary to the second-hand impression of reviews and press commentary, he did focus attention on these aspects of the new regime, which were as little noted or understood in the media as the impact of the U.S war.[207]

The real conditions of Cambodian peasant life are of little concern in the West. The brutality of the civil war and the U.S. attack, though dramatic and unquestionable facts of very recent history, are rapidly passing out of memory. Note that Ponchaud, while not guilty of the outrageous deception of Barron-Paul and others like them who excise the Western role and responsibility from history, nevertheless downplays it; U.S. bombers did not merely strike rubber plantations, nor did the French simply bring "order and peace."[208]

When we move from the mainstream of commentary that reaches a mass audience to studies by people who know and care about Cambodia, the picture changes. Ponchaud's book, as already noted, is quite different from most of the media comment it elicited. Chandler's article is another case in point. One of the small group of scholars concerned with Cambodia, Michael Vickery, reviewed the course of recent Cambodian history in an effort to explain why the revolution evolved "in a manner so contrary to all predictions":

> For all wise old Indochina hands believed that after the war had been won by the revolutionary forces—and there was no doubt by 1972, at the latest, that they would win—it would be the Vietnamese who would engage in the most radical and brutal break with the past. In Cambodia it was expected that both sides, except for a few of the most notorious leaders, would be reconciled and some sort of mild, tolerant socialism would be instituted...Among the Indochina countries only Laos has come out of the war true to form, while Vietnam and Cambodia have behaved in ways nearly the opposite of what had been expected. What this means first of all, of course, is that the Vietnamese and Cambodians were misunderstood and that the facets of their culture and history which might have revealed an unexpected capacity for tolerance in the one and vindictiveness in the other were missed.[209]

He examines what was missed; notably in Cambodia, "in spite of its heady atmosphere as the last exotic Asian paradise, it was rent by political, economic, and class conflicts." The war that seemed to explode in 1970 "proceeded naturally from trends in the country's political history over the preceding twenty-five years, a period characterized by intense efforts of the traditional elite to frustrate any moves toward political, economic or social modernization which would threaten its position."

Vickery suggests a degree of caution in assessing the postwar situation: "A blackout on information has been imposed by the new government, what the refugees, the only first-hand source of news, say is contradictory, and contributions from other sources, principally the Cambodian community in Paris, alternate between the trivial and the absurd."[210]

Vickery gives a detailed account of how Sihanouk and his right wing supporters proceeded to "rule alone," with ample resort to repression. Lon Nol, later premier after the March, 1970 coup, "established himself solidly as a power figure" in Battambang Province bordering Thailand, assuming command of the region with the rank of colonel after the withdrawal of French military forces in 1952: "During the next two years this area was the scene of operations by government forces against Issaraks[211] and Viet Minh characterized by gratuitous brutality." Recall that this is one of the areas where the worst atrocities were later recorded. Vickery continues:

> As related to me by a participant, [government forces] would move into villages, kill the men and women who had not already fled and then engage in individual tests of strength which consisted of grasping infants by the legs and pulling them apart. These events had probably not been forgotten by the men of that area who survived to become the Khmer Rouge troops occupying Battambang in 1975 and whose reported actions have stirred up so much comment abroad

—where, we may add, they are attributed to "Marxism," a much more convenient origin for the purposes of Western ideology, however dubious in the case of Cambodian peasants who had lived through such experiences in their "gentle land."

The "conservative ideology" of Sihanouk's Sangkum party, which effectively ruled after 1955, was clear at once, Vickery continues. In accordance with its "authoritarian philosophy," "natural leaders should rule," namely, "the rich and powerful who enjoyed such a situation in the present because of virtuous conduct in previous lives...The poor and unfortunate should accept their lot and try for an improved situation in the next life through virtuous conduct in the present." As we have noted, a major theme of Ponchaud's book, cited if at all with the implication that the beautiful traditional culture is being obliterated by savage monsters, is that these conceptions were being replaced by a new egalitarianism and emphasis on peasant self-reliance.

From the election of 1955, won by Sangkum by a resort to repression and deceit, power "remained solidly in the hands of the old right"; the elite wasted the country's wealth through "conspicuous consumption," "expensive foreign products," "frequent trips abroad, [and] hard currency bank accounts." Meanwhile foreigners were mesmerized by the famous Khmer smile. "Skeptics might wish to ask why the system didn't break down... In fact, it did break down, and that is why Cambodia passed through a war and revolution."

The Issaraks were the inheritors of the tradition of warfare of the colonial period, turning themselves into "fighters for independence against the French." "For all but a tiny minority who had truly absorbed European intellectual values, modernization meant the type of growth exemplified by Bangkok and Saigon— lots of chrome and concrete, streets clogged by cars, a plethora of luxurious bars, and everyone dressed in western clothes." It was this tiny minority who, together with the forgotten peasants of inner Cambodia, later brought the old era crashing to the ground with bitterness and violence. Meanwhile the United States, while remaining the chief supplier for the Cambodian army, often mistook Sihanouk for a "communist" in the grip of their "Dullesian hysteria."

The political and economic situation worsened through the 1960s as the right consolidated its power and repression and corruption increased, and with it, discontent among the peasants and some urban intellectuals:

> The discontent was accompanied by repression, the secret police were omnipresent, people mysteriously disappeared, and by 1966 Cambodia, though still smiling and pleasant for the casual visitor, was a country in which everyone lived in fear.

"The first large peasant revolt broke out in western Battambang province in the spring of 1967 and was suppressed with bloodshed which was reminiscent of the 1950s and prefigured that of 1975." There were further revolts and disappearances and by 1969 insurgency was widespread though scattered.[212] The coup of 1970 that overthrew Sihanouk was led by men who "had always been among the big guns of the Cambodian right who had sabotaged democracy, opposed the Geneva Accords, organized the Sangkum, and helped maintain Sihanouk's absolute rule from 1955." In the subsequent war, they lost to a large extent "out of sheer greed and incompetence."

The outright U.S. intervention sharply intensified the conflict, particularly, with the escalation of U.S. bombardment of the countryside in 1973:

> Particularly during the severe U.S. bombing which lasted throughout the first eight months of 1973, and which produced no reaction in Phnom Penh[213] other than relief, it must have seemed to FUNK [the guerrillas] that their urban compatriots were quite willing to see the entire countryside destroyed and plastered over with concrete as long as they could enjoy a parasitical existence as U.S. clients. It is certain that FUNK policy became much harsher after the bombing. Whereas in 1971-1972 they showed considerable efforts at conciliation and in general Cambodian villagers did not fear them, from 1973-4, with all allowance for government propaganda there are authentic accounts of brutal imposition of new policies without ideological preparation of the population.[214]

Vickery points out that the Kissinger-Nixon policy during the last two years of the war was "a major mystery," for which he suggests an explanation that appears to us quite plausible. Referring to the "Sonnenfeldt Doctrine," which holds that "pluralistic and libertarian Communist regimes will breed leftist ferment in the West," he suggests that "when it became clear [to U.S. leaders] that they could not win in Cambodia, they preferred to do everything possible to insure that the post-war revolutionary government be extremely brutal, doctrinaire, and frightening to its neighbors, rather than a moderate socialism to which the Thai, for example, might look with envy." In short, though it was understood that the United States had lost the war in Cambodia (even though it was, quite clearly, still trying to win it in Vietnam[215]), destruction of rural Cambodia, by imposing the harshest possible conditions on the eventual victors, would serve the two classic ends: retarding social and economic progress, and maximizing the brutality of the eventual victors. Then the aggressors would at least be able to reap a propaganda victory from the misery they had sown.[216] This explanation for the insistence on battering Cambodia to dust after the war was lost seems particularly reasonable against the background of the basic rationale for the U.S. war in Indochina, namely, the rational variant of the "domino theory" which held that social and economic successes in countries that extricated themselves from the U.S.-dominated global system might cause "the rot to spread" to other areas, with severe long-term consequences for U.S. power and privilege. Unable to retain control over Indochina, the United States could at least reduce the terrifying prospects that viable societies might emerge from the wreckage.[217]

Vickery points out that "the success of this policy [in Cambodia] may perhaps be seen in the [1976] Thai elections, in which the defeat of the socialist parties has been attributed in large measure to fear of a regime like that in Cambodia."

Writing of the Nixon-Kissinger bombing policy of 1973 at the time, Laura Summers pointed out that it followed the Nixon administration's refusal "to accept Prince Sihanouk's invitation for negotiations in January and February, 1973." U.S. B-52s "pounded Cambodia for 160 consecutive days, dropping more than 240,000 short tons of bombs on rice fields, water buffalo, villages (particularly along the Mekong river) and on such troop positions as the guerrillas might maintain," a tonnage that "represents 50 per cent more than the conventional explosives dropped on Japan during World War II." In spite of the enormous destruction, "the bombing had little effect on the military capacity of the Cambodian guerrillas." She concludes, surely accurately, that "American policy and American bombing have placed a small country's physical and political survival in escrow for many years to come, not for the benefit of the people who live there nor in defense of any laudable ideal."[218]

The fact that the Khmer Rouge ideology and practice became harsher in 1973 as a direct result of the intensified bombing was also noted by David Chandler in his congressional testimony.[219] The interpretation just suggested apparently seems credible to Cambodians. Summers remarks that "in 1973, Khmers loyal to the resistance believed the major purpose of Nixon's six-month bombing campaign was to destroy the emerging productive potential and the social security of the liberated zone ..."[220] We suspect that the goal of increasing the harshness of the Khmer Rouge, a predictable consequence, was also quite probably an intended one.

The study of the revolutionary movement in Cambodia from 1970-1974 by Kenneth Quinn of the National Security Council is quite revealing in this regard.[221] Quinn was resident in a South Vietnamese province bordering Cambodia from 1972-1974 studying refugees arriving from Cambodia. He reports that from early 1973—that is, from the time that the extraordinarily heavy bombing attack began—

> the Khmer Communists drastically accelerated and intensified their program to radically alter society. Included in this effort were mass relocations of the population, purges of lenient cadres, the use of terror, and extensive remodeling of the economic system...events occurred within Cambodia which sent the first group of refugees fleeing into South Vietnam [beginning in 1973].

We have already discussed his comments on the measures undertaken by the Khmer Communists at that time. What is now relevant is the timing. Nowhere in his article does Quinn mention the bombing among the "events [that] occurred within Cambodia" from early 1973, or its possible significance for understanding the sharp modification of policy that he describes. The omission is as interesting as the timing he indicates, from his well-placed vantage point.

Stephen Heder has suggested (personal communication) that the radicalization of 1973 in response to the U.S. bombing might well have been motivated by a desire to win popular support and encourage willingness to sacrifice on the part of the poor majority of the population, who would bear the brunt of the attacks and would also stand to gain the most from these policies, as is sufficiently clear even from the hostile account by Quinn cited above.[222]

Whatever the explanation may be for the fierce bombing of 1973, the available facts lead to one clear conclusion: every bomb dropped added its contribution to the postwar record of revenge by the battered peasant society. Meanwhile the perpetrators—who remain beyond the reach of retribution—receive awards for their humanitarian contributions[223] as they denounce the unaccountable savagery of the Khmer Rouge.

Turning to the policies of the new regime, Vickery remarks that

> they may be usefully compared with the recommendations of a "Blueprint for the Future" prepared by an anonymous group of western and Thai social scientists and published in the conservative *Bangkok Post* [in February 1976]. Their suggestions, in order for Thailand to avoid a breakdown of its society and a revolution, were that people should be taken out of the cities and put back on the land, decentralization should give more power to local authorities, much more investment should go into agriculture, and the old elite should lose some of its wealth and political power. Now this is precisely what Cambodia has done, though of course on a much more massive

scale than envisioned by "Blueprint," but it illustrates that the basic policies are considered by "bourgeois" economists and political scientists to be rational and practicable for a country with problems similar to those of Cambodia.

Of course, there is also a major dissimilarity: Cambodia had been savaged by U.S. terror, and faced imminent disaster with the termination of the U.S. dole for the millions of people who had been subjected, in their turn, to the "forced-draft urbanization and modernization" that so entranced U.S. ideologists of the period.

Vickery was cautious in assessing the current situation though relatively pessimistic, and was willing to hazard few predictions. The postwar Khmer Rouge regime, he observed, "will certainly have no trouble teaching their people that Cambodian suffering was mainly due to foreign intervention"—we may add, from our different perspective, that the propaganda organs of the West have been busily at work convincing *their* people that any such charge is a "simple-minded myth" or a case of wallowing in "the politics of guilt."[224] He concludes finally:

> Although one may legitimately ask whether the new egalitarian society could not have been established with less deliberate destruction of the old, there are ample reasons why the new leadership might answer in the negative.

Vickery's analysis of the backgrounds of the war and the sources for the harshness of the new regime was as foreign to the media as was his skeptical caution with regard to the developing situation. But it has not been uncommon in commentary by people whose concern is with the facts rather than with fanning hysteria in the West about the dangers of "socialism" or "Marxism"—we stress again the absurdity of the major theme of press propaganda: that the atrocities committed by Khmer peasants simply flow from "Marxism" or "atheism," as dire consequences of liberation from the grip of Western benevolence.[225]

A rather similar perception is expressed in the prepared re-

marks by Charles Meyer at the April, 1978 Hearings on Cambodia in Oslo.[226] Meyer, conservative and anti-Communist, is the
author of scholarly studies on Cambodian history and contemporary Cambodia. His writings, based on long residence in Cambodia and intimate knowledge, have been ignored in the United
States.[227] Discussing the evidence presented at the Hearings,
Meyer concludes that it suffices to show that "Democratic Kampuchea has been the stage of hasty executions" and that its people
live under a regime that violates the International Declaration of
Human Rights. But he adds some significant words of caution:

> One knows that the colonial powers have often used the ar-
> gument of "wildness" in order to impose their domination and
> their "civilizing mission." They have today successors, who are
> pushed by the same ambitions. It is only the vocabulary that
> has changed.[228]

As for the "wildness" of the Cambodian leaders, he has this to say:

> Today, like yesterday, whether they are monarchists, republi-
> cans or revolutionaries, the Khmers have an extreme suscep-
> tibility, which makes relations with them often difficult. Our
> Cambodian friends who are present here will not contradict
> me. Those who at present govern Cambodia have not escaped
> from this national characteristic. But they are not mad people
> nor monsters demanding blood—I have known several among
> them. Most of them sons of peasants, more or less formed in
> the French Marxist school, rebelling against a system which
> has remained feudal, they have the sentiment among the peo-
> ple of the countryside to have received a veritable illumina-
> tion and found the road to the new. Perhaps I will shock many
> among you. But I believe that these Red Khmer leaders incar-
> nate really a part of the peasants, who recognize themselves
> in them.[229]

These leaders, Meyer argues, "maintain the tradition of their
predecessors just before them" and in their "immoderation" reflect deep-seated currents in Cambodian history and culture,
though again he urges caution: "In reality the records re Cam-

bodia are not so simple and many pieces are missing." As in his book, he observes that "it is important to destroy the picture in the West that the Cambodians are non-violent by nature and filled with Buddhistic benevolence." On the contrary, "behind that smile violence is slumbering and...it is dangerous to wake it up," as happened in 1967 with the "brutal repression of a rising of peasants in the region of Battambang and the revolt of the minorities in the region of Rattanakiri." Furthermore:

> The American airforce gave the [military regime calling itself republican] its support by destroying the Cambodian plains through heavy bombing without for this being accused of genocide. The following events should not let us forget this. [As] regards the fratricid[al] fights with ties from one side as well as from the other to Vietnam in periods, they were without mercy, [as] is usual in all civil wars.

Today, as previously, "one should be extremely careful in one's analysis of the politics" of the victors, considering "the weight of the past, the ideology of the leaders, the menaces from outside, and, naturally, the psychological factors as well as the economical, religious and other ones"—a perception foreign to the mass media.

The summary executions of officials of the old regime "is in reality the application of the Cambodian penal code of 1877," including the brutal means employed: "This punishment was used between 1965 and 1970 for 'Red Khmers' who were caught and would have been used still more systematically, if the government had won the victory." Furthermore, "it seems to me that we should accept with reservations the balance in figures of the victims...[and]...admit that any estimation at present is impossible." He insists that "there are no simple explanations or clear and evident ones and that peremptory affirmations should always be avoided." He sees the war as a rising of the peasants against the cities, the symbol of corruption and repression: "One must further know that Cambodian city-dwellers were in reality Western colonials and Chinese [traders]."

Meyer is highly critical of the "radicalism and the excesses" of the revolutionaries. His concern to explain the postwar events in terms of Cambodian history and tradition is, however, in striking contrast to Western fulminations, though not uncommon among specialists on Cambodia, as is his attention to the factors that "contributed to harden the [internal] politics of the revolutionary leaders."

We learn still more about these factors in a paper by Laura Summers cited earlier.[230] She discusses the destructive impact of French colonialism, which violated the "corporate integrity" of the Khmer people: "its indigenous legal system, pattern of land possession and national administration were dismantled." During the national uprising of 1885-1886, "French authorities with the aid of Vietnamese infantrymen succeeded in reducing the Khmer population of the *Protectorat du Cambodge* by 195,000 (20% of the entire Khmer population)."[231] "The French displayed little remorse over the fate of this people whom they believed doomed to extinction," as they brought a form of what Ponchaud calls "order and peace" to the land in fulfillment of their "colonial mission." The impact on the countryside was particularly destructive. While most peasants owned some land, vast numbers of family holdings were insufficient for subsistence requirements by the early 1950s. Yields were among the lowest in the world "and barely met the subsistence requirements of the rural population in 1965, 1966 and (especially) 1967."[232] At that time, annual rates of interest for loans ranged from 100% to 200%; "the total effect of the credit structure in agrarian economy was to make the peasant worse than a tenant on his own property" while village and urban elites lived in luxury. Sihanouk's attempts at some social reform had little impact. Particularly scandalous was the lack of medical care and the practice of charging exorbitant fees to peasants or denying them services or hospital treatment. The judiciary was no less corrupt and urban-based civil servants with no interest in peasant affairs enjoyed the amenities offered the rich by the colonial system while the mass of peasants sank deeper into poverty and suffering. "It is...not surprising that the revolution was violent for in addition to the human destruction heaped upon the community by intensive American bombing, there were profound social grievances and scores to be settled." In an accompanying demographic analysis, Summers estimates the number of "postwar deaths from exhaustion, disease and execution in the range of two hundred thousand, an estimate which is based on an extremely difficult to determine *status quo ante bellum.*"

It is quite evident that to understand the events in the aftermath of the war it is necessary to pay attention to the historical background of the peasant revolution, which was further inflamed and deeply embittered by the U.S. attack culminating in the bombing of 1973, that Meyer hints might be considered genocidal in character. The sensational press accounts of atrocities that entirely ignore that background, while at the same time relying on highly dubious or sometimes fabricated evidence, may be useful contributions to the revival of imperial ideology; but they are of little value in conveying any understanding of the postwar situation.

We have already mentioned the peasant rebellions in Battambang in the west and the tribal provinces of the northeast in the late 1960s. The sources of these revolts in peasant discontent resulting from penury, oppression and corruption under the increasingly right wing central government have been explored by the Australian scholar Ben Kiernan.[233] These revolts were no small affair; Sihanouk cited a figure of 10,000 deaths (a figure which he may well have exaggerated for rhetorical effect), and it is estimated that about 4,000 peasants fled their homes in June 1967 "in the wake of severe army repression of their protest against harsh local conditions," as "aircraft bombed and strafed villages and jungle hideouts" and villages were burned to the ground and surrounded by troops, their inhabitants massacred. By the time that Sihanouk was overthrown in the March 1970 coup, there was "a sophisticated, powerful and indigenous resistance movement well entrenched in many parts of Cambodia." After the coup, there were peasant uprisings interpreted in the West as indicating support for Sihanouk. In an analysis of the locale and character of these protests, which were brutally suppressed by military force (including Khmer troops trained by the CIA in South Vietnam), Kiernan concludes that they reflect in part the ongoing anti-government rebellion, though loyalty to Sihanouk was no doubt a factor as well.[234]

In several studies, Kiernan suggested a picture of early postwar events in Cambodia that is rather different from what has been featured by the press.[235] Specifically, he took issue with horror stories published in *Time* (26 April, 1976), which alleged that 500-600,000 people had died under the rule of the Khmer Rouge, "one of the most brutally murderous regimes in the world" which rules Cambodia by "a chilling form of mindless terror." Like others, he notes that most of the atrocity stories come from areas of little Khmer Rouge strength, where orders to stop reprisals were disobeyed by soldiers wreaking vengeance, often drawn from the poorest sections of the peasantry. He discusses the fake photographs,[236] and gives examples of fabrication of atrocity stories by refugees "in order to persuade the Thai border police to admit them." He also deals with other fabrications that have appeared in the Western press. He suggests that, "untrained and vengeful, and at times leaderless, some soldiers in the northwest of Cambodia have terrorized soldiers, city dwellers, and peasants. This has been aggravated by the threat of widespread starvation, and actual starvation in some parts." He questions the assumption that there was central direction for atrocities as well as the assumption that the stories from specific areas where, in fact, the Khmer Rouge had little control, can be freely extrapolated to the country as a whole. His conclusions are based in part on interviews with refugees in Thai camps and in Bangkok, and like Vickery in Thailand and Fraser in Vietnam, he reports quite a range of refugee judgments on the nature of the regime. He also gives an analysis of the class background and region of the refugee flow, relating these factors to the social and economic situation that had prevailed.

Kiernan's detailed conclusions suggest why attending to these questions might be useful, at least for those whose concern is truth. Consider his analysis of the composition of Cambodian refugees in Thailand in August 1976. Note that this date is well after what Ponchaud describes as the worst period of terror, and that these refugees form a substantial part of the population sampled by Barron-Paul and Ponchaud.[237] Kiernan concludes:

> There were 10,200 Cambodian refugees in Thailand in August 1976. A tiny handful of these belong to that category of over half the population who, at the end of the war, had lived in Khmer Rouge areas for several years. The great majority of the refugees can be divided into three groups: former Lon Nol soldiers, former urban dwellers, and farmers from Battambang and Siemreap provinces.[238]
>
> Unsurprisingly, over a third of the 3,000 refugees in the Aranyaprathet camp in Thailand are former Lon Nol soldiers, and many of the refugees are former *Khmer Serei*, commandos trained and financed by the CIA.

In Battambang, Kiernan writes, the "thin and undernourished" Khmer Rouge troops headed directly to the airport and broke up four T-28 bombers into pieces,[239] "remembering the agony in the trenches, the hunger in the countryside because the paddy fields were full of bomb craters, and their terrible fear of asphyxiation bombs."[240] "For many months after that," he continues, "refugees reported that Lon Nol soldiers were hunted down, particularly in northwest Cambodia—a few refugees were eyewitnesses to executions."

Kiernan believes there is little evidence that the government planned and approved a systematic large-scale purge. The evidence indicates, he believes, that "apart from the execution of high-ranking army officers and officials, the killing reported by refugees from the northwest after April 1975 was instigated by untrained and vengeful local Khmer Rouge soldiers, despite orders to the contrary from Phnom Penh." "Most of the brutality shown by local Khmer Rouge soldiers is attributable to lack of training and the difficulty of forging a disciplined organisation in the Cambodian countryside, especially after the bombing of 1973," though "it is also quite probable that some Khmer Rouge local cadres harbour the...conception of the priorities for Cambodia's survival...[with]...the emphasis on hard work, sacrifice, and asceticism which this dynamic form of Khmer nationalism entails" and which "has dismayed some Cambodians," among them some cadres "who ensure peasant co-operation with their policies through force." The killings were concentrated in "exceptional" areas where living conditions were harshest (he cites concurring judgments by Patrice de Beer of *Le Monde* and Ponchaud), regions where the Khmer Rouge were "organisationally and numerically weak." He feels that "it is little wonder that several thousand *peasants* have fled from northwest Cambodia" (his emphasis), whereas "very few peasants, if any, have fled to Thailand from other parts of Cambodia, while soldiers and former city dwellers have arrived in Thailand from eastern and central Cambodia as well as from the northwest." The reason is that "at the end of the war, farmers in the northwest were in for a very difficult period" because of the drastic shortage of food, exacerbated by the flow of refugees to the towns. In contrast, in areas that had been administered by the Khmer Rouge, canals and dams had been built enabling two crops to be brought in, and some rice had been stockpiled, a subject analyzed by Hildebrand and Porter, to whom he refers. Furthermore, these regions were unique in the inequity and exploitation of the poor: "With class divisions as stark as this, and after a brutal war, equally brutal revenge was taken by poor peasants" many of whom had joined the Khmer Rouge (though many bandits "passed themselves off as Khmer Rouge" as well, not an unusual phenomenon in comparable situations). He quotes one Khmer refugee who said that in Battambang the rich were being "persecuted" while the poor were better off than before, and adds that "where the Khmer Rouge were better organised, 'persecution' of the rich was much less violent."

This analysis covers the period of the worst terror according to Ponchaud, the period that provides much of the basis for the best-publicized accounts (Barron-Paul, Ponchaud, and reviews and references to Ponchaud).[241] Therefore the situation that Kiernan describes is crucially significant for an analysis of the response in the West to postwar events in Cambodia. We know of no comparable analysis from a later period, though this in any event would not be relevant to our major concern—the workings of the Western propaganda system.[242]

The Southeast Asia correspondent of the *Far Eastern Economic Review*, Nayan Chanda, presented his assessment of the situation at about the same time in several articles.[243] In the *FEER*, he estimated that in the 18 months of postwar bloodletting, which according to refugee reports and "most observers" was largely over, "possibly thousands of people died," including not only the top figures of the Lon Nol regime but also "large numbers of lower-strata civilian and military personnel of the former administration [who] have been executed in the Khmer Rouge's cleansing process."[244] But the actual numbers are "impossible to calculate." The estimate of "possibly thousands" presumably refers to those killed, not the victims of starvation or disease or unexploded ordnance. In his May, 1977 article,

Chanda discussed the "human cost" of what the regime had so far accomplished in these terms:

> One will probably never know exactly how many human lives have been cut down by political execution, starvation and disease. The tendency of refugees to exaggerate their troubles to attract sympathy, the active presence of the intelligence services in the refugee camps and the Bangkok press—the most important source of information about the massacres—and the contradictory testimony of the last foreigners present in liberated Phnom Penh make a precise evaluation impossible.[245] But the consistency of refugee stories in Thailand and Vietnam and the testimony from socialist sources leaves no doubt: the number of deaths has been terribly high.

On the necessity for the evacuation of Phnom Penh and the question whether the executions were a result of deliberate policy or local initiative, Chanda comments that opinions vary and takes no explicit stand himself (*Le Monde diplomatique*), though he suggests a point of view not unlike Kiernan's. Chanda quotes a diplomat who spent four years in Cambodia until the Khmer Rouge victory and who attributes the massacres in part to the bitterness of the war and in part to "the action of the have-nots against the haves." Chanda adds that the 1970-1975 war "was probably the most savage in Indochina, with soldiers of both sides giving no quarter" (*FEER*):

> To the thirst for vengeance must probably be added the relative numerical weakness, political inexperience, and lack of organization of the Khmer Rouge, who suddenly became the rulers of a land ravaged by the war. In the absence of political work and a clandestine organization among the population controlled by Lon Nol, force more than persuasion was naturally used as the method of government. Suspicion, indeed profound hatred on the part of the Khmer soldiers—young peasants many of whom had lost their homes and families under the bombs—towards an urban population that was richer and more numerous also seems to have played a role (*Le Monde Diplomatique*).

Fear of sabotage was also an element.[246] "The elimination of the former regime's officials and the dispersal into the countryside of the educated urban middle class has created a vertical power structure," with a "tiny group of French-educated elite...at the top dictating policy, while young and often illiterate farm boys—the grassroots cadres—are expected to implement the decisions. It is hardly surprising that these cadres rely on disciplinary action rather than persuasion or ideological motivation."[247]

As for the postwar dead, who are listed simply as Khmer Rouge victims in the mainstream Western media, Chanda comments that disease was an extremely serious problem during the war (including a million suffering from malaria in 1972) and that the massive U.S. rice shipments which were the sole sustenance of the cities swollen with refugees did not suffice even then for more than a part of the population. He cites a source close to the U.S. government who predicted a million deaths from starvation in Cambodia in the event of a Khmer Rouge victory—approximately the number of deaths later reported by Ponchaud and many others on the basis of alleged estimates from U.S. government and other Western sources.[248] Recall that these numbers, often inflated by imaginative reporters and congressmen, are consistently attributed to the barbarism of the Khmer Rouge, who allegedly "boast" about these deaths.

Chanda quotes one observer who says: "If you consider the sheer magnitude of the problem faced by the Khmer Rouge in April 1975 and the dire prediction from Washington that 1 million Cambodians could die of starvation, this is no mean achievement."[249] He also describes the economic and development programs undertaken by the new regime and the beginnings of trade and foreign contacts,[250] the obsessive self-reliance and the conversion of the country into a labor army. His own view is evidently along the lines indicated by an observer whom he quotes: "They might have read a lot of Marx, Lenin, and Mao, but the ideology of the present leadership is virulent Khmer nationalism" (*FEER*).

In commenting on the contradictory testimony of the last foreigners to leave Phnom Penh, Chanda cited a letter by W. J. Sampson,[251] an economist and statistician in Phnom Penh who is the author of a number of technical reports on the Cambodian economy and who worked in close contact with the government's central statistics office until March 1975, and was thus well-placed to comment on events of the period. Both the contents and the subsequent history of this communication are interesting. Sampson cites a UN estimate that the population of Cambodia in mid-1974 was 7.89 million, which agrees with his independent estimate.[252] He further believes that the figures offered of war casualties are much inflated, estimating civilian killings at "perhaps in tens of thousands." Turning to the postwar situation, Sampson finds the figure of 2.2 million dead mentioned in the press "questionable."[253] After leaving Cambodia, he writes, he visited refugee camps and kept in touch with Khmers. "A European friend who cycled around Phnom Penh for many days after its fall saw and heard of no other executions" beyond the shooting of some prominent politicians and "the lynching of hated bomber pilots in Phnom Penh." As far as he could determine, refugees offered no first-hand evidence of elimination of collaborators. He believes that "such executions could be numbered in the hundreds or thousands rather than in hundreds of thousands," though in addition there was "a big death toll from sickness" and there were food shortages.

This communication, from what seems a credible source, appeared just at the time that the Barron-Paul book and Lacouture's review of Ponchaud were causing a great sensation in the media about the murder of 1-2 million Cambodians by the Khmer Rouge. The letter was specifically brought to the attention of journalists who cited Lacouture's statement that the Khmer Rouge had "boasted" of having killed a quarter of the population: 2 million people.[254] With one exception they were unwilling to cite it.[255] Porter mentioned Sampson's letter in congressional testimony when challenged by Rep. Solarz on his skepticism about the *Famiglia Cristiana* "interview."[256] Solarz dismissed this by saying: "So, for all you know, this fellow could be a psychotic, right?" No such question was raised about unknown priests or reporters who circulated faked photographs and interviews from such sources as *Famiglia Cristiana,* or who drew conclusions from interviews with prisoners in Thai police cages.

Solarz's question and Porter's correct response ("theoretically, yes") were cited by William Shawcross in a context that is even more remarkable than his willingness to cite this disreputable insinuation.[257] Shawcross argues that both sides of the "propaganda battle" have failed to examine their evidence carefully. The two sides are Barron-Paul, condemning the new Cambodian regime, and Hildebrand-Porter, defending it (the latter book, he writes, is "in some ways...a mirror image" of Barron-Paul). In this context, he alleges that "Hildebrand and Porter's use of evidence can be seriously questioned." As his sole evidence to substantiate this charge he offers the fact that Porter cited the Sampson letter, with its estimate of casualties, as "documentation" in the Congressional hearings when asked why he was skeptical about charges leveled at postwar Cambodia. But, Shawcross continues, "Porter had to agree with Congressman Solarz that Sampson could in theory be 'a psychotic.'" Shawcross then reports that he spoke to Sampson by telephone to inquire into his views. He quotes Sampson as having "said that altogether 'deaths over and above the normal death rate would not be more than half a million.'" Shawcross interprets this as an estimate of victims of the Khmer Rouge, concluding: "Mr. Sampson thus seems an unconvinced and unconvincing witness on behalf of Khmer Rouge moderation. Neither side of the propaganda battle has carefully examined all of the sources that it wishes to exploit."

Note carefully the reasoning. First, whatever Porter might

have said in the May 1977 Hearings, it can hardly be offered in support of the charge that "Hildebrand and Porter's use of evidence can be seriously questioned" in their 1976 book (worse still, as the sole support for this charge). Sampson's letter was published subsequent to the book and obviously not mentioned in it. Secondly, Sampson's letter is, most definitely, "documentation," however one chooses to evaluate it. Furthermore, Shawcross does not question that Porter quoted it quite accurately and appropriately. As for Porter's being compelled to agree that Sampson could in theory be a psychotic, Shawcross's willingness to cite Solarz's absurd question is remarkable; Porter would—or should—have responded in the same way if asked whether Ponchaud, or Shawcross, or the authors of this book, etc., might be psychotics: "Theoretically, yes." Furthermore, consider Shawcross's inquiry concerning Sampson's views. He argues that since Sampson has allegedly changed his mind in a telephone call subsequent to Porter's correct citation of his views, that shows that Hildebrand and Porter's book (which makes no mention of Sampson) is unscholarly and that their "use of evidence can be seriously questioned." The logic is mindboggling.

But putting logic to the side, did Sampson in fact change his views, thus showing himself to be an "unconvinced and unconvincing witness?" The answer to the question depends on how we interpret the telephone statement by Sampson that Shawcross quotes. Given Sampson's known views on the general tendency to inflate figures, it might be supposed that his figure of deaths altogether above the normal is a reference to the total number of deaths throughout the war and the postwar period. In fact, in response to a query, Sampson stated quite explicitly in a letter dated March 6, 1978 that this was exactly his intent.[258] This letter was immediately transmitted to Porter, Shawcross and the editor of the *New York Review*. Aware of these facts, Porter in response to Shawcross wrote correctly that Sampson had intended to refer to all deaths—wartime and afterwards—when citing the half-million figure.[259] Equally aware of the facts, Shawcross responded by repeating his claim that Sampson had offered the figure for deaths "since the end of the war." This is, surely, a rather curious "use of evidence."

There is much more evidence from sources that seem to deserve a hearing but have been ignored by the media. We have noted the selectivity in choice of refugee reports. We will mention two additional examples of eyewitness reports that were available to the media, in addition to those already cited, but that they chose to disregard. Liberation News Service (New York) carried a dispatch from George Hildebrand (one of the co-authors of the Hildebrand-Porter study) reporting an interview with "one of the few people in the U.S. today who can speak from direct experience," namely, a Cambodian refugee named Khoun Sakhon who "spent the better part of a year traveling through Cambodia's populous central provinces and working in a number of rural areas in the developing western region of Cambodia," after having lived both in Phnom Penh and in liberated zones in earlier years. He also witnessed the evacuation of Phnom Penh in April, 1975.[260] Sakhon "saw no massacres or abandonment of sick and elderly people" during the evacuation of Phnom Penh and claims that what the *Reader's Digest* described as "looting" was in fact "the soldiers' opening luxury shops and rice stores to the people."[261] He states further that during the evacuation, "trucks distributed rice and medicine to the people and the people were free to join the cooperatives they passed or to move on." He lived in a commune, with, he claims, an 8-hour work schedule, adequate food and medical services, and generally fair treatment. His account of the "revolutionary culture" and the conditions of life and work is generally favorable, and he expresses regret that he joined a group of urban young men who escaped, saying: "I don't know what I'm doing here. I feel I belong back there." A press concerned to determine the facts about postwar Cambodia might have chosen to explore this lead.

Another example that would appear to merit attention is a lengthy and detailed account of the evacuation of Phnom Penh by Chou Meng and Shane Tarr.[262] The forced evacuation of Phnom Penh has served as proof of the near-genocidal intent and practice of the Khmer Rouge ever since it was graphically reported by journalists at the time.[263] It is featured in the books by Barron-Paul and Ponchaud and by many others. According to these accounts, based on refugee reports and what journalists observed largely from their confinement in the French embassy in Phnom Penh, the evacuation was a hideous atrocity. Hildebrand and Porter cite eyewitness accounts by Westerners that paint a different picture, but their book has been ignored, along with the published sources they cite. The account by the Tarrs, which is the only published account by participants that provides substantial detail, to our knowledge, tends to corroborate the sources cited by Hildebrand-Porter. Shane Tarr is from New Zealand; his wife, Chou Meng, is Cambodian. Both joined the mass evacuation to the countryside on April 18, returned to Phnom Penh on April 21, and then travelled through the countryside with the convoy of journalists and others on their way to Thailand. They write that they attempted to contact the media on their return to New Zealand to present their story, "but generally speaking news editors were not interested in hearing what we had to say unless we denounced communism in general and 'painted a picture' of Khmer Rouge atrocities in particular." Several articles of theirs nevertheless appeared, but apart from the left wing press, all were "heavily censored so as to make our articles unintelligible and contradictory," they allege.

The Tarrs claim that people were told that they would have to leave Phnom Penh because there was insufficient food. "Refugees we talked to were happy at the prospect of returning to their homes" though "city-dwellers were far less enthusiastic," at least those who had some food (the very poor were "quick to leave ..."). The initial orders were polite; subsequently they "became more like demands than requests," though they saw no sign of force. After comparing notes with other evacuees, they conclude "that force was used only on isolated occasions." They report that prior to liberation, they had visited the hospitals and found that only one (Calmette) was functioning properly, and that "the revolutionary forces continued to operate it after they took over" though most of the medical personnel had fled.[264] They believe that patients were evacuated to "more hygienic surroundings," a belief that cannot be dismissed out of hand in the light of the eyewitness account by Swain and others. They continue with a virtually hour-by-hour account of their trip to the countryside with the evacuees, then back to Phnom Penh where they joined other foreigners at the French embassy. They report many friendly contacts with villagers, refugees, cadres, and soldiers and say that they "witnessed no executions or other atrocities, and saw no attempts to intimidate people with weapons."

On their return to the French embassy on April 21, the Tarrs report, they were questioned for several hours by journalists who had been there since the 17th of April. "But when it became clear that we had no sensational stories to tell of mass executions, rape, pillage and suicides many of these journalists became quite disappointed." Specifically, they contend that Sydney Schanberg of the *New York Times* (who later won the Pulitzer Prize for his report of these days) dismissed their positive account with sarcasm; it did not enter his subsequent reports, including a long story (9 May 1975) on foreigners at the French embassy. With a few exceptions, the Tarrs report, "for most of the time we spent in the French embassy we were the object of abuse and fear by those who had nothing but contempt for the

Kampuchean people."

Although Schanberg does not mention the Tarrs or their experiences during their participation in the evacuation, Swain does refer to them. He writes that Shane Tarr is so contemptible that "we—who have abandoned our Cambodian friends—do not wish to pass the time of day" with him. "He is full of nauseating revolutionary rhetoric" and he and his wife "fraternise with the Khmer Rouge guards over the walls." Shane Tarr "has a low opinion of us members of the capitalist press, we of his hypocrisy. He is shunned." Swain also apparently has a low opinion of the experiences of the Tarrs during the evacuation; these are never mentioned. We will see in a moment how "scholarship" deals with the account by the Tarrs.

The Tarrs then describe their evacuation to Thailand. They describe the tremendous destruction in the countryside and conversations with villagers. They claim to have seen no signs of coercion, but rather people working "according to their capabilities and the needs of the group."

We quote their conclusions:

> From our observations and understanding of the events of Kampuchea from 17th April, when we evacuated Phnom Penh, to our arrival in Poipet on 3rd of May, we can make the following points:
>
> 1. We saw no organised executions, massacres, or the results of such like. We saw about fifteen bodies in Phnom Penh, of soldiers killed in the fighting.
>
> 2. There was very little intimidation of Phnom Penh's population by the revolutionary army. Many saw it not as an occupier but as a liberator.
>
> 3. We can refute the claims of the imperialist media that the liberation army indulged in a mass orgy of looting and destruction.
>
> 4. The march to the countryside was slow and well organised. People who had no relatives to stay with were put up by other villagers in the liberated areas, until they were assigned elsewhere. They were provided with food.

5. The aged and the ill were not expected to join in the march. We saw very few who were old or sick on the road; those that we met elsewhere told us that the revolutionary organisation catered for their needs.

We saw the destruction of five years of war and of intense U.S. bombing. But we also saw dams, irrigation canals, rice paddies, and people who, while having to struggle very hard, were proud to have liberated Kampuchea from imperialism and were now the masters of their destiny.

Again, we may ask why the eyewitness report of Chou Meng and Shane Tarr does not enter the record, as shaped by the selective hand of the media and mainstream scholarship?

The question deserves a closer look. The account by the Tarrs of their evacuation in the convoy from the French embassy to Thailand is not unique; many reporters were present and wrote extensively about this trip. But their account of their participation in the earlier evacuation from Phnom Penh is indeed unusual. As we have seen, journalists simply ignored it, though at the time this was virtually the only direct evidence concerning what was happening beyond the view from the embassy. There is also apparently a conflict of opinion—represented by the Tarrs on the one hand and Swain and Schanberg on the other—about the situation inside the embassy where foreigners and some Cambodians were confined. The Tarrs are, incidentally, not alone in their view. Richard Boyle of Pacific News Service is a correspondent with considerable experience in Vietnam, and author of an important but unread book.[265] On reaching Thailand he filed a report from Bangkok published in the New York *Guardian* that did not appear in the mainstream press in the United States, to our knowledge. Boyle reports that he was asked by AP to take over their bureau and file for them as well as PNS after the U.S. departure:

> I reported what the Cambodian staff reported to me: that the "Khmer Rouge" troops told Phnom Penh government soldiers that they were "brothers" and that they did not want to kill

them. There were eyewitness accounts by Cambodian AP staffers of "Khmer Rouge" and Phnom Penh troops embracing on the battlefield, yet when I filed this it was censored by AP. After that the story was killed. AP reported that the liberators burned down refugee huts two days before the fall of Phnom Penh, yet the Cambodian AP staffers who visited the front all day could not confirm the report.[266]

Boyle states that "stories of a bloodbath, as reported by other news agencies, cannot be verified and there is every indication that the accounts are lies." He cites as an example an AP report "that French women were raped and brutalized," though he asserts that French doctors and nurses "never saw any rape victims."[267] He also says that French mercenaries and Americans with CIA and DIA connections were permitted to take refuge in the embassy and to leave in safety, though they were regarded by the Khmer Rouge as war criminals. One of them, Douglas Sapper, a former Green Beret, "publicly boasted he was planning to take a Swedish submachine gun...and raise the American flag at the U.S. embassy killing as many 'commies as I can.'" Yet he "was one of the first Americans to seek refuge in the embassy" and was permitted to leave, along with other journalists rumored to be working with intelligence, though the Khmer Rouge knew of these threats (Schanberg refers fondly to Sapper as one of those who "performed constructive roles" in the embassy; Barron and Paul cite him simply as an "American businessman"). Boyle questions the atrocity reports and gives a positive account of the occupation and evacuation, adding that the French prevented fraternization with Khmer Rouge troops who wanted to visit journalists. His account of the situation in Phnom Penh and within the embassy is similar to that of the Tarrs.

Returning to the theory of the Free Press, we see that there are conflicting reports of all these events. Swain and Schanberg present their view in the London *Sunday Times* and *New York Times*; the Tarrs and Boyle give their conflicting account in *News from Kampuchea* (international circulation 500) and the left wing New York *Guardian*, also with a tiny reading public. The detailed participant account by the Tarrs of the actual evacuation from Phnom Penh as they perceived it, which is quite unique, is not so much as mentioned in the mass media; their reports appeared without distortion, they claim, only in tiny left wing journals in New Zealand. Boyle reports that AP refused to publish his stories when he had taken over their bureau, choosing instead accounts of atrocities that neither he, nor French doctors or nurses, nor Cambodian AP staffers could verify. But there is no censorship in the Free Press, such as we find in totalitarian states.

We are aware of only one reference to the report by the Tarrs in the mainstream media in the West. It is worth reviewing as an indication of how academic scholarship deals with evidence that departs from the prevailing line. The well-known Cambodia specialist Michael Leifer reviewed Barron-Paul in the *Times Literary Supplement*.[268] In a letter commenting on this review,[269] Torben Retbøll noted that Leifer "seems to accept, somewhat uncritically, the charges put forward in the book" despite serious questions about its accuracy and selective treatment of available data— questions that are quite pertinent, as we shall see. Specifically, Retbøll cited eyewitness reports that question the Barron-Paul account of the evacuation of Phnom Phenh, including that of the Tarrs. Leifer responded rather haughtily that by "eyewitness" Retbøll "presumably...means foreigners who sheltered in the compound of the French embassy. He does not confirm whether any of these so-called eyewitnesses had actual experience of participation" in the evacuation.[270] Evidently, Leifer was unaware of the fact that the account by the Tarrs—published six months earlier— made quite explicit that they were direct participants in the evacuation prior to being sheltered in the embassy on their return to Phnom Penh. Retbøll then reported the Tarrs' account correctly, quoting the conclusions just given, in a letter which furthermore gave the citation to their report in *News from Kampuchea*.[271] In response, Leifer asks whether Retbøll "is aware of the fact that Tarr and his wife were among those confined to the compound of the French embassy in Phnom Penh"—which of course he was, though the relevant point is that prior to this they participated in the evacuation. Leifer then cites Swain's account of how the Tarrs were evacuated from the embassy concluding that "on the basis of this experience, it would seem impossible for the Tarrs to have compiled a report at first hand." He says that "at one stage, there was every prospect that Mrs Tarr would be separated from her husband because of her nationality and dispatched out of the capital on foot," but "the weeping couple" were smuggled on board a convoy by a French diplomat (citing Swain).[272] Nowhere does Leifer mention the fact that the Tarrs participated in the evacuation on foot before they returned to Phnom Penh and the French embassy from which they were evacuated, and had published a detailed report of this experience. Leifer's first letter indicates that he was simply unaware of their account. His second letter cannot be explained on this basis; rather, it reveals that he was simply unwilling to look into it, preferring to insinuate that their detailed story must have been invented out of whole cloth, evidently in complete ignorance of what they had reported. At this point he knew exactly where their account appeared. A striking example of careful and dispassionate scholarship. Retbøll's response correcting the factual record was not published.

In citing Swain's contemptuous account of the Tarrs and the alleged circumstances of their evacuation, Leifer simply presents it as fact, never mentioning that their own account differs radically. Typically, an insulting account of the Tarrs reaches a mass audience, while their own version of events in which they were involved—including their participation in the evacuation and their relations to journalists—is not permitted to enter the public record. In this case scholarship surpasses journalism in deceit. The journalists simply did not refer to the Tarrs' experiences, while condemning them for their "nauseating revolutionary rhetoric" and contemptible efforts to fraternize with the Khmer Rouge. The Cambodia scholar goes a step further, pretending that their account does not exist even when he knows precisely where it is to be found.[273]

To complete the story, we turn finally to the major sources of information that have reached the general public, the books by Barron-Paul and Ponchaud.

As already noted, the Barron-Paul book and their earlier *Reader's Digest* article have reached tens of millions of readers in the United States and abroad and are undoubtedly the major source of information for the general public. They have also been widely and generally quite favorably reviewed and have been the subject of extensive comment apart from reviews, also to a mass audience, ranging from a front-page horror story in the *Wall Street Journal* to an article in *TV Guide*[274] (circulation more then 19 million) by Ernest Lefever, a foreign policy specialist who is otherwise known for his argument before congress that we should be more tolerant of the "mistakes" of the Chilean junta "in attempting to clear away the devastation of the Allende period" and his discovery of the "remarkable freedom of expression" enjoyed by critics of the military regime.[275] The book has been described as "impeccably-documented"[276]; the authors "deserve substantial credit, however, for the exhaustiveness and meticulousness of their research."[277] The London *Economist* wrote that "the methods and documentation" of the authors "will convince any save the most dedicated sceptics that at least 1m people have died since the fall of Cambodia as a direct result of the excesses of the *Angka Loeu*"; "It may be the best book there ever will be" on this subject.[278] In the United States, the press response in editorials and commentary was also substantial and largely unquestioning.[279]

Not all reviewers have been completely uncritical.[280] Martin

Woollacott noted that the estimates of dead are "guesswork" and that their sample of refugees "is disproportionately drawn from the middle-class and the north-west of the country."[281] William Shawcross commented that their figure of dead "is that of the Carter Administration."[282] Elizabeth Becker objects that they "pepper their book with facile polemics," turning it "into a Cold War propaganda piece."[283] A number of reviewers have remarked on their infantile discussion of Khieu Samphan's alleged impotence and its significance as well as their failure to refer to the U.S. role; when they speak of "the murder of a gentle land," they are not referring to B-52 attacks on villages or the systematic bombing and murderous ground sweeps by U.S. troops or forces organized and supplied by the United States, in a land that had been largely removed from the Indochina conflict prior to the U.S. attack. But in general, their conclusions have been taken as overwhelmingly persuasive, if not definitive.

To evaluate the Barron-Paul account in a serious way, one must first consider its credibility where verifiable. Their case is largely built, as it must be, on refugee accounts. How much faith we place in their rendition of these accounts and the conclusions they draw from the samples they present will be determined by their credibility where what they say is subject to check. We stress again the importance of avoiding a gross but common error of reasoning: since the refugee accounts far outweigh in significance the supporting documentation, one might erroneously conclude that even if the latter collapses the main charges remain intact. The error is transparent; it is only the independently verifiable material that gives some indication of the trustworthiness of their account of what they claim to have heard and found.

We have already seen several examples of their exhaustive, meticulous, and impeccable scholarship, including their reliance on the *Famiglia Cristiana* "interview" and their uncritical handling of the edict allegedly put forth by a Khmer Rouge commander; they are not, of course, to be faulted for the fact that their source, Ponchaud, has since modified and then silently withdrawn this "quote," though for the reasons we reviewed, there was ample reason for skepticism about this and other sources that they cite—quite selectively, as we shall see, as fits their purposes. We have also mentioned their method of finding "promising" subjects under the "guidance" of Thai ministry officials and "elected" camp commanders, a critical admission as to methodology that should have at once alerted reviewers and commentators that this study is hardly to be taken too seriously.

In fact, this reliance—whether naive or cynical—on the guidance of Thai authorities is typical of their research. In his preface, Barron reviews the "diverse sources" that "all" assured him that "the communist conquerors of Cambodia had...put virtually everybody to work tilling the soil under deathly conditions." These "diverse sources" are, *in toto*: specialists at the State and Defense Departments, the National Security Council, and three unnamed foreign embassies in Washington.[284] The Acknowledgements supplement these remarkably diverse sources as follows: a representative of the Thai Ministry of the Interior, whose "knowledge and advice additionally provided us with invaluable guidance"; Cambodian specialists in the U.S. Department of State, the National Security Council, and the U.S. Army General Staff, who "made available large quantities of their own data, guided us to other sources, answered innumerable questions and favored us with authoritative criticism"; and Ponchaud, who "put at our disposal his immense store of knowledge about Cambodia, generously shared with us the results of his own research, saved us from errors through scholarly criticism[285] and on several occasions assisted Ursula Naccache as an interpreter in the conduct of important interviews."[286] Can one imagine a researcher limiting himself to comparable sources on the other side of the fence for a critical study of U.S. imperial violence, then to be lauded for his meticulous and exhaustive scholarship? The same concept of "diverse sources" also sets the limits of their "impeccable documentation," to which we return.

No less remarkable than their search for "promising" interviewees and their concept of "diverse sources" is the short shrift they give to pre-1975 Cambodia. They explain that they "have referred to [events prior to April 17, 1975] only to the extent we thought such references were necessary to an understanding of what has transpired since then,"[287] reasonable enough until we see what they omit as unnecessary to such understanding. The U.S. role, for example—surely known to them if they read the journalistic sources they cite and hardly a great secret to readers of the daily press—is off the agenda as irrelevant to subsequent events.[288] Also unnecessary to the understanding of postwar Cambodia in their view are such minor matters as the backgrounds of the revolutionary movement in peasant society and social conflict. That a study of postwar Cambodia resting on such a historical vacuum can be regarded as an outstanding work of scholarship or even a useful study of current Cambodia is remarkable indeed. The framework that they set reveals with crystal clarity that their story, where unverifiable, is to be taken about as seriously as an account of the U.S. war in Vietnam produced by the World Peace Council. Correspondingly, it is treated as seriously by the Free Press as WPC studies are on the other side of the Iron Curtain.

There is, of course, method in the Barron-Paul research methodology; it is not as stupid as it looks at first glance. If Cambodian history, internal social conflict, the nature of peasant society, French colonialism, and U.S. intervention are all excluded by fiat as unnecessary for the understanding of what has transpired since April 1975, then the stage is fully set to blame everything on the evil Communist leaders: revenge killings, disease, starvation, overwork, unexploded ordnance, the B-52 craters that have "churned up...the entire countryside" (Swain), everything. Given their framework, we hardly need inquire into the details to predict the conclusions that these scholars will reach. All deaths in Cambodia in the postwar period, all penury and suffering and strife, will necessarily be attributed to the sole factor that is not eliminated from consideration *a priori*: the Khmer Rouge leadership. And of course that is exactly what the authors conclude. The absurdity of this procedure apparently has not been perceived by the many commentators who take this transparent propaganda exercise seriously.

The methodology for estimating postwar deaths, which has so impressed the editors of the London *Economist* and other ideologists, is hardly more than a joke; one does not have to be a "dedicated sceptic" to question their basis for concluding that "at least 1m people have died since the fall of Cambodia *as a direct result of the excesses of the Angka Loeu*" (our emphasis); mere rationality suffices, since all other factors were eliminated as irrelevant. What of the numbers? These are determined on the basis of such notable sources as Khieu Samphan's alleged admission that "roughly a million Cambodians died,"[289] and beyond that, estimates offered with no stated basis by various named and unnamed "Western observers," various guesses based on no cited evidence about the proportion of "educated people" massacred, other guesses about deaths from starvation and disease, and so on.[290]

By such routes Barron and Paul concoct their estimate that "at the very minimum, more than 1,200,000 men, women, and children died in Cambodia between April 17, 1975, and January 1, 1977, *as a consequence of the actions of Angka Loeu.*"[291] The breakdown of numbers includes "100,000 or more in massacres and by execution" and most of the rest—roughly a million—from disease and starvation.[292]

The "dedicated sceptic" might, at this point, raise eyebrows over the fact that 1.2 million is the figure allegedly produced by the U.S. embassy in Bangkok, since repeated widely in the press.[293] And the figure of a million deaths from disease and starvation happens to correspond to the prediction by U.S. government sources of the numbers who would starve to death after the Khmer Rouge victory, as we have seen[294]—an estimate based on an assessment of the ravages of the war, specifically, the destruction of the economy by the United States.

Very little in the Barron-Paul book is subject to possible verification. Therefore an assessment of the credibility of their primary evidence (refugee reports) rests very largely on the accuracy of their brief historical remarks. Several reviewers have commented on the striking inadequacies of these remarks, failing to draw the obvious conclusion, however: if what can be checked turns out to be false or misleading, what are we to conclude about claims that are subject to no verification? Turning to their version of history, we find the standard clichés about this "once happy country" now devastated by Khmer Rouge atrocities, the "faithful, kindly believers in Theravada Buddhism" who produced annual rice surpluses in the plentiful land "without overly exerting themselves," the "Phnom Penh residents, who had been known for their spontaneity and gaiety, their uninhibited curiosity and friendliness," etc.[295]; compare the accounts of peasant life, the exploitative existence of the Phnom Penh elite, and the history of violence in Cambodia mentioned earlier, which pass here without notice. Barron and Paul, unlike every serious commentator, make no effort to find out what lies behind the "Khmer smile," and they do not seem intrigued by the fact that the very reporters they cite speak of the surprise of urban residents when dark-skinned country boys in traditional garb looking like creatures from another planet entered Phnom Penh in April, 1975.

Turning to the Khmer Rouge, Barron and Paul claim that

"there is no evidence that the communists ever enjoyed the voluntary support of more than a small minority of Cambodians, in either the countryside or the cities" (a standard propaganda cliché of the Vietnam War applied to the NLF, although known to be false by official experts).[296] Rather, the Khmer Rouge programs "alienated the peasantry affected" so that families "fled to the cities" in a "mass migration"—not from the U.S. bombing but rather from Khmer Rouge cruelty. Their "mute and phlegmatic" soldiers include children "impressed into the revolutionary army at age ten or eleven when the communists had overrun their villages."[297] On the assumption that these remarks accurately characterize the Khmer Rouge relation to the peasantry, the "difficult question" of how they now maintain control becomes an imponderable mystery, not to speak of their rise from a tiny movement to a substantial army under the most horrendous conditions and their success in defeating the Lon Nol army backed by massive U.S. force. But no such problems trouble these thinkers. The Khmer Rouge succeeded by skillful propaganda, exploiting the U.S. "limited incursion" and the B-52 raids directed against the North Vietnamese and Vietcong sanctuaries.[298] The Khmer Rouge, they explain,

> had new opportunities. To escape the spreading fighting, people started swarming from the countryside into the cities, spawning economic and social problems for the Lon Nol government. The American intervention and B-52 raids (the latter continued until August 1973) enabled the communists somewhat more convincingly to depict the North Vietnamese as "our teachers,"[299] the United States as the "imperialist aggressor" and the Lon Nol government as "a lackey of the imperialists." The *Far Eastern Economic Review* observed: "From being widely regarded as the dogmatic disciples of a Marxist ideology alien to Khmer national traditions and culture, the Khmer Rouge became patriots."[300]

After their "conjecture" that the awful fate visited upon postwar Cambodia results from the "chronic impotence" of Khieu Samphan, Barron and Paul add the following explanation of the success of the Khmer Rouge despite their terrorizing the country-side:

> But what is in doubt is not so important as what is certain. Khieu Samphan and a few kindred people, who neither by achievements nor by ideas had ever attracted any substantial following, absconded into the jungles, assumed leadership of an insignificant, ineffectual little guerrilla force, captured control of a political coalition and through it absolute control of an entire society.[301]

Sheer magic.[302]

The "impeccable documentation" in this major work omits the many published sources that explain how the Khmer Rouge were recruited by the U.S. bombardment of the civilian society, a factor that the authors would have us believe is as irrelevant to an understanding of postwar Cambodian history as the actual situation in the countryside or the history of internal conflict.[303]

Apart from their historical comments, there is a possibility of independent verification of Barron-Paul's evidence only in the case of the occupation of Phnom Penh, when many reporters were present at first in the city itself and later confined in the French embassy. We will therefore consider perhaps the most striking claim that they put forth from this period.

Barron and Paul claim that there was a major bloodbath. In Phnom Penh, they assert, some people saw "summary executions" and

> virtually everybody saw the consequences of them in the form of corpses of men, women and children rapidly bloating and rotting in the hot sun. The bodies, sometimes grotesquely contorted in agony, yielded a nauseating, pervasive stench, and they had a transfiguring effect on the hundreds of thousands of people being exiled...[turning them into]...a silent, cowed herd...[304]

Evidently, something so dramatic would be hard to miss, so one would indeed expect "virtually everybody" to have seen it.[305]

Their supporting documentation falls into the two familiar categories: (1) a list of names of Cambodians; (2) verifiable documentation, namely: "*Sunday Times* (London), May 8, 1975; *Mirror* (London), May 9, 1975, AP dispatch from Bangkok, May 8, 1975."[306] Turning to the verifiable documentation, consider first the *Sunday Times*, May 8. There is no such document. Presumably, they are referring to Jon Swain's report in the *Sunday Times*, May 11. Assuming so, we turn to Swain's account. There is no doubt of his fury over the "enormity and horror" of what he describes in gory detail, but he seems to have missed the consequences of summary executions described so eloquently by Barron and Paul as he was walking through Phnom Penh or observing from the embassy. He does not report having seen any signs of summary executions. He does transmit stories he heard about killings by soldiers, but that is all.

One of these stories is cited by Barron-Paul, with a little embellishment, as an example of a "summary execution." Swain presents it as follows:

> A newly-arrived French teacher says that at 8:30 this morning he was on his way to the embassy when a Khmer Rouge patrol ran out of an alley and cut a line of refugees in half, splitting a family. When the parents protested the leader raised his rifle and shot them in the chest.

This second-hand report, if correct,[307] would serve as a second-hand example of a "summary execution" under a broad interpretation of this concept, but provides no support for the far more dramatic claim that virtually everybody saw the consequences that Barron and Paul so vividly describe. Furthermore, this example does not support the major thrust of their argument, that the "summary executions," here and elsewhere, were commanded from on high as part of a systematic policy of genocide, perhaps a consequence of Khieu Samphan's "chronic impotence." Rather, it appears to be a case of a murderous act by soldiers of a conquering army, horrifying no doubt, but unfortunately all too common—for example, the "robbery and murder" committed by U.S. troops occupying Japan or their participation in mass murder of members of the anti-Japanese resistance in the Philippines, to take a case where the armed forces in question and the society from which they were recruited had not suffered anything remotely like the savagery that the Khmer Rouge had endured.[308]

Actually, Swain does discuss the matter of bloodbaths, though Barron and Paul do not refer to these remarks. Commenting on the assurance by U.S. diplomats "that the revenge would be dreadful when the Khmer Rouge came," he writes:

> I can only say that what I have heard and seen provides no proof of a bloodbath (and I would question the reliability of reports of mass executions that almost from the start have circulated outside Cambodia)...What has taken place, though equally horrific, is something different in kind. My overriding impression—reinforced as we journeyed through the countryside en route to the Thai border—was that the Khmer Rouge military authorities had ordered this mass evacuation not to *punish* the people but to *revolutionise* their ways and thoughts. Many thousands will no doubt die. But whatever else, this does not constitute a deliberate campaign of terror, rather it points to poor organisation, lack of vision and the brutalisation of a people by a long and savage war.

In this connection, Swain has something to say about a bloodbath that escaped the attention of Barron and Paul completely:

> The United States has much to answer for here, not only in terms of human lives and massive material destruction; the rigidity and nastiness of the un-Cambodian like fellows in black who run this country now,[309] or what is left of it, are as much a product of this wholesale American bombing which has hardened and honed their minds as they are a product of Marx

and Mao...The war damage here, as everywhere else we saw, is total. Not a bridge is standing, hardly a house. I am told most villagers have spent the war years living semi-permanently underground in earth bunkers to escape the bombing. Little wonder that this peasant army is proud of its achievements... The entire countryside has been churned up by American B-52 bomb craters, whole towns and villages razed. So far I have not seen one intact pagoda.[310]

His final thoughts are also perhaps worth quoting:

In the last five years, Cambodia has lost upwards of half a million people, 10 per cent of its population, in a war fueled and waged on its soil by outside powers for their own selfish reasons. The people who run, live in and try to reconstruct the heap of ruins they have inherited in Cambodia today deserve the world's compassion and understanding. It is their country and it was their sacrifices. They have earned themselves the right to organise their society their own way.

In brief, Barron and Paul are careful not to cite Swain for what he does actually say, though it is highly relevant to their alleged concerns.[311] Furthermore, this source lends no support to their claim that "virtually everybody" saw the hideous consequences of summary executions, or that the "summary executions" were a matter of government policy.

Perhaps we will do better with Barron and Paul's second source: "*Mirror* (London), May 9, 1975, AP dispatch from Bangkok, May 8, 1975." The *Daily Mirror*, May 9, contains no AP dispatch (this journal contains little international news). There is, however, a report by an unidentified *Mirror* reporter, nestled amidst such items as "My secret agony, by girl's mum," and "Men's Lib at the Altar." This story is based on reports by evacuees from the French embassy and refugees. The reporter does not seem to have been in Cambodia, so he could not have witnessed the scene described by Barron-Paul. Nor did the people he interviewed. But he does have this to say: "The refugees heard reports of wholesale executions of Cambodians. But they never saw any themselves."

So much for the second bit of impeccable documentation. Perhaps Barron and Paul, in the somewhat misleading citation quoted above, had in mind an AP dispatch from another source. There is, in fact, an AP dispatch from Bangkok (May 8, 1975) filed by Jean-Jacques Cazaux and Claude Juvenal on their arrival after evacuation from Cambodia.[312] They say nothing about executions in Phnom Penh and report that "not a single corpse was seen along our evacuation route, however."[313]

Perhaps there are other May 8 Bangkok AP reports relevant to the Barron-Paul claim quoted above,[314] but the sources they cite plainly are not. Rather, these sources either say nothing about a bloodbath that should have been hard to miss on their account, or express skepticism about bloodbath reports. There is no shred of evidence from this documentation in support of their claim about what "virtually everybody saw" or even in support of their general claim that the government was responsible for "summary executions." We are left with the unverifiable documentation: alleged interviews with Cambodians.

Other sources that Barron-Paul cite in a related context also do not bear out their claims about the signs of a bloodbath that virtually everybody saw. They cite Cazaux (AFP, Hong Kong, May 8, 1975) under the related heading "Transformation of Phnom Penh into a wasteland." We have been unable to locate this report and doubt that it exists, but there is an AFP report filed by Cazaux on May 8 from Bangkok, where he actually was. Here he says that there were rumors that 200 heads were lying in the marketplace and thousands of bodies rotting along Highway 5 leading north, "but latecomers to the embassy said that nothing of the kind [i.e., massacres] had taken place."[315] Similarly, Sydney Schanberg, whom they cite under "Evacuation of Phnom Penh," notes "unconfirmed reports of executions of senior military and civilian officials" and the prospect that many will die on the march to the countryside; "But none of this will apparently bear any resemblance to the mass executions that had been predicted by Westerners." He cites reports of executions, "but none were eyewitness accounts." He saw bodies on the road from Phnom Penh but says "it was difficult to tell if they were people who had succumbed to the hardships of the march or simply civilians and soldiers killed in the last battles."[316]

Still another lengthy account (which Barron-Paul do not cite) was given by Patrice de Beer of *Le Monde*.[317] De Beer urges caution with refugee or secret service reports ("how badly mistaken they were is only too well known"). He is skeptical about the reports of executions. "One instance cited is that of Oudong, which we went through on April 30, and where we saw nothing of the sort." He is also skeptical of monitored radio messages, "when you recall that the day after Phnom Penh fell a clandestine transmitter on the Thai border announced that a score of journalists had been killed by the Khmer Rouge, when in fact they were all alive." He describes "an unknown world" in the countryside, peaceful despite the devastation, turning to the task of reconstruction.

We hardly find here an "impeccably documented" account of how "virtually everybody" saw the horrendous scenes that Barron-Paul describe. In fact, their documentation reduces to category (1): unverifiable reports of alleged interviews with refugees.[318] The fact appears to be that virtually nobody whose reports can be checked, including sources that they are clearly aware of since they cite them in related contexts, saw the scenes that they describe.

The fact that their claim was undocumented was noted by Torben Retbøll in letters commenting on the reviews of the Barron-Paul book in the *Economist* and the *Far Eastern Economic Review*. Barron and Paul have each responded.[319] Each produces the obligatory insults ("one of the world's few remaining apologists for the Cambodian communists," etc.), with a touch of hysteria that stands in marked contrast to Retbøll's letters, which quietly point out errors in the book and express skepticism about its claims. We will not review their huffing-and-puffing in an effort to evade the issue, but the upshot is that the claim to which Retbøll referred, which we have just discussed, is not supported by the verifiable documentation that they cite. It is, furthermore, a fairly sensational claim, and one of the few that is subject to possible verification. Furthermore, even the second-hand story of an atrocity that they cite more or less accurately lends no support to their thesis about the "summary executions," as we have seen.

Perhaps this is enough to indicate that Barron and Paul's impeccable documentation and exhaustive and meticulous scholarship, which has so impressed reviewers, will not withstand scrutiny. The historical comments are worthless and their effort to document what might have been observed reduces to the testimony of refugees, that is, unverifiable testimony. They do offer what to the superficial reader may appear to be "documentation," but we discover on analysis that it is irrelevant or contrary to their claims, where it exists. Recall that this is apparently the best that could be achieved with the ample resources of the *Reader's Digest*. In the case of reporters of demonstrated integrity, reports of what refugees are alleged to have said must surely be taken seriously. In the present case, the very framework of analysis makes it clear that this is not a serious piece of work. At any point where their contribution can be evaluated, it is found seriously wanting if not entirely absurd. People who are willing to place their trust in what Barron and Paul report where no supporting documentation is available (i.e., essentially all the crucial cases) merely reveal that their preconceived bias overwhelms any critical judgment. Nevertheless, their work, both in the *Reader's Digest* with its mass international circulation and in this widely-reviewed and much-praised book, remains the major source of evidence on which the Western media and the general public have relied, a remarkable bit of evidence in support of the theory of the Free Press that we have been elaborating here.

Ponchaud's book, the second major source for Western audiences on postwar Indochina, is a more serious work and deserves more careful study and critical analysis. Before discussing it, a word about its reception and impact is in order. In fact, it is not quite accurate to say that Ponchaud's book itself has been a major source despite the numerous references to it: rather, the impact of this book has been through the medium of reviews and derivative commentary, primarily, a very influential review by Jean Lacouture, who has compiled an outstanding record as a historian and analyst of contemporary affairs in Vietnam and the Middle East, apart from other important work. The English translation of Lacouture's French review appeared shortly after the Barron-Paul *Reader's Digest* article, followed within a few months by their book and his corrections.[320] The already quite extensive press commentary on Cambodia, which had been denouncing the Cambodian horror chamber and Gulag since the war's end, reached a crescendo of outrage and indignation at this time—always coupled with an agonized plea to "break the silence" that could barely be heard above the din of protest. The congressional hearings of May and July followed immediately. This escalation of the already high level of protest was caused, no doubt, by this "one-two punch"; Barron-Paul for the masses in the *Reader's Digest,* and Lacouture for the intellectual elite in the *New York Review of Books.* To appreciate how unusual all this is, compare the reaction to benign and constructive bloodbaths, as in the case of Timor.

As we have already mentioned, it is rare—indeed, unprecedented—for a French book on Indochina to receive such rapid and wide notice in the English-speaking world. Lacouture's book on postwar Vietnam was neither translated nor, to our knowledge, ever mentioned in the press, though it was an eyewitness account based on long-demonstrated expertise; in contrast his version of a report by a hitherto unknown French priest concerning a country with which Lacouture had considerably less familiarity became a major literary and political event. Similarly, earlier French studies that give much insight into the developments that have led to the present situation in Cambodia have never been translated and were only mentioned far from the mainstream.[321] And postwar French publications that give a more positive view of the Khmer Rouge are unnoticed and untranslated.[322]

It would be difficult to argue that Ponchaud's book has been translated and so widely discussed because of its unique excellence as a work of scholarship or interpretation. Whatever its merits, one would hardly maintain that it is in a class by itself in this regard. Nor is the reason for its uncommon fame that it records horrible atrocities; the same was surely true of the work of Pomonti-Thion and Meyer, for example, who dealt with the U.S. war. Nor can the reason be humanitarian concern, since the latter books were far more relevant than Ponchaud's (all questions of merit aside) on any moral scale, for reasons that are simple and obvious: the information that they conveyed could lead to direct action that would impede or halt ongoing atrocities, while it is difficult to see what Westerners could do to improve the lot of those who were subjected to repression or worse in Cambodia, as specialists have commonly observed.[323] To "speak out" about Cambodian atrocities in the West, joining the chorus of protest, is easy enough—as easy as it would be for a Russian intellectual to condemn the atrocious acts of U.S. imperialism.[324] It cannot be that some moral imperative affords Ponchaud's book its unique fame.

In fact, it is clear enough why this study has been singled out for special attention: its message, accurate or not, happens to conform perfectly to the needs of current Western ideology.[325] These comments are no criticism of the book, of course. Rather, they relate to its remarkable reception, and thus are relevant to our primary concern: the workings of the Western propaganda system.

Ponchaud's book appeared in France in January 1977. A review by Jean Lacouture in *Nouvel Observateur* was immediately translated and appeared in the March 31 issue of the *New York Review of Books*, probably a record for speed in reviewing a French book. Lacouture's review had a considerable impact. Ponchaud himself writes that it "provoked considerable reaction in all circles concerned about Asia and the future of socialism."[326] Our own interpretation of the impact would be a bit different. Most of those who reacted to Lacouture's review in the media by lauding the contribution of the book that they had never seen had shown little concern for the future of socialism; or for Asia, except in the sense that a fox is concerned with a brood of chickens.

Others have also commented on the influence of Lacouture's review, which has indeed been unprecedented. William Shawcross writes that it had "enormous impact particularly because it was written by a former supporter of the Khmer Rouge (he issued a *mea culpa*) for a paper which had consistently opposed the war. It was taken up by dozens of papers ..."[327] In its review, the London *Economist* wrote that Ponchaud's book "gained considerable notoriety because of an extraordinary review in the *New York Times* [sic] *Review of Books* written by Jean Lacouture, a French journalist."[328] Lacouture's corrections (a "bizarre episode")[329] "added—a bit illogically—to the controversy that was already well advanced over whether the book itself was adequately researched and the refugees' evidence viewed with sufficient scepticism."

These comments bring out several interesting themes which, as we have seen, crop up constantly in discussion about postwar

Indochina. Consider the *Economist*'s reference to the "contro-versy that was already well advanced" over Ponchaud's book. There was no controversy. It was quite impossible for there to have been a controversy at the time when Lacouture's review appeared. The book itself had just appeared; for all we know there was not a single person in the English-speaking countries who had read the book, let alone engaged in controversy over it, at that time (and precious few afterwards, when the unread book was having its "enormous impact" on the press); nor was there any controversy "well advanced" in France a few weeks after publication. Furthermore, there has been very little con-troversy over the book since. Reviews have been consistently favorable, our own review in the *Nation* included, as Ponchaud remarks in the author's note to the American translation,[330] though we raised several questions about it. But it is, as we have seen, a staple of media coverage of postwar Cambodia to pretend that a major intellectual battle is in progress, com-parable perhaps to the debate over Stalinist crimes years ago. Such pretense provides a useful backdrop to the incessant plea that the story is "untold," everyone remains silent, etc., a per-formance that would have an air of low comedy were it not for the seriousness of the subject.

Shawcross's observation that part of the impact of the review was due to Lacouture's former support for the Khmer Rouge and the fact that the *New York Review* had consistently opposed the war is very much to the point. But the matter deserves a closer look. In fact, much has also been made of Ponchaud's early sym-pathy for the Khmer Rouge as evidence that his criticism has unusual force.[331] Lacouture does describe himself as someone "who supported the Khmer Rouge cause,"[332] and "advocated the cause of the Khmer Rouge in their struggle against the corrupt Lon Nol regime."[333] His previous writings indicate, however, that he was a supporter of Sihanouk, who was a bitter enemy of the

Khmer Rouge until they joined forces against Lon Nol in 1970 and whose subsequent relations with the Khmer Rouge are not at all clear.[334] In fact, it is difficult to see how a Westerner could have supported the cause of the Khmer Rouge, since virtually nothing was known about it. One should beware of the "God that failed" technique.[335] It is a common error, as we have pointed out several times, to interpret opposition to U.S. intervention and aggression as support for the programs of its victims, a useful device for state propagandists but one that often has no basis in fact. As for the *New York Review*, it is true enough that it consistently opposed the war and was at one time open to writers connected with the peace movement and the U.S. left (along with a wide range of others), but it rejoined the liberal consensus in these respects years ago. It may be that the impact of Lacouture's review derived in part from the fact that it appeared in the issue immediately following the André Gelinas article on Vietnam that we discussed in chapter 4. This too was influential, and its impact was enhanced, as we have seen, by the pretense that the journal in which it appeared had been an "organ of celebration" for the Communists, a typical lie of the propaganda institutions.[336]

Finally, as concerns Ponchaud, it is quite true that he writes that he listened to Khmer Rouge proposals "with a sympathetic ear," since "I come of peasant stock myself."[337] As far as we know, however, during the years Ponchaud lived in Cambodia he never publicly expressed this sympathy and also apparently felt that no purpose would be served by any public comment or protest over the war—specifically, the foreign attack—while it was in progress; we are aware of nothing that he wrote on the war apart from several articles and his book all after the war's end. Furthermore, he describes nothing that he did that might have been to the benefit of the peasants of Cambodia.

It apparently has not been noticed by the many commentators who have cited Ponchaud's alleged sympathy with the

Khmer peasants and the revolutionary forces that if authentic, it is a remarkable self-condemnation. What are we to think of a person who is quite capable of reaching an international audience, at least with atrocity stories, and who could see with his own eyes what was happening to the Khmer peasants subjected to daily massacre as the war ground on, but kept totally silent at a time when a voice of protest might have helped to mitigate their torture? It would be more charitable to assume that Ponchaud is simply not telling the truth when he speaks of his sympathy for the Khmer peasants and for the revolution, having added these touches for the benefit of a gullible Western audience or for the benefit of apologists who can then write that the atrocity stories have "impressed even those such as François Ponchaud,...who was sympathetic to the Communists when they first took over."[338]

In short, neither Lacouture, nor Ponchaud, nor the *New York Review* had ever, to our knowledge, identified with the Khmer Rouge or their "cause." While it is true that the impact of Lacouture's review of Ponchaud's book in the *New York Review* derives in part from such loose associations as those just mentioned, that is more a commentary on the media than on the facts.

Lacouture's review has indeed been extremely influential. The corrections, in significant contrast, have been little noted.[339] Two samples from the national press illustrate the media response.

Basing themselves on a review of a book that they had never seen, by an unknown author, the editors of the *Christian Science Monitor* published an editorial stating that "the loss of life" had been reported to be "as high as 2 million people out of 7.8 million total." They quote Lacouture's rhetorical question: "What Oriental despots or medieval inquisitors ever boasted of having eliminated, in a single year, one quarter of their own population?"[340] Surely enough time had passed to enable the *Monitor* editors to do what several private individuals had done upon reading Lacouture's review: namely to check his source for this remark, and find that it did not exist. The *Monitor* also cites the faked photographs discussed above (the fakery had been publicly exposed a year earlier), noting merely that they "have not been positively verified." They quote Lacouture's conclusion that "Cambodia's leaders have been 'systematically massacring, isolating and starving city and village populations whose crime was to have been born when they were,'" never troubling—here or elsewhere—to inquire into the evidence for this allegation, or to ask what curious aberration might impel Cambodia's leaders to systematically starve and massacre the population of the country, or how a small group of leaders might be able to achieve this strange purpose. They conclude that "for the outside world to countenance such barbarism and remain officially silent about it, in a sense diminishes respect for humanity and its rights everywhere." To fully appreciate their reaction one would have to review the shabby editorial record of this journal[341] in countenancing the barbarism of the United States over many years.[342]

Lacouture, like Ponchaud, takes note of the brutality of the U.S. war, surely a major factor in what followed. These references disappear from the *Monitor* editorial, which like Barron-Paul pretends that the current suffering in Cambodia takes place in a historical vacuum, a mere result of Communist savagery. We have already quoted their earlier editorial based on Barron-Paul, which avoids any reference to U.S. responsibility, though there is much moralizing about those who are allegedly indifferent to Khmer Rouge terrorism against the "engaging people" of Cambodia.[343]

To mention a second example, the liberal columnist of the *New York Times*, Anthony Lewis, devoted a column to Lacouture's review.[344] Lewis was an outspoken and effective critic of the U.S. war from 1969 and has since explained that "by 1969 it was clear to most of the world—and most Americans—that the intervention had been a disastrous mistake"[345]—not a crime. He commented on the "painful honesty" of Lacouture's article which "lends ghastly conviction to its terrible conclusions." He then quotes Lacouture's conclusions: the new rulers "have invented something original—auto-genocide," a new and more horrible form of genocide: "After Auschwitz and the Gulag, we might have thought this century had produced the ultimate horror, but we are now seeing the suicide of a people in the name of revolution; worse: in the name of socialism." Apparently a greater horror than Auschwitz or the Gulag, not to speak of the Indonesian massacre of 1965-1966 or the U.S. massacres in Indochina (but then, as Lewis has explained, these were only a "disastrous mistake"). Lewis also quotes approvingly Lacouture's claim that the "group of modern intellectuals, formed by Western thought, primarily Marxist thought" are systematically massacring and starving the population, and his further claim that these monsters "boast" of having "eliminated" some 2 million people, along with other citations that happen to be inaccurate. As distinct from the *Monitor*, Lewis cites Lacouture's reference to the U.S. role, and like his colleagues warns that "to remain silent in the face of barbarism as enormous as Cambodia's would be to compromise our own humanity"—as if there had been silence, as if it is "our own humanity" that is at stake, as if we do not compromise our own humanity by describing "American decisions on Indochina" as "blundering efforts to do good" (see note 345) after having remained silent about them apart from timid queries during the period of the worst barbarism. "In today's world," he concludes, "we ignore mass murder anywhere at our own peril."

The allegations that Lewis quotes are severe indeed. As a legal scholar, he might have troubled to inquire into the source of the allegations that he is reporting from a book he had never seen by an author of whom he knows nothing, before broadcasting them in such a manner to a mass audience. Had he done so, he would have quickly discovered that his specific citations had no basis in the text of the book, as we shall see. And for all his expressed concern about compromising our own humanity, it is only "our own peril" that concerns this moralist (who concedes "that there is not much hope of affecting the Cambodian government"), not the consequences for Third World peoples who are potential victims of the hysteria that he is helping to inflame with his unexamined charges based on misquotations and errors.

The *Monitor* was unwilling to print corrections of the false statements in its editorial or the conclusions based on them, despite evidence provided to them that established the falsity beyond question. They did, however, publish (prominently) a letter correcting some of these errors[346]; retraction would have been the honorable step. After Lacouture's corrections had appeared, Lewis (who had also had in hand for several weeks the documentary evidence showing that his quotes were baseless) noted them at the end of a column.[347] His corrections were only partial, and he did not make clear that full corrections eliminate entirely the evidentiary basis for the conclusions he proclaimed. Nor did he indicate whether this fact bears on the "ghastly conviction" lent to Lacouture's "terrible conclusions."[348]

Since the media have relied heavily on the contents of Lacouture's review, regardless of the corrections,[349] it is important to see exactly what kind of information they are offering to the reading public. We are not concerned here with Lacouture's interpretation of what he read, but rather with the evidence that was available to the many journalists who made use of this evidence without troubling to investigate its character and accuracy. Such evidence, plainly, consists of Lacouture's more or less explicit references to the book. These references turn out to be false or highly misleading in every instance. Hence the journalists were writing on the basis of no serious evidence whatsoever.

Furthermore, subsequent inquiry has revealed that some of the material in the book that was the basis for Lacouture's distorted account was quite dubious at best—again, a pattern that we have noticed earlier; evidence about Cambodia has a way of crumbling when one begins to look at it closely, a fact that should raise some questions about the examples that have not been investigated because of their lesser prominence in the international campaign. What reached the public was a series of reports by journalists of Lacouture's misreading of statements by Ponchaud that are themselves questionable in some instances (even forgetting the additional link in the chain of transmission, namely, the refugee reports). It is therefore of some interest to review these cases one by one.

The review contains the following references that can be related to something that appears in the book itself:

(1) "What Oriental despot or medieval inquisitors ever boasted of having eliminated, in a single year, one quarter of their own population?"

(2) Ponchaud "quotes from texts distributed in Phnom Penh itself inciting local officials to 'cut down,' to 'gash,' to 'suppress' the 'corrupt' elites and 'carriers of germs'—and not only the guilty but 'their offspring until the last one.' The strategy of Herod." [Lacouture's emphasis]

(3) Ponchaud "cites telling articles from the government newspaper, the *Prachachat*,...which denounced the 're-education' methods of the Vietnamese as 'too slow.' 'The Khmer method has no need of numerous personnel. We've overturned the basket, and with it all the fruit it contained. From now on we *will choose only the fruit that suit us perfectly*. The Vietnamese have removed only the rotten fruit, and this causes them to lose time.' [Lacouture's emphasis.]

"Perhaps Beria would not have dared to say this openly; Himmler might have done so. It is in such company that one must place this 'revolution' as it imposes a return to the land, the land of the pre-Angkor period, by methods worthy of Nazi Gauleiters."

(4) "When men who talk of Marxism are able to say, as one

quoted by Ponchaud does, that only 1.5 or 2 million young Cambodians, out of 6 million, will be enough to rebuild a pure society, one can no longer speak of barbarism [but only] madness."

These quotes exhaust the alleged evidence available to the journalists on whom this review had such a powerful impact, and provide the basis for their further commentary.

Let us now review the status of this evidence. We have already discussed case (4), noting that the source, if any, is so unreliable that Ponchaud deleted the reference from the American edition. Case (1) is simply false, as Lacouture points out in his corrections.[350] There was no Khmer Rouge boast reported, and no figure of one quarter of the population "eliminated" or even an allegation of that number of postwar deaths.

Turning to case (2), as Lacouture acknowledges in his corrections, the source is not texts distributed in Phnom Penh but something much more vague; this is true not only of the single case he discussed in the "Corrections," namely, the injunction to suppress "their offspring until the last one," but also of the others cited.[351] The one case that Lacouture discusses in his corrections is presented, as he says, as a "leitmotif de justification" in the French text. The other examples we are unable to locate in Ponchaud's French text, though similar quotes are offered as "slogans used, both on the radio and at meetings." What their status may be is not made clear. The radio reports are not identified (others are elsewhere in the book), so they are perhaps refugee memories. Plainly this must be true of the slogans reported. Thus what we have is memories transmitted at second-hand by Ponchaud, modified by Lacouture, and presented as texts distributed in Phnom Penh.

What of the one example that Lacouture corrects, which expresses "the strategy of Herod"? Does this judgment still hold if it is a "leitmotif" without explicit source rather than an official text? Without pursuing that question, we note that the American translation of Ponchaud's book softens the reference still further. There is no quote given at all; rather, the text reads: "the theme that the family line must be annihilated down to the last survivor is recurrent in such reports." The relevant "reports" are identified only as "several accounts"—presumably, refugee memories. Ponchaud's paraphrase of a theme that several refugees have allegedly reported does not seem to us to provide very powerful support for denunciation of a regime as employing "the strategy of Herod."[352]

We are left with one single bit of evidence, namely case (3). This case turns out to be rather interesting. In his "Corrections," Lacouture acknowledges that *Prachachat* is not a Cambodian "government newspaper" but rather a Thai newspaper—a considerable difference, which suffices to undermine the comment that he appends to this quote. In the corrections he writes that this Thai paper, in its issue of June 10, 1976, "carried an interview with a Khmer Rouge official who said, as Ponchaud writes, that he found the revolutionary method of the Vietnamese 'very slow,' requiring 'a lot of time to separate the good people from the counter-revolutionaries.'" It was the Thai reporter, he adds, who drew the conclusion he quoted that the Khmers had "overturned the basket ..."[353]

This is a fair rendition of what Ponchaud reports.[354] Ponchaud writes: "In an interview in the Thai newspaper *Prachachat* of 10 June 1976 a Khmer Rouge official said that the Vietnamese revolutionary method was 'very slow,' and that 'it took a great deal of time to sort out the good from the counter-revolutionaries.'"[355] Ponchaud then cites the conclusion of the reporter of *Prachachat*, and adds this final comment as a separate paragraph, closing the chapter: "This is the 'Great Leap Forward' of the Khmer revolution."

The American version is a bit different. The final ironic comment is deleted entirely. Furthermore, he says here that the interview with the Khmer Rouge official was "cited" in *Prachachat*; that is, there is still another link in the chain of transmission. Note that this interview and the Thai reporter's comment are considered rather significant; the chapter heading is: "The Overturned Basket."

When we first read Ponchaud's original, we assumed that the Thai journal *Prachachat* must be a right wing journal giving a criticism of the Khmer Rouge. That is what Ponchaud's account suggests, in particular his final ironic comment, now deleted in the American edition. We wrote in the *Nation* (25 June 1977) that the chain of transmission was too long to be taken very seriously and we raised the following question: "How seriously would we regard a critical account of the United States in a book by a hostile European leftist based on a report in *Pravda* of a statement allegedly made by an unnamed American official?" (Correspondingly, how seriously should we regard a critical account of Cambodia in a book by Ponchaud based on a report in *Prachachat* of a statement allegedly made by an unnamed Khmer Rouge official?) The answer is: not very seriously. Whatever one thinks of this, it is evident that the basis for the extreme criticisms that Lacouture appends to this "quote" disappears when it is properly attributed: to a Thai reporter, not a Cambodian government newspaper.

Several people (Heder, Ponchaud, Vickery) have pointed out to us that we were mistaken in assuming that *Prachachat* was a right wing newspaper critical of the Khmer Rouge. The fact is that it was a left wing newspaper, and the actual text[356] is not a criticism of the Khmer Rouge, but a defense of the Khmer Rouge against foreign criticism, something that could hardly be guessed from Ponchaud's account and is certainly worth knowing, in this context. Furthermore, it turns out that there is indeed another link in the chain of transmission; Ponchaud's revision of his French text in the American (but not British) translation is correct. *Prachachat* did not interview a Khmer Rouge official. Rather, it cites a report by a person described as "a neutral individual" in Paris who says that "a Khmer official of the new government, residing in Paris, said to me ..." Here, then, is an improved version of our original analogy: How seriously would we regard a critical account of the United States in a book by a hostile European leftist based on a report in *Encounter*[357] of comments by a "neutral person" who reports statements of an unnamed American official? Again, not very seriously.

Note that the unnamed Khmer Rouge official in Paris is quite possibly a member of the pro-revolutionary Cambodian community in Paris, whose information is itself second or third-hand (perhaps through Peking), as Heder points out.[358] Furthermore, given the context it is not so clear what interpretation to give to the comment about the Vietnamese methods being "very slow." Lacouture's reference as well as Ponchaud's text suggest that what is intended is that the methods are too slow in eliminating people (at least, that is how we read them). The full context of the original article in *Prachachat*, however, suggests that what is in fact meant is that the Vietnamese method is too slow in returning former collaborators (including professionals and even former military men) to normal lives to help build the new society; again, a vast difference. The gist of the article seems to be a call for rapid proletarianization of the urban bourgeoisie—who, as every rational observer agrees, had to be moved to productive work in a country that had no economy,[359] and had no way of feeding millions of people who had been driven into the cities by U.S. "forced-draft urbanization." No one could guess from Ponchaud's citation that this may well be the intended sense of these remarks.

Furthermore, the context and the proper wording suggest a rather different sense for the paragraph quoted from the Thai journal's conclusion; recall that the article was intended as a defense of the Khmer Rouge against criticism.[360] As Lacouture gives the quote, following Ponchaud, the Thai journalist says that "the Khmer method has no need of numerous personnel." The implication is rather similar to that conveyed by the widely quoted remark about needing only 1-2 million people to build the new society (Lacouture's case (4), already discussed): namely, not many people are needed; the others can be eliminated. Evidently, Lacouture understood it this way (we did as well)—hence his comment about Beria, Himmler and Nazi Gauleiters. But the context omitted from Ponchaud's text makes it clear that this interpretation is entirely false. The immediately preceding paragraph and the one in question read as follows:

> If we may make a comparison, we see that the Vietnamese method requires numerous personnel to supervise the population; it may even turn out that it will not succeed everywhere, and the authorities will thus be charged with a very heavy burden.[361]
>
> In contrast, the Khmer method does not need numerous personnel; there are no burdens; because they have removed all the burdens out of the city ...

Then comes the comparison of overturning the basket.

Note two crucial points. Placed in context, it is obvious that the reference to the Khmer method not needing numerous personnel means that not many people are needed as supervisors, not that most of the population can be eliminated. Whatever one may think of this, it hardly justifies the remarks about Beria, Himmler and the Nazi Gauleiters. Ponchaud's citation, eliminating the relevant context, radically changes and severely harshens the sense. Secondly, note that the phrase "they have removed all the burdens out of the city," which plainly means that the burdens of the authorities have been removed from the city, is translated by Ponchaud as follows: "there are no heavy charges to bear because everyone is simply thrown out of town."[362]—obviously, the connotations are quite different.

When the proper context is introduced and Ponchaud's mistranslation is corrected, we find that the journalists of *Prachachat* are indeed giving what they take to be a defense of the Khmer revolution. We will not go into the question of whether this defense is adequate. Rather, our point is that what they are saying is radically different from the impression conveyed by Ponchaud—which explains why Lacouture, and we too, were so seriously misled as to the character of the *Prachachat* article. Thus this final item in the list of Lacouture's references (number (3)), goes the way of the others. It provides no basis whatsoever for his charges, but rather shows that Ponchaud has once again flagrantly misrepresented a quotation, the very one from which he took the chapter heading.

Two conclusions emerge from this discussion. First, journalists who have been relying on Lacouture's review (with or without corrections) have built their case on sand. Furthermore, inquiry reveals that when we proceed beyond his published correction to a full list of corrections, and beyond that to correction of Ponchaud's original text to which he referred, the sand turns to jelly.

The original French has been considerably modified in the American edition. Specifically, in the list just given, item (4) is dropped entirely; the central example of (2) is changed from a quote to a paraphrase; the final ironic comment based on the translation of *Prachachat* is deleted and it is correctly stated that the article did not contain an interview with a Khmer Rouge official but rather that such an interview was cited. Item (1) was simply an error based on a misreading of a false statement by Ponchaud. Item (2) was also a misreading of Ponchaud. As for item (3), not only was Lacouture's reference to Ponchaud seriously in error, but Ponchaud's original translation from *Prachachat* is in part extremely misleading and in part flat wrong.

All in all, not a very impressive performance, either at the source or in the review.[363] But it is this material that has had such a major impact on Western journalists, perhaps second only to the Barron-Paul book that we have already discussed.

Returning now to Lacouture's point that it is a matter of secondary importance to decide "which person uttered an inhuman phrase, and whether the regime has murdered thousands or hundreds of thousands of wretched people," we believe that this review of the facts strengthens our earlier argument that it does matter indeed. It appears that the "inhuman phrases" in question may not have been uttered at all, or when uttered, were hardly so inhuman as Lacouture and Ponchaud suggest. It remains an open question whether the "regime has murdered" those who died from disease, starvation or overwork—or whether we have murdered them, by our past acts. It is also unclear on Ponchaud's evidence whether "the regime" has murdered the victims of "summary executions" (by government design? or peasant revenge? or soldiers out of control?).

We have now reviewed the two major sources of information for U.S. and indeed Western readers: Barron-Paul and Lacouture's rendition of Ponchaud. We turn next to Ponchaud's book itself. Again, we face the usual problem of logic: the trust we place in unverifiable material, which includes the essential and the most serious charges, depends on the trustworthiness of material that can be verified, here or elsewhere. In this case, we are restricted to the book itself, as the few articles we know of add little. As we have seen, Ponchaud plays fast and loose with numbers and is highly unreliable with quotations. This discovery naturally raises questions about sources that cannot be checked. As in the case of Barron-Paul, we can turn to his account of the history and background to assess the credibility of his reporting and conclusions. There is a vast difference between the two books in this regard. Ponchaud at least makes an effort to deal with these crucial matters. He offers virtually no documentation, which again reduces the possibility of assessment, but much that he recounts seems plausible both on grounds of inner consistency and what is known from other sources. We have mentioned a few cases where we find his historical account unsatisfying; namely, in reference to the colonial impact and the U.S. role, though these are at least mentioned. On his account of Khmer culture and the ideology of the post-revolutionary society, briefly mentioned above, we are not qualified to comment.

In his historical comments, Ponchaud tends to keep closely to the version of events offered by the U.S. propaganda system. Consider, for example, his discussion of the U.S. and Vietnamese involvement in Cambodia. Since he gives no sources, we do not know on what information he relies; plainly, not direct experience in these cases. The major studies[364] give a general picture of the following sort: Cambodia had been subjected to attempts at subversion and direct aggression by its U.S.-backed neighbors, Thailand and South Vietnam, from the 1950s. Diem's troops had attacked border regions in 1957. A CIA-backed plot to dismember Cambodia in 1958-1960 was foiled. There were provocations from the Thai side of the border, but the Vietnamese frontier posed a much more serious threat. "From 1957, but particularly from 1964, American-South Vietnamese forces attacked posts and villages, bombed rice fields, machine-gunned trucks, napalmed or defoliated the Cambodian side of the frontier," causing hundreds of casualties each year (Pomonti-Thion). Meyer reports that "at the end of 1963, the 'Khmers Serei,' equipped and trained by the CIA, made more frequent incursions into Cambodian territory from bases in South Vietnam and Thailand," and a few years later "the American-South Vietnamese attacks, ever more murderous, multiplied against the frontier villages of Cambodia." After the massive and destructive U.S. military operations in nearby areas of South Vietnam, particularly in January-February 1967, Vietnamese peasants and guerrillas took refuge in narrow border areas, leading to cynical charges from Washington about Communist encroachment into neutral Cambodia. According to Meyer, by March, 1970, when the coup that overthrew Sihanouk took place, they were scattered along border areas to a maximum depth of perhaps 25 kilometers in the extreme northeast provinces which were to a considerable extent under the control of indigenous guerrillas. Other sources concur. Relations between the Cambodians and the Vietnamese in the "sanctuaries" were generally friendly at that time, and there were few military conflicts. The first evidence of Vietnamese encampments on the Cambodian side of the border was discovered in late 1967, a few kilometers beyond an unmarked border. While hypocrites in Washington and the press fumed in public about "North Vietnamese aggression," the internal view was different. From the *Pentagon Papers* we learn that as late as May 1967—i.e., well after the major U.S. military operations cited above—high officials believed that Cambodia was "becoming more and more important as a supply base—now of food and medicines, perhaps ammunition later" (John McNaughton). A year earlier a U.S. study team discovered the results of a U.S. helicopter attack on a Cambodian village (first denied, later conceded when eyewitnesses including a CBS television team reported the facts), one of several such cases discovered accidentally. In March 1969 the massive "secret bombing" began.

It is intriguing to consider the reactions in the United States to the occasional revelations that Cambodia had been attacked by U.S. forces. Roger Hilsman, who was director of the Bureau of Intelligence and Research in the State Department and later Assistant Secretary of State for Far Eastern Affairs in the Kennedy administration, describes an attack by U.S. bombers on a Cambodian village on January 21, 1962, with an unknown number of civilian casualties. He describes this as a "tragic error in map-reading": the real intent was "to bomb and strafe the cluster of huts near the Cambodian border" where it had been reported that there were Viet Cong guerrillas. It would not have been a "tragic error" if a Vietnamese village had been bombed by U.S. planes in January, 1962, with an unknown number of civilian casualties. Hilsman's sole criticism concerning this bombing attack against a defenseless village (apart from the tragic error in map reading, which led to the wrong peasants being killed) is that though "the plan was well and efficiently executed" it was not well-designed for guerrilla warfare: "The greatest problem is that bombing huts and villages will kill civilians and push the population still further toward active support for the Viet Cong."[365] Hilsman is widely regarded as a "dove."

On 25 March 1964, the *New York Times* published a report by Max Frankel, now an editor, with the interesting title: "Stomping on U.S. Toes: Cambodia Typical of Many Small Nations Putting Strain on a Policy of Patience." What aroused Frankel's ire was that Cambodia had "borrowed a leaf from Fidel Castro's book and demanded tractors and bulldozers as compensation for the killing of Cambodians by South Vietnamese in a frontier attack." He is referring to the Cambodian response to a Vietnamese ground and air attack on a Cambodian village in which they were accompanied by U.S. advisers. A U.S. Army pilot "was dragged from the wreckage" of an L-19 observer plane "shot down in the action," and "diplomats who rushed to the scene confirmed Cambodian reports that at least one troop-carrying helicopter had landed at Chantrea with three Americans on board." The Cambodian village of Chantrea was bombed and attacked by 12 armored cars, according to Cambodian sources; seventeen persons were reported killed and 13 injured.[366] It was not the attack, but Cambodia's response that enraged Frankel, who explains as follows:

> It is open season again for the weaker nations to stomp on
> the toes of big ones...Leading the pack in big-power bait-
> ing these days is one of the smallest of nations, the South-
> east Asian kingdom of Cambodia...What Cambodia is up
> to seems to turn on what Cambodia's young leader, Prince
> Norodom Sihanouk, is up to. Washington has always re-
> garded the 41-year-old Premier-Prince as a clever, head-
> strong, erratic leader who wishes to serve his people, defend
> their independence and develop their resources. It has also
> found him lacking some of the talent and temperament for
> the job...For the most part, the Administration's instinct has
> been to try to save a wayward young nation's independence
> in spite of itself and, at times, despite its own leaders. Offi-
> cials remark privately that Indonesia is more important than
> Sukarno, Ghana more important than Nkrumah, Cambodia
> more important than Sihanouk.

But now Washington is "not only alarmed and saddened, but
confused." Of course, "Cambodia's current effort to force the
United States into a major conference that would embarrass its
Thai and Vietnamese friends will be resisted"; the reference is to
a conference that would settle border questions and guarantee
Cambodia's neutrality and integrity in a period when the United
States was desperately seeking to undermine international efforts to neutralize South Vietnam, Laos, and Cambodia so as to
avert the major war towards which the United States was clearly
driving.[367] But what was most irritating was the Cambodian effort to "stomp on U.S. toes" by asking for reparations after a village was attacked by forces trained, supplied and advised by the
United States, and accompanied by U.S. military advisers and
aircraft. It was this unmitigated gall that was trying the patience
of the U.S. government while calling forth a reaction in the *New
York Times* that is remarkable as much for the paternalism and
racism of its style, so typical of the annals of colonialism, as for
the response to the actual events discussed.

In his rather sketchy historical review, Ponchaud passes over all of these events of the 1950's and 1960's in silence. His only comment is that the "Vietnamese revolutionaries were becoming a real menace to Cambodia,"[368] hardly an adequate summary. He says that "in his desire to stop the infiltration along Cambodia's borders, [Sihanouk] disclosed the location of Vietcong bases, which were then bombed by the American air force. He called it a scandal and a crime over Radio Phnom Penh, but nobody was deceived"[369]; the reference is to the 1969 bombings. Actually, Ponchaud is deceived. Keeping strictly to the position of U.S. propaganda, he fails to indicate that Sihanouk vigorously and publicly denounced the bombing *of Khmer peasants.*[370] Turning to the March 1970 coup, Ponchaud has little to say about the background. His few comments are, furthermore, inconsistent: the coup was "presumably backed by the Americans" and "the United States was not sure what attitude to adopt in the Cambodian crisis. Sihanouk's downfall was bad news ..."[371] The first of these two contradictory claims seems to us the more likely correct, given what little evidence is available, but Ponchaud does not pursue the issue—a rather important one. He makes no mention of US-ARVN military intervention from two days after the coup of March 18. As for the "incursion" of April 30, he says only that the South Vietnamese took advantage of it to avenge the murder of Vietnamese by the Lon Nol government: "their savagery drove a number of Cambodian peasants over to the Khmer Rouge."[372] Not a word about the savagery of the U.S. attack, which was amply reported at the time. Ponchaud asserts that the North Vietnamese "[swept] up young Khmers to be trained in revolutionary warfare,"[373] ignoring entirely the eyewitness reports by U.S. correspondents in captivity that the U.S. bombing was recruiting Khmers, both young and old, to the Khmer Rouge. Pomonti-Thion remark appropriately that "the mechanism by which American bombs create resistance is too well known for us to describe here."

With regard to the war in Vietnam, Ponchaud also keeps closely to the U.S. government propaganda line in his scattered remarks. Discussing the "North Vietnamese" withdrawal from Cambodia by 1971, he says that they "returned to their conquest of South Vietnam"[374]—the sole reference to that struggle, astonishing in its misrepresentation of the background that is so well-documented and familiar that we need not elaborate here. Referring to Sihanouk's attitude towards the struggle in Vietnam, he says that at the time of the Tet Offensive, "when he saw how fiercely the population in the south defended itself he wavered, and began to think the north might be defeated."[375] Again, an amazing distortion of well-known facts that are easily documented from U.S. government sources. There is overwhelming evidence from these sources and elsewhere that the Tet Offensive was primarily a struggle between the U.S. Army and South Vietnamese guerrillas—indeed, the fact is not seriously disputed. In the Mekong Delta, for example, where some of the fiercest battles were waged, there were no North Vietnamese regular forces, and in fact the total number of North Vietnamese who had been drawn into the war by the U.S. bombardment of North Vietnam (exactly as planners anticipated) was at approximately the level of the South Korean and Thai mercenaries at that point, vastly outnumbered (and even more vastly outgunned) by the U.S. Expeditionary Force that had for years been attempting to conquer South Vietnam and to destroy the society in which the indigenous revolt was rooted. Furthermore, during the Tet Offensive, the U.S. military continually lamented their difficulties in encouraging ARVN to reenter the countryside, particularly in the Delta. To describe the Tet Offensive in Ponchaud's terms is a gross falsification and a remarkable capitulation to the U.S. propaganda machine.

Such examples as these do not increase one's faith in the veracity of material that is not subject to independent confirmation, to say the least, and should alert any serious reviewer. We have seen no mention of any of this in a single review or comment.

Turning to material that is closer to the focus of Ponchaud's book, as in the case of Barron-Paul, the only section subject to independent verification is the one dealing with the evacuation of Phnom Penh. Here too serious questions arise. We have already noted how severely Ponchaud's account was distorted by Donald Wise in a review.[376] Turning to his own account, there are many dubious elements. Thus Ponchaud reports the explanation given by the revolutionary government: that the evacuation was motivated in part by impending famine. He rejects this argument on the grounds that rice stocks in Phnom Penh would have sufficed for two months for a large part of the population with careful rationing.[377] The book cites none of the evidence from Lon Nol and U.S. government sources that gives radically smaller estimates, namely 6-8 days' supply,[378] one of the many cases where the lack of documentation in the book conceals a rather casual attitude towards crucial facts. We questioned Ponchaud's two-month estimate in our review already cited. In a letter in response, Ponchaud informed us that his estimate included food illegally stored and "may be somewhat excessive"; he also suggests that the 8-day estimate of the Lon Nol government may have been exaggerated in an effort to obtain more aid, which is possible, though their demand at the time was primarily for arms rather than "humanitarian assistance," and in any event that still leaves the estimate of USAID officials that there was only a six-day supply of rice. Even if Ponchaud's possibly "excessive" two-month estimate were correct, it remains unclear how famine could have been averted after two months had the cities not been evacuated, though the methods were extremely brutal, judging by most of the eyewitness accounts. As we have already noted, sources in or close to the U.S. government concur.[379]

On the question of whether the atrocities in Cambodia, which Ponchaud graphically records from the testimony of refugees, were the result of a centralized policy of massacre or were rather, as many close observers suspect, in significant measure the result of localized peasant revenge and the acts of undisciplined troops, Ponchaud comes down squarely on the side of systematic and centralized policy:

> The liquidation of all town and former authorities was not improvised, nor was it a reprisal or expression of wanton cruelty on the part of local cadres. The scenario for every town and village in the country was the same and followed exact instructions issued by the highest authorities.[380]

And elsewhere, after reporting a refugee account of the massacre of officers and sick or invalid soldiers, he writes: "So many accounts contain similar statements that it can safely be affirmed that the revolutionaries had simply decided to kill off the bulk of the former civilian and military establishment in the hours following the capture of Phnom Penh."[381]

One may, perhaps, be skeptical that Ponchaud has reviewed the scenario "for every town and village in the country" as is claimed in the cited remark. As for the "exact instructions issued by the highest authorities," this is presumably his reconstruction from the alleged similarity of refugee accounts—he offers no direct evidence—and is as trustworthy as these accounts, his report of them, his interpretations of what he reports, and his judgment about the similarity of accounts of which, naturally, he can offer only a sample. The cautious reader, bearing in mind the serious inaccuracies of his quotes and citations where they can be checked and his careless treatment of historical fact, may want to reserve judgment on the question at issue. Ponchaud's own conclusions, it is by now clear, cannot be taken very seriously because he is simply too careless and untrustworthy. It is hardly in doubt that work of this calibre would be dismissed out of hand, if it were critical of the United States.

It is also worth recalling in this connection that according to published refugee testimony that Ponchaud does not cite, executions had been ordered halted by mid-1975,[382] though we do not know how reliable this testimony is, or, if reliable, whether such orders were observed or changed. As for the similarity of refugee accounts, we have already noted reasons for skepticism. Other Cambodia watchers and scholars who have visited refugee camps and interviewed refugees have expressed different judgments, and we have cited a few examples that have been generally ignored by the media that also raise questions. Ponchaud himself naturally gives only a sample of the accounts he has assembled.[383] Even the examples he cites do not substantiate his firm conviction that central direction rather than localized cruelty or revenge has been clearly established. To mention a few examples, he cites a Khmer pharmacist who escaped in June 1975—that is, well after "the revolutionaries had simply decided to kill off the bulk of the former civilian and military establishment in the hours following the capture of Phnom Penh"—who reports: "The attitudes of the Khmer Rouge varied enormously from one to the next, and we got the impression that their orders were not very specific." Later he is quoted as saying: "You had to understand [the villagers]; they had suffered a lot from the government air force. Several people in every family had been killed in the bombardments."[384] Perhaps this observation, far from unique, accounts for some of the subsequent killing and oppression. The same pharmacist speaks of the unaccustomed hard work and lack of food, concluding: "The Khmer Rouge were decent enough but if anyone resisted them or didn't obey at once, it meant death."

In his *Le Monde* articles, Ponchaud was less certain about the alleged "central direction." Here he writes of the Khmer

Rouge cadres that "it is difficult to know whether they receive orders coming from the government or whether they act on their personal initiative."[385] In general these articles give the same account as the book, though obviously in less detail.[386] What did Ponchaud learn in the interim that caused him to change his mind on this crucial point?

In other connections too Ponchaud refers to diversity of policy. On the matter of "marriage customs," the subject of much denunciation in the Western press, Ponchaud writes that "refugees' accounts differ widely on this point, presumably because of variations in regional practice."[387] And on revenge as a possible factor for killings, he observes that during the Samlaut *jacquerie* of the late 1960s the police and military

> were heavy-handed, killing many villagers and burning their homes. The population fled into the forest, with intensified loathing for the unjust administration that was leaving a trail of death wherever it went...when the Samlaut peasants took to the mountains [in 1968], they were firmly resolved to pay back a hundredfold the evil that had been done to them.[388]

Recall again that this was one of the areas where the worst atrocities were later reported, and where Khmer Rouge control is said to have been very limited.

Such examples as these, which can readily be supplemented from the literature, raise serious questions about Ponchaud's certainty with regard to the central direction of the massacres. There seems ample evidence that other factors—peasant revenge, for one—were involved, and it seems to us far from clear, on the evidence that he and others put forward, that practices were as uniform as he claims. We note once again that not one single reviewer or other commentator in the mainstream press, to our knowledge, has expressed any skepticism about these conclusions, and some have elaborated them considerably, e.g., Lacouture, who informs us that the group of intellectuals who proclaim their Marxist ideology as they lead the country to ruin are systematically massacring and starving the population and that the "auto-genocide" of the new rulers shows us that we were wrong when we thought that Auschwitz and the Gulag were "the ultimate in horror." Ponchaud's reference to Lacouture's review expresses no reservations on these or other conclusions, so we may perhaps assume that he regards them as justified. They go far beyond any evidence that he presents (and as noted, are in part inconsistent with this evidence) and are subject to serious question in the light of other evidence to which he does not refer.

In the author's note to the American translation, Ponchaud writes: "I am an exegete by training and profession; I have long been accustomed to applying the methods of source criticism to a body of reported events in order to elicit the historical truth from them."[389] This self-characterization hardly seems appropriate to the work we have been discussing, with its carelessness with regard to quotes, numbers, and sources. We have ourselves been led to undertake some unexpected exegesis in comparing the various texts that Ponchaud has produced: the *Le Monde* articles and the French book; the French original and the American and British translations; the *Prachachat* article and Ponchaud's severely distorted version of its contents. The discrepancies between the British and American translations deserve a further look, as we try to assess the credibility of the unverifiable material that constitutes the bulk of Ponchaud's case.

We have noted several discrepancies between the British and the American translations. In each case, the British translation remains true to the French original whereas the American translation introduces changes that are not trivial, in the light of the way in which the material deleted or modified has been exploited in the international condemnation of the Khmer Rouge. It is a little strange, to begin with, that there should be these discrepancies. None are indicated. There is a single translator: Nancy Amphoux. The author's notes for the two translations are dated on the very same day: September 20, 1977, Paris. Presumably they were written at the same time.[390] Why then should the two translations differ? The differences are systematic: where a question was raised about the French text in the course of the effort to trace Lacouture's references, the American translation has been modified while the British translation has been left as in the original. We note, finally, that the queries were raised in the United States, and that by an international trade agreement the British translation cannot be purchased in the United States and will not be found in U.S. libraries; the British version is the world edition. Perhaps it is worthwhile to undertake a more systematic review of the discrepancies, in an effort to understand just what is going on.

To review so far, we have noted the following examples:

(1) The British translation includes (in the text, and as modified by Lacouture, on the cover) the alleged quote: "One or two million young people are enough to make the new Kampuchea" (Ponchaud's revision of his Le Monde citation) and the appended statement that the Khmer Rouge are "now grimly turning" this "blood-chilling boast...into a reality." All of this is eliminated from the American translation.

(2) The "quote" that is described as an official text by Lacouture, namely, that "their line must be annihilated down to the last survivor," has been softened to a "recurrent theme" of refugee reports without quotes in the American translation, but left in quotes as a "leitmotiv of justification" in the British version, as in the French.[391]

(3) With reference to the Thai journal Prachachat, the American translation indicates correctly that there was no interview in the paper with a Khmer Rouge official, as both the French and British versions assert, but rather that such interview was

"cited" in the journal, which gave a second-hand report. Furthermore, the American translation deletes the final ironic comment about the "Great Leap Forward," again softening the impact, while the British version keeps it. We emphasize again that these discrepancies are insignificant in comparison to the gross distortion of the Thai original and the crucial omission of relevant context that remains in the French original and both translations, and is further distorted in Lacouture's review, where it reached a general audience.[392]

(4) There is a further striking case in which the American and British translations diverge, in perhaps a still more curious way. Recall that the author's notes for the English and American translations are dated on the same day and are translated by the same person. They are also largely identical, but not entirely. The American version begins as follows:

> On March 31, 1977, *The New York Review of Books* published an account of my book under the signature of Jean Lacouture, which provoked considerable reaction in all circles concerned about Asia and the future of socialism. With the responsible attitude and precision of thought that are so characteristic of him, Noam Chomsky then embarked on a polemical exchange with Robert Silvers, Editor of the *NYR*, and with Jean Lacouture, leading to the publication by the latter of a rectification of his initial account. Mr. Chomsky was of the opinion that Jean Lacouture had substantially distorted the evidence I had offered, and, considering my book to be "serious and worth reading, as distinct from much of the commentary it has elicited" [reference to the review cited in note 100], he wrote me a personal letter on October 19, 1977 in which he drew my attention to the way it was being misused by anti-revolutionary propagandists ...

The British version, dated the same day, begins as follows:

> Even before this book was translated it was sharply criticized by Mr Noam Chomsky [reference to correspondence with Silvers and the review cited in note 100] and Mr Gareth Porter

[reference to *May Hearings*]. These two "experts" on Asia claim that I am mistakenly trying to convince people that Cambodia was drowned in a sea of blood after the departure of the last American diplomats. They say there have been no massacres, and they lay the blame for the tragedy of the Khmer people on the American bombings. They accuse me of being insufficiently critical in my approach to the refugees' accounts. For them, refugees are not a valid source ...

The British version then includes the following passage:

After an investigation of this kind, it is surprising to see that "experts" who have spoken to few if any of the Khmer refugees should reject their very significant place in any study of modern Cambodia. These experts would rather base their arguments on reasoning: if something seems impossible to their personal logic, then it doesn't exist. Their only sources for evaluation are deliberately chosen official statements. Where is that critical approach which they accuse others of not having?

None of this appears in the American version.

The contrast between these two texts, both dated September 20, 1977, is quite striking. Our favorable reference to Ponchaud's book in the American version becomes a sharp attack in the British version. The "responsible attitude and precision of thought" that receive such fulsome praise in the American version become complete irrationality, refusal to consider evidence, blind dogmatism, lack of any critical approach, and faked "expertise" in the simultaneous British version.

The accusations in the British version are false, and Ponchaud knows very well that they are false, as is sufficiently clear from the American version penned—it appears—on the same day. Far from saying that "there have been no massacres," we wrote in the article to which he refers that there undoubtedly had been massacres though their scope and character were subject to debate, which we briefly reviewed, including Ponchaud's "grisly account of what refugees have reported to him about the barbarity of their treatment at the hands of the Khmer Rouge" in a book that we described as "serious and worth reading." We concluded that "we do not pretend to know where the truth lies amidst these sharply conflicting assessments," all of which, incidentally, assume substantial atrocities and thousands or more killed. As for Porter, in the reference that Ponchaud cites he begins by writing: "There were undoubtedly large numbers of killings in the newly-liberated areas immediately after the war by soldiers of the victorious army ..." and "it may well be true" that there were summary executions by local officials, though "an adequate picture" will be impossible to construct for many years. Ponchaud's statement that according to Chomsky and Porter "refugees are not a valid source" is also an outright falsehood, as he knows perfectly well. In the reference Ponchaud cites, we wrote: "While [refugee] reports must be considered seriously, care and caution are necessary"; exactly his own explicit conclusion in the book, as we have seen. Porter takes the same position: after giving examples to illustrate the care that must be taken with refugee reports, he writes, in the very reference that Ponchaud cites: "This does not mean that refugee accounts are always false or even grossly exaggerated. But in judging the credibility of assertion based on a refugee report, one should take into account ..."—then follow considerations that would be second nature to any serious journalist or scholar. Ponchaud's final remarks merit no comment, though they give some further insight into his reliability and precision.[393]

This comparison, which strikes us as quite remarkable, explains why the editors of the *Economist* were misled into writing that Ponchaud "forthrightly included some of the main attacks as a footnote to the English-language preface,"[394] referring to our review which described the book as "serious and worth reading," and thus hardly qualifies as an "attack"—recall Ponchaud's citation in the American edition. They were, of course, reviewing the British edition, and naively trusted the author, in this respect as in others. Further questions remain unexplained. Why the stream of falsehoods, surely known to the author to be false, in the British edition, replaced in the simultaneous American edition by a show of courtesy and praise? We note again that the British edition is not obtainable through commercial channels in the United States and is not to be found in American libraries, while conversely, readers of the British edition are unlikely to be familiar with the references to U.S. publications that Ponchaud cites in his series of false accusations.

This kind of petty deceit is unworthy of discussion except insofar as it provides some indication of the credibility of a person who is building a case on largely unverifiable evidence. That issue is important, given the enormous impact of his work and its effect, as it has been amplified through the international propaganda system, in reconstructing attitudes and ideology in the West.

We gain some further insight into Ponchaud's scholarly practice by looking at subsequent translations of his book. The Norwegian translation contains reference to events of May, 1978, and therefore evidently went to press long after the British and American translations were completed, indeed after they had appeared.[395] The material deleted or modified in the American translation appears in the Norwegian translation, as it did in the French original and the British translation. Evidently, it is only the reader in the United States who is to be spared the material that has been questioned in the United States, and that Ponchaud knows to be indefensible.

In a review of Ponchaud's book that is fairer than most, William Shawcross writes that "Chomsky has pointed out some inconsistencies and mistakes in Ponchaud's book" (referring, presumably, to private correspondence and our published review), "but they are of a minor nature and do not in any way affect that judgment."[396] The judgment to which he refers is Ponchaud's comment in the author's note to the American translation, which reads: "I was compelled to conclude [in the book], against my will, that the Khmer revolution is irrefutably the bloodiest of our century. A year after the publication of my book I can unfortunately find no reason to alter my judgment."[397] The evil demon that bedevils quotations about Cambodia has been at work once again. We are, by now, perhaps not surprised to discover that Ponchaud has misrepresented himself. The conclusion stated in the book is not, as he alleges in the author's note, that the Khmer revolution "is irrefutably the bloodiest of our century" but rather a distinctly different one: "the Khmer revolution is one of the bloodiest of the twentieth century."[398] Actually, we concur with the judgment expressed in the book itself ("one of the bloodiest"), although we feel that the context requires *immediate* complementary mention—lacking in Ponchaud's book—of the no less bloody U.S.-sponsored counter-revolution and direct assault that precipitated the bloody revolution. Shawcross seems to be implying that we do not concur with the judgment in the book, why, we have no idea; certainly not on the basis of anything we have written.

As for the inconsistencies and mistakes in Ponchaud's book, how seriously one takes them is, of course, a matter of judgment. While we find the conclusion in the book itself valid enough—and are indeed unaware of any contrary view—we want to point out the fallacy of reasoning that leads Shawcross to accept Ponchaud's misrepresentation of the conclusion of his book. The fact is that Ponchaud's book is highly unreliable where an independent check is possible. It is also true that the errors are "of a minor nature" as compared with the bulk of the evidence he presents: unverifiable refugee reports. As we have further noted, even these reports, on which he relies, do not support his unqualified conclusions on the serious question of central direction and planning of atrocities,[399] and the material that has proven unreliable plays a large role in his argument for central direction and intent. We stress again that it is the verifiable evidence, of however minor a nature it may be, that determines how much faith a rational person will place in material that is subject to no check. This point Shawcross seems to have missed.

In his author's note for the American translation, Ponchaud writes that although "we, the French and the Americans, bear part of the responsibility for the Cambodian drama," nevertheless "we cannot make use of the deaths of millions of Khmers to defend our own theories or projects for society," referring to unnamed "accusing foreigners."[400] Shawcross ends his review with the second of these statements and then adds: "In fact, of course, it can be and is being done." Shawcross does not say who is "of course" making use of the deaths of millions of Khmers to defend their own theories or projects for society, nor does Ponchaud tell us who are those "accusing foreigners" to whom his injunction is directed. The lapse is not accidental.[401] It would be difficult indeed to find anyone *defending the Khmer Rouge* (as distinct from those who exploit and magnify Cambodian atrocities to demonstrate the evils of Communism or liberation) whom this description fits.

The logic should be carefully considered. Shawcross's statement is a plain falsehood and Ponchaud's comment on which it is based is at best seriously misleading, with a presupposition that is plainly false.[402] There are, to be sure, people who are skeptical of the implicit claim that "millions of Khmers" have died as a result of the policies of the regime—surely nothing that Ponchaud reports substantiates this estimate, which is in fact far higher even than his own assessment of casualties, as we have noted.[403] There are other people, though they are few indeed, who have defended the Khmer revolution on the basis of their own "theories or projects for society." We know of few people, in fact, who have offered more positive comments than Ponchaud himself does, in his discussion of the emphasis on self-reliance, the dignity of labor, the "new mentality" with its "spirit of responsibility" and "inventiveness," etc. But to fall under Ponchaud's injunction or Shawcross's obviously false claim, a person would have to *both* agree that millions have died at the hands of the regime *and* justify this fact on the grounds of his social theories. We seriously doubt that any such person exists. All of this is simply another of the desperate efforts to create an opposition, which we have observed throughout this review.

In fact, there is a different interpretation of Ponchaud's comment and Shawcross's elaboration which can be justified, though one at variance with their intention. There are indeed people—a great many of them—who claim that millions have died (or have been killed) in Cambodia and who are making use of this alleged fact to defend their own theories and projects for society. It is, in fact, one of our main themes that the mass media of the West have discovered Cambodia's travail (previously ignored, understated or suppressed when the direct responsibility was incontestably Western) precisely because of its ideological serviceability. The populace of the West can be mobilized to fear the consequences of "radicalism," attention can be diverted from the proliferating terror within the U.S. sphere, and the case can be reaffirmed that the West must be prepared to intervene to prevent such awful events as the removal of some "gentle land" from the Free World.

Returning to Ponchaud's book, despite flaws that seem to us quite significant, we still believe, as we wrote in the earlier review cited, that it is "serious and worth reading, as distinct from much of the commentary it has elicited" and as distinct from propaganda tracts such as Barron-Paul which have aroused general enthusiasm in the West, for reasons that are all too obvious. A fair review of informed opinion about postwar Cambodia would, in our opinion, include this book as a serious though also seriously flawed and obviously unreliable contribution, in some (but not all) respects, to be placed at the more extreme critical end of the spectrum of specialist judgment and analysis. Such a review would not, however, single this book out (still less, Barron-Paul) as the repository of unchallenged truth, as the media coverage generally suggests. In fact, as we have seen, insofar as its statements cannot be independently verified, they should be regarded with a degree of skepticism, given the fate of those examples that are subject to independent verification.

It is noteworthy that not only the media but also governments appear to have relied uncritically on Ponchaud, despite his evident unreliability. A British government report, released by the Foreign Office, stated that "many hundreds of thousands of people have perished in Cambodia directly or indirectly as a result of the policies of the Communist government," according to the press summary.[404] The Foreign Office report "cited 'reputable observers' for this estimate." Only one such observer is cited in the *Post* account: "Father Francois Ponchaud, a French authority on Cambodia." A careful look at Ponchaud's work—specifically, his way with figures (his estimates are cited by the Foreign Office)—shows that it must be regarded with considerable caution; it is at best suggestive, hardly authoritative. If the press account of the British government report is accurate, proper caution was not taken, though an analysis of Ponchaud's work should not have been beyond the resources of the British Foreign Office, had it been concerned with finding the truth.

To complete the review of books about postwar Cambodia, we should mention briefly a third—actually the first to appear—namely the Hildebrand-Porter study to which we have referred several times.[405] This book differs from the later studies by Ponchaud and Barron-Paul in a number of respects: (1) it is virtually unread (by mid-1977, when we discussed it in the cited review, it had sold about 1,000 copies); (2) it has been almost entirely ignored by reviewers and political commentators apart from occasional abuse; (3) it is carefully documented from

Western and Cambodian sources. Factors (1) and (2) are explained by a fourth striking difference: this book gives a rather favorable account of Khmer Rouge programs and a detailed picture of the impact of the U.S. war—a continuing impact, as the authors show. The fourth factor alone suffices to eliminate it from the record, whatever its merits or deficiencies. Published in 1976, the book was well received by the journal of the Asia Society.[406] In *Choice*[407] it is described, in a brief note, as "A rare combination of humanitarianism and scholarly research." Apart from these notices, the book has to our knowledge been reviewed only in our 1977 *Nation* article (very briefly) and in the *New York Review* by Shawcross a year later,[408] where its "use of evidence" was challenged in the manner we described. It has not been used as the basis for editorial comment, with one exception. The *Wall Street Journal* acknowledged its existence in an editorial entitled "Cambodian Good Guys,"[409] which dismissed contemptuously the very idea that the Khmer Rouge could play a constructive role, as well as the notion that the United States had a major hand in the destruction, death, and turmoil of wartime and postwar Cambodia. In another editorial on the "Cambodian Horror," the *Journal* editors speak of the attribution of postwar Cambodian difficulties to U.S. intervention as "the record extension to date of the politics of guilt."[410] On the subject of "unscrambling Chile," however, the abuses of the "manfully rebuilding" Chilean police state are explained away as an unfortunate consequence of Allendista "wrecking" of the economy.[411] In brief, Hildebrand and Porter attribute "wrecking" and "rebuilding" to the wrong parties in Cambodia.

In his foreword to the book, Asian scholar George Kahin of Cornell University observes that

> in their documented and comprehensive account, George Hildebrand and Gareth Porter provide what is undoubtedly the best informed and clearest picture yet to emerge of the des-

perate economic problems brought about in Cambodia largely as a consequence of American intervention, and of the ways in which that country's new leadership has undertaken to meet them....Anyone who is interested in understanding the situation obtaining in Phnom Penh before and after the Lon Nol government's collapse and the character and programs of the Cambodian government that has replaced it will, I am sure, be grateful to the authors of this valuable study.

The Free Press, however, is not grateful for an account of the results of the U.S. intervention or the efforts to overcome them, and has shielded the general public from any perception of postwar Cambodia that focuses on these issues.

Since this book does not form part of the media barrage concerning what must be believed about postwar Cambodia, we will not subject it to any further analysis, given our specific concerns here.

It is difficult to convey properly the deep cynicism of the all-too-typical reporting that obscures or completely eliminates the U.S. role in turning Cambodia into a land of massacre, starvation, and disease. While journalists prate about morality, people are dying in Cambodia as a direct result of policies that many of them supported and concealed, and now eliminate from history. It is hardly in doubt that the malnutrition and disease caused by the U.S. war, not to speak of the legacy of hatred and revenge, will have lasting effects upon this "lovely land" with its "engaging people."[412]

It is difficult to conjure up in the imagination a statement from a Cambodian source that would not have served as proof of Communist iniquity as it entered the U.S. propaganda system. On the anniversary of the Khmer Rouge victory, Khieu Samphan gave a talk over Phnom Penh radio in which he said that agricultural production had improved and people now get enough to eat "to take care of their health and fatten them up." How was this received and interpreted in the United States? An

AP dispatch from Bangkok cites this comment, adding that he "made no reference to the starvation, disease and widespread executions reported by many Cambodian refugees. But he *admitted* that the country...had 'suffered untold difficulties' since the Communist victory."[413] The reader is presumably to conclude that this "admission" of untold difficulties such as starvation and disease supports the charges against the Communist regime. And just this conclusion is drawn by the *Christian Science Monitor* in the editorial on Cambodia already cited: "Reading between the lines is illuminating," the editors inform us, repeating the wording of the AP dispatch and commenting: "All this calculated mistreatment of a people in order to make a nation self-sufficient ought not to go unnoticed ..."[414] Presumably, they prefer the situation in Laos where the United States withholds all but a trickle of aid in the face of overwhelming disaster,[415] or Vietnam where the refusal is total and even initiatives to normalize relations have been rebuffed by the United States. Recall the widespread acknowledgement that the new regime had considerable, perhaps "spectacular" success in overcoming the food crisis caused by U.S. bombing, considerably more so than the other countries of Indochina. It was hardly irrational for the Cambodian regime to suppose that the United States would leave the country to starve after destroying its agricultural system. If the *New York Times*, the *Christian Science Monitor*, and the media in general were expressing any human concern, instead of simply grasping at any straw to find a way to denounce an official enemy, they would be in the forefront of the drive to bring the U.S. government to alter radically its inhuman policy of withholding sustenance from the countries it has destroyed, instead of gloating over the suffering of our victims in one of the most hypocritical displays in modern history.

Bertrand Russell was one of the early critics of Bolshevism after a visit to Russia in 1920. But he also had this to say:

Every failure of industry, every tyrannous regulation brought about by the desperate situation, is used by the Entente as a justification of its policy. If a man is deprived of food and drink, he will grow weak, lose his reason, and finally die. This is not usually considered a good reason for inflicting death by starvation. But where nations are concerned, the weakness and struggles are regarded as morally culpable and are held to justify further punishment...Is it surprising that professions of humanitarian feeling of the part of the English people are somewhat coldly received in Soviet Russia?[416]

Similarly, when poor peasants are driven into the jungle from villages destroyed by bombing, they may seek revenge. How much more apt are Russell's words when applied to the United States, which bears direct responsibility for bitter suffering throughout Indochina and now refuses to aid the victims because they do not meet its finely discriminating standards of human rights. It would require at least the talents of a Jonathan Swift to do justice to this scene.

To appreciate fully the cynicism of the press and editorial comments, it is necessary to recall the role of the U.S. mass media in supporting the "secret war" against Cambodia. Prior to the Nixon-Kissinger administration, Cambodia had been subjected to U.S. or U.S.-supported armed attack and subversion, but not on a regular and systematic basis. The massive assault against Cambodia began with the B-52 operations, initiated, according to the official record, on March 18, 1969. On March 26 the Cambodian government, recognized by the United States, issued statements condemning the bombing and strafing of "the Cambodian population living in the border regions...almost daily by U.S. aircraft," with increasing numbers of people killed and material destroyed, alleging that these attacks were directed against "peaceful Cambodian farmers" and demanding that "these criminal attacks must immediately and definitively stop ..."[417] Prince Sihanouk called a press conference on March 28 in which he emphatically denied reports circulating in the United States that he "would not oppose U.S. bombings of communist targets within my frontiers." He went on to say that Communists are not the only victims; "Unarmed and innocent people have been victims of U.S. bombs," including "the latest bombing, the victims of which were Khmer peasants, women and children in particular." He then issued an appeal to the press: "I appeal to you to publicize abroad this very clear stand of Cambodia—that is, I will in any case oppose all bombings on Cambodian territory under whatever pretext."[418]

The "secret bombings" continued, along with defoliation attacks for which no agency of the U.S. government has as yet admitted responsibility. On January 3, 1970 the Cambodian government issued an official White Paper giving specific details of U.S. and U.S.-client attacks on Cambodia up to May, 1969 by air, sea and land, with dates, places, specific numbers of casualties, photographs, etc. Occasional cases of U.S. bombing of Cambodian villages (including destruction of well-marked hospitals, bombing of ambulances attempting to retrieve wounded, etc.) became public knowledge when discovered by Americans who happened to be on the scene; the usual technique was for the government to deny these reports, then concede them if American eyewitnesses were found to be present.[419] Throughout this period, the press remained virtually silent. Neither Sihanouk's appeal nor the official White Paper which documented murderous U.S. government attacks on a "friendly" country were considered worthy of comment by the press; we know of no reference to the White Paper in the mainstream U.S. press, though it was hardly a secret.[420] The "secret bombings" continued, concealed by the U.S. press which was later to claim that it was Richard Nixon who kept the bombings secret from the press and the U.S. public, thus undermining the foundations of our democracy.[421]

There was one notable exception, namely, a *New York Times*

report by William Beecher which reported B-52 raids on "Vietcong and North Vietnamese supply dumps and base camps in Cambodia," citing U.S. sources and stating falsely that "Cambodia has not made any protest," disregarding Sihanouk's impassioned appeal and his protest against the murder of "Khmer peasants, women and children in particular."[422] Beecher's report also said that "in the past, American and South Vietnamese forces had occasionally fired across the border and even called in fighters or helicopter gunships to counter fire they received from enemy units there"; not mentioned is the somewhat more important fact that U.S. aircraft attacked Cambodian villages and that according to the "friendly" government of Cambodia, there were such incidents as an attack by U.S., South Vietnamese, and Korean armed forces on a Cambodian village along with aircraft of the same armed forces, after which U.S. and South Vietnamese troops invaded and burnt the villages, among other examples.[423]

Now the same media that helped conceal these and earlier U.S. attacks on Cambodia, as elsewhere in Indochina, are retrospectively eliminating the U.S. role from history and attributing the consequences of the U.S. attack to its surviving victims.

The peasant army that captured Phnom Penh did not conform to the colonialist cliche. They were not gentle folk with a delightful Khmer smile:

> The troops that seized Phnom Penh were dark-skinned peasants. Their close-cropped hair was covered by the traditional checkered peasant headcloth, their uniforms the faded remnants of what had once been olive green fatigues...They neither talked nor smiled. Some appear to be as old as 25 or 30, but a majority seem to be between 12 and 15 years old...Many had probably never seen a city street or a lawn before. Their appearance was equally shocking to many of the residents of Phnom Penh.[424]

They had suffered bitterly in a war that had been fought with no quarter. Their enemy was a foreign power that had come to de-

332   NOAM CHOMSKY AND EDWARD S. HERMAN

stroy their villages and land, and an urban society, hardly less foreign in their eyes, a colonial implantation that they know only as a murderer and a remote oppressor. In the regions where there had been brutal suppression of peasant revolts, there were many scores to settle. In the dark recesses of peasant life and history, unstudied and unknown beyond, there no doubt lay the roots of many more. The latent conflict was churned to a tempest of violence by the armed might of the United States, striking its savage blows directly or by the hands of its local clients. In Vietnam and Laos, where the circumstances were different though comparable, there appears to have been little murderous vengeance—little, that is, by historical standards. In Cambodia, however, the dark-skinned peasants exacted a fearful toll. Of that, there is little doubt.

Beyond that, evidence is slight and unreliable, and informed opinion ranges over quite a wide spectrum. At one extreme, we find Ponchaud—or rather, several different Ponchauds. One of them estimates "peace deaths" at over a million (including more than 100,000 killed); a second alleges that the Khmer Rouge were making good their formidable boast to eliminate 5-7 million people; and a third speaks of "the deaths of millions of Khmers." He regards it as established that a centralized plan dictated a systematic program of terror, massacre and oppression in every town and village, and apparently accepts Lacouture's interpretation that a small group of men who proclaim their Marxist ideology were systematically massacring and starving the people of Cambodia.

Across the spectrum opinions vary. Many, including State Department experts, are quite skeptical of a toll of "millions of Khmers"—we wonder, frankly, whether Ponchaud really believes such figures—and offer estimates of killed ranging from "thousands" upwards, with many more deaths from starvation and disease, though perhaps not the million such deaths predicted by U.S. government sources before the war's end. Many specialists suspect that executions were heavily concentrated in regions of little Khmer Rouge control and unusual peasant discontent and hatred, intensified by war and the U.S. bombings, particularly those of 1973.

There are also varying opinions on the character and effectiveness of Khmer Rouge social and economic programs and the roots of postwar Cambodian society in the traditional culture, Khmer nationalism, and the ideology of the leadership.

We suspect that the main body of informed opinion would accept the tempered comments of such critics of the Khmer Rouge as Charles Meyer that "one should be extremely careful in one's analysis of the politics" of the Khmer Rouge, whose leaders "incarnate really a part of the peasants, who recognized themselves in them," considering carefully such factors as "the weight of the past, the ideology of the leaders, the menaces from outside, and, naturally, the psychological factors as well as the economical, religious and other ones."[425] Informed opinion would also not dispute the judgment of Laura Summers that "...the Khmer revolution is the expression of deep cultural and social malaise unleashed by a sudden and violent foreign assault on the nation's social structure."[426]

If a serious study of the impact of Western imperialism on Cambodian peasant life is someday undertaken, it may well be discovered that the violence lurking behind the Khmer smile, on which Meyer and others have commented, is not a reflection of obscure traits in peasant culture and psychology, but is the direct and understandable response to the violence of the imperial system, and that its current manifestations are a no less direct and understandable response to the still more concentrated and extreme savagery of a U.S. assault that may in part have been designed to evoke this very response, as we have noted. Such a study may also show that the Khmer Rouge programs elicited a positive response from sectors of the Cambodian peasantry because they dealt with fundamental problems rooted in the feudal past and exacerbated by the imperial system with its final outburst of uncontrolled barbarism. Such a study, however, has yet to be undertaken. The West is much more concerned to excise from history the imperial role and to pretend that the history of contemporary Cambodia begins in April 1975 in a manner that is disconnected from the imperial legacy and must be explained by the lunacy of "nine men at the center" who were systematically massacring and starving the population in a form of "auto-genocide" that surpasses the horrors of Nazism.

While many questions remain open about Cambodia during the 1975-78 period that we have reviewed, on another question, the one that primarily concerns us, we feel that the facts are clear and overwhelming. The theory of the Free Press that we have been discussing throughout these two volumes is once again dramatically confirmed. The media, in this case as in others reviewed earlier, are serving in effect as a propaganda agency for the state. It is a fair generalization that the more extreme the condemnation of Cambodia, the more confident the claim that "Communism" lies at the roots of its present travail, the more diminished the U.S. share and responsibility—then the greater the exposure. The nature and quality of the evidence presented is of little moment. It is an astonishing fact that where evidence is subject to some independent check, it repeatedly and with remarkable consistency turns out to be fabricated, misleading, or dubious. Furthermore, exposure of falsehoods and fabrication is dismissed as insignificant and unimportant or is even condemned as apologetics for terror. Known fabrications and material of a most dubious nature continue to be exploited long after exposure. The extreme condemnations that constitute the standard fare in the media rest almost entirely on reports that cannot be checked, transmitted by sources that are revealed to be of extremely low credibility where they are subject to some verification.

Critics are not sent to concentration camps; Western societies are indeed free in this respect. Rather, they are permitted to speak to one another, within tiny circles. Meanwhile an image is concocted of a mighty force that must be vigorously combated by those courageous souls who try to stem the flood of apologetics; or it is claimed, with equal merit, that these lone voices must somehow find a way to penetrate the barriers of silence and unconcern. The propaganda system has been committed to eke what profit it could from the misery of Cambodia. Questions of truth are secondary. The serious moral issues that arise—the issues of the real locus of responsibility, the obligations to the victims, and the probable human consequences of the media barrage—have been entirely beyond the comprehension or concern of those who preach in the most strident tones of moral obligations. What enters history in the United States (and, we believe, the West generally, though we have not examined the media systematically elsewhere) is a version of the facts that suits the ideological requirements of dominant social groups; other interpretations, whatever their merits, are simply swept aside. The central theme that liberation from Western domination is a fate to be avoided at all costs is constantly and persistently drilled into popular consciousness. So effective is the awesome system of indoctrination and thought control that even many people who have been critics or skeptics are caught up in the well-orchestrated hysteria.

When the facts are in, it may turn out that the more extreme condemnations were in fact correct. But even if that turns out to be the case, it will in no way alter the conclusions we have reached on the central question addressed here: how the available facts were selected, modified, or sometimes invented to create a certain image offered to the general population. The answer to this question seems clear, and it is unaffected by whatever may yet be discovered about Cambodia in the future.

We urge once again that the reader concerned with the workings of Western propaganda compare the treatment of Cambodia—and the other societies of Indochina as well—with the attention given to other cases where the evidence available, the scale and character of the atrocities alleged, and even the time frame is comparable: Timor, for example. We stress again that in the case of Cambodia, as all observers of even moderate seriousness agree, what happened in the 1975-78 period under review, whatever it may have been, lay beyond our control, whereas in the case of Timor and other ongoing benign and constructive bloodbaths, that is far from true. Perhaps evidence will be forthcoming to support the claim of the British Foreign Office that "many hundreds of thousands of people have perished in Cambodia directly or indirectly as a result of the policies of the Communist government," evidence more credible than the material on which they uncritically relied. There is no doubt that many hundreds of thousands, if not millions of people have perished in other third world countries in the same period as a direct or indirect result of the policies of Western powers, victims of aggression, starvation, disease, hideous conditions of work, death squads, etc. Furthermore, this will continue, with continuing Western responsibility but without government protest or media exposure. The conclusions from such a comparison seem obvious.

Finally, perhaps we should stress some obvious points about what the future may reveal. We speculated in the preface that the Vietnamese invasion may prove disastrous for Cambodia. Any assessment of the resulting conditions should be carefully compared with what visitors observed just prior to the invasion— specifically, with their general assessment that food supplies appeared adequate and that there were certain constructive developments, whatever one may think of the regime.[427] If there is a deterioration in the conditions of Cambodia, this is very likely a consequence of the invasion itself; and here again the Western contribution cannot be ignored, including the special role played by the propaganda hysteria and climate of opinion of 1975-78, discussed at length above. A no less obvious point is that for some time at least, the Vietnamese (like the Pol Pot regime) are likely to permit only a guided and selected view, so that interpretation of any evidence that may become available will necessarily have to be subjected to critical analysis. The media record hardly encourages optimism, in this regard.

7

Final Comments

We have explored some of the ways in which the propaganda systems of the West, primarily that of the United States, have faced the major tasks noted in chapter 1 of this volume. Not surprisingly, inquiry reveals a highly selective culling of facts and much outright lying. Some areas of the world are almost entirely blacked out, where disclosure of major abuses would disturb both pliable clients and the U.S. economic, military and political interests that find this pliability advantageous. As we have described throughout the two volumes, the first principle of the Free Press is the averting of the eyes from benign or constructive terror, along with a general avoidance of invidious language and a sympathetic understanding for the difficult problems faced by the terrorizing elites backed by the United States. In sharp contrast, countries that ordinarily evoke minimal Western interest are thrust into the limelight when "enemy" terror and the evils of Communism can be revealed, and other useful lessons drawn. Thus the second principle of the Free Press is the intense and dedicated search for nefarious terror, which can be brought into focus without giving offense to any important groups and which contributes to domestic ideological mobilization.

Further devices used in handling nefarious terror, as we have described, include the stripping away of historical context, fabrication, and myth creation. Useful myths, once successfully instituted,

339

are virtually immune to correction. In focusing on refugees fleeing from Indochina and the prevailing harsh conditions there,
the Western media employ a third principle of the Free Press,
namely, "agent transference." That is, the critical role of the
United States in maintaining internecine conflict from 1954, and
its more direct shattering of the Indochinese societies and their
economic foundations, is acknowledged only occasionally and as
an afterthought. The only "agents" to whom responsibility is in-
dignantly attributed for the suffering in Indochina are the new
regimes that came into power in a presumably normal environment in 1975. Death and suffering from malnutrition and disease
in societies brought to ruin by U.S. intervention are displayed as
proof of the evil nature of Communism. Meanwhile, in the U.S.
sphere of influence working conditions of extraordinary severity,
massive dispossession of the peasantry, child labor, near slavery,
starvation in the midst of rapid economic "growth," and similar concomitants of development in accord with the Free World
model are, if noted at all, dismissed as an unfortunate element
of the process of modernization. And the hundreds of thousands
of refugees from Latin American subfascism, or the plight of the
victims of Indonesian aggression in East Timor or other benign
and constructive terror in Southeast Asia and elsewhere, and the
causes of their plight, are studiously ignored, in recognition of
the friendly client status of the official terrorists and the absence
of any useful lessons to be drawn from their depredations.

There are further and more general aims to be served by
the extensive effort to dispel what the *Wall Street Journal* calls
the "simple-minded myth" that Indochina's suffering is somehow
related to U.S. actions over the past thirty years. For the groups
that dominate economic, social, political and intellectual life in
the United States, it is a matter of urgency to ensure that no
serious challenge is raised to their predominant role, either in
ideology or in practice. While mild social reforms have been in-

troduced in the United States, others now conventional in Western Europe (e.g., national health insurance, minimal "worker participation" in industry, etc.) have been effectively resisted here, and there has been remarkable success in designing policy so that state intervention in the economy and social life serves the needs of the wealthy and powerful. We have noted that the absence of an organized left opposition in the United States has facilitated the work of the system of thought control and indoctrination. U.S. ideologists have been unusually successful in conducting "the engineering of consent," a technique of control that substitutes for the use of force in societies with democratic forms.[1] To serve this end, every effort must be made to discredit what is called "socialism" or "communism." In its more vulgar forms, the argument is that "socialism" or "Marxism" (which in practice means unwelcome social reform, since radical institutional change is hardly an immediate issue) leads inevitably to Gulag. The process of agent transference has made more plausible the doctrine that socialism must inevitably become tyranny. A recent media favorite is the group of Paris "new philosophers," whose congenial message that Marxism equals Gulag has assured them a ready and uncritical audience in the United States and Western Europe. In fact, their critique of authoritarian elements in Marxism-Leninism is remarkably shallow as compared with the long tradition of left-wing libertarian thought that has been virtually ignored in the West, and their enormous success in France reflects in part conditions specific to French intellectual life,[2] but U.S. media have little care or understanding for any of this. The access of this group to the media and the receptivity to their slogans is a perfect counterpart to the curtain of silence drawn over the proliferating Gulags in the U.S. sphere, as well as the agent transference in Indochina.

There is, to be sure, an element of absurdity in the constant refrain that socialism equals Gulag, as revealed by events in the underdeveloped societies. A comparison of the problems facing such societies as Vietnam, Laos, Cambodia, Cuba, Mozambique, etc., with the situation in the industrial West would simply be ridiculed in societies that were not subjected to such effective ideological control as ours. But despite the inherent absurdity of attributing, say, revenge killings by Cambodian peasants who were bombed out of their homes by Western force to "Marxism" or "atheism," the practice is common and quite successful as a tactic in engineering consent to the priorities and structures of contemporary state capitalism.

In the United States, this tactic has become a virtual reflex. Bolshevik and later Stalinist crimes have regularly been exploited as a weapon against movements seeking reform or revolutionary change. During the Red Scare after World War I, which was quite effective in controlling labor militancy and eliminating radical intellectual currents, the *Wall Street Journal* wailed: "We talk of parlor Bolshevists, but what of those other Bolshevists, in the Cabinet, or at any rate near the throne?" Similar accusations, loosely associating reform Democrats with Stalinist crimes despite the eager and frightened collaboration of many liberals were common during the era mislabelled "McCarthyism." Harry Truman even denounced the civil rights movement of the 1950s as a Communist plot—conceding, in response to inquiry, that he had no proof, but explaining: "I know that usually when trouble hits the country the Kremlin is behind it."[3] The 1970s campaign against "Big Government" (understood to cover health and welfare activities but not the police and military establishment) is likewise facilitated by a propaganda barrage carrying the implicit message that "socialism equals Gulag." In this context, too, it is an effective tactic to focus attention on real or invented atrocities committed in underdeveloped ex-colonies that use the phrase "socialism" in reference to their programs of mass mobilization under authoritarian state control to carry out industrialization and modernization.

One final factor merits a few words of comment. So-called "North-South conflicts" do not necessarily take the form of imperial intervention. At various levels and in a multitude of interactions there is a continuing struggle over access to resources, terms of trade, opportunities for international capital and other problems. A general public mood of hostility to the Third World is useful to the managers of the industrial democracies as they attempt to manipulate these conflicts to their benefit. In contrast, the sympathy towards Third World independence movements that developed during the post-World War II struggles for national liberation, brutally repressed primarily by France and the United States, is an impediment to the imposition of measures that will meet the requirements of the world's wealthy industrial powers. In this context, it is useful to engender hatred, contempt and moralistic outrage directed against the nationalist movements of the Third World, particularly those that have recently escaped from the domination of the United States. It should hardly come as a surprise, therefore, that a major effort should be directed towards reversing the worldwide currents of sympathy towards the people of Indochina that were aroused by the assault of the U.S. war machine. That struggle came to be perceived as symbolic of the conflicts between the industrialized West and the former colonial domains, and it imposed barriers to the mobilization of public support for the traditional measures that may be required to preserve a favorable investment climate in the coming era.

These remarks bear directly on the framework of Western propaganda. They do not touch another and very different question: how should one evaluate the programs and character of the countries that have been liberated from Western domination, or respond to developments there? Our primary concern here has been U.S. global policy and propaganda, and the filtering and distorting effect of Western ideology, not the problems of reconstruction and modernization in societies that have been victimized by Western imperialism. Correspondingly, we have not developed or expressed our views here on the nature of the Indochinese regimes. To assess the contemporary situation in Indochina and the programs of the current ruling groups is a worthwhile endeavor, but it has not been our objective.

As for appropriate response, its central component in the current situation should be a committed and very substantial effort to help the victims, insofar as this is possible: those who are oppressed, those who have fled, those who are seeking to reconstruct some kind of viable existence from the wreckage. Such response is not to be discerned among the dominant classes and states of either East or West.

There is no single cause for the misery and oppression that we find in every part of the world. But there are some major causes, and some of these are close at hand and subject to our influence and, ultimately, our control. These factors and the social matrix in which they are embedded will engage the concern and efforts of people who are honestly committed to alleviate human suffering and to contribute to freedom and justice.

The success of the Free Press in reconstructing imperial ideology since the U.S. withdrawal from Indochina has been spectacular. The shift of the United States from causal agent to concerned bystander—and even to leader in the world struggle for human rights—in the face of its empire of client fascism and long, vicious assault on the peasant societies of Indochina, is a remarkable achievement. The system of brainwashing under freedom, with mass media voluntary self-censorship in accord with the larger interests of the state, has worked brilliantly. The new propaganda line has been established by endless repetition of the Big Distortions and negligible grant of access to non-establishment points of view; all rendered more effective by the illusion of equal access and the free flow of ideas. U.S. dissenters can produce their

Samizdats freely, and stay out of jail, but they do not reach the general public or the Free Press except on an episodic basis. This reflects the power and interests that benefit from the uncontrolled arms race, the status quo of domestic economic arrangements, and the external system of multinational expansion and collaboration with the Shahs, Suhartos, Marcoses in the contemporary "development" and sacking of the Third World. Change will come only when material facts arouse sufficient numbers to force a reassessment of policy. At the present time, the machine expands, the mass media adapt to the political economy, and human rights are set aside except in rhetorical flourishes useful for ideological reconstruction.

Notes

Preface to the 2014 Edition

1. Among other publications, see E.S. Herman and N. Chomsky, *Manufacturing Consent*, 1988, Pantheon; second edition with new introduction, 2002. N. Chomsky, *Necessary Illusions*, 1989, South End. Edward Herman and Robert McChesney, *Global Media: the Missionaries of Global Capitalism*, 1997.

2. For review, see N. Chomsky, "'Green Light' for War Crimes," in Chomsky, *A New Generation Draws the Line* (Verso, 2000). Richard Tanter, Mark Selden, and Stephen Shalom, eds., *East Timor, Indonesia, and the World Community*, Roman & Littlefield, 2000 (in which a slightly different version of "'Green Light' for War Crimes" also appears). For detailed review of the early years, in addition to the chapter reprinted here, see Chomsky, *Towards a New Cold War* (1982).

3. See *Manufacturing Consent*.

4. Fallows, *Atlantic*, June 1982. Power, *"A Problem from Hell: America and the Age of Genocide*, Basic Books, 2002.

5. Moynihan with Suzanne Weaver, *A Dangerous Place*, Little, Brown, 1978.

6. John Holdridge (State Dept.), Hearing before the Subcommittee on Asian and Pacific Affairs of the Committee on Foreign Affairs, House of Representatives, 97th Congress, 2nd sess., Sept. 14, 1982, 71.

7. Melvyn P. Leffler and Odd Arne Westad, ed., *Cambridge History of the Cold War*, Cambridge University Press, 2010.

8. Open Society Foundation, *Globalizing Torture: CIA Secret Detention and Extraordinary Rendition*, Feb. 2013.

9. Greg Grandin, "The Latin American Exception," http://www.tomdispatch .com/blog/175650/.

Preface

1. Peter Weintraub, "The exodus and the agony," *Far Eastern Economic Review,* 22 December 1978.

2. *Ibid.*

3. Editor's Comment, "Refugees, blackmail and a remedy," *Far Eastern Economic Review,* 5 January 1979.

4. President Carter, explaining that "as long as I am president, the government of the United States will continue throughout the world to enhance human rights. No force on earth can separate us from that commitment," which is "the soul of our foreign policy." Presumably, the force that has separated us from that commitment in Iran, Indonesia, the Philippines and elsewhere is extra-terrestrial. Edward Walsh, "Carter Asserts Human Rights Is 'Soul of Our Foreign Policy,'" *Washington Post,* 7 December 1978.

5. See chapter 6, note 228.

6. Nayan Chanda, "Cambodia: Fifteen days that shook Asia," *Far Eastern Economic Review,* 19 January 1979.

7. "Ho's will is done," *Economist,* 13 January 1979. The same was true quite generally. Thus the *Washington Post* commented editorially that while the Vietnamese invasion "was not, of course, a direct response to Sen. McGovern" (who had called for military intervention several months before), nonetheless "it probably did arise in part from a perception that Pol Pot's demise would be accepted as a deliverance in every corner of the international community except Peking"—as it was by the *Post.* Editorial, "Phnom Penh falls," 9 January 1979.

8. Jay Mathews, "Sihanouk to Aid Ousted Rulers," *Washington Post* (9 January 1979), reporting from Peking.

9. John Fraser, *Toronto Globe and Mail,* reporting from Peking, reprinted in the *Christian Science Monitor* (12 January 1979).

10. Jay Mathews, "Sihanouk: 'We Were Privileged, Compared to the Rest,'" *Washington Post* (9 January 1979).

    According to a direct transcript of the tape that we have received from journalists who were present, the omitted material reads: "If you allow me to speak about the common people, the common people, food, cooking: the cooking is good, clean, clean. The dining rooms are clean. They have good hygiene, Asian hygiene..." Sihanouk added that "the conditions of life are good. At the beginning, yes, we were in difficulty because of the war, the revenge of the war. But now it is good! Now? Before the conquest of our country by the Vietnamese the conditions were good, were good, I can say, I can assure you."

    We have kept in the text to the rendition of Sihanouk's remarks that appeared in the U.S. press. These are not always exactly accurate, according to the transcript, but they convey the sense accurately, though many of Sihanouk's more favorable comments concerning the regime do not appear. Thus he said that "I would like to see my government, the government of my country, presided over by Pol Pot and the Communist Party of Cambodia...it is right of the Pol Pot regime to do what they have done, since the people accept their status...I do not pretend to say that they have violated human rights. Perhaps they are right, I don't know. Sincerely, I do not know. I have not the right to condemn them. I could not condemn them." Responding to a question from Fox Butterfield of the *New York Times,* Sihanouk made it clear that he opposed the internal regimentation, lack of communication, and other restrictions. But though "my conscience is not in agreement with my friends the Khmers Rouges,...it seems to me that the majority of the people agree with Pol Pot and his team so far as the regime is concerned. In fact—there is it seems a better social justice. Why? Because the rich, there are no more rich, and the poor, they are less poor, so there is a movement of unification of Cambodian society. There is no rich, there is no poor. This is, I think, what pleases the Cambodian people—I say. I think the majority...I think there are some disadvantages. But for the poorest I think there are advantages, because you know their houses are better—their food is better."

11. Mathews, "Sihanouk to Aid Ousted Rulers."
12. Norodom Sihanouk, address to the UN Security Council, representing Democratic Kampuchea, *Guardian* (New York), 24 January 1979. The week before the *Guardian* had reprinted the entire program of the Kampuchean National United Front for National Survival (KNUFNS; the Khmer group placed in power by the Vietnamese). It is remarkable that one has to turn to the tiny Marxist-Leninist press to find a record of such documents in the media.
13. Mathews, "Sihanouk to Aid Ousted Rulers."
14. *Guardian, op. cit.*
15. Mathews, "Sihanouk: 'We Were Privileged, Compared to the Rest.'"
16. William Borders, "Task Facing India: Easing Misery of Masses," *New York Times* (2 January 1979), quoting the well-known nutritionist Jean Mayer. The report describes families who are seriously undernourished while high-quality wheat that they cannot afford to buy is stored "in sheds and warehouses all over the country." This is not an atrocity by Western standards, but rather a difficult problem yet to be solved.
17. Ho Kwon Ping, "Thailand's broken ricebowl," *Far Eastern Economic Review,* 1 December 1978.
18. *Ibid.*
19. See Stephen R. Heder, "Origins of the Conflict," *Southeast Asia Chronicle,* no. 64, September-October 1978, and for further detail, Heder's article "The Historical Bases of the Kampuchean-Vietnam Conflict: Development of the Kampuchean Communist Movement and Its Relations with Vietnamese Communism, 1930-1970," *Bulletin of Concerned Asian Scholars,* volume 11, no. 1, 1979.
20. In an accompanying article in the same issue of the *Southeast Asia*

Chronicle (see note 19), Heder reviews the history of the delineation of the border, which had been readjusted by the French to the detriment of Cambodia for two main reasons: Cambodia was only a protectorate while Cochinchina (approximately the southern third of re-united Vietnam) was a full colony viewed by the French "as literally French territory"; "The commercial agricultural interests of the French colonists in Cochinchina were much stronger and much better organized than those in Kampuchea," and therefore were able to impel the French imperial rulers to adjust the boundary in their favor. As a result, many ethnic Khmer areas were included in Cochinchina.

21. It was certainly obvious to any visitor to Hanoi during the war. The Vietnamese, while clearly trying to maintain a balance in the Sino-Soviet dispute and to contribute to healing it if possible, went out of their way to express their concern over potential Chinese expansionism, often rather symbolically, for example, by elaborate references to much earlier history.

22. For further discussion of the international aspects of the conflict, see Lowell Finley, "Raising the Stakes," in the *Southeast Asia Chronicle*, no. 64.

23. Bernard Weinraub, "Vietnamese Said to Shatter a Big Cambodian Force," *New York Times* (3 December 1978).

24. "Vietnam Offensive Reportedly Starts in Northeast Cambodia," *Washington Post* (5 December 1978), datelined Bangkok.

25. Nayan Chanda, "Words, not deeds, from Peking," *Far Eastern Economic Review*, 22 December 1978.

26. Nayan Chanda, "Cambodia: Fifteen Days that Shook Asia."

27. *Ibid.*

28. William Chapman, "Cambodian resistance builds," *Washington Post* (18 January 1979) citing a "source" who reports that "The Vietnamese have the towns, and the Cambodians have the countryside" and reporting surprise by "informed sources" in Bangkok at the "swiftness with which [guerrilla counter-attack] has flourished in so many places." Richard Nations, "Pol Pot Forces Regroup, Harass Vietnamese in Cambodian Countryside," *Washington Post* (26 January 1979) and "Major Khmer Rouge Attacks on Vietnamese Yield Success," *Ibid.*, (31 January 1979), reporting that the Vietnamese hold "an almost empty strategic shell" while the Khmer Rouge move with considerable freedom "among the population in the countryside," with serious fighting throughout much of the country: "the Khmer Rouge appear to have 'jerked the anvil out from under the Vietnamese hammer blow,' in the words of one veteran Indochina analyst" while another estimates that 60,000 men have regrouped in large units of the Cambodian army; "rice has had to be airlifted into Battambang and Siem Reap—the traditional granaries of Cambodia—a good indication that the Vietnamese either cannot move into the countryside or find no food when they arrive" and that "the Khmer Rouge appear to have denied their enemies the stocks of

fuel and food the Vietnamese appear to have been counting on"; "It now looks like a far longer, bloodier and more expensive operation than Hanoi probably counted on," one observer said. See also Henry Kamm, "Vietnamese Army Is Said to Face Vigorous Cambodian Resistance," *New York Times* (2 February 1979).

29. Elizabeth Becker, "Offensive Threatens Cambodia's Capital," *Washington Post* (6 January 1979).

30. Kamm, *op. cit.*

31. The standard assumption of the Western media is that "the Khmer Rouge government in Cambodia was presumably hated by almost everybody" (London *Economist,* 27 January 1979). This was written at the same time that Western intelligence was issuing analyses of the sort indicated in note 28. The *Economist* adds that "the Khmers Rouges are physically isolated from a source of supplies to a degree that Vietnam never was after the early days of the French war." That is accurate, and may lead to the crushing of resistance whatever the actual level of popular support may be, a question that is considerably more open than the standard line of the media indicates.

32. Malcolm W. Browne, "Red Clash on Cambodia: Big Hit at the U.N.," *New York Times* (13 January 1979).

1 The Setting

1. For details concerning this remarkable episode, see N. Chomsky, "The Peace Hoax," *Liberation,* January 1973: "Endgame: the tactics of peace in Vietnam," *Ramparts,* April 1973; "Reporting Indochina: the news media and the legitimation of lies," *Social Policy,* September-October 1973. On the history of the negotiations and their aftermath, see Gareth Porter, *A Peace Denied,* Indiana, 1975.

2. Cf. AP, "U.S. Trade Embargo Against Hanoi Quietly Extended by President," *Washington Post,* 14 September 1978: "President Carter, rebuffing persistent signals of friendship from Vietnam, is quietly extending the U.S. trade embargo against Hanoi." Officials concede that there are "sound economic arguments for lifting the embargo," since "trade with Vietnam could help cut back on the U.S. trade deficit." But the importance of punishing the Vietnamese and internal political considerations far outweigh these concerns.

3. On these matters, see Gabriel Kolko, *The Politics of War,* Random House, 1969; Joyce and Gabriel Kolko, *The Limits of Power,* Harper & Row, 1972. On the United States and the European labor movement, see Ronald Radosh, *American Labor and United States Foreign Policy,* Random House, 1969; Alfred W. McCoy et al., *The Politics of Heroin in Southeast Asia,* Harper & Row, 1972, chapter 2; Fred Hirsch and Richard Fletcher, *CIA and the Labour Movement,* Spokesman, 1977; Roy Godson, *American Labor and European Politics,* Crane, Russak, &

Co., 1976. This last work, based on internal AFL documents, explains how the AFL exploited postwar starvation to transfer power to its own associates by keeping food from their opponents, employed gangsters as strike breakers to split the labor movement, undermined efforts of French labor to block shipments to the French forces attempting to reconquer Indochina, and so on. All of this is presented in glowing terms as a great humanitarian achievement in defense of democracy, liberty, and a free trade union movement.

4. *Trialogue,* journal of the Trilateral Commission, no. 18, Summer, 1978, p. 15.

5. Richard West, "Re-fighting the Vietnam war," *Spectator,* 16 July 1977. West was one of the more perceptive and independent-minded of the foreign correspondents in Vietnam for many years. On the consequences for the U.S. Army, see David Cortright, *Soldiers in Revolt,* Doubleday, 1975.

6. See the references of footnote 1.

7. Joseph Buttinger, *Vietnam: The Unforgettable Tragedy,* Horizon, 1977, p. 148.

8. T.D. Allman, "The U.S. refugee policy," *Manchester Guardian Weekly,* 12 April 1975. It is interesting to compare the euphoric descriptions regularly offered by apologists. See e.g., P.J. Honey, "Viet Nam Argument," *Encounter,* November 1965, for a typical example, in midcourse.

9. For details, see N. Chomsky and E.S. Herman, "Saigon's Corruption Crisis," *Ramparts,* December 1974; Porter, *op. cit.*; Buttinger, *op. cit.*; Maynard Parker, "Vietnam: The War That Won't End," *Foreign Affairs,* January 1975; Frank Snepp, *Decent Interval,* Random House, 1977.

10. Bernard Fall, *Last Reflections on a War,* Doubleday, 1967, pp. 33-34.

11. On the role of this prime candidate for a war crimes trial, as depicted largely in his own words, see N. Chomsky, *For Reasons of State,* Pantheon, 1973, pp. 87ff. Komer is now a respected official in the Human Rights administration.

12. Snepp, *op. cit.,* p. 568. This book should be read with caution. Though Snepp resigned from the CIA and is critical of U.S. errors, he writes completely within the general framework of the state propaganda system and, despite his alleged expertise, repeatedly offers propaganda fabrications as fact. For example, Snepp repeats standard myths with regard to the North Vietnamese land reform and the Hue massacre (pp. 211, 354); his account suffers further from internal inconsistency in the numbers game. See Volume I, chapter 5, sections 2.2, 2.3. See also chapter 2, footnote 9, below.

13. 4 May 1977. The same editorial laments that the Northerners who "are streaming down to manage the reconstruction" are "dispersing the discontented middle classes, appropriating the consumer goods while denouncing them as alien"; while in Cambodia, Communist purges are

"said to have taken hundreds of thousands of lives" and in "lovely little Laos,...the elites are fleeing to Thailand." We return below to the question of how the *Times* reacted when it learned that "lovely little Laos" was being "secretly" bombed by the state it serves and to the alleged facts in this editorial about "what we have learned."

14. See Volume I, chapter 5. The media do most of their editorializing in what are called "news reports," a far more effective device since propaganda is disguised as objective fact. Thus in a column by *Times* Asia correspondent Fox Butterfield we read that "the Communist victory last year and the coming formal unification evidently have made the fiction of a separate southern movement no longer necessary," *New York Times* (25 April 1976). That the separate southern movement was a fiction was, of course, a staple of U.S. propaganda, dutifully repeated by obedient journalists though rejected by many serious analysts; Bernard Fall, for example. Typically the *Times* simply intones government propaganda without qualification. *Times* correspondents could hardly be expected to take note of the fact that the southern movement, however one may debate its status, was destroyed by the U.S. aggression that the *Times* supported; how much more convenient to exploit this consequence as proof that it was a fiction no longer needed by the devious communists.

15. John Pilger, "Vietnam: Do not weep for those just born," *New Statesman*, 15 September 1978; Canadian officials reported by 1965 that Vinh, a city of 60,000, had been flattened; cf. Fall, *Last Reflections*, pp. 232-33. See Jean and Simonne Lacouture. *Vietnam: voyage à travers une victoire*, Seuil, 1976, for a graphic eyewitness description of the extent and character of the damage to property and persons throughout Vietnam. The literature on the consequences of the U.S. war is substantial. See, among others, E.S. Herman, *Atrocities in Vietnam: Myths and Realities*, Pilgrim Press, 1970; J.B. Neiland, et al., *Harvest of Death*, Free Press, 1972; J.C. Pomonti, *La Rage d'etre Vietnamien*, Seuil, 1974; and many other sources.

16. Internal documents, in contrast, make it clear that the United States explicitly intended, from immediately after the "disaster" of the Geneva Accords, to use military force "to defeat local Communist subversion or rebellion not constituting armed attack," in direct defiance of the "supreme law of the land" which restricts the use of force to self-defense against armed attack, and to extend the use of such force elsewhere, including China, if need be. NSC 5429/2, August 1954. These crucial and explicit recommendations were too hot to handle for the Pentagon Papers historians, who seriously misrepresented the contents of the document, and they are consistently ignored by academic scholarship, no doubt for similar reasons. Cf. *For Reasons of State*, pp. 100f.

17. Despite the massive destruction caused by the war, the NLF-PRG nevertheless was able to play a substantial role to the end. See, for

example, the eyewitness report of the capture of Quang Ngai by southern PRG forces, with barely a shot being fired, by Earl S.
Martin, a Mennonite social worker in Vietnam who was fluent in Vietnamese;
Reaching the Other Side, Crown, 1978. The press generally referred only
to a North Vietnamese invasion.

18. See Volume I, chapter 5, section 1.2. See also London *Economist,* "The
bottle stayed corked," 13 May 1978: "The original purpose of that long,
inefficient war was to keep Indochina as the 'cork in the bottle'" (our
emphasis). The choice of adjective is revealing: would the *Economist*
speak of the German bombing of England merely as "inefficient"? The
distinction reflects the deep racist and imperialist assumptions that
permeate Western liberal thought. We return directly to the quite comparable "pragmatic" opposition to the war on the part of U.S. "doves."
For detailed analysis of this strategy, based on internal documents, see *For Reasons of State,* chapter 1, section V; also R.B. DuBoff,
"Business ideology and foreign policy," in *The Pentagon Papers,* Gravel
edition, vol. 5, N. Chomsky and H. Zinn, eds., *Critical Essays,* Beacon,
1972. The rational imperial planning that always lay behind the U.S.
intervention in Vietnam has been effectively written out of history by
U.S. scholars, as inconsistent with the image of U.S. benevolence (or
perhaps, "tragic error") that "responsible scholarship" must convey.
For some recent discussion see Chomsky, *'Human Rights' and American Foreign Policy,* Spokesman, 1978; *Intellectuals and the State,* Het
Wereldvenster, 1978.

19. This scandalous policy is based in part on rational imperial strategy,
and in part simply on chauvinist pique of the sort expressed by Asian
scholar Robert Scalapino of Berkeley, who said in Hong Kong that
"We Americans have got used to the idea of aiding those we defeat in
war, but I find it unacceptable for the U.S. to aid a country which has
defeated us." *Far Eastern Economic Review,* 15 July 1977.

20. Gavin Young, "The nonviolent war in Southeast Asia; Let's see which
system works best, say the members of ASEAN, a five-nation, non-
communist bloc, which is working to obliterate communism, not with
bombs but with prosperity," *London Observer,* reprinted in the *Boston
Globe* (15 October 1978).

21. For discussion of these matters, see N. Chomsky, *American Power and
the New Mandarins,* Pantheon, 1969; *'Human Rights' and American Foreign Policy.* See Charles Kadushin, *The American Intellectual Elite,* Little,
Brown, 1974, for detailed analysis of attitudes of a certain group of
intellectuals towards the war.

22. Mitchell S. Ross, *New Republic,* 18 June 1977.

23. We cannot take the space here to explore the astonishing comparison
between the support of volunteers for the Spanish Loyalists against
Franco's Moroccan army backed by military forces from Nazi Germany and Fascist Italy, with U.S. government intervention to impose

and support client fascism in South Vietnam. Notice how, in Peters' account, the U.S. military forces that were bombing South Vietnamese before we "began to go wrong" in 1965 have become "volunteers" who were "help[ing] the South." By the term "South," Peters is referring to the client regime established by the United States, not the people of South Vietnam, who, as U.S. analysts at the time and later were well aware, had little use for the U.S. creation and to a substantial extent supported the NLF (about half the population, according to U.S. analysts, a higher proportion than supported the American rebels in the revolutionary war; see chapter 2, section 2).

24. "Deliverance," editorial, *Washington Post* (30 April 1975).

25. *New York Times* (21, 24 April, 1 May 1975).

26. Richard Strout (TRB), *New Republic*, 25 April 1975.

27. The real ends of U.S. intervention in Indochina, as disclosed by state documents, indicate an almost total amorality and willingness to use force in complete disregard of law to achieve balance of power and economic objectives. Democracy, independence, self-determination and the welfare of Indochina were useful manipulative symbols, but their relevance to policy decisions of U.S. leaders approached zero in value.

28. *Dissent,* Summer 1964; Russell's criticism is reprinted in Bertrand Russell, *War Crimes in Vietnam,* Monthly Review Press, 1967.

29. Editor's comment, *Dissent,* Spring 1975. They have yet to comment on their confident prediction that "all" of the millions of people who fought against the Communists would be slaughtered, their reason for supporting the U.S. "intervention," which by 1964 already involved major U.S. military activities, massive forced-population removal, and other atrocities.

30. *Dissent,* Fall 1978. They explain that while *they* do not accept the premises of the question, others are raising it, so that it should be discussed; evidently, they consider it a serious question, worthy of discussion. On the ambiguity of their own current attitudes towards the exercise of force and violence by the United States, see the comments by the editors on the question of military intervention.

31. See chapter 6, footnote 7.

32. Cited by Marilyn Young, "Critical Amnesia," *Nation,* 2 April 1977, from the *New Republic,* 22 January 1977. Young discusses this and other comparable reviews of Emerson's book in the *New York Times* and the *New York Review of Books.*

33. Arthur M. Schlesinger, Jr., *The Bitter Heritage: Vietnam and American Democracy, 1941-1966,* Houghton Mifflin, 1966.

34. On the so-called "McCarthyite period," a term that minimizes the role of cold war liberals, see David Caute, *The Great Fear: the Anti-Communist Purge under Truman and Eisenhower,* Simon and Schuster, 1978; Mary S. McAuliffe, *Crisis on the Left: Cold war Politics and American Liberals, 1947-1954,* University of Massachusetts, 1978; Robert J.

Goldstein, *Political Repression in Modern America*, Schenkman, 1978. See also Richard M. Freeland, *The Truman Doctrine and the Origins of McCarthyism*, Knopf, 1972; Michael P. Rogin, *The Intellectuals and McCarthy: the Radical Specter*, MIT, 1967. On the extensive and quite effective repression by the national political police (FBI) during the 1960s, see Morton H. Halperin *et al.*, *The Lawless State*, Penguin, 1976; N. Blackstock, ed., *COINTELPRO*, Random House, 1976; Dave Dellinger, *More Power than We Know*. Doubleday, 1975. The scale of FBI activities can be appreciated from one minor revelation. In civil suits charging the FBI with illegal surveillance it was revealed by the Bureau that in the Chicago office alone—one of 59 field offices—there were 3,207 linear feet of files under the "subversive" and "extremist" classifications, an estimated 7.7 million pages. From 1966 the Chicago FBI office paid out more than $2.5 million to 5,145 informants. These classifications do not include sedition, sabotage, or other criminal investigative files. In the "subversive" classification there are such organizations as the American Civil Liberties Union; under "extremists" we find CORE, NAACP, the Afro-American Patrolmen's League, Rev. Jesse Jackson's operation PUSH, etc. Rob Warden, *Washington Post* (9 April 1978). The Chicago documents also acknowledge an FBI break-in at the offices of the Chicago Committee to Defend the Bill of Rights, which was formed during the "McCarthy" period to oppose government repression. *Washington Post*, AP (21 January 1978). On the efforts of the FBI in Chicago to incite murder of Black leaders and their involvement in political assassination when these efforts failed, see the references cited above. FBI surveillance was the least significant of the disruptive and often violent acts initiated by the Federal Government as opposition to its policies developed. On the "staggering dimensions" of FBI actions to ruin the personal lives of dissenters, foment violence, etc. see William M. Kunstler, "Writers of the Purple Page," *Nation*, 30 December 1978.
35. *Internews International Bulletin*, 13 February 1978.
36. See for example the *New Republic* editorial, 29 April 1978, a defense of Carter against criticism which is coupled with a complaint that he and his advisers have only "vague notions about the East-West conflict which remains the central fact of international relations today." The editors continue: "We thought we saw the beginnings of a coherent strategy in Carter's 'tough' talk several weeks ago at Winston-Salem, North Carolina. But then the neutron bomb decision indicated that the president had been only talking."
37. Theodore Draper, "Appeasement & Détente," *Commentary*, February 1976.
38. John Stockwell, *In Search of Enemies*, Norton, 1978. Stockwell was CIA station chief in Angola. He provides authoritative evidence that, despite the claims of Carter and the mass media, Soviet intervention in

Angola *followed* that of the United States (pp. 66-67). He resigned in protest from the CIA after Katangese based in Angola invaded their native province in Zaire (apparently, with considerable local support). According to Stockwell, the CIA had warned of such retaliation if the United States persisted in supporting attacks on Angola mounted from Zaire, but the warning was ignored by Kissinger, who seems to have been interested in developing an international confrontation with the Russians as his efforts to subvert the Paris agreements collapsed in Vietnam. Cf. John Stockwell, "Why I am Leaving the CIA," *Washington Post* (10 April 1977). See Seymour M. Hersh, "Kissinger-Colby Briefings on C.I.A. Called Misleading by Senate Panel," *New York Times* (16 July 1978), on how Kissinger and Colby "misled Congress about the extent of the Central Intelligence Agency's activities in the 1975 civil war in Angola, according to sources with first-hand knowledge"—to put it more bluntly, lied to Congress, the least significant but most discussed element of this sordid affair.

39. Cited by Clayton Fritchey, "Encore for Pax Americana," *Washington Post* (25 March 1978). Fritchey is critical of the renewal of interventionist ideology.

40. Stephen S. Rosenfeld, "The case for using force against the third world," *Washington Post* (5 May 1978), citing a Rand Corporation study by Guy J. Pauker. See also C. Cooper et al., The American Experience with Pacification in Vietnam: an Overview of Pacification, NTIS, U.S. Department of Commerce, March 1972, a study of pacification commissioned by the Pentagon and undertaken by the Institute for Defense Analysis, a university-based consortium, which "derives doctrinal and operational lessons from the US experience with pacification in South Vietnam to guide US policy-makers in providing technical assistance and advice in the future to a friendly government facing an internal security problem." The study explains the problems caused, for example, by the threat of "political struggle" from 1956 (13), and later, "the vast swarms of refugees from Viet Cong controlled or bombed-out villages" (xvi; "most [refugees fled] from battle-ravaged and bomb-destroyed hamlets and villages" (48), which confounded "American and Vietnamese humanitarian efforts" (xvi)), and by the "local bully boys...[who]... have made Saigon into a seething social jungle"(49). Other problems are caused by "our strong sense of social justice and morality" which leads us to take over programs best left to the friendly government (43). Some of the techniques suggested "should be tried on a pilot basis in one or two other insurgency situations (e.g., the Philippines)" (61).

41. Cf. Richard B. Du Boff and E.S. Herman, "The New Economics: Handmaiden of Inspired Truth," *Review of Radical Political Economics,* August 1972; Richard J Walton, *Cold War and Counterrevolution: the Foreign Policy of John F. Kennedy,* Penguin, 1973.

2 Precedents

1.   For example, the outstanding study *Israel, La fin des mythes* (Albin Mi-
     chel, 1975) by Amnon Kapeliouk, an Israeli journalist who is a regular
     correspondent for *Le Monde*, which was unable to find a U.S. publisher;
     or *The Gun and the Olive Branch* (Harcourt Brace Jovanovich, 1977) by
     David Hirst of the *Manchester Guardian*, published in the United States
     but virtually ignored. There are many other cases.

2.   Isaiah Berlin, "The Bent Twig," *Foreign Affairs*, October 1972. Though
     the context suggests that he was referring to the statist intelligentsia
     of "the left," the term and accompanying analysis apply quite gener-
     ally. See N. Chomsky, *Intellectuals and the State*, for some discussion of
     the typical role of those who Bakunin called "the new class" a century
     ago—a concept that is periodically rediscovered and distorted in ways
     appropriate to contemporary ideology.

3.   William Harper and James Henry Hammond, quoted in Drew Gilpin
     Faust, "A Southern Stewardship: The Intellectual and the Proslavery
     Argument," *American Quarterly*, forthcoming.

4.   H.C. Peterson, *Propaganda for War: The Campaign against American
     Neutrality, 1914-17*, University of Oklahoma Press, 1939, pp. 29, 175-
     76. See also Arthur Ponsonby, *Falsehood in Wartime*, Dutton, 1928.
     Compare the record of popular attitudes toward the U.S. war in Viet-
     nam, which shows a somewhat similar pattern. See Bruce Andrews,
     Public Constraint and American Policy in Vietnam, SAGE Publications,
     International Studies Series, vol. 4, 1976; Andrews observes, however,
     that popular "pacifism" was often of the "win or get out" variety.

5.   James Morgan Read, *Atrocity Propaganda: 1914-1919*, Yale, 1941,
     p. 201. The following account relies on Read's judicious study, from
     which the quotes are taken; pp. 201ff.

6.   On the problems of obtaining an accurate record from refugees, given
     their generally dependent and vulnerable position, see Chomsky, *At
     War With Asia*, pp. 240-41, a discussion of refugee reports of U.S.
     atrocities in Laos. (See also Volume I, chapter 3, section 4.4, and the
     discussion in chapter 6 below.)

7.   "Who Willed American Participation," *New Republic*, 14 April 1917,
     cited in Clarence Karier, "Making the World Safe for Democracy: An
     Historical Critique of John Dewey's Pragmatic Liberal Philosophy in
     the Warfare State," *Educational Theory*, Winter, 1977.

8.   Cf. Carol S. Gruber, *Mars and Minerva: World War I and the Uses of the
     Higher Learning in America*, Louisiana State University Press, 1975,
     pp. 128f., 151f. The practice continues. A case recently exposed by
     the Senate Committee on Intelligence involves the Penkovsky Papers,
     actually "prepared and written by witting Agency assets who drew on
     actual case materials" and "sold to a publisher through a trust fund
     established for the purpose," the publisher remaining "unaware of any
     U.S. Government interest." Cited from the Senate report by Stephen

S. Rosenfeld, *Washington Post* (30 April 1976). Rosenfeld was expelled from Moscow in protest over publication of the CIA fabrication in the *Post*. The Russians alleged—correctly, as we now discover—that the book was a "coarse fraud, a mixture of provocative invention and anti-Soviet slander" (Rosenfeld). The book's "editor," Frank Gibney, pledged that proceeds would go to a fund "to further the cause of genuine peace and friendship between the American and Russian peoples," which must have caused a few laughs in CIA and KGB circles.

9. See Volume I, chapter 5, section 2.2. What is remarkable is not so much that Chi's account was believed at the time, but that belief persists even after the exposures, as we discussed. See particularly note 168, discussing Guenter Lewy's parody of scholarship. In this case, the intelligence fabrications may well have deluded the CIA as well. Snepp, who is described on the jacket of his book as "the agency's principal analyst of North Vietnamese political affairs," refers to "some 30,000 to 50,000 intransigent peasants and landowners...killed or imprisoned" in the land reform program of the mid-1950s (p. 354). The fact that he offers one of the more restrained estimates suggests, however, that he may be continuing to purvey the myth, rather than expressing his belief in it. Frank Snepp, *Decent Interval,* Random House, 1977.

10. *Portrait of a Cold Warrior,* Putnam, 1976. A defense of the CIA, the book is not devoted to an exposure of its practices. Nevertheless, it contains much of interest, including an account of electoral manipulation in the Philippines, the anti-Castro crusade (which, he claims, was being escalated by Kennedy just before his death but was reduced in scale by Johnson), and other matters. As for the more humanitarian aspects of U.S. policy, Smith concludes that "despite the idealistic Alianza para el Progreso prattle, U.S. policy and CIA activities in Latin America were shaped by U.S. business interests and investments." This conclusion, produced in reference to the CIA's role in putting Frei into office in Chile in 1964, is interesting because of its source, though hardly novel. (See also Volume I, chapter 2, note 38.)

11. Cf. Volume I, chapter 5, sections 2.2, 2.3.

12. See, for example, John K. Fairbank, "Our Vietnam tragedy," *Newsletter,* Harvard Graduate Society for Advanced Study and Research, June 1975. He writes that "a factor of ignorance" lies at the source of "our Vietnam tragedy." We did not realize that the Vietnamese revolution was "inspired by the sentiment of nationalism" and we misguidedly "embarked on an anti-nationalist effort," and later misconceived "our role in defending the South after 1965," conceiving it as aimed at blocking aggression from North Vietnam and "forestalling a southward expansion of Chinese Communism." A judicious scholar, he also remarks that our "greatly accelerating the urbanization of Vietnam" after 1965 was "not necessarily to our credit or to the benefit of the South Vietnamese," referring to the policy of bombing the population into

the cities to destroy the rural society and thus deprive the NLF of its support. See also Edwin O. Reischauer ("Back to Normalcy," *Foreign Policy*, Fall, 1975), who also claims that the U.S. government was unaware of the nationalist character of the Viet Minh and its successors: "The real lesson of the Vietnam war is the tremendous cost of attempting to control the destiny of a South-east Asian country against the cross-currents of nationalism"—the cost to us, that is. To thoroughly appreciate the character of this historical nonsense (putting aside its moral level), one must recognize that Fairbank and Reischauer are the "deans" of Asian scholarship, with solid liberal credentials.

13. Chomsky, *For Reasons of State*, pp. 51f., and for the relevant background, the references of chapter 1, note 18 of this volume.

14. Cf. note 9, this chapter; also chapter 1, note 12.

15. This phrase is the propaganda term, invariably applied by the press and scholarship, to the client regime installed by the United States in South Vietnam; useful in its implication of a positive connection with the population rather than the actuality of a minority instrument of a foreign power.

16. On occasion, alert reporters commented on the fabrications. For example, Daniel Southerland cabled from Saigon "that so far he has been unable to verify reports of executions of officials and others in occupied areas. Mr. Southerland does report cables from the U.S. embassy in Saigon to Washington reporting alleged executions, but says one monk supposed to be an eyewitness is nowhere to be found. Another alleged eyewitness in Da Nang told Mr. Southerland he had seen no such thing. The embassy's cables have the apparent aim of persuading Congress to vote more aid, Mr. Southerland reports." Interpolated in Godfrey Sperling Jr., "Will Saigon become election issue?" *Christian Science Monitor* (21 April 1975).

17. Snepp, *op. cit.* pp. 301f. This operation, in which Britain and Australia also played a part, was described by Richard West as a "nauseating charade...this sudden concern for orphans is the most disgusting sham I have witnessed in nine years in Vietnam" (*New Statesmen*, 11 April 1975). Martin Woollacott described it as "one of the most hideous aspects of these last days of Saigon—the way in which children are suddenly being used as a propaganda weapon...the orphanages of Saigon are now being scoured by people whose only purpose is to make some kind of capital out of the present situation" (*Manchester Guardian Weekly*, 12 April 1975). The Vatican accused the United States "of engaging in international kidnapping, abusing the children for propagandistic purposes and engaging in a national 'guilt trip' to compensate for America's role in Southeast Asia" (*New York Times*, 13 April 1975). A group of Buddhist orphanages denounced the "exploitation of the orphans for political aims"; the airlift "has stirred great sympathy among Americans but it has raised a storm of protest in Vietnam

itself" (Daniel Southerland, *Christian Science Monitor*, 23 April 1975). The Red Cross condemned the operation as contrary to the Geneva conventions and the Buddhist An Quang Pagoda called it "a shameful act" (*Washington Post*, 10 April 1975). Many non-Communists in Saigon called it "a 'criminal act' akin to kidnapping," while the effort of the *Daily Mail* (London) "to get in on the orphan act" by rounding up orphans was called "a grotesque stunt" (H.D.S. Greenway, *Washington Post*, 15 April 1978). "...most Vietnamese reacted with anger at the American babylift last week" while Deputy Prime Minister Phan Quang Dan admitted that "it was a good way to get sympathy for additional American aid to Vietnam," noting that Ambassador Martin had "intervened personally" to send the orphans abroad so as to "help swing American public opinion to the advantage of the Republic of Vietnam" (Fox Butterfield, *New York Times*, 13 April 1975). Jane Barton, a Vietnamese-speaking staff worker of the AFSC, interviewed children who said that they were not orphans but had been separated from their parents in refugee camps and then flown to the United States. They reported that families were arbitrarily broken up with children sent to different countries; in three visits to orphans arriving in San Francisco she did not meet one child who had lost both parents (AFSC report, 14 April 1975). Desmond Smith, director of CBC TV in Montreal, described the "body snatching" as perhaps the most "revolting" act yet in the war. He quotes a Canadian relief worker who describes it as "like getting meat in a meat market." He points out further that up to two months before it "was not fashionable" to save real orphans, and also discusses the disgusting spectacle of Americans who would not dream of saving an orphan from a U.S. ghetto or a Calcutta slum but who now just must have a Vietnamese child kidnapped from Saigon: "The final indignity for the Vietnamese is that after we have bombed, strafed, napalmed and maimed half the population, we now take their children from them" (*Nation*, 19 April 1975). The actual evacuation was described by a doctor aboard the chartered Pan-Am aircraft as "the most incredible scene of deprivation and illness I've ever seen." Children suffered from dehydration, pneumonia, diarrhea and viral disease, while staff members on the aircraft were running out of liquids to treat dehydration cases (Douglas Kneeland, *New York Times*, 7 April 1975). A year later, the *Washington Post* reported (25 April 1976) that only nine of over 2,000 "orphans" had been legally adopted, because it turned out that perhaps 2/3 are not orphans (*Nation*, 8 May 1976). In a San Francisco court, court-appointed experts testified that 18 of 25 randomly selected "babylift" children were illegally removed from Vietnam by private adoption agencies, many with parents who had signed no release. Sixty-nine are being given a fundamentalist Christian upbringing in a Baptist church where the pastor refuses repatriation to their parents because "Vietnam is communist now" (Liberation News

Service, *Guardian,* New York, 26 November 1975). See also, Richard Flaste, *New York Times* (9 April 1975); Judith Coburn, "The War of the Babies," *Village Voice* (14 April 1975); Gloria Emerson, "Operation Babylift," *New Republic,* 26 April 1975. Among the more sordid scenes in this squalid affair was the sight of President Ford tearfully welcoming "orphans" and Hugh Hefner's "Big Bunny" flying 40 orphans to the United States to be carried off the plane by Playboy bunnies (*Washington Post,* 10 April 1975).

18. The *Times* refused to open its letters column to comments on this interesting gambit, though it published quite a wide range of responses to the editorial, including even a call for nuclear war. One letter that was not published, our own, read as follows:

> An editorial in the *Times,* April 5, observes that "a decade of fierce polemics has failed to resolve this ongoing quarrel" between two contending views: that "the war to preserve a non-Communist, independent South Vietnam could have been waged differently," and that "a viable, non-Communist South Vietnam was always a myth." There has also been a third position: That apart from its prospects for success, the United States has neither the authority nor competence to intervene in the internal affairs of Vietnam. This was the position of much of the authentic peace movement, that is, those who opposed the war because it was wrong, not merely because it was unsuccessful. It is regrettable that this position is not even a contender in the debate, as the *Times* sees it.
>
> On a facing page, Donald Kirk observes that "since the term 'bloodbath' first came into vogue in the Indochinese conflict, no one seems to have applied it to the war itself—only to the possible consequences of ending the war." He is quite wrong. Many Americans involved in the authentic peace movement have insisted for years on the elementary point that he believes has been noticed by "no one," and it is a commonplace in literature on the war. To mention just one example, we have written a small book on the subject (*Counter-revolutionary Violence: Bloodbaths in Fact and Propaganda,* 1973), though in this case the corporation (Warner Brothers) that owned the publisher refused to permit distribution after publication. But quite apart from this, the observation has been made repeatedly in discussion and literature on the war, by just that segment of opinion that the *Times* editorial excludes from the debate.

19. Among the most persuasive examples of the subservience of the press are those that it regards as its proudest moments; e.g., Watergate, a fact that is obvious enough if one looks just a bit below the surface. See Chomsky, introduction to Blackstock, ed., *op. cit.* (see chapter 1, footnote 34); Chomsky, "Nixon's defenders do have a case," *More,* December 1975.

20. Peter Braestrup, *Big Story: How the American Press and Television Reported and Interpreted the Crisis of Tet 1968 in Vietnam and Washington,* 2 volumes, Praeger, 1977.

21. See the entry for Freedom House in E.S. Herman, *Great Society Dictionary*, Philadelphia, 1968: "A small fabricator of credibility; a wholly-owned subsidiary of the White House." (See Volume I, chapter 4, section 1, for an example of Freedom House's devotion to freedom.)

22. Braestrup succeeds in portraying the media as unduly "pessimistic" by extensive fabrication of evidence and misrepresentation of his own documents, as is shown in detail in N. Chomsky, "The U.S. Media and the Tet Offensive," *Race and Class*, XX, 1978; large parts appear in *More*, June 1978. See the same review for documentation on the subjects of this paragraph. Reviews and comment in the *New York Times* and *Washington Post* lauded this incompetent and hopelessly inaccurate work as "one of the major pieces of investigative reporting and first-rate scholarship of the past quarter century," a "conscientious" and "painstakingly thorough study," etc.

23. Cf. Saburo Ienaga, *The Pacific War*, Pantheon, 1978, pp. 236f. Ienaga's book is primarily a critique of Japanese fascism, aggression and atrocities. His documentation of crimes of the U.S. occupying army has yet to be mentioned in a review in the United States, to our knowledge. In the U.S. colony in the Philippines, meanwhile, the United States was engaged in dismantling the popular peasant-based anti-Japanese resistance and restoring to power the wealthy elites that collaborated successively with the U.S. occupiers, the Japanese, and then again the United States. In the course of these operations, U.S. military forces took part in a massacre of 109 peasant guerrillas who were rounded up, ordered to dig a mass grave, then shot "with the knowledge and consent of American [Counterintelligence Corps] officers present at the time." The perpetrator of the massacre was then appointed mayor by the United States. Benedict J. Kerkvliet, *The Huk Rebellion*, University of California Press, 1977, p. 113, a valuable study of the origins of the Huk rebellion in peasant discontent intensified by U.S. colonialism, suppressed with the aid of U.S. military intelligence headed by Major Lansdale, later of Vietnam fame, regarded in the United States as a deep thinker with great insight into the peasant mind but in fact a typical colonialist fantasy-monger. Cf. *Ibid.*, p. 147, for an example.

24. Richard H. Minnear, *Victor's Justice: the Tokyo War Crimes Trial*, Princeton, 1971, p. 6.

25. Cf. Adolph Frank Reel, *The Case of General Yamashita*, Chicago, 1949.

26. Report to President Roosevelt, cited by Minnear, p. 16.

27. Judgment of the Tokyo Tribunal, cited by Minnear, p. 199. (See also p. 72.)

28. Cited by Minnear, p. 54. For further discussion of Pal's dissent, and the moral ambiguities of the Pacific war, cf. Chomsky, *American Power and the New Mandarins*, chapter 2. Pal, incidentally, was the only Justice at Tokyo with any background in international law, and the only Justice who dissented from the entire judgment.

29. For details, see Stephen Salaff, "The Diary and the Cenotaph: Racial and Atomic Fever in the Canadian Record," *Bulletin of Concerned Asian Scholars*, April-June 1978. The racist sentence was concealed until the lapse of a 30-year prohibition on the publication of secret government papers. The example illustrates rather well what is often considered "a state secret." On the racism of Western leaders during World War II, see Christopher Thorne, *Allies of a Kind*, Oxford, 1978. One wonders how Canadian (or Western) historians will deal with a comparable revelation concerning Prime Minister Lester Pearson, who is highly regarded in the West for his humanism. In released but unpublished sections of the *Pentagon Papers* it is revealed that Pearson was approached by the U.S. government in mid-1964 when the bombing of North Vietnam was under close consideration in the hope that the DRV might exert its influence to restrain the southern forces that were preventing the U.S. conquest of the South. The Nobel Peace Prize winner replied that nuclear weapons would be excessive, but conventional bombing would be quite legitimate. On the Canadian record of support for the United States in Indochina, see Claire Culhane, *Why is Canada in Vietnam?*, NC Press, Toronto, 1972; D.R. SarDesai, *Indian Foreign Policy in Cambodia, Laos, and Vietnam*, California, 1968.

30. Salaff, *op. cit.*

31. Telford Taylor, *Nuremberg and Vietnam: an American Tragedy*. Quadrangle, 1970. For discussion, see Chomsky, "The rule of force in international affairs," *Yale Law Journal*, vol. 80, no. 7, June 1971; reprinted with revisions in *For Reasons of State*.

32. Nuremberg Charter, cited by Minnear, p. 94; emphasis added.

33. *The Present State of Denazification*, reprinted in Constantine Fitzgibbon, *Denazification*, Norton, 1969, p. 133. These figures exclude war criminals. Directors of the great corporations who took part in Hitler's atrocities, however, received only light sentences (while the U.S. corporations that aided them during the prewar period were, naturally, entirely exempted), and some later became respected figures in the German "economic miracle." See Joseph Borkin, *The Crime and Punishment of I.G. Farben*, Free Press, 1978.

34. Data and quotes from Henry Faulk, *Group Captives: The Re-education of German Prisoners of War in Britain, 1945-1948*, Chatto & Windus, 1977, pp. 17, 32, 35, 47, 65, 69. The ultimate release of the POWs was impelled in part by a campaign by the same British groups that later opposed nuclear weapons and the war against Vietnam. Cf. Peggy Duff, *Left, Left, Left*, Allison & Busby, 1971, p. 20. In addition to Germans there were also Italian POWs, not discussed in Faulk's study.

35. Jawaharlal Nehru, *The Discovery of India*, Asia Publishing House, Bombay, 1961, p. 326.

36. Judith M. Gansberg, *Stalag: USA*, Crowell, 1977, p. vii.

37. Pp. 14f, 43. In explaining the importance of her study, Gansberg notes

that except for "horrible atrocities" such as "the inhumanity of the North Vietnamese," war prisoners are usually forgotten when war ends (p. 14). It does not occur to her, apparently, that the treatment of German POWs in the United States was hardly a model of humanity as she describes it, even putting aside the fact that the U.S. pilots were shot down while destroying towns and villages in North Vietnam, which was not exactly parallel to the case of the German POWs in the United States.

38. Robert Aron, *France Reborn, The History of the Liberation*, Scribner's 1964; chapter V: "The Summary Executions," pp. 417-24. Translated from the French original.

39. John Ehrman, *History of the Second World War, Grand Strategy V*, London, 1956, pp. 330ff.

40. *Boston Globe* (19 October 1977). Defeated Japan "condemned the show attack as being in bad taste and offensive to the Japanese people the preceding year, according to this 20-line report, but to no effect.

41. Bernard Crick, "On Rereading [Hannah Arendt's] *The Origins of Totalitarianism,*" *Social Research*, Spring 1977, citing G. M. Gilbert, *The Psychology of Dictatorship*, Ronald Press, 1950, p. 246.

42. It is a tribute to the effectiveness of U.S. propaganda that the question could even be raised, given the transparent absurdity of the U.S. claim. The American revolutionary war, Fall wrote, "entirely fits the bill of the many revolutionary wars which afflict the middle of the twentieth century...it was a military operation fought by a very small armed minority—at almost no time did Washington's forces exceed 8,000 men in a country which had at least 300,000 able-bodied males—and backed by a force of 31,897 French ground troops, and 12,660 sailors and Marines manning sixty-one major vessels." *Last Reflections on a War*, p. 276. For some further discussion of analogies between the American revolution and "modern revolutionary wars in Indochina and elsewhere," see John Shy, *A People Numerous and Armed*, Oxford, 1976, pp. 196f. Shy is a military historian. This essay resulted from a Pentagon-sponsored project on "Isolating the Guerrilla" from his civilian supporters, about which Shy writes that he was "skeptical."

43. Carl Van Doren, *The Secret History of the American Revolution*, Viking, 1941, p. vi.

44. Claude Halstead van Tyne, *The Loyalists in the American Revolution*, MacMillan, 1902, p. 105. (Reprinted, Peter Smith, 1929; quotes from this edition).

45. Shy, *op. cit.*, p. 184, citing Robert R. Palmer, *The Age of the Democratic Revolution*, Princeton, 1959-65, I, 188-190. He also notes Palmer's suggestion "that, measured by the relative numbers of refugees from revolution, the American may have been as violently intolerant as the French."

46. Shy, *op. cit.*, citing Paul H. Smith, "The American Loyalists: Notes on their Organization and Numerical Strength," *William and Mary Quarterly*, 3rd series, XXV (1968), pp. 259-77. Another standard reference

is John Adams's estimate that 1/3 of the population supported the revolution, 1/3 opposed it, and 1/3 were neutral (Shy, 166). Shy's own analysis leads him to the conclusion that "almost certainly a majority of the population, [the great middle group of Americans] were the people who were dubious, afraid, uncertain, indecisive" and unwilling to risk the hazards and suffering of revolutionary struggle; "the prudent, politically apathetic majority of white American males was not eager to serve actively in the militia" (pp. 215, 217).

47.   "At first divided and vacillating, the bulk of the Indians were eventually driven by events to fight for their 'ancient protector and friend' the king of England" (Francis Jennings, "The Indians' Revolution," in Alfred F. Young, ed., *The American Revolution: Explorations in the History of American Radicalism*, Northern Illinois Univ. Press, 1976, p. 341). He explains why in vivid detail, concluding that "heedless of theories, Americans began the building of their empire with an inheritance of ethnocentric semantics that made logic valid to themselves out of the strange proposition that invasion, conquest, and dispossession of other peoples support the principle that all men are created equal" (p. 344).

The same curious logic, with regard to Blacks, was noted by Samuel Johnson, who asked: "How is it that we hear the loudest *yelps* for liberty among the drivers of negroes?" Cited by Ira Berlin, "The revolution in black life," in Young, ed., *ibid.*, p. 356, an essay devoted to the Black response to the revolution. (See footnote 51, this chapter.)

48.   See Ronald Hoffman, "The 'Disaffected' in the Revolutionary South," in Young, ed., *ibid.*

49.   Benjamin Franklin, "after recounting the atrocities of the French and Indian wars,...called for the 'extirpation' of the French in Canada because of their manifold wickedness" (Shy, 238). Later, colonists raised an outcry against a 1774 act of the British Parliament concerning Quebec, stressing "the horrors of 'Papacy,' because it permitted Canada's Catholics to worship without disturbance" (Jennings, *op. cit.*, p. 339). "After the battles of Lexington and Concord," Jennings continues, "the Second Constitutional Congress made an address to 'the oppressed inhabitants of Canada,' in which the Congress 'perceived the fate of the protestant and catholic colonies to be strongly linked together'—so much for the popish menace—and appealed to the Canadians to overthrow the yoke of their 'present form of tyranny.' A few months later, the Congress's armies invaded Quebec to confer the boon of liberty upon those poor, deserving Catholics" (340).

50.   Kamm is the reporter assigned by the *New York Times* to record the misery of those who escape from postwar Indochina. We return to his reporting below. Compare his rather different approach to refugees in Timor from U.S.-backed Indonesian terror. (Volume I, chapter 3, section 4.4).

51.   Though not as familiar as it should be, the treatment of Blacks and

Indians after the war of independence is well enough known so that we need not recount it here. Recall that the first emancipation proclamation applying to American slaves was issued by the British in November, 1775, offering to free "all indentured servants, Negroes or others...able and willing to bear arms..." A. Leon Higginbotham, Jr., *In the Matter of Color*, Oxford, 1978; excerpts in the *Washington Post* (21 May 1978). Slaveholders, in response, urged slaves to "be content with their situation, and expect a better condition in the next world." Small wonder that thousands of Blacks joined the British forces, and "when the British left America at the end of the war, they carried thousands of blacks to freedom in Great Britain, the West Indies, Canada, and, eventually, Africa." (Berlin, *op. cit.*, pp. 353-55.)

An early draft of the American Declaration of Independence contained a condemnation of the slave trade, but this was deleted "in complaisance to South Carolina and Georgia" (Jefferson). The British ridiculed the colonists for their protest against their alleged "enslavement" to England—their constant claim that "we are slaves" under British oppression (Josiah Quincy, and many others); see footnote 47. The rhetoric of the American revolutionaries was, however, used effectively by the abolitionists and others in later years. See Higginbotham, *op. cit.* Now a federal judge, Higginbotham was first impelled to study this subject, he writes, as a college student when his protest over the refusal to allow Black students to live in campus dormitories at Purdue University was met by the following response by President Edward Charles Elliott: "Higginbotham, the law doesn't require us to let colored students in the dorm, and you either accept things as they are or leave the university immediately." But in fairness we must add that this was, after all, only 160 years after liberation. Matters have since improved, as a result of the courageous struggles of Blacks in the 1950s and 1960s, but it is still possible for the state to murder Black leaders with impunity and imprison civil rights activists for long periods, with no public outcry and (in the latter case) no interest on the part of President Carter, whose concern for human rights looks selectively outward. See references of chapter 1, footnote 34 and Chomsky, *'Human Rights' and American Foreign Policy*, pp. 69f.

52. Clarence J. Karier, Review of Lawrence A. Cremin, *Traditions of American Education*, Basic Books, 1977; *Paedagogica Historica*, XVII/2, 1977 (Netherlands).

3 Refugees: Indochina and Beyond

1. 17 June 1978. The Laotians are largely Hmong Tribemen, organized by the CIA to fight against the Pathet Lao and then abandoned when they were no longer needed. (See chapter 1, section 1; and chapter 5.) By the end of the 1975-1978 period under review in this volume, the total

number of refugees from Indochina remaining in Asia was estimated to be 333,500, including 150,000 refugees from Cambodia in Vietnam. Another 130,000 had been resettled in the United States, France, and elsewhere. These figures do not include the 135,000 airlifted from Vietnam by the United States in April 1975. Cited from the UN High Commissioner for Refugees in the *Los Angeles Times*, 8 January 1979. On the causes of the accelerated flight of refugees from Vietnam in mid and late 1978, see the preface to this volume.

2. The reference is presumably to East Asia.

3. Among them are some 250,000 refugees from Zaire prior to the invasion of May, 1978, according to the UN High Commissioner for refugees, "mostly farmers who had arrived empty handed," in some cases whole villages. "The Cold War in Africa," *Peace Press*, London, July/August/September, 1978. The same report cites the observation of a Belgian refugee in the *London Guardian* (22 May 1978): "What the government troops did to the population down here after [the arrival of the Moroccan troops flown in by the French to expel the Katangese rebels in May 1978] was unbelievable. One whole village was massacred. Even the Moroccans...were disgusted." President Mobutu of Zaire, maintained in power by French, Belgian and Moroccan forces backed by the United States, offered an amnesty to exiles from his rule. "Mobutu offers Amnesty to 200,000 Refugees," *Washington Post* (25 June 1978). Upon their return, many thousands of these refugees were taken to detention centers, where they were subjected to interrogation and frequent beatings, all in "flagrant violations of the amnesty," according to international officials on the scene. John Darnton, "Zaire Is Reported to Violate Shaba Refugees' Amnesty," *New York Times* (5 February 1979).

4. William Mattern, "Refugees: Burma's brand of apartheid," *Far Eastern Economic Review*, 14 July 1978.

5. Maurice Lafite, "Still in fear of the dragon," *Far Eastern Economic Review*, 3 November 1978. In a rare reference to the flight of refugees from Burma, the *Christian Science Monitor* carried a Reuters dispatch from Bangladesh (16 November 1978) reporting that more than 5,000 of the Burmese Muslim refugees had been repatriated, though 190,000 "were still living in 13 improvised camps set up by the Bangladesh Government," according to UN officials. In December 1978, one of the torrent of articles on refugees from Indochina then appearing mentioned the "bizarre tale of almost 200,000 Moslems who fled last May from Burma to Bangladesh ..." Richard M. Weintraub, "Asia's Refugees: A New Wave of Human Migration," *Washington Post*, 12 December 1978, the second of two long articles; most of the article was devoted to the refugees from Indochina, as was (in its entirety) the first article of the series the preceding day and a second article that also appeared on December 12. A third article on December 12 noted that at the UN meeting in Ge-

neva devoted to "the Indochina refugee problem," the U.S. government "called on governments around the world today to provide homes for the flood of Indochinese refugees."

6. See Volume I, chapter 4, section 1. In mid-July, China estimated the number of ethnic Chinese who fled Vietnam to China at 140,000. *New York Times* (15 July 1978). Later reports are higher; it seems that most ethnic Chinese were fleeing not to China but elsewhere in late 1978. Most of the increasing number of "boat people" in late 1978 are reported to be Chinese.

7. *Far Eastern Economic Review*, 5 August 1977. See also *FEER*, 12 May 1978, citing reports that "Filipino refugees [to Sabah] are being turned back to their troubled homeland."

8. Peter Weintraub, *Far Eastern Economic Review*, 16 December 1977. Compare the London *Economist* report of class backgrounds noted above. An analysis from Australia points out that there are many "doubts about identity" of refugees. A Catholic relief worker notes that "there have been white collar workers, public servants as well as army officers, who have said they were fishermen." The Laotian and Cambodian refugees "come from a higher class, representing the 'finest families imaginable,'" according to Berenice Lenze of the Indochinese Refugee Association. A large proportion of the refugees are Chinese— few of the Vietnamese who arrived even spoke Vietnamese. *National Times* (Australia), week ending 10 June 1978.

9. Frederic A. Moritz, "The *other* refugees in Asia," *Christian Science Monitor*, 30 March 1978. By "other" the *Monitor* means: "other than boat people"; not refugees from areas in Asia other than Indochina.

10. See Jonathan C. Randal, *Washington Post* (20 March 1978). These are useful weapons against such targets as the Rashidiyeh Palestinian refugee camp, where "hours after the raid, an Israeli helicopter flew over the camp south of Tyre no more than 20 feet off the ground and was not fired upon" (Randal). The Israeli use of CBUs aroused some mild protest in the United States, presumably, on the grounds that only the United States has the right to use such weapons against defenseless people.

11. H.D.S. Greenway, "Vietnam style raids gut South Lebanon," *Washington Post* (25 March 1978). Interviewed in Israel about the attacks on the civilian population, Israeli Chief-of-Staff Mordechai Gur commented that these were nothing new: "For 30 years, from the War of Independence until today, we have been fighting against a population that lives in villages and cities." *Al-Hamishmar* (10 May 1978).

12. *Maariv*, 16 May 1978. This emigration is important for Israel because of the "demographic problem" posed by the presence of Arabs in a Jewish state, a very substantial minority given the intention since 1967 to maintain control of large parts of the West Bank and Gaza. Much of the "emigration" is far from voluntary.

13. Jean-Pierre Clerc, *Le Monde* (3 November 1978); Pierre Simonitsch,

Tages Anzeiger (Switzerland), 13 October 1978, citing official Costa Rican estimates that 10,000 refugees fled to Costa Rica in September joining 100,000 Nicaraguan refugees already in this country of two million people. The estimate for Honduras is about 8,000 refugees in September. Clerc writes that the refugees who fled to Costa Rica had to escape through barbed wire laid by Nicaraguan armed forces and that those in Honduras are suffering severe deprivation despite assistance from Austria.

14. "U.N. Seeks Solution for 'Boat People,'" *New York Times* (11 November 1978).

15. Richard Holbrooke, address excerpted in the *Christian Science Monitor,* (20 December 1978).

16. Ira Gollobin, "Asylum for 'boat people,'" *Rights* (newsletter of the National Emergency Civil Liberties Committee, March/June 1978). Gollobin is General Counsel for the American Committee for the Protection of the Foreign Born and now Counsel for the National Council of Churches in the Haitian refugee case.

17. For recent discussion of the U.S.-Haiti relationship, see Wendell Rawls, Jr., "'Baby Doc's' Haitian Terror," *New York Times Magazine* (14 May 1978).

18. Jon Nordheimer, "Illegal Tide of Haitians Arriving on U.S. Shore," *New York Times* (18 July 1978). The report was occasioned by the arrival of 33 "boat people" who were "rounded up by the police." It claims that Haitian "boat people" are no longer imprisoned and that "confusion over the changing regulations, meanwhile, has slowed down the deportation of Haitians unable to show that they were political refugees *from a country with friendly ties with the United States*" (our emphasis), always the crucial consideration.

19. Robert M. Press, "U.S. crackdown seeks to bar fleeing Haitians," *Christian Science Monitor* (29 August 1978).

20. 2,000 people attended a funeral in the Bahamas for 23 refugees who died at sea fleeing to Florida to avoid deportation to Haiti. *Militant* (1 September 1978), which also carries a report of a demonstration in Miami protesting "racist attacks" against Haitian refugees. The mainstream press rarely carries such news.

21. The U.S. Immigration and Naturalization Service works in an interesting fashion. Its timing in the expulsion of victims of friendly tyrannies, for example, has a curious way of coinciding with union organizing. Thus in September, 1978, a group of Haitian custodians were arrested by INS just a day before contract negotiations for custodians were to begin. "The negotiations are now up in the air," Martha Cooley reports; "I-Men Raid Quincy Market for Illegal Aliens, Impede Union Drives," *Real Paper,* Cambridge (14 October 1978). This is one example of a pattern described in the article, mere coincidence according to INS.

22. News conference, March 24, 1977; reprinted in the *New York Times,*

March 25 without comment. Carter was asked by a CBS newsman whether the United States "has a moral obligation to help rebuild Vietnam." At first he evaded the question. When it was reiterated he gave this response: we have no obligation because "the destruction was mutual." Since "we went to Vietnam without any desire...to impose American will on other people" but only "to defend the freedom of the South Vietnamese," there is no reason for us "to apologize or to castigate ourselves or to assume the status of culpability." Nor do we "owe a debt." One learns a good deal about the United States—indeed, the Free World—from the fact that such a statement made by the apostle of Human Rights can pass without notice.

23. See Volume I, chapter 1, section 16.
24. *Christian Science Monitor* (18 April 1978).
25. The advisory board overturned the jury nominations in 5 of 10 cases. The others are also interesting. The prize for commentary went to William Safire, the extreme rightwing commentator of the *New York Times*, who was not even a finalist. The prize for editorial writing was awarded to Meg Greenfield of the *Washington Post*, who has specialized in urging a renewal of a harsher cold war stance, again overruling the jury recommendation. We have already discussed Kamm's first published article after he received the Pulitzer Prize, namely, his report from Jakarta on Timor (Volume I, chapter 3, section 4.4).

4 Vietnam

1. Recall the confident prediction of the editors of *Dissent* that all of those who fought the Communists would be slaughtered—i.e. many millions of people—tacitly reiterated again in the spring of 1975, but never specifically recalled since; see chapter 1 note 29. (See also Volume I, chapter 2, section 2.2.)
2. Cited from *Vietnam: If the Communists Won*, Saigon, Vietnam Council on Foreign Relations, 1972, in *The British Press and Vietnam*, Indochina Information No. 3; written by a group of working journalists in the British media and published by the Indochina Solidarity Conference, 1973, the source of the background on this authority.
3. *New York Times* (31 May 1978).
4. Presumably, the source for the Tass dispatch is the Vietnam Press Agency, 26 January 1978, giving official statistics of 260,000 montagnards in the South of a total of 800,000 who have been resettled. Nayan Chanda, "Le communisme vietnamien en marche," *Le Monde diplomatique*, April 1978. Chanda, regular Southeast Asia correspondent for the *Far Eastern Economic Review*, has been a perceptive commentator on affairs of the region for many years. His report of a visit to Vietnam in fact provides some basis for the claim made on purely *a priori* grounds in the *New York Times*. Certain montagnard areas, he

writes, were closed to visits for security reasons, apparently because of montagnard discontent over the resettlement policy and the institution of Vietnamese as a common language for the whole country.

5. Butterfield informed us that the wording in question was not his, but was added by "overly eager editing." He apparently regards it as accurate, however, as we see directly.

6. Cf. *Pentagon Papers*, Gravel Edition, Beacon, 1971, vol. II, section 2; Roger Hilsman, *To Move A Nation*, Delta, 1967, chapter 29, Milton Osborne, *Strategic Hamlets in South Vietnam*, Cornell University, 1965. Dean Rusk claimed that almost half the population had been relocated by 1963; cited in Chester Cooper, *The Lost Crusade*, Dodd, Mead, p. 201. On the cynicism of liberal commentary on the strategic hamlet program, cf. Chomsky, *For Reasons of State*, p. 106.

7. Dennis J. Duncanson, *Government and Revolution in Vietnam*, Oxford, 1968, p. 321.

8. For these and further references, see *For Reasons of State*, pp. 80f.

9. Gerald Cannon Hickey, "The Lost Montagnards," *New York Times*, Op-Ed, (16 August 1973).

10. Martin, *Reaching the Other Side*, Crown, 1978, pp. 165-166. Some of the montagnards did escape back to their home. Of the remainder, one-seventh died during the four months the Martins were working with them as relief workers in the camps.

11. But there have been protests, for example by the French anthropologist Georges Condominas, who worked with hill tribes that were virtually wiped out by U.S.-backed atrocities. (*We Have Eaten the Forest*, Allen Lane, 1977, introduction). In fact, the Vietnamese Communists seem to have a far better record than the various U.S.-imposed regimes in dealing with the hill tribes, and while many montagnards allied themselves with the United States (much as American Indians did with the British) because of fear of any Vietnamese, others fought with the Communists. For example, the capture of Ban Me Thuot, which began the final 1975 offensive, was reported by an escaped Catholic priest to have involved local montagnards but no North Vietnamese troops. Cf. *Washington Post* (15 March 1975), cited by Buttinger, *Vietnam: the Unforgettable Tragedy*, p. 150.

12. See Chomsky, *For Reasons of State*, pp. 84f. for explicit recommendations on generating refugees, from the highest sources. See also pp. 5f. and elsewhere for relevant background.

13. Butterfield states that the purposes of the resettlement program are "to relieve the major unemployment problem in parts of the south, to overcome chronic food shortages in the north by opening new farmland and to improve police control of the population by moving malcontent members of the bourgeoisie out of the cities." He makes no reference to the "cost in human terms" of leaving millions of people to starve in the cities to which they were driven by U.S. programs of "forced-draft

urbanization" and "modernization" (Harvard Professor Samuel Huntington's euphemism for bombing the rural population into U.S.-controlled cities; cf. Chomsky, *At War with Asia*, pp. 54f.).

14. Butterfield is, in fact, one of the more serious U.S. correspondents writing about Southeast Asia, and the *New York Times*, apart from its national stature, is perhaps on the liberal side of the narrow spectrum of the U.S. media. In the admittedly rather silly Freedom House study of the press discussed above, p. 34, the *Times* is described as an "antiwar journal." See Volume I, chapter 2, note 101, for the consequences of its allegedly "leftist" positions, as perceived by U.S. business interests.

15. Butterfield writes that "many highly trained and educated southerners, between 50,000 and 100,000, analysts estimate, remain imprisoned in so-called re-education camps."

16. Compare, in contrast, the behavior of the U.S. and Britain in detaining hundreds of thousands of German POWs in "reeducation camps" where they could be used for forced labor for up to three years after World War II, or the execution of hundreds of Japanese and massive purges in Japan and Germany, regarded as proof of Western humanitarianism. (See above, chapter 2, section 2.)

17. See, among many other examples, Fox Butterfield, "Shortages, Misrule and Corruption Said to Plague Vietnam's Economy," *New York Times* (9 June 1978), (reporting, *inter alia,* a 10 to 12% rise in industrial production in each of the past two years; but this was "from a very low base, largely reflecting recovery from war damage rather than new growth," analysts in Hong Kong believe); Peter Hazelhurst, "Old-style corruption begins to taint new regime in Saigon," *London Times* (24 April 1978), describing how the daughter of "a wealthy Chinese jeweller" was able to purchase travel documents to escape through bribery, and the problems that face the formerly wealthy as the black market is suppressed.

18. The United States is unlikely to attend to these lessons, for obvious reasons, but people who live in its neo-colonial domains may come to heed them, realizing the longstanding fears of U.S. planners with regard to the "ideological successes" of Communist regimes, the rational version of the "domino theory." See chapter 1, section 2, and the references cited there. It is interesting to compare the situation in the Caribbean. See, for example, Mike Phillips, "Cuba's shifting image lends a new model to the Caribbean," *New Statesman,* 18 April 1978. While in the West, Phillips comments, "Cuba is most often seen as a tool of Soviet policy and, as such, fatally discredited within its own sphere of influence," in fact, "the reverse is very nearly true" and there is "a renewed pro-Fidel groundswell among Latin American nationalists," not because of Castroite propaganda but rather because the effect of U.S. policies in Latin America is all too obvious to their victims while "Cuba now offers the

Caribbean the choice between attempting to transform its own economies and continuing to accept the model of dependency," with its "torture, poverty, the suppression of human rights, financial bankruptcy or
the overall dependence (in most of the smaller countries) on the whims
and necessities of foreign capital." One can see the logic in the intensive but failed efforts of the United States to subvert Cuban social and
economic development by poisoning food supplies, trying to assassinate
Castro, terrorist attacks, etc. (See Volume I, chapter 2, note 94.)

19. *New York Times* (9 April 1978). The situation seems still worse in other
nearby U.S. colonies, where Filipino workers have been murdered
"under mysterious circumstances." Few of the Filipino and Korean
workers have been willing to report abuses for fear of deportation, since
even under these conditions ("like slavery") they "can usually make
more in an hour than they could for a full day's work, say, in Manila,"
where workers benefit from the fruits of a U.S. humanitarian effort
that began 80 years ago. Cf. Volume I, chapter 4, section 3. An ACLU
observer on Guam states that immigration officers and the code they
apply have given contractors and their agents "virtually total power over
their workers, a licence to steal and beat the men without restraint,"
while female immigrants, according to the labor department official
cited, "have been forced to have sexual relations with immigration officers to keep from being deported."
     This report, a rare example of serious journalism, aroused no com-
ment and quickly passed from memory.

20. *New York Times*, "Our Vietnam Duty is Not Over," editorial (28 February 1978). See also "The Indochina debt that lingers," editorial (15
April 1978) (cited above, chapter 3, p. 64).

21. David Anable, *Christian Science Monitor*, "UN Report says Vietnam
needs rural resettlement" (7 June 1976).

22. See also Patrice de Beer, *Le Monde* (26-28 January 1976), translated in
the *Manchester Guardian Weekly* (11 July 1976): "It is realized in Saigon today that Operation Phoenix, conducted by the Americans, which
involved the elimination of Communist Party officials, together with
the bombings had been fearfully effective. The number of revolutionary
cadres is said to have dropped from the 80,000 or so before the United
States intervened to a maximum of 50,000 in 1975, most of them soldiers. Party cells were successively wiped out in the rural districts and
decimated in the cities. At the beginning of the new regime, there were
5,000 militants in Saigon, of whom 2,000 were cadres, not necessarily
the best, but those who had managed to survive Nguyen Van Thieu's
repression machine. 'In the last few years of the war,' Nguyen Huu Tho,
the president of the Front, told me, 'our activities declined because our
comrades had been eliminated...The best of us were sacrificed, and we
did not have enough cadres to run the cities after the liberation. We had
to take people who had revolutionary fervour, but no experience, and to

bring personnel down from the North.'" (See chapter 1, section 2, and Volume I, chapter 5, section 1.5.)

23. "Vietnam Communists Inter Once-Vital 'Front' Group," *Washington Post* (5 February 1977), reprinted from the *Manchester Guardian*. Woollacott is unusual in that he recognized that "the Front was an enormous human achievement and a formidable instrument of war."

24. Long An happens to be a particularly well-studied province because of the outstanding work of Jeffrey Race, who described Communist success there prior to the U.S. invasion of 1965. See further, Volume I, chapter 5.

25. For an eyewitness description of these regions today, see John Pilger, *op. cit.* (chapter 1, note 15).

26. See chapter 1, notes 9 and 12.

27. Cf. Martin Woollacott, "Vietnam: still two nations," *Manchester Guardian Weekly* (25 April 1976). He writes that "South Vietnam now has, for the first time, something like a true health service." He cites a Catholic sister who had worked in the Central Highlands for 20 years and "described with admiration how within weeks of taking over, the Communists had established clinics in every village and new 50-bed hospitals in the towns. People who previously had no chance of hospital treatment at all were now getting it." See note 97. See also the report of the study mission to Vietnam by Senator Edward Kennedy for comment on achievements of the health program and the enormous problems caused by lack of supplies and the legacy of the war. *Congressional Record*, S 14007f., 22 August 1978. Also, Hearing before the Committee on the Judiciary, U.S. Senate, Ninety-Fifth Congress, second session, 22 August 1978, in which members of the study mission testified, reporting determined and in some cases encouraging efforts to meet health and nutrition problems despite deplorable conditions. Mildred Kaufman summarized what appears to be their general impression: "I was very impressed with the rather stark conditions under which the people of Vietnam are valiantly struggling to overcome the aftermath of the war" (p. 25).

Health care developments under the extremely onerous conditions of Indochina are especially interesting for the contrast with conditions under subfascism. We have discussed in Volume I the absolute decline of public health expenditures under the auspices of the Brazilian generals, and the similar disregard for the health conditions of the majority in the Philippines, Indonesia and elsewhere in the subfascist empire. We are awaiting a Butterfield-Kamm study comparing medical care in the countryside of Indochina with that in, say, Indonesia or South Vietnam under U.S. rule, taking into account both the facts and the resources available.

28. See chapter 1, note 15.

29. Richard Dudman, *St. Louis Post-Dispatch*, October 30, October 31,

November 1, 2, 3, 4, 6, 7, 8, 9, 1977.

30. *Time* the same day quotes Secretary of Defense Harold Brown who explains that "a lesson we learned in Vietnam is that we should be very cautious about intervening in any place where there is a poor political base for our presence." *Time* (23 May 1977). If there is a good political base, as the Russians claim to have found in Czechoslovakia in 1968, then the use of massive U.S. force to destroy "local Communist subversion or rebellion that does not constitute armed attack" in violation of the supreme law of the land is, presumably, quite appropriate. (Cf. chapter1, note 16).

31. Fox Butterfield, "Vietnam, 2 Years After War's End, Faces Painful Problems of Peace," *New York Times* (1 May 1977).

32. Butterfield follows standard Western practice in identifying southerners who hold key decision-making positions in the Hanoi regime as "northerners." That Vietnamese adhere to these imperialist conventions is perhaps open to question.

33. See the reports of Snepp, Casella, de Beer, and Dudman cited above. "One possible factor behind the continued dominance of Northerners in the reunified Vietnam," Butterfield speculates, "is that the old ethnic prejudices between Northerners and Southerners have persisted." Another possible factor is that the United States decimated what it always recognized to be the only mass-based *political* force in the South, but this factor is not fit to print.

34. See also the AFP report carried by the *New York Times* (16 March 1978) on a road trip from Hanoi to Saigon which reveals "a startling new look to this country a little less than three years after the end of hostilities"—new construction, rice fields and coffee plantations, and homes that "have sprung up in areas that two years ago still resembled lunar landscapes," in areas that were "like a desert because of the bombing." The report continues: "Provincial authorities in the south reported large surpluses of rice but did not explain why the surplus had not been sent north." No speculation on the reasons is offered.

35. A personal experience may be relevant. After a few days in Vientiane, one of us (Chomsky) was brought into contact with underground Pathet Lao cadres and sympathizers in the city, including a teacher in a Buddhist school (who was, shortly after, picked up by CIA agents), a guerrilla from northern Laos, and a minister in the U.S.-backed government who was hoping for a Pathet Lao victory. Cf. *At War With Asia*, chapter 4, where identities were concealed in the midst of the ongoing U.S. war. The attitudes of such people could barely have been known to readers of the Free Press, which also virtually ignored the hundreds of thousands of rural and urban poor, who are rarely considered when assessments of attitudes are given by Butterfield and others.

36. As contrasted with the hordes of Vietnamese correspondents freely roaming about the United States, which was never invaded and de-

molished by Vietnam. Even a Vietnamese nun visiting Canada was apparently denied entry into the United States. See Don Luce's Congressional testimony in the Hearings to which we return (see note 70).

37. *New York Times* (20 September 1977). This ridiculous pretense was abandoned by the *Times* shortly after, with the publication of reports by Ian Mather (reprinted from the *London Observer*), October 13, 14, 18, 27, 1977; and Horst Faas, October 13, 16, November 13, 1977. As we will see in chapter 6, Kamm adopts a similar pretense in the case of Cambodia. In the case of East Timor, however, Indonesian officials are the principal source of information for the *Times* correspondent. See Volume I, chapter 3, section 4.4.

38. Gabriel Kolko, personal communication.

39. Jean and Simonne Lacouture, *Vietnam: voyage à travers une victoire,* Seuil, 1976.

40. Ibid. pp. 182, 194. It should be added that Vietnam was "irremediably miserable" not because of God's wrath, but as a direct result of the vicious practices of French colonialists, documented in painstaking detail by Ngo Vinh Long, *Peasant Revolutionary Struggles in Vietnam in the 1930s,* Harvard University Ph.D. Dissertation, May, 1978; see also his *Before the Revolution: the Vietnamese Peasants Under the French,* MIT Press, 1973, which includes a revealing account of these years as seen by peasants themselves. The revolutionary struggles of the 1930s, as Long fully documents, were part of an impressive struggle for independence and democratic control of social life, intensified by the miserable conditions resulting from French rule which led to mass deaths from starvation in the 1930s, while the French (working in part through their local allies among landlords and village officials) compelled the starving peasants to purchase alcohol from their monopoly, withheld aid, prevented the rebuilding of dikes and wantonly murdered those who stood in their way. Now, Western reporters bewail the fact that Indochinese revolutionaries who studied in Paris failed to absorb the traditional "humanism" of Western civilization. See Martin Woollacott, *Boston Globe* (2 October 1977) excerpted from the *Manchester Guardian.*

41. Nayan Chanda, "Vietnam: idéologie révolutionnaire et pragmatisme économique," *Le Monde diplomatique,* March 1977.

42. See above, chapter 3, note 22.

43. Like drug addiction, venereal disease was virtually unknown prior to the U.S. invasion. See Don Luce's congressional testimony to which we return. We may note, in this connection, some recent concern in the United States over the fact that many war veterans appear to be developing symptoms associated with excessive use of defoliants. See, for example, *Boston Globe* (25 March, 8 October 1978); *New York Daily News* (11 June 1978). Notably missing from these reports is any concern for the possible effects on the Vietnamese, who were surely subject to far heavier doses, or for U.S. responsibility to offer them some medical as-

sistance. On this matter see the comments by Arthur Galston, a plant physiologist at Yale University, in the private hearings cited in note 56. In the *Far Eastern Economic Review*, 11 August 1978, Tom Grundfeld reports Galston's conclusions on his return from the most recent of his many trips to Vietnam. Apart from the ecological damage caused by bombing and chemical warfare, what particularly concerned him was the extensive use of herbicides containing dioxin, which causes cancer. "Galston said that liver cancer is now the second most common cause of death in Vietnam, where before the war it was rare."

44. Recall again the interesting list of the sole violators of human rights that deserve such punishment by the U.S. guardians of global morality: Vietnam, Laos, Cambodia, Cuba, Mozambique, Angola—and Uganda, thrown in for good measure, and something of a joke, since the United States is "Uganda's largest free world trading partner, buying one third of its coffee exports in 1977 (price tag: $245 million) and thereby providing the hard currency essential to keeping Amin's repressive regime in power." Senator Lowell Weicker, "Stop subsidizing Amin's murders," *Christian Science Monitor* (21 August 1978). Coffee sales amount to over 85% of the government's revenues, according to Weicker. Among the other current contributors to Idi Amin are "a mysterious Israeli tycoon and the Mossad, Israel's intelligence service," who "appear to have provided Idi Amin's Uganda Airlines with its two Boeing 707 jetliners as part of an Israeli effort to spy on Libya," an absurdity, since it is well known to the Libyans so that "nobody is fooling anybody in this affair," though "Idi Amin must be delighted with a cut-rate service that transports Ugandan coffee, officials and their mistresses to Europe and brings back whiskey, machine tools, livestock, and Mercedes Benz limousines." "But the big winner in this operation appears to be Shaul Eisenberg, the elusive Israeli entrepreneur at its center." Eisenberg works in close collaboration with the Israeli Aircraft Industry, a subsidiary of the Israeli Defense Department; his trading firm is also supported by "the U.S. Export-Import Bank, which is supposed to make loans to promote American exports." He is also "the sole beneficiary of what in Israel is called 'the Eisenberg law' [which] exempts from tax certain companies that do business abroad. So far, it fits only Eisenberg." "Ugandan Plane Deal Believed Key to Israeli Spy Operation," *Washington Post*, London (11 September 1978). Presumably the author is Bernard Nossiter; see his "How the CIA keeps Idi Amin in whiskey," *New Statesman*, (13 October 1978), virtually the same article, but with the additional information on CIA involvement, or perhaps coordination.

45. *Fellowship*, December 1977.

46. Henry Kamm, "Vietnam Asks Help from Asian Bank, but Early Action is Held Unlikely," *New York Times* (24 April 1977). The United States also cast a negative vote (as is the practice) when the World Bank approved a $60 million loan for irrigation in Vietnam. Cf. Jean Mayer's testimony in the August 22, 1978 Hearings cited above (note 27), p. 7.

47. The cynical exploitation of the MIA issue by the United States merits little comment. Reporting on Carter's Commission to Hanoi to inquire into the MIA matter, the *Washington Post* sermonized that "it is ghoulish for the Vietnamese to trade on heartbreak," but we must understand that "'the losses they themselves suffered—losses that they define as an American responsibility—left them with little else to trade" (how odd that they should define these losses as "an American respon sibility"). But they can expect no more than "token direct assistance from Washington," given their human rights record, the *Post* explains. ("Vietnam Mission," *Washington Post*, 23 March 1971). Nayan Chanda ("Laying the MIA issue to rest," *Far Eastern Economic Review*, 11 March 1977) reports the same story in a slightly different way. The report of the U.S. Select Committee on the Missing Persons in Southeast Asia, he writes, "clearly shows how Hanoi has been pressed to supply information about people lost in non-hostile circumstances, on the open sea and unknown to the Vietnamese authorities." The existence of such cases "erodes the credibility of the United States' data base... it may appear to the Indochinese leaders that the United States has deliberately requested information which they cannot furnish in order to embarrass them or to prevent meaningful talks" (quoted from the Committee reports).

48. Cited by Nayan Chanda, "New Delhi wants to offer help," *Far Eastern Economic Review*, 25 February 1977, another report that escaped the attention of the U.S. press.

49. *Times of India,* July 10, 17, 24, 1977. Excerpts appear in *Atlas World Press Review,* October 1971.

50. *Le Monde,* January 21-22, translated in the *Manchester Guardian* (8 February 1976).

51. *Fraternité Vietnam* is a charitable organization founded by the Vietnamese community in Paris in March, 1975, functioning also in Canada; 18, rue du Cardinal Lemoine, 75005, Paris; 1040 Jean Dumetz, Ste-Foy, Quebec, G1W4K5. Apart from its aid projects for Vietnam, it has circulated considerable information on wartime and postwar Vietnam.

52. He reports that he visited several parishes where he saw "with my own eyes that the Churches are full, with both young and old."

53. Recall, for example, the AP report that accompanied Butterfield's 1977 survey.

54. *New York Times* (13 March 1977).

55. The *Times* account asserts that Collett "said its members did not go to Vietnam on an inquisitorial mission to check on allegations of repression ..." but then quotes him as having inquired into repression.

56. The transcript appears in the *Congressional Record, Senate,* 29 March 1977.

57. *New York Times,* editorials of 28 February and 15 April 1978, cited above.

58. See *New England Peacework*, April, May, 1977. A detailed report is also available from the American Friends Service Committee (AFSC), 1501 Cherry St., Philadelphia, PA 19102. A private account has also been circulated. Their reports and films are also discussed in Robert K. Musil, "Vietnam Today: Problems and Challenges," *WIN*, 17 November 1977, along with reports by James Klassen and Don Luce (see below). *WIN*, published with the support of the War Resisters League, is unusual among U.S. journals in that it has been open to a wide range of reports, opinion, and discussions of postwar Indochina. It gives a rare insight into what a free press might be like, if such a phenomenon were to exist.

59. See Volume I, chapter 5, section 1.3.

60. "Meeting with Ngo Cong Duc, Ho Ngoc Nhuan and Ly Chanh Trung, 1 February 1977." Ngo Cong Duc was a member of the Saigon Assembly until 1971. A Catholic and cousin of the Archbishop of Saigon, he was editor of *Tin Sang* until it was banned by Thieu and then escaped to Europe. He is now once again editing *Tin Sang*. Ho Ngoc Nhuan was a member of the Saigon Assembly. Ly Chanh Trung is a well-known Catholic intellectual. For a lengthy quote from a speech he delivered at the Saigon Student Center in 1968, see Chomsky, *At War with Asia*, pp. 65-66. Parts of the transcript appear in *Vietnam South East Asia International*, ICDP, 6 Endsleigh St., London WC 1, February-April, 1977.

61. In an interview with Richard Dudman, Duc "said that he had more freedom now than under the old government. He prints articles critical of the government and publishes translations of foreign affairs analyses from *Le Monde* of Paris, the *New York Times* and the *Washington Post*. The Thieu regime cut off his newsprint, confiscated his property and sentenced him to prison for doing that sort of thing." He claims that there is no censorship, but adds: "I am a self-censor—I know what we should publish in the interests of the country and the Vietnamese people." Such self-censorship can be equivalent to censorship, or worse (if accompanied by the delusion of freedom), as readers of the Free Press should be aware. *St. Louis Post-Dispatch* (2 November 1977).

62. A statement that she gave to the Swedish delegation appears in *Vietnam South East Asia International*, op. cit.

63. As antiwar activists have long been aware, there is a way for them to gain access to the Free Press—namely, when they take a position that happens to conform to the current needs of Western propaganda. This is one reason why some, at least, refused to participate in a public statement released to the U.S. press. For some discussion of the issues, see N. Chomsky, "Vietnam Protest and the Media," *Resist Newsletter #112*, 1977.

64. George McArthur, "Hanoi hints at reeducation' scope; At least 110,000 South Vietnamese said to be in camps," *Boston Globe—Los Angeles Times* (10 April 1977). We wrote to McArthur to inquire as to

the source of the material to which he refers, but received no response. This is the same correspondent who informed his readers that the victims of the Indonesian massacre of 1965-66 had "subjected" Indonesia to the massacre. See Volume I, chapter 4, section 1.

65. Martha Winnacker, "Recovering from Thirty Years of War," *Southeast Asia Chronicle*, May-July 1977.

66. James Klassen, "Religion in Viet Nam Today," privately circulated by James Klassen, RR 2, Box 102A, Newton, Kansas 67114.

67. Catholic missionaries have long been notorious for their role in colonial oppression. For example, during the peasant uprisings in 1930-1931 French priests led "pacification" teams. Others usurped communal land and brought soldiers to intimidate and kill resisting peasants. The heavily censored Saigon press in 1938 reported that the manager of an estate of a French Catholic priest closed canals that were the communication routes for peasants in the area and forced them to pay tolls or hand over possessions, resorting to savage beatings if they refused, with no action by the French authorities despite much publicity. Long, *Peasant Revolutionary Struggle* (pp. 50, 212, 225).

The dubious role of the Catholic Church during the war has been discussed in the *National Catholic Reporter,* a leading church weekly, after a year-long investigation of the Catholic Relief Services by its Washington correspondent, Richard Rashke. Rashke alleges that "during much of the Vietnam War, Catholic Relief Services abandoned its apolitical humanitarian role and became an adjunct of the American military effort," turning over "vast quantities of relief supplies...to both U.S. and South Vietnamese military units to be used as pay for irregular forces and incentives for intelligence gathering" and allowing U.S. military personnel to work in relief offices where they had access to "information valuable to military intelligence but possible disastrous to the Vietnamese civilians whom the organization was chartered to help." The report charges that 90% of the church relief agency's budget came from the US AID program "on a *quid pro quo* basis, which presupposed the church agency would reciprocate 'by accepting U.S. policy without criticism and by sharing information with US AID personnel.'" US AID was admittedly a CIA cover in Laos from 1962, and perhaps elsewhere as well. Catholic Relief Services also supplied rations for interrogation centers and political prisons, including the Con Son prison with its "tiger cages." It was incorporated into the U.S. refugee program which forced "Vietnamese civilians from homes and farms into refugee camps, which were supplied by the organization." After earlier criticisms in this regard, the organization "merely changed the accounting procedures," Rashke alleges. Quotes from Marjorie Hyer, *Washington Post* (13 December 1976). See also Kenneth A. Briggs, *New York Times* (14 December 1976).

Western visitors to Indochina (including one of us) have observed the cruel and inhuman attitude of some Catholic missionaries towards the population, which has a long history. It is remarkable that the testimony of Catholic missionaries condemning alleged practices of Indochinese revolutionaries is so commonly accepted without question in the West.

On the role of missionaries in Vietnam and elsewhere, see the interview with Doug Hostetter, "An Insider's Story: Religious Agencies in Viet-Nam," in NACLA's *Latin America and Empire Report*, December 1973: *Christian Mission for the Empire*; Rev. Richard Edwards, "The CIA and Christian Mission: Can We Get the CIA Out of the Church," *Signs of the Times*, Winter, 1978. Both articles review evidence of what Hostetter calls the "nice hand-in-glove relationship between the Christian clergy and the U.S. military" and the CIA. Cf. also Volume I, chapter 3, section 4.3.

68. The Catholic Church seems to be taking the same stand. At the Synod of Bishops in Rome, October, 1977, the Archbishop of Saigon who attended and then travelled in Europe along with Cardinal Trin Nhu-Kue of Hanoi, discussed the problems faced by the church in operating in a "marxist milieu": "Instead of theoretical discussions, the communists want only concrete facts. The christians therefore have to show a new countenance, the authentic countenance of Christ and the Church." Accordingly, "In July, 1976 at the Episcopal Conference of the two ecclesiastical provinces of Hue and Saigon we bishops unanimously and without ambiguity launched an appeal to all the Catholics, inviting them to take the way of commitment, i.e., contribute to the construction of society." The Pope, in response, urged Catholic relief organizations to offer assistance to Vietnam and encouraged Catholics in Vietnam to take part with all their strength in "the great work of reconstruction" (*L'Osservatore Romano*, 9 December 1977); distributed along with the statement of the Archbishop by *Fraternité Vietnam*—see note 51, this chapter).

See Henry Tanner, "Saigon Archbishop Says Coexistence with Reds is Vital," *New York Times* (10 October 1977). On the "reconciliation between the anti-communist Roman Catholic Church of the south and the unified communist government," see Nayan Chanda, "Clergy and comrades link arms," *Far Eastern Economic Review*, 8 October 1976. Chanda discusses the goodwill shown by the government towards the church after the dismantling of a counterrevolutionary group discovered with arms and equipment for counterfeiting currency in a southern church; see Chanda, *Far Eastern Economic Review*, 27 February 1976 and Turley (see note 72, this chapter). Chanda also cites a letter from the Saigon Archbishop to a Paris Catholic newspaper in which he explains the cooperation of the church with the Communists on grounds that religious freedom "has really been respected" including liturgical ceremonies and conversions to Catholicism.

69. G. Gianni, mimeographed, Hong Kong. "Vietnam, Vietnam: A Missionary's reflections after liberation."

70. A few of the many hints that the press might have followed up had it chosen to do so, apart from those already cited: Bill and Peggy Herod, "Vietnam Observations from Hong Kong," *The Disciple*, 17 April 1977; H. Lamar Gibble of the Board of World Ministry, "Report on consultations with religious leaders in Vietnam," 4-11 May 1977; Rev. George W. Webber, Chairperson of Clergy and Laity Concerned, letter, *Washington Post*, 12 January 1977; representatives of the AFSC and church groups who lived in or visited Vietnam after liberation, who testified in Congressional Hearings: Hearings before the Subcommittee on International Organizations of the Committee on International Relations, House of Representatives, Ninety-Fifth Congress, First Session, June 16, 21 and July 26, 1977 (among them Don Luce, who had lived and worked in Vietnam for many years as head of International Voluntary Services and as a journalist, is fluent in Vietnamese, and met privately with "at least 50 former friends," generally Third Force people, including friends who had returned from reeducation centers); and many others.

71. The group is small for many reasons, one of them being the inability of many young scholars who depart from mainstream ideology to obtain employment, a matter that amply merits a careful study; there are many examples that illustrate a minor academic purge.

72. William S. Turley, "Urban transformation in South Vietnam," *Pacific Affairs*, Winter, 1976-77.

73. The term "ironic" seems out of place, in the light of the systematic policies of the United States throughout its far-flung subfascist domains.

74. We have found no record of this. As far as we can determine, Hoan was a minor member of a neutralist Buddhist group. Don Luce, who was well-acquainted with Third Force leaders, testified in the Hearings that he did not know Hoan "as an outspoken antigovernment figure there." Whatever his role may have been, he never achieved the prominence of such non-Communist dissidents as Ngo Ba Thanh, Ngo Cong Duc, Ly Chanh Trung, Father Chan Tin, Huynh Tan Mam, or others now reported to be active in southern Vietnam, whose reports are ignored.

75. In his testimony before the same committee, Nguyen Van Coi of the militantly anti-Communist Hoa Hao Buddhist sect estimates the number of prisoners at one million. Actually his testimony is in some respects more convincing than that of Hoan, since he recounts numerous personal incidents of torture and abuse during almost a year in detention centers and forced labor camps before his escape in October 1976, whereas Hoan offers almost no direct testimony.

The official government position is that there are about 50,000 people imprisoned "for security reasons." *International Herald Tribune*, 5 February 1977. Reports on the character of "reeducation camps" vary widely. Compare the testimony of Coi with the observations of McCleary and Meinertz in the Congressional Hearings (see note 70, this chapter), and the subsequent remarks of Luce (115) on conversations with people released from camps. (See also Chanda, p. 68, and similar reporting in Lacouture, *op. cit.* and elsewhere.) In the private hearings cited above (note 56), Luce quotes the report of one American, Jay Scarborough, who spent five months in a camp and described the treatment as humane. Actually, there is no direct inconsistency among these radically conflicting reports; it is possible that the camps vary widely in character.

The Lacoutures conclude that the camps "are evidently not Gulag—not l'école des Roches [a finishing school] either." Richard Dudman, who describes a visit to one camp, reports the view of several Western diplomats in Hanoi that the reeducation program seems "to have been an effective trade-off that avoided any possibility of the bloodbath" that had long been predicted after a bitter civil struggle. "Several individual non-Communist Vietnamese who could be questioned privately said that they had been amazed at the leniency of the victorious Communists." *St. Louis Post-Dispatch*, "Vietnam's Dismal New Camps," (3 November 1977). See also, Casella, *op. cit.*

76. This was offered in response to a question by Rep. Smeeton about the "50,000 to 500,000 people...killed during the 'refashioning' of the North's agriculture and economy" in the 1950s. In an earlier session, Turley had testified on these exaggerated propaganda claims, offering the estimate of probably 5,000 killed on the basis of Moise's careful study. Cf. Volume I, chapter 5, section 2.2. As is so often true, mere fact is never allowed to get in the way of useful propaganda concerning the enemy.

77. In Africa, the Middle East, and Taiwan, Hoan said, referring to unidentified press reports.

78. See the eyewitness reports of Ediger, Klassen, Tran and many others. In the same Congressional Hearings Don Luce reported that he had seen religious materials published in South Vietnam and had attended churches in Hanoi and Saigon that were functioning with parishioners. He also recalled that the Archbishop of Hanoi was recently made a Cardinal by the Vatican, and stated that the former teachers continue to teach in Catholic Schools. Paul F. Mcleary, Executive Director of the World Church Service Delegation, testified that he "went unexpectedly to a 6 a.m. mass at a Roman Catholic Church. It was filled." The Archbishop said that "there were over 100 studying in a major seminary to go into the priesthood, that they were not decreasing in terms of the size of the church, but he felt they were now growing....At this point, the leadership of the Buddhist community, the Roman Catholic Church, and the Protestant Church...seem supportive of the present political situation, the present government, and did not give indications that these kinds of pressures existed upon them, or that there were restraints on their activities." In the 22 August 1978 Hearings (see note 27, this

chapter) Archbishop Philip M. Hannan described his attendance at a crowded mass. (See notes, 52, 68, 70, 83, this chapter.)

79. Snepp, *op. cit.*, pp. 147, 433, 14. The White House "flatly denied" the last charge and U.S. Ambassador Bunker was also quoted as denying it, but it is correct, as revealed by a CIA memo in a pretrial deposition in a government suit against Snepp. Charles R. Babcock, "CIA Memo Confirms U.S. Offer to Fund '71 Viet Candidate," *Washington Post* (28 May 1978). For more information on Buu's association with Diem's Can Lao Party and such notorious pro-imperialist and anti-labor groups as the AFL-CIO international relations operations (see chapter 1, note 3) and the Christian Democratic Konrad Adenauer Foundation in West Germany, his gross corruption, and the service of his union for the privileged rather than the poor, see *Der Spiegel* (16 April 1973), based on information by a West German who worked with an affiliate of the Adenauer Foundation in Vietnam from 1969-72. See Chomsky and Herman, "Saigon's corruption crisis: the search for an honest Quisling," *Ramparts,* December 1974, for some details.

80. Cf. Turley, *op. cit.*, for discussion on relative popular participation under Thieu and the new regime, which suggests rather different conclusions.

81. See references of note 6, this chapter.

82. See Turley, *op. cit.*, for a comparison of the Thieu programs with those of the new regime.

83. Several examples have been mentioned and we return to others. One further well-known example is Richard Hughes, who continued his work with orphans while living with the Vietnamese until he left in August, 1976. Even during the war, American visitors to Vietnam were free to speak privately to Vietnamese whom they met through professional and other contacts and the absence of overt security was remarkable under the circumstances, as we know from direct experience and the testimony of friends. For example, one of us (Chomsky) spent many hours with professional colleagues in Hanoi and walked unaccompanied through both urban and remote village areas. Hoan's claim requires us to believe that policies have radically changed in the postwar period, despite substantial testimony to the contrary. We have heard privately from reputable journalists who have visited Vietnam that friends from earlier years seemed afraid to talk to them, but that is considerably short of Hoan's blanket claim. Others do not report anything of the sort. For example, John Fraser of the *Toronto Globe and Mail* reports that he spent two weeks "in and around Ho Chi Minh city," left to his own devices insofar as he chose. He "covered nearly all the districts of the city, by day and night, and talked to a great number of people." He found "the willingness of so many people to talk openly about their frustrations and complaints...exhilarating—a journalist's gold mine," though ultimately this openness was "oppressive" since he "had no help or remedies to offer" to their discontents. His tes-

timony too is radically inconsistent with Hoan's claims.

As for the "discontent" so openly voiced in Saigon, Fraser found that "the complaints were rarely what we in the West would describe as human rights problems" but rather "huge gripes about the declining standard of living," that is, the decline in the "subsidized and materialistic standard of living [that] had been provided for this city" (or at least those elements of the city with whom journalists were familiar). Like other commentators concerned with fact, he too points out that the Communists have gone out of their way to maintain the artificial economy of Saigon, despite the grinding poverty elsewhere: "For all the talk of revenge, people in Saigon eat better, dress better, work less and have more trinkets to play with than the people of Hanoi, whose poverty remains real and painfully obvious." Fraser was particularly struck by the Saigon "cowboys," "some of the toughest young people I have ever encountered," the gangster element created by the U.S. invaders who now refuse to work and constitute a continuing social problem. Fraser found the new Saigon/Ho Chi Minh city to be neither at the extreme of "a city groaning under oppression" nor a city with "a new dignity," though it had "aspects of both." Reprinted in the *Christian Science Monitor* (5 December 1978), from the *Toronto Globe and Mail* (25 November 1978). This is part 2 of a seven-part series (24, 25, 26, 27, 28, 29, 30 November and 1 December). In other sections, he describes the horrendous problems facing this "blighted land" of "grinding poverty" in the North and a "declining standard of living" for those in the South who have to "come to terms with the reality of Vietnam's overall poverty." The problems include the legacy of the war, open warfare along the Cambodian border and a dangerous confrontation with China, catastrophic flooding and "the prospect of famine," and "an almost complete lack of foreign funds to pay for its modest plans in modernization." The ethnic Chinese, he believes, are not persecuted in the North, "while in the South, the actual persecution of ethnic Chinese is based exclusively on class and economic divisions." But the problem was handled quite clumsily, he believes. In contrast, "the Catholic question is being managed with considerable sophistication and finesse" in the South, and he gives a interesting account of Church-State accommodation and conflict. He also relates conversations with Mme. Ngo Ba Thanh and Father Huynh Cong Minh, "also a member of the National Assembly as well as the editor of a national Catholic newspaper," both non-Communists who struck him "as deeply troubled and sincere people struggling to come to terms with present-day reality in Vietnam," basically supportive of the regime and its policies.

84. The "redeployment" of the population towards new economic zones in unsettled areas oft he South, announced shortly before by the government, was to include 150,000 Northerners. *Le Monde* (15 January 1977).

85. Bishop Thuan is in fact held under police custody in Hanoi, according to a letter from Archbishop Nguyen Van Binh of Ho Chi Minh City

(Saigon) that was "slipped out" to the Vatican "under the noses of Communist officials." Thuan is a nephew of former President Diem and "an outspoken anti-Communist." Archbishop Binh wrote that he had met with Thuan just before his trip to Rome (see note 68). He wrote that Thuan is "in good health, although a little thinner, and alert in his mind" and quoted him as saying that he was well-treated: "I am quite well today, so please, when you go to Rome, explain to the Pope and to the archbishop who is in charge of preaching and to others what is the truth in the Socialist Republic of Vietnam. I say these things, not because of the presence of this cadre in Hanoi but because it is the truth." Richard Dudman, *St. Louis Post-Dispatch* (7 November 1977). Dudman was informed of the letter by Father Chan Tin in Ho Chi Minh City.

86. David Tharp, "Political defector blasts Viet repression," *Christian Science Monitor* (4 May 1977).

87. Don Luce, who is fluent in Vietnamese, reported that "I could go to the marketplace by myself and talk to whomever I wanted to there. I went to visit friends of mine in their homes alone and could talk to them about their views on what was happening there." Congressional Hearings, June-July, 1977, *op. cit.*, p. 114. See also the reports by the Vietnamese visitors from Canada, the AFSC workers, Hughes, Ediger, Klassen, and other Americans fluent in Vietnamese. (See also notes 83 and 97).

88. Henry Kamm, "Defector From Hanoi Depicts Conditions," *New York Times* (18 May 1977).

89. Or the local Japanese press. Rep. Derwinski quoted from an article about Hoan in the Japanese press in the Congressional Hearings, *op. cit.* p. 137-138.

90. Henry Kamm, "Vietnamese Who Fled To Speak Out Find It Isn't Easy," *New York Times* (10 June 1977).

91. Theodore Jacqueney, "Hanoi's Gulag Archipelago: Human Rights in Vietnam," *AFL-CIO Trade Union News,* September 1977.

92. See the report of the Indochina Resource Center replying to Jacqueney, Appendix 2 of the Congressional Hearings on Vietnam; see note 70. For supplementary information, see Chomsky and Herman, "Saigon's corruption crisis." Whatever one may think of the arrest of Thanh after the Vinh Son affair, Jacqueney's characterization of him gives some insight into his own standards of evaluation.

Another person alleged by Jacqueney to be a prisoner is Tran Ngoc Chau, who was arrested by the Thieu regime and imprisoned in 1969. Chau had been Program Director of Revolutionary Development, a pacification program designed to gather intelligence on the NLF infrastructure, and in his trial claimed to be a supporter of Thieu and Nixon (see Indochina Resource Center report, cited above). Jacqueney does not report the fact that Chau was framed with the collaboration of William Colby, CIA Station Chief Theodore Shackley and Ambassador Ellsworth Bunker, and that the CIA in Washington refused to evacuate him from Vietnam (Snepp, *op. cit.*, p. 15; recall Casella's observation, p. 84 above). Richard Dudman reported from Vietnam that "A well-informed Vietnamese said that Chau had been under house arrest until early October but now was free" (*St. Louis Post-Dispatch*, 3 November 1977).

93. The reason cannot have been that U.S. journals do not review French books or that Lacouture is unknown. For example, Father François Ponchaud's highly critical account of postwar Cambodia became an instant media hit when it was reviewed in the *New York Review* by Jean Lacouture, with considerable embellishment, only a few weeks after its publication in Paris. We return to this book and its reception in the West in chapter 6.

94. According to the *New York Review*, he arrived in Vietnam "in December 1948 and stayed on for twenty-eight years." He himself says that he arrived in Vietnam in 1957 and "starting in 1963, and for 13 years without interruption, I was on the staff of the Alexander-de-Rhodes Student Center...(Congressional Hearings, June-July, 1977, p. 81). Later he claims to "have lived with the people for 19 years" (p. 22). *The Globe and Mail* introduces him as having spent 19 years in Vietnam. The issue is not particularly important in itself, but gains some interest in the context of the more general question of the credibility of Gelinas's report and the media treatment of it.

   According to a detailed curriculum vitae provided by Father Tran Tam Tinh of *Fraternité Vietnam* in a letter of 15 March 1977, Gelinas spent the years 1958-59 and 1965-76 in Saigon. In 1957 and 1964 he was in Taiwan and from 1960-63 at Columbia University in New York. Basically the same account appears in *Seven Days*, 9 May 1977 in an article by Jon Steinberg.

95. Cited by Robert K. Musil, "Vietnam and the press," Appendix 7 of the Congressional Hearings of June-July, 1977.

96. Quotes henceforth are from the English translation in the *New York Review*.

97. To our knowledge, no visitor or resident in Vietnam apart from Gelinas has reported mass suicides in September-October, 1975 following the currency regulations. Ms. Forsythe, however, has some other things to say based on her three years in South Vietnam, including 6 months after the war when "I was free to travel anywhere in the city, and did so...by public bus or on foot...[which]...gave me ample chance to meet ordinary people and observe the impact of the new government on the daily lives of people." She reports having seen children suffering from severe malnutrition under the U.S.-Thieu regime, eating only leaves, apparently because the Saigon armed forces were hoarding rice purchased by the United States for distribution to the needy, and children killed or wounded by ARVN soldiers for revenge or "target practice." She also describes the many false rumors that circulated during and after the war

about Viet Cong atrocities, discussions with neighbors who returned to ordinary lives after "study and practice" (i.e., "reeducation"), the impressive spirit of students who were engaged in social and economic reconstruction, and the substantial improvement in health care for the poor people who "are benefactors of any aid that is flowing into that country" which, for the first time, has honest officials. She denies most of what Gelinas reports, saying "It is very hard for me in listening to Father Gelinas to square what he says with my own experience," the standard reaction, as we shall see. Her report, as distinct from that of Gelinas, did not exactly become an international media sensation.

98. Cited by Musil, *op. cit.* This did not appear in the *New York Times* report of 16 December cited above.

99. Musil, *op. cit.,* his emphasis.

100. See Volume I, chapter 5, section 2.2.

101. Cf. Musil, *op. cit.*

102. Cf. Musil, *ibid.,* for further discussion.

103. Compare the report by Father Gianni (cf. note 69), who left Vietnam at the same time as Gelinas. "I remember the day on which many of us were invited to a meeting with the civil authorities. They thanked all of us foreign religious for the many years missionaries from abroad had been working in Vietnam. But since they claimed that the number of native Vietnamese priests, sisters and religious was sufficient, we were no longer needed, and so they invited us to return to our own native countries...Here, as in many other cases, when the socialist government of Vietnam invited foreign missionaries to leave, this brought into focus a situation in need of correction for many years in Vietnam."

104. *Toronto Globe and Mail* (23 March 1977).

105. Don Braid, "Viets 'pray for war,'" *Montreal Star* (26 March 1977). Excerpts of the *L'Express-New York Review* interview are reprinted, and the journal notes that this "highly unflattering report...has appeared in mass-circulation newspapers and magazines in France, Italy, England and the United States." Here Gelinas is said to have "lived in Vietnam for 15 years" (see note 94), and he has become the "director of the Alexander of Rhodes Education Center."

106. Martin, who remained in Vietnam after the war ended, is the author of *Reaching the Other Side;* cf. note 10, this chapter. Many of the same charges by Gelinas are refuted, on the basis of direct eyewitness observation, by Forsythe, Hughes, and the Canadian Vietnamese visitors; for example, his claims about a "coup d'état against the PRG" on July 19-20, 1975, when "the city woke up in a state of siege," and the PRG headquarters "was surrounded by armored cars" (he expands on this "coup" in his congressional testimony). During this "coup," Martin reports, "friends and I rode bicycles freely around town" observing nothing except somewhat enhanced security arrangements in expectation of demonstrations and violence that did not eventuate; he also points out

that Gelinas mislocated the PRG headquarters. Forsythe also reports that while there was street gossip about a possible "coup," it "never took place" and "there was no unrest" and "never a purging of the PRG from any level in Saigon" to her knowledge. Hughes adds that not only was there no "coup d'état against the PRG," but in fact any such coup "would have resoundingly failed because, among other things," the place mentioned by Gelinas is "not where their 'headquarters' was" (they actually had no headquarters, he adds, but rather leadership was "decentralized into a plethora of almost autonomous 'offices' (themselves broken down into smaller teams), functions, and locations." Hughes also comments on the absurdity of the belief that tanks and infantry could have rounded up "a widely scattered, guerrilla leadership who, for years, had resisted one of the world's most sophisticated war machines." The remainder of Gelinas's charges suffer a like fate, according to eyewitnesses who were not, like Gelinas, living behind what Hughes calls "the barred entrance of the walled-off Western style Alexandre-de-Rhodes center."

107. Recall that this claim is expressly denied by numerous independent observers, cited above. It is worth noting, perhaps, Gelinas's statement that "the churches have never been fuller," contradicting the claims of the other media favorite, Nguyen Cong Hoan; but this is because "many Vietnamese find solace in prayer." The contradictions on this score between Gelinas and Hoan have not troubled the journalists and editors who cite them both as giving the true picture of life in Vietnam, an interesting example of the ability of the faithful to tolerate counterevidence. According to Hughes, Gelinas told him: "people were ordered to have a good Christmas [in December, 1975], to have religious services." There was no written order, he added in response to questioning, but local authorities "gave the churches Christmas trees. To show the world, you see."

108. "'Liberation' Comes to Vietnam," New York Times editorial (21 March 1977).

109. Cf. the Times retrospective assessment of the war, discussed in chapter 2, section 1.

110. See note 94.

111. Editorial, "Harvest in Vietnam," (21 April 1977).

112. Consistent with their general concern for factual accuracy, the editors misspell his name throughout.

113. Vietnam South East Asia International, March-April 1977. "Only about ten people attended and a number of those walked out in protest."

114. Recall a point that is quite significant in this connection. Gelinas was completely unknown. His various accounts cite no evidence or documentation, and their credibility therefore depends entirely on his credibility, as judged by comments of his that are subject to check. To appreciate properly the Western reaction to Gelinas, consider the

following hypothetical case: imagine that Russian forces were driven out of Hungary next year, and that a Russian who had worked for many years in a Russian cultural center in Hungary came forward in the Soviet Union, deploring the situation in Hungary after liberation without citing any evidence that could be checked, offering reports that are entirely at variance with eyewitness accounts of others during the same period, and describing Hungary under Russian rule as a land of freedom and wealth, now suffering under the yoke of an oppressor. Under such hypothetical circumstances, no one familiar with the Soviet propaganda system would be surprised to discover that his reports receive wide publicity and much acclaim and are used by editorialists as a club to beat Russian dissidents who denounced Russian rule in Hungary, the 1956 invasion, etc. The Western treatment of Gelinas is quite comparable, and once again gives an insight into the workings of the Free Press.

115. He is predictably silent on the decimation of southern forces by the United States.

116. Gelinas tells us little about his ministrations to his flock during his years in Vietnam. An American visitor to the bookstore he ran remembers him as "the only priest who was a hawk and who seemed more interested in business than in religious matters. Books of the neutralist Third Force were not sold in his store, but he did have a government monopoly on all translations of government books into Western languages." Jon Steinberg, *op. cit.* (see note 94). Gelinas's bitterness towards the government that forced him to leave is understandable, Steinberg adds, while "Those who print his stories as truth have less excuse."

117. See note 83. Recall that Fraser interviewed non-Communist activists who had defended political prisoners under the Thieu regime and who, contrary to what Paringaux wrote, had not "now become silent" but expressed their support for the general policies of the regime. Fraser's account also conflicts with the well-publicized French reports in other significant respects. His reaction to their reports appears in part four of his seven-part series, 28 November 1978.

118. CBS news, 6 p.m. (5 October); Jim Browning, "Repression in Vietnam growing?," *Christian Science Monitor* (6 October); Editorial, "Vietnam's 'Gulag Archipelago,'" ibid., 10 October; Joseph Fitchett, "Saigon Residents Found Intimidated by 'Occupation Force,'" *Washington Post* (6 November 1978), reprinted from the *International Herald Tribune*. October 28, 29, citing reports by four French journalists who recently spent 10 days [in Saigon], gaining the most extensive access of any Western reporters since 1975." The *New York Times* was then on strike. Both CBS and Browning refer to *Le Monde* as a left-wing newspaper, but otherwise, their reports were generally accurate.

The editorial is about what one would expect in a journal that not long ago was featuring discussions by one of its saner commentators

(Joseph Harsch) on the relative merits of bombing trucks and dams (the latter so much more satisfying to the pilots, who come home "with a feeling of accomplishment" when they see the waters "pour through the breach and drown out huge areas of farm land, and villages, in its path" and so much more effective in "hurt[ing] people"). For lengthy quotes, see *American Power and the New Mandarins*, p. 14; for analogies, see the Nazi archives.

119. It is less appropriate, however, to ignore the subsequent discussion in *Le Monde*, including the reply of the Vietnamese Ambassador to France, November 10. See the extensive discussion and analysis in *Vietnam South East Asia International*.

120. See *At War with Asia*, pp. 96f., for quotes and discussion. The text appears in N.S. Adams and A.W. McCoy, eds., *Laos: War and Revolution*, Harper and Row, 1970.

121. See chapter 5, note 12.

122. *Le Monde hebdomadaire* (18-24 January 1968).

123. *New Statesman*, 1 December 1967.

124. Cf. Chomsky, *American Power and the New Mandarins*, pp. 249, 285. Other comparable examples of effective press self-censorship are reported there. In most of the cases mentioned, including the ones we cite here, much effort was expended in trying to convince the media to publish the facts, with no success.

125. For a comparable example, see chapter 6, note 102.

5 Laos

1. See Bernard Fall, *Anatomy of a Crisis: The Laotian Crisis of 1960-61*, Doubleday, 1969, for a detailed exposure of some of the more ludicrous incidents in the early phases of the U.S. war; this exposure, like others, had no detectable effect on subsequent reporting.

2. See the reports by Henry Kamm in the *New York Times*, cited below; or for example a Sunday feature story by Ogden Williams, "The Tragic Plight of our Abandoned Allies," *Washington Post* (24 September 1978). Williams is identified as a former CIA officer who also worked with USAID in Vietnam—quite possibly, a distinction without a difference in this case, since as was finally conceded in public, the aid program, in Laos at least, was providing a CIA cover from 1962. He claims that the Hmong army organized by the CIA was tying up two divisions of North Vietnamese regulars in Laos. Comparable claims are common, but tend to evaporate on investigation; cf. the references of footnote 4 for detailed analyses. Sources close to the U.S. government estimate perhaps one combat regiment of North Vietnamese soldiers in northern Laos, where the CIA army was fighting, in 1968.

3. See Fred Branfman, *Voices from the Plain of Jars*, Harper and Row, 1972; Walter Haney, "A Survey of Civilian War Casualties Among Refugees

from the Plain of Jars," U.S. Congress, Senate, Committee on the Judiciary, Hearings before the [Kennedy] Subcommittee on Refugees and Escapees, 92nd Congress, 1st session, 22 July 1971, Appendix 2; "A Survey of Civilian Fatalities Among Refugees from Xieng Khouang Province, Laos," Kennedy Subcommittee Hearings, 92nd Congress, second session, 9 May 1972, part 2, "Cambodia and Laos," Appendix 2; see also his paper "The Pentagon Papers and U.S. Involvement in Laos," in N. Chomsky and H. Zinn, eds., *The Pentagon Papers, Critical Essays*, vol. 5 of the Senator Gravel edition of the *Pentagon Papers*, Beacon, 1972. See also the references of footnote 4.

4. For a detailed analysis of the material just briefly reviewed, see N. Chomsky, *At War with Asia*, Pantheon, 1970, chapter 3; *For Reasons of State*, Pantheon, 1973, chapter 2; and references and documentary evidence cited there. The scholarly literature is useful but must be treated with care, since as demonstrated in the sources just cited the conclusions reached often derive from the most dubious evidence, sometimes sheer fabrication on the part of government officials who are taken quite seriously despite their long record of prevarication.

5. See John Everingham, "Press war creates problems for Laos," *Far Eastern Economic Review*, writing from Vientiane before his expulsion on the "hostile and inaccurate Thai press coverage of Laotian affairs" that "may convince those not on the spot," and on the questionable "principle of reporting Laos from Thailand," where one finds a "stream of anti-Lao hysteria and falsities."

6. *Laos Recovers from America's War*, Southeast Asia Chronicle, no. 61, March-April 1978, P.O. Box 4000D, Berkeley, California 94704. Most of the material in this issue is by the Hieberts. Other material is supplied by Mennonite missionaries still in Laos.

7. "How now, Laos?," *Christian Science Monitor* (10 June 1975).

8. Hieberts, *op. cit.* These features of lovely little Laos, and of other "small old places," have intrigued thoughtful U.S. observers like Reasoner much less than the eroticism, which, as visitors to Vientiane quickly learned, was a major preoccupation of the press corps, many of whose members seemed to divide their time between the U.S. Embassy (where they received "the news"), the hotel bars, and the local house of prostitution. As elsewhere in Indochina, there were noteworthy exceptions.

9. See footnotes 1 and 4.

10. Wolfgang Saxon, "Long Fratricidal Strife in Laos Was Intensified by Outsiders," *New York Times* (24 August 1975).

11. E.g., Phoumi Nosavan's "proclaimed anti-Communism won him military aid from the Eisenhower administration and the Thai government" in 1960. In fact, Phoumi was armed and backed by the United States in his successful effort to overthrow the government recognized by the United States, and thousands of Thai troops (virtually, U.S. mercenaries) were apparently fighting in Laos (see *At War with Asia*). The U.S.

role in overthrowing the 1958 political settlement in which the Pathet Lao emerged as the dominant force is not so much as mentioned, though it is entirely beyond controversy. See, for example, Hugh Toye, *Laos: Buffer State or Battleground*, Oxford, 1968; Charles Stevenson, *The End of Nowhere: American Policy towards Laos Since 1964*, Beacon, 1972.

12. See T.D. Allman, *New York Times* (1 October 1969) reporting on the testimony of refugees from the Plain of Jars and concluding that "the rebel economy and social fabric" are now the main target of the U.S. bombardment, which is claimed to be a success: "The bombing, by creating refugees, deprives the Communists of their chief source of food and transport. The population of the Pathet Lao zone has been declining for several years and the Pathet Lao find it increasingly difficult to fight a 'people's war' with fewer and fewer people." On the same day *Le Monde* (weekly selection) reported that this "battering" of Laos had been going on for over five years and that "the United States Air Force carries out more than 12,500 raids a month." As already noted, eyewitness reports of the U.S. attack on the rebel economy and social fabric had been reported by Jacques Decornoy of *Le Monde* in July 1968, and repeatedly brought to the attention of editors of the *New York Times* and other journals, to no effect. See p. 134, above.

See also the eyewitness report by T.D. Allman at just the time when Air Force Secretary Robert Seamans, visiting the same areas, reported that "I have seen no evidence of indiscriminate bombing." Allman's report of massive destruction from highly discriminate bombing aimed at civilian targets appeared in the *Far Eastern Economic Review* and the *Manchester Guardian*; Seaman's failure to see anything was reported in the *Washington Post*. Direct reporting from the ground by Michael Morrow did not appear in the U.S. press at all, to our knowledge, as befits observations of U.S. atrocities by a Western reporter who concludes that "it is unlikely that Americans are or will ever be around to pick up the unexploded pieces of the most extensive bombing campaign in history," a campaign that is now being expunged from the historical records. See *At War with Asia*, pp. 95f; *For Reasons of State*, pp. 173f. For the Decornoy report and much other valuable material that is conveniently ignored in the United States, see N.S. Adams and A.W. McCoy, eds., *Laos: War and Revolution*, Harper, 1970.

13. Given what is known about CIA control and activities, it seems likely that this was part of a U.S. intelligence campaign. This places the subsequent show of compassion for the refugees—see footnote 2—in a still more ugly light.

14. Daniel Southerland, "Lao tribesmen moving out," *Christian Science Monitor* (30 May 1975). Southerland was one of the small group of correspondents in Indochina who maintained a high level of professional integrity throughout. We are indebted to Louis and Eryl Kubicka of the AFSC, who spent three years in Laos (including two and one-half

years after the war), for additional information about Lyteck and for helpful comments and information about other matters. The Kubickas have made extensive efforts to bring information about postwar Laos to the U.S. press, to little effect. They inform us that their accounts were seriously distorted by *New York Times* reporters Paul Hoffman and David Andelman, "by the device of omission and by taking the negative side of balanced statements we made" and other standard Free Press techniques. An important analysis of Thai perception of U.S. moves to undermine Thai democracy prior to the October 1976 military coup (see Volume I, chapter 4, section 2) was submitted to the *New York Times, Washington Post* and other journals, but rejected. For their own account of the postwar situation in Laos, see Louis Kubicka, "Laos: Resettlement Begins on Bombed-Out Plain of Jars—Minus U.S. AID," *Los Angeles Times* (1 March 1976); "War Hangover in Laos," *Eastern Horizon*, March 1978; "From the Plain of Jars," *Progressive*, March 1978.

15. "Learning to Love the Pathet Lao," *Washington Post* (27 October 1975).

16. Norman Peagam, "Communist Changes in Laos Upset Easy-Going Way of Life," *New York Times* (3 May 1977).

17. Interviews with two refugees who returned are reported by John and Beulah Yoder of the Mennonites, writing from Vientiane in February, 1978 in *Laos Recovers from America's War*. One, a Hmong tribesman now in a teacher training college, recalls "the intense anti-Lao propaganda in the Thai camps" and the "many lies about Laos" spread in France. In the Thai camp, "we lived like pigs. No one had enough to eat" and the Thai military attempted to recruit refugees to fight communism, possibly in Laos, while camp guards beat or imprisoned anyone trying to escape. The second says that he fled to Thailand "because I didn't understand the policies or goals of the new regime. In the old regime we were taught only to make ourselves rich. We were not taught love for our nation." Living in France, he "learned about the goals of the new Lao regime" from the Lao student organization. "He realized they had a vision for Laos which he could share." On the Thai camps, see footnote 24 below.

18. Since these important elements of the "prisoners" in "re-education camps" are a legacy of Western imperialism, they are regularly disregarded in Western commentary.

19. "Political repression reported in Laos," *Boston Globe* (10 February 1978). (See footnote 5, above.)

20. Henry Kamm, "Hill People Who Fought for U.S. Are Fleeing Laos," *New York Times* (28 March 1978); "Laos Said to Battle Internal Resistance," *New York Times* (29 March 1978). Both stories are filed from Thailand.

21. A phrase of rare accuracy from this pen, though one wonders whether the author comprehends its meaning.

22. See chapter 1, note 16. In the documents cited there, it is proposed that Thailand be developed "as the focal point of U.S. covert and psycholog-

ical operations in Southeast Asia." The proposal was implemented, and Thailand also became a major base for direct U.S. military operations against Laos and Vietnam, and for CIA-backed groups attempting to undermine the neutralist government of Cambodia. (See Volume I, chapter 4, section 2; chapter 6, below, and references cited there).

23. On the "growing Vietnamese influence," always a staple of U.S. reporting—it has been "growing" in the U.S. press for some 25 years—see footnote 4, and also pp. 147, 151-53, below, and note 31.

24. On the Thai refugee camps, see John Burgess, "City of broken lives," *Far Eastern Economic Review,* 26 May 1978. According to refugees, some "use the camp as a base to support the guerrillas harassing the communist government in Laos" though most are more interested in finding another country, usually the United States, to take them in. "People leave Laos for varied reasons: some because they are threatened with reeducation, some because they have records as prostitutes or criminals, others because they cannot find jobs." The underworld is thriving in the camp, where Thai police "claimed to have discovered a syndicate...that was producing Laotian women for the brothels of Bangkok," and the drug trade flourishes. 41% of the people in the camp "claimed direct or indirect membership in U.S.-affiliated agencies, mostly the old Laotian armed forces." A few of the camp's people intend to join the anti-Communist resistance in Laos, and "one well-placed refugee" reports that small numbers "pass in and out of Laos with help and equipment from the Thai military." A Hmong veteran of the CIA army reports that "his village had been destroyed by artillery" while others claim that the Lao government used poison gas against them.

25. It is superfluous to note that Vietnam's attempts "to establish normal links with the West" have been blocked at every turn by the U.S. government, since Hanoi has not yet succeeded in meeting the exalted standards set by the United States, to the applause of the Free Press.

26. Peter Kovler, "Laos's need: U.S. rice," *New York Times* (14 March 1978). The Op-Ed page of the *Times* is the spot where all sorts of odd opinions are permitted occasional expression.

27. See footnote 6. This is the only press reference to the Hieberts that we have noted, though their eyewitness report from a country virtually closed to the West would have been featured in a country enjoying a free press.

28. The reference, presumably, is to the Plain of Jars, where the vast U.S.-inflicted war damage remains unrepaired (if indeed it can be repaired).

29. The impending starvation is a result of the U.S. attack and also the natural disasters that have afflicted Southeast Asia in the past several years.

30. In what it called "a humanitarian aid decision in keeping with the Administration's policy of answering basic human needs," the Carter Administration agreed to send 10,000 tons of rice in August and Sep-

tember of 1978; UPI, "U.S. giving $5m in rice to Laos," *Boston Globe* (2 June 1978); Don Oberdorfer, "U.S. Will Give Laos $5 Million in Food Aid To Avert a 'Disaster,'" *Washington Post* (1 June 1978). The last U.S. aid was in 1974, when 24,000 tons of rice were sent. The 10,000 tons allegedly forthcoming would supplement the 80,000 tons pledged by other countries. Note that the fear of jeopardizing the canal treaties was past, at this time.

It appears, however, that even this tiny gesture towards "humanitarianism" was a fraud. When the State Department announced that a piddling 10,000 tons of food would be released for the starving Lao on May 31, it was assumed that this munificence would be in addition to the regular contribution of the United States to the World Food Program of the United Nations, which had pledged 30,000 tons of food to Laos. But it seems that the U.S. donation is to be "merely a *part of* its normal biannual contribution to WFP, and no more." The estimated need in Laos to avoid disaster is at least 120,000 tons of emergency food. Roger Rumpf and Jacqui Chagnon, AFSC representatives in Laos, letter, *Washington Post* (14 October 1978). There appear to be no limits to the cynicism of the Human Rights Administration.

31. Nayan Chanda, "Laos keeps up a cold front," *Far Eastern Economic Review*, 15 April 1977. Vietnamese influence in Laos has no doubt been growing, for several reasons, among them, punitive U.S. policies towards Laos and Vietnam and the Vietnam-China conflict. Occasionally, propaganda fabricated with no concern for fact may be accurate—in this case, in part as a consequence of the brutal policies supported or concealed by the media.

32. Nayan Chanda, "Drought Worsens Laotian Plight," *Far Eastern Economic Review*, 26 August 1977.

33. The situation may have somewhat improved in subsequent months, as the Thai government moved to a more "liberal" anti-Communist policy.

34. Norman Peagam, "Letter from Vientiane," *Far Eastern Economic Review*, 6 May 1977. No aid donor countries offered to supply the DDT required for malaria control after the U.S. aid cut-off. Peagam adds that the health problem is exacerbated by efforts to encourage hill tribes to move down to the lowlands in order to conserve the forests and "sending civil servants into the countryside for political seminars and manual work."

35. Among them, Thai journalists, accurately for once. Theh Chongkhadikij, "Fears of Imminent Famine in Laos," *Bangkok Post* (1 March 1977), reporting the fear of "ambassador-level sources in Vientiane" that Laos faces starvation within a few months, largely because of the drought. Similar fears have been repeatedly expressed in the *Far Eastern Economic Review*.

36. For a review of some of these, see *At War with Asia*, chapter 3.

37. "Drought Worsens Laotian Plight" (see footnote 32).

38. Nayan Chanda, "Lao-Thai gulf is still wide," *Far Eastern Economic Review*, 26 August 1977.

39. Nayan Chanda, "Laos Gears up for Rural Progress," *Far Eastern Economic Review*, 8 April 1977.
40. Nayan Chanda, "Putting the pieces back together," *Far Eastern Economic Review*, 23 December 1977. See Branfman, *op. cit.*, for the view from the wrong end of the guns.
41. Properly, Chanda places the word "secret" in quotes. As we have seen, the "secrecy" was a matter of decision by the Free Press.
42. Recall that the bombing in the Plain of Jars had nothing to do with North Vietnamese supply trails, as loyal correspondents for the *New York Times* and other specimens of the Free Press continue to pretend. Rather, its purpose was to destroy a civilian society that was undergoing a mild social revolution. See the references of notes 3 and 4.
43. "War Hangover in Laos." (See footnote 14).
44. *Los Angeles Times* (1 March 1976). (See footnote 14).

6 Cambodia

1. We would like to thank Stephen Reder, Ben Kiernan, Torben Retbøll, Laura Summers, Serge Thion and Michael Vickery for important information and very helpful comments on an earlier draft of this chapter.

   During the period of this review—mid-1975 to the end of 1978— the regime used the name "Democratic Kampuchea." With some misgivings, we will continue to use the conventional English spelling, "Cambodia," throughout. Again with misgivings, we will use the term "Khmer Rouge" to refer to the revolutionary movement of Cambodia and to the regime during the period of our review. See Volume I, chapter 1, note 56.

2. François Ponchaud, *Cambodia: Year Zero*, Holt, Rinehart and Winston, 1978; a revised and updated translation of his *Cambodge: année zéro*, Julliard, 1977, which became perhaps the most influential unread book in recent political history after a review by Jean Lacouture, to which we return. It is also unusual in that it is the only recent French book on Cambodia to have been not only widely quoted and misquoted, but also translated. In contrast, important French studies of the colonial period and the U.S. intervention have gone unreviewed, unnoticed and untranslated, as was the case with Lacouture's book on Vietnam, mentioned above: for example, Charles Meyer, *Derrière le sourire Khmer*, Plon, 1971; Jean-Claude Pomonti and Serge Thion, *Des courtisans aux partisans*, Gallimard, 1971 (for some discussion of these books, see Chomsky, *For Reasons of State*, chapter 2). Ponchaud, a French priest who lived in Cambodia for ten years, is the best-informed and most careful of those who have done extensive critical work on postwar Cambodia, though his study is not without serious flaws. For tens of millions of readers in the United States and throughout the world, the major source of information is no doubt John Barron and Anthony

Paul, *Murder of a Gentle Land: the Untold Story of Communist Genocide in Cambodia*, Reader's Digest Press, Crowell, 1977, expanded from an article in the *Reader's Digest*, February 1977. Subsequent references to Ponchaud will be to the U.S. edition cited above, unless explicitly noted. We stress that references are to the U.S., not the British edition, which differs in crucial respects, as we shall see.

3. We will return to a few examples. As one indication of the power of the U.S. propaganda system, consider a study of the "Ten Best Censored Stories of 1977" described as "a nationwide media research project" with "a panel often nationally recognized individuals"; one of us (Chomsky) was among them, along with journalist Shana Alexander, Ben Bagdikian of the Graduate School of Journalism at Berkeley, Congresswoman Shirley Chisholm, Nicholas Johnson (chairman of the National Citizens Communications Lobby), Victor Marchetti (former CIA agent who has written important exposés of the intelligence system) and other well-known journalists, writers, and media specialists. The panel selected "Massacre in Cambodia and Vietnam" as one of the ten best censored stories (news release, Office of Public Affairs, Sonoma State College, 9 August 1978). Putting aside any question as to the facts of the matter, this story does not even merit consideration in a study of "censorship," given the actual media coverage.

4. We do not want to imply that this is the only reason why journalists sought out dissenting opinion. In the case of Cambodia, as in the other cases we have discussed, there remains a current of honest journalism though it is often buried under the avalanche of propaganda.

5. Ponchaud, Author's note for the American translation, dated 20 September 1977, *op. cit.*, p. xvi.

6. For example, Morton Kondracke, "How Much Blood Makes a Bloodbath?' *New Republic*, 1 October 1977: "Perhaps the United States does bear some responsibility [note the admirable caution], but the doves themselves had better explain why similar things haven't happened in Vietnam... ." Why is it the responsibility of those who opposed the U.S. intervention that converted a civil struggle into a murderous war to "explain" the consequences that ensued?

7. *Dissent*, Fall 1978. Evidently, the question can be raised only if one accepts two assumptions: 1) the U.S. intervention in Indochina would have prevented a Cambodian bloodbath or was designed for this purpose; 2) the United States has the right to use force and violence to prevent potential crimes—and thus, *a fortiori*, to resort to force to prevent actual crimes by invading Indonesia, much of Latin America, etc. It is difficult to decide which of the two assumptions that are jointly required for the question even to be raised is the more absurd.

8. *Human Rights in Cambodia*, Hearing before the Subcommittee on International Organizations of the Committee on International Relations, House of Representatives, Ninety-Fifth Congress, First Session,

3 May 1977 (henceforth, *May Hearings*), p. 40; see also the Hearing before the same subcommittee, 26 July 1977 (henceforth, *July Hearings*). Government Printing Office, Washington, 1977.

9. See his prepared statement, *July Hearings*, pp. 19-32. See also George C. Hildebrand and Gareth Porter, *Cambodia: Starvation & Revolution*, Monthly Review Press, 1976.

10. In fact, Pike is a State Department propagandist whose effusions are often simply embarrassing. For some examples, see Chomsky, *American Power and the New Mandarins*, pp. 365-66.

11. AP, *Boston Globe*, 22 August 1978. See also *Washington Post*, August 22; editorial, *Boston Globe*, August 23, reprinted in the *Christian Science Monitor*, August 28; *Wall Street Journal*, August 22 and editorial August 23; William F. Buckley, *Boston Globe*, 29 August 1978. The *New York Times* was on strike and not publishing.

12. *Congressional Record*, 22 August 1978, S 14019.

13. McGovern introduced the transcript into the *Congressional Record*, August 22, S 14020.

14. *Congressional Record*, 25 August 1978, S 14397.

15. We choose a factor of a hundred for illustration because of Jean Lacouture's observation, to which we return, that it is a question of secondary importance whether the number of people killed was in the thousands or hundreds of thousands.

16. See note 53, this chapter. Given the wording McGovern used, it is likely that his actual source was a widely quoted allegation by Jean Lacouture that the regime was "systematically massacring, isolating and starving" the population and had "boasted" of having killed some 2 million people. See the reference of note 17. As we shall see, even after Lacouture published a correction, stating that there was no basis for the latter charge, it continues to be reiterated by people who are aware of the correction, along with his more general claim, for which he also provided no evidence that withstands inquiry.

17. See his "The bloodiest revolution," *New York Review of Books*, 31 March 1977, a review of Ponchaud's *Cambodge: année zéro*, translated from *Le Nouvel Observateur*. See also his "Cambodia: Corrections," *New York Review*, 26 May 1977. Also his review of Barron-Paul, *New York Times Book Review*, 11 September 1977.

18. Ponchaud, *op. cit.*, p. xvi. His estimate of refugees is conservative as compared with some others. We noted earlier a recent estimate of 14,000 Cambodians in Thai refugee camps (others have already been resettled) in addition to an alleged 150,000 who have fled to Vietnam. According to Vietnamese sources, there have been 330,000 refugees and displaced persons from Cambodia since April 1975, including 170,000 of Vietnamese origin, almost all women, children and older people (UN High Commissioner for Refugees, Information Note, Hanoi, 31 July 1978). Based indirectly on this source, the U.S. press

has given estimates of 500,000 refugees from Cambodia (Editorial, *Boston Globe*, 23 August 1978; the record will show that Hanoi sources have rarely been given such credence and publicity; in this case, the journal was unaware of the original source.) On the exodus of Vietnamese refugees from Cambodia, see Laura Summers, "Human Rights in Cambodia," paper delivered at the International Studies Association, Washington, D.C., February 1978. She estimates that the Vietnamese population of Cambodia was about 450,000 before the war in 1970 and 310,000 were expelled or fled (along with 20,000 detained) during "the racialist campaign against Vietnamese Kampucheans by Lon Nol's 'Khmer Republic'" (her source is the well-known demographer Jacques Migozzi, *Cambodge: faits et problèmes de population*, CNRS, Paris, 1973). See T.D. Allman, cited in Volume I, chapter 3, note 20. Note that this exodus of over 300,000 people during the racialist campaign by the government backed by the United States has been quietly absorbed by the propaganda system, and that Lon Nol is now apparently offered as a serious source for allegations backing a proposal for military intervention in Cambodia. We return to Lon Nol's earlier exploits.

19. See chapter 2, section 2.
20. Ponchaud, *op. cit.*, p. xvi.
21. Henry Kamm, "Cambodians, Held in Thai Police Cages for IJlegal Entry, Await Future Apathetically," *New York Times*, 10 May 1978. See also note 170 of this chapter. On Kamm's Pulitzer Prize, see p. 58, above.
22. *Op. cit.*, p. 211.
23. *Ibid.*, p. xiii.
24. To be precise, Porter cites a similar comment from their *Reader's Digest* article, where they write that the "promising subjects" were selected with the "guidance" of the campleader. *May Hearings*, p. 23.
25. *Op. cit.*, p. 187.
26. Richard C. Holbrooke, Assistant Secretary for East Asian and Pacific Affairs, Department of State, *July Hearings*, p. 23.
27. *July Hearings*, p. 6.
28. See the discussion in chapter 2, section 1.
29. *May Hearings*, p. 22, citing CBS Evening News, 26 January 1976; *Washington Post* (8 April 1977). See also the letter to the *Economist* (London) by Torben Retbøll, 26 August 1978.
30. 20 January 1978, in Washington. This is a private group supporting U.S. military build-up.
31. *Battleline*, May 1978, publication of the American Conservative Union, featured in an issue devoted to atrocities in Cambodia.
32. Excerpts appear in *Worldview*, May 1978.
33. *AIM Report*, May 1978, Part II, reprinted as a full-page advertisement in the *Washington Post* (2 June 1978). Accuracy in Media, which publishes the *AIM Report*, is a well-financed right-wing group which is

concerned that the media do not adhere to the doctrines of state propaganda with sufficient loyalty, and under the guise of defending "accuracy" exerts pressures of various kinds to overcome this unfortunate situation. The alleged failure of the media to give sufficient attention to "the Cambodian holocaust" is one of their staples.

34. *Le Monde*, 7, 8 September 1977, 25 October 1977. There was, in fact, a CIA-run secret school in Laos for training Cambodian Army guerrillas that was closed down by the agency when a high-ranking officer who was an aide to the brother of Prime Minister Lon Nol was arrested by the Lao police for heroin smuggling. See Alan Dawson, *Pacific Stars & Stripes,* 12 October 1971.

35. "Cannibalism in Cambodia doubted," *Bangkok Post* (24 January 1978).

36. Neil Kelly, "Vietnamese refugee walked 350 miles across Cambodia to Thailand," *London Times* (30 January 1978).

37. Note that he should have witnessed or learned directly of the worst excesses. According to Ponchaud, "the early months were those of blackest terror....The executions continued after the early months of the massive purge of the former regime's civilian and military cadres and the many recalcitrant elements, but they became less frequent and less summary" (pp. 64, 69). Other sources agree, as we shall see below. Even people who should be ranked among outright propagandists agree that there must have been "some diminution of the killings" (Leo Cherne, *MacNeil/Lehrer Report*; see note 53). Cherne explains this on the grounds that the population had been reduced from 8 to 5 million, so that there were just fewer people left to kill. On his source for the 5 million figure, see note 118.

38. *Aftenposten* (Norway), 22 April 1978, translated in FBIS, 28 April 1978, Cambodia, H1-2.

39. John Fraser, "Pushy Russian replaces Ugly American," *Toronto Globe and Mail* (27 November 1978).

40. Michael Vickery, personal letter of September 24, 1977, which he has authorized us to cite. In this letter he expresses his pessimism about developments in Cambodia, along with a good deal of skepticism about finding out the truth.

41. See, for example, *Wall Street Journal*, editorial (18 July 1978), which offers "Prof. Chomsky's heroic efforts to disprove the Cambodian bloodbath through textual criticism of witnesses' statements" as an example of "intellectual levitation" on a par with apologetics for Mao, scholastic debate over the Shaba incursion, or the "passionate" argument of specialists on Africa that "Mau Mau outbreaks in Kenya were a spontaneous response to colonial oppression." Putting aside these interesting examples, the fact is that apart from letters to journalists who have invented or spread known falsehoods, these "heroic efforts" reduce to the single article cited below (note 100), which notes that refugee reports "must be considered carefully" though "care and caution are

necessary" for obvious reasons. No attempt whatsoever was made to "disprove the Cambodian bloodbath." The article states that "we do not pretend to know where the truth lies amidst these sharply conflicting assessments" cited by experts, of which the more extreme are selected (and distorted) by the press. Furthermore, these perhaps less than heroic efforts contain no specific discussion of witnesses' statements but rather document falsehoods and misrepresentations by those who have made use of these statements, as well as the continuing efforts by the *Wall Street Journal* and others to devise apologetics for atrocities within the U.S. sphere. Excerpts from a letter correcting these typical falsehoods appeared in the *Wall Street Journal*, 7 August.

42. See, for example, Norman Peagam, "Good crops and grim terror in Cambodia," *New Statesman*, 4 August 1978, or his briefer report in the *New York Times* (19 July 1978). Peagam makes the important point that "refugees in Thailand and Vietnam give virtually identical accounts," which he reports graphically—and in this case, credibly.

43. As noted above, p. 134, the Free Press preferred to ignore these reports too, though they were certainly known to editors of leading journals.

44. Leo Cherne, "The Terror in Cambodia," *Wall Street Journal* (10 May 1978).

45. Leo Cherne, "Why we can't withdraw," *Saturday Review*, 18 December 1965. On a government-sponsored study of how U.S. air and artillery attacks by causing "damages and casualties to the villagers" impel them "to move where they will be safe from such attacks...regardless of their attitude to the GVN," and the reaction by U.S. officials and apologists, see Chomsky, *For Reasons of State*, pp. 5, 142. In the same article, Cherne observes that "there should be no illusion about the consequences" of "an American withdrawal from Vietnam": "There will be a bloody purge of the non-Communist leaders and intellectuals."

46. "Cambodia: Corrections." See note 17 of this chapter. The significance of his reference to "deciding exactly which person uttered an inhuman phrase" will be explained below.

47. On Operation SPEEDY EXPRESS, see Volume I, chapter 5, section 1.3.

48. As we shall see, the evidence he reported was seriously in error throughout, and the sources on which he relied prove to be quite dubious on further inquiry. Lacouture's corrections, which were partial and somewhat misleading, were published in the United States when the errors were brought to his attention here, but never in France, where the article originally appeared.

49. See chapter 2, section 2. Recall the estimate by the "victim of the liberation," Pleyber-Grandjean, that the resistance had massacred 7 million people; quite evidently an exaggeration, though with some factual basis in tens of thousands of killings, but at least not widely disseminated as authoritative in the mass media of France and Germany, and not

beyond correction.
50. This quote from Lacouture appears on the cover of the U.S. version of Ponchaud's *Cambodia: Year Zero*.
51. To illustrate the issues at stake, consider the following example of a very general phenomenon in the industrial West. A U.S. newspaper in 1978 ran a cartoon showing a picture of a confused Nicaraguan citizen with Somoza on one side and a guerrilla with a gun on the other. The caption defined the alternatives he faced: Somoza's corruption and oppression on the one hand, "liberation or worse" on the other. It is important in the current phase of the Western system of indoctrination to establish in the popular mind the principle that liberation is a terrible fate for subject peoples, a major reason for the current campaigns of abuse and deceit with regard to Indochina.
52. Or, where possible, on independent evidence as to the credibility of those who present reports and interpretations.
53. Here are some scattered examples. From the *New York Times:* (9 July 1975) editorial "scores genocidal policies of Cambodia's Khmer Rouge rulers," comparing them to "Soviet extermination of Kulaks or with Gulag Archipelago" and "says silence by US Cong[ress] members and UN must be broken" (quoted from index); (20 October 1975) editorial with similar content; (27 March 1976) editorial contends that Cambodia is a "vast slave labor camp" ruled by "fanatical Communist leaders"; (12 April 1976) article cites *Time* report that 500,000 Cambodians have perished since April 1975; (3 June 1976) citing a journalist of *France Soir:* "the figure of a million victims since April 17, 1975, the day of the 'liberation' of Phnom Penh, is plausible, if not certain"; David A. Andelman (2 May 1977) "The purges that took hundreds of thousands of lives in the aftermath of the Communist capture of Phnom Penh on April 17, 1975, have apparently ended, for the most part..."; (27 July 1977) "Up to 1.2 million people may have been killed under the Communists in Cambodia, a high State Department official said today," citing Richard Holbrooke, who in fact testified that "Journalists and scholars...guess that between half a million and 1.2 million have *died* since 1975" (our emphasis, *July Hearings*, p. 2); C.L. Sulzberger (27 August 1977): "estimates of the number deliberately slaughtered by the Communist regime run from two hundred thousand to one million"; editorial (3 July 1978): "The estimates are that many hundreds of thousands, perhaps even 2 million Cambodians out of a population of 8 million, have been killed or allowed to die of disease and starvation." *Christian Science Monitor:* editorial (26 April 1977), "Reports put the loss of life as high as 2 million people out of 7.8 million total"; editorial (31 August 1978) citing State Department officials: "The U.S. government is confident that scores, probably hundreds of thousands of people have been killed." *Washington Post*, Don Oberdofer (20 April 1978) citing the former minister of Information

of the Lon Nol government: "1 million Cambodians have been 'slaughtered' and another million 'appear to have perished from disease and starvation'"; Jack Anderson (2 May 1978): "Competent sources have offered estimates ranging from 1.8 million to 2.5 million...who...have died from mistreatment and execution"; Jack Anderson (3 May 1978): "The death toll from beatings shootings, starvation and forced labor may have reached 2.5 million victims ..."; Smith Hempstone (7 May 1978): "It appears certain that between 500,000 and 2 million Cambodians...have been executed, starved or worked to death, died of disease or been killed while trying to flee ..." *Boston Globe:* UPI (17 April 1977): "Most foreign experts on Cambodia and its refugees believe at least 1.2 million persons have been killed or have died as a result of the policies of the Communist regime...Some experts...believe as many as 3.5 million people—half of the total population—have been killed or have died in the past two years;" (12 September 1977): Lon Nol reports that "more than 2.5 million Cambodians have been killed since the Communist Khmer Rouge conquered his country." *Business Week,* 23 January 1978: "As many as 2 million may have died out of a population of 5.5 million." *MacNeil/Lehrer Report* (TV, 6 June 1978): "In the worst accounts some two million people are said to have been killed by the new Communist regime" (the government specialist Timothy Carney estimated the number of deaths, not by "mass genocide" but by "brutal, rapid change" at "hundreds of thousands"). Many similar examples can be given overseas; to select just two: *Die Zeit,* (23 April 1976): "500,000 to 1.5 million people have died, been executed or starved"; *Izvestia,* (9-10 December 1978) alleging 2 million "executions" in Cambodia (*Le Monde,* 12 December 1978).

We will return to a few other examples of the great many that might be cited from the fall of Phnom Penh to the present.

54. AP, 22 August 1978. See note 11 of this chapter.
55. *July Hearings,* pp. 4, 15.
56. *May Hearings,* pp. 40-41.
57. *Ibid.,* p. 14.
58. *Ibid.,* p. 17.
59. See Volume I, chapter 3, section 5.4, for discussion of his role.
60. Kenneth M. Quinn, "Political Change in Wartime: The Khmer Krahom Revolution in Southern Cambodia, 1970-1974," *Naval War College Review,* Spring 1976.
61. See note 108, this chapter.
62. *Le Monde,* 8 September 1977.
63. Compare the contemptuous remark of another refugee, who complained that "Now all village chiefs are selected from among the poorest and the most illiterate," cited by Laura Summers, "Defining the Revolutionary State in Cambodia," *Current History,* December 1976, from *Le Monde,* 18-19 April 1976. Such comments perhaps give some

insight into Twining's "difficult question."
64. The same is true of the fierce resistance to the full-scale Vietnamese invasion of December 1978-January 1979. See the preface to this volume. We will keep here to the time frame preceding this invasion, as throughout this chapter. On the border conflicts, see Heder's articles cited in note 19 of the preface.
65. *Washington Post* (22 August 1978).
66. See note 12 of this chapter.
67. *Philadelphia Inquirer* (7 May 1978).
68. Frederic A. Moritz, "Cambodia's surprising 'win' over Vietnam," *Christian Science Monitor* (28 March 1978).
69. David Binder, "Cambodia-Vietnam Battles Spur U.S. Concern over 'Proxy' War," *New York Times* (25 December 1978). Note that this analysis, which appeared on the day that Vietnam stepped up its dry season offensive to a full-scale attack with 100,000 troops, appeared well after Vietnamese efforts to establish a Cambodian liberation front, with a program tailored to what are assumed outside of Cambodia to be the needs and concerns of the local population. See Nayan Chanda, "Pol Pot eyes the jungle again," *Far Eastern Economic Review*, 15 December 1978. Chanda points out that "None of the 14-member central committee of the KNUFNS [the Vietnamese-established front]...are nationally known figures." The one well-known Cambodian whom rumor had associated with KNUFNS, So Phim, "who was earlier reported to be leading anti-Pol Pot resistance, is dead." Chanda, *FEER*, 26 January 1979. As noted in the preface, the Vietnamese plainly do not believe that the KNUFNS can control the population without an army of occupation that far outnumbered the Pol Pot forces even before the massive Vietnamese assault that is reported to have destroyed a substantial part of the Cambodian army.
70. Recall the experience of Russia during World War I, or even World War II, when Hitler succeeded in raising a substantial army in support of the invasion of Russia and, according to some analysts, might have achieved his ends if Nazi atrocities had not helped organize the massive resistance that played the major role in the ultimate allied victory. Or recall even the experience of Western Europe, where Germany had little difficulty in organizing local support after its conquests.
71. *Op. cit.* (see note 11). He is referring to the unwillingness of a refugee who had allegedly seen nine members of his immediate family killed to support a foreign invasion.
72. *Op. cit.*, pp. 139-143. Recall some of Henry Kissinger's thoughts on the inability of people of the Third World to comprehend "that the real world is external to the observer" because their "cultures...escaped the early impact of Newtonian thinking," leading to a "difference of philosophical perspective" that is "the deepest problem of the contemporary international order." For discussion of these and comparable

profundities, see Chomsky, *"Human Rights" and American Foreign Policy,* Spokesman, 1978, chapter 1.

73. Lewis M. Simons, "Experts list disease as No. 1 killer in Cambodia today," *Washington Post* (24 July 1977). In congressional testimony, Twining questioned Simons's "source on this reevaluation" while agreeing with the contents of this "otherwise excellent article." Specifically, "I am convinced that the number of people who have died from disease and malnutrition has been even greater than those executed" (*July Hearings,* p. 8). On the number killed, he offers the estimate: "Certainly thousands or hundreds of thousands." Twining blames the government of Cambodia for the deaths from disease, claiming that they rejected drugs and medicines. Ponchaud reports that from August 1976, with the resumption of foreign trade, medicines have been imported, along with U.S.-produced DDT, including antimalaria drugs sent in 1976 from the AFSC (pp. 94-97, 116). See also the corrections to Twining's statement by Richard Holbrooke, *July Hearings,* p. 16; also the references of note 250, below.

74. *July Hearings,* p. 2.

75. *Ibid.,* p. 23.

76. *MacNeil/Lehrer Report;* see note 53.

77. See Poole's remarks on the evacuation, p. 176 above.

78. *New York Times* (9 May 1975).

79. *New York Times* (14 July 1975).

80. This is one of the arguments offered by Cambodian authorities for the forced evacuation of the urban centers. The second reason regularly advanced is the fear of CIA-backed subversion by groups left in Phnom Penh (cf. Ponchaud, *op. cit.,* p. 19, citing a statement of September, 1975). These reasons are continually rediscovered by the U.S. press: e.g., *New York Times* (29 July 1978), reporting that "for the first time" the government alleged that "the revolutionaries considered the city to be full of agents, ammunition dumps and conspiracies to undermine the new regime, and therefore felt total evacuation to be necessary for defense." The second argument has more force than is commonly alleged. See Snepp, *Decent Interval,* pp. 339-40, who reports that the evacuation "left American espionage networks throughout the country broken and useless." As for the first motive, Ponchaud disputes it. We return to his reasons below, 313.

81. See note 9 of this chapter. Quotes are from pp. 25-29. See pp. 30f. on the U.S. role in the politics of starvation for the mass of the population while the elite pursued the good life.

82. *May Hearings,* p. 30. Porter cites a U.S. intelligence study on Cambodia leaked to the press by Henry Kissinger, discussed in the *Washington Post* (23 June 1975) and *Far Eastern Economic Review,* 25 July 1975. A U.S. AID report of April 1975 concluded that widespread starvation was imminent and "Slave labor and starvation rations for half the nation's

people...will be a cruel necessity for this year, and general deprivation and suffering will stretch over the next two or three years ..." William Shawcross, *Sideshow*, Simon & Schuster, 1979, p. 375.

83. On this matter, Laura Summers comments (*op. cit.*, see note 63): "By all accounts, however, universal conscription for work prevented a post-war famine." This appeared in December, 1976. Perhaps by now one should write "by all serious accounts," or at least the vast majority of them. We have already cited Poole and Simons (with Twining's concurrence). Comparable judgments from sources by no means sympathetic with the regime will be noted below.

84. "McGovern the Hawk," *Wall Street Journal* (23 August 1978). Note that it is only the end of the Indochina campaign that was "sordid," and that the *Journal* feels no need to observe the injunction of silence, after its disgraceful record of subservience to state power and apologetics for barbarism. Note also the suggestion of the editors that it was the *critics* who took us through the painful contortions of the Vietnam war, not the war managers. The *Journal* also pretends that the silence of the activists is of their own choice, rather than a case of simple refusal of access by the mass media.

85. One of us (Chomsky) was approached by *Time* in the preparation of this article in a transparent effort to elicit a favorable comment from a "supporter of the Khmer Rouge." Instead, *Time* was offered a (very partial) record of fabrications with regard to Cambodia for which *Time* and other journals are responsible.

86. In his review of U.S. wartime journalism, Peter Braestrup comments that "In 1962-66,...*Time* policy on Vietnam was hawkish, even euphoric" (*Big Story* Volume I, Westview Press, 1977, p. 45). While this study contains so many errors that little in it can be assumed to be true, in this case Braestrup is correct. See the references of note 22, chapter 2 of this volume. Later, *Time* policy was no longer euphoric, though it remained hawkish.

87. Richard Dudman, "The Cambodian 'People's War,'" *Washington Post* (24 April 1975).

88. Richard Dudman, *Forty Days with the Enemy*, Liveright, 1971. He reported here that "the bombing and shooting was radicalizing the people of rural Cambodia and was turning the countryside into a massive, dedicated, and effective revolutionary base," p. 69, referring to the U.S. attack, an insight that has been rapidly forgotten and is in fact denied in some of the more disreputable literature on postwar Cambodia.

89. Lewis M. Simons, "The Unknown Dimensions of the Cambodian Tragedy," *Washington Post* (19 February 1978).

90. It is worth noting that the northwestern areas were then subject to Thai-supported anti-Communist guerrilla sabotage activities (see Stephen Heder, "Thailand's Relations with Kampuchea: Negotiation and Confrontation along the Prachinburi-Battambang Border," mimeo-

graphed, Cornell University, December 1977). An internal Amnesty International paper of 14 June 1976 notes that in that region "there are still many aspects of civil war." During the period 1972-75 parts of this region were under Thai military domination in part sanctioned by agreements with the Lon Nol government, and there were also instances of land grabbing. The Thai had also annexed and plundered the region in collaboration with Japanese fascism in 1941-45. We are indebted to Laura Summers for this information. The CIA-supported Khmer Serei also operated in this area from Thai bases for many years. As we shall see below, Lon Nol conducted brutal attacks on the peasants of the region in the early 1950s. Thus there is a long historical background that helps explain why this region should be the focus of violent revenge.

91. *July Hearings*, p.22.

92. Cf. Poole, p. 176, above, and the evidence cited on pp. 182f.

93. See the *Economist* (London) 21 October 1978, reviewing the effects of the floods in Southeast Asia: "As usual, there is no reliable information about what goes on inside Cambodia, but agricultural experts say it could be the worst hit of all. At one time, most of the country looked like a gigantic lake. Much of the vast Tonle Sap-Mekong basin is still under water. There seems little doubt that the waters have brought new hardships to this unhappy country." To the surprise of most observers, the grim prediction does not appear to have been realized, though we have yet to read a comment on this fact or its import in the major media.

94. See p. 239 below. Also, *FEER Asia 1979 Yearbook*.

95. Presumably, he has in mind Lacouture's remark on the relative insignificance of a factor of a hundred and his original allegation that the regime had "boasted" of having killed some 2 million people.

96. During the U.S. war in Vietnam, it was common for reporters and others to comment on the curious "xenophobia" of the Vietnamese, which makes it so hard to deal with them. Apparently it is a curious trait of peasant culture, as yet unexplained by contemporary scholarship, to react with a demonstration of xenophobia when foreign powers drop cluster bombs on villages after many years of colonial domination. Yet another aspect of the mysterious Asian mind.

97. See below, p. 250.

98. Berkeley, 25 April 1977.

99. Douglas Z. Foster, "Photos of 'horror' in Cambodia: fake or real?" *Columbia Journalism Review*, March/April 1978. No date is given. Foster also reviewed the basic facts briefly in *More* (February 1978).

100. N. Chomsky and E.S. Herman, "Distortions at Fourth Hand," *Nation*, 25 June 1977.

101. We are concentrating on fabrications and distortions in the U.S. press, but it should be noted that the phenomenon is worldwide. For some documentation on fabrications in the French press and television,

which elicited no comment or explanation when they were exposed, see Pierre Rousset, "Cambodia: Background to the Revolution," *Journal of Contemporary Asia*, vol. 7, no. 4, 1977. See also note 48.

Another example is a widely published photo taken by the West German journalist Christopher Maria Froder, showing a Khmer Rouge soldier brandishing a weapon, according to the photographer, to prevent looting of shops in Phnom Penh after its liberation on 17 April 1975. The picture appeared in the *Far Eastern Economic Review*, 14 April 1978, with the caption "Khmer Rouge takeover: Savage Repression." The *Review* refused to publish a letter by Torben Retbøll noting that after the photo had appeared in *Die Welt* (West Germany, 9 May 1975) with the claim that the soldier was looting, and in *Der Stern* (29 April 1976) with the caption: "After the victory, there followed the revenge against the rich," the photographer protested the falsification on German TV (the facts were correctly reported in the West German *Befreiung*). But on 15 August 1976, the *Sunday Telegraph* (London) again published the photo as an illustration of Khmer Rouge brutality as did *Newsweek* in the issue just cited. Retbøll's appeared in *News from Kampuchea* (Australia), vol. 2, no. 2, November/December 1978, to an international audience of 500 people. The same picture appeared in the *Washington Post* (9 May 1975, with the caption: "Khmer Rouge soldier angrily orders Phnom Penh shopkeepers into streets"), and again in the *New York Times Magazine* (Henry Kamm, "The Agony of Cambodia," 19 November 1978), this time with the caption: "Conquering Pnom [sic] Penh in 1975, a Khmer Rouge soldier rounds up merchants," illustrating that a good piece of propaganda never dies.

102. There are many others. For example, one of the fabricated photographs appears in the Soviet journal *Literaturnaja Gazeta*, 4 October 1978, in an article devoted to atrocities in Cambodia that quotes extensively from the U.S. press. Torben Retbøll has informed us of a number of Western European examples: *Der Spiegel*, 30 January 1978, who refused to print a letter of correction, like their U.S. counterparts; the Danish journal *Ekstra Bladet*, on three separate occasions (3 May 1976, 28 December 1977, and 4 January 1978); the *London Observer* (30 October 1977) on the front page.

103. George Orwell, "Notes on nationalism," 1945. In Sonia Orwell and Ian Angus, eds., *The Collected Essays, Journalism and Letters of George Orwell*, vol. III, Harcourt Brace & World, 1968, p. 371.

104. Communiqué du Ministre de l'information et de la propagande (*Hu Nim*), 31 March 1976. Hildebrand and Porter (op. cit., p. 70) cite a government report of 15 April 1976 alleging that several hundred thousand draught animals were killed in rural areas. Whatever the actual numbers may be, they are surely not small. As we have seen, the same is true throughout Indochina.

105. Ponchaud, *op. cit.*, p. 55. See also chapter 5, on similar conditions in Laos.

106. *New York Times* (14 June 1976).
107. *Op. cit.*, p. 340n. As noted earlier, this is only one of several cases where Snepp offers evidence based on what may very well be intelligence fabrications.
108. Richard Holbrooke informed the Congressional Committee in the *July Hearings* that Twining, Carney and Kenneth Quinn, "form to my mind, the American core of expertise on Cambodian affairs today in the U.S. Government" (p. 2). As we shall see, Quinn also refers to this alleged interview, and may well be the source of its wide dissemination. Twining, when asked what public statements the Cambodian government has made about executions, replied: "The little that has been said publicly, when Khieu Samphan was in Colombo, for example ..." (p. 12). It is not clear whether he is referring to the "interview" or to Khieu Samphan's statements at the Colombo meetings. Thus of the three specialists who form "the American core of expertise on Cambodian affairs today in the U.S. Government," two cite this "interview" as genuine, perhaps three, depending on what Twining had in mind in this reference.
109. *July Hearings*, p. 22.
110. 1 May 1977.
111. Barron and Paul, *op. cit.*, p. 202. In their article in the *Reader's Digest*, February 1977, the story is reported slightly differently. For a full discussion of the various versions and their authenticity, see Torben Retbøll, "Cambodia—the Story of a False Interview," unpublished ms., 1978. Retbøll, a Danish historian, is one of the small number of people in the West who care enough about the facts to pursue the details and write to journals that print false or dubious information, and like others, has been regularly subjected to vilification and abuse for this unwelcome commitment to the truth.
112. This was a personal letter to Chomsky commenting on the article cited in note 100.
113. Barron says: "Ponch [sic] assisted us extensively in our interviews in France. He compared data with us, criticized our work, and challenged in some cases our findings." *May Hearings*, p. 48. Paul cites a letter from his research colleague on the book who claims to have been "in almost daily contact with Father Ponchaud." (*FEER*, letter, 9 December 1977). We cannot comment on the authenticity of these remarks for reasons discussed below.
114. *Cambodia: Year Zero*, p. xvi. Ponchaud cites one of these letters in his note for the American translation, p. xiii. See below, p. 318.
115. See p. 158, above.
116. William Shawcross, "The Third Indochina War," *New York Review of Books*, 6 April 1978.
117. See among others, Ieng Sary (interviewed in *Der Spiegel*, 9 May 1977, by Tiziano Terzani), who estimated the population at 7,760,000 and explicitly denied the reports by Barron-Paul and others of massacres (it is

curious that one constantly reads that the Cambodian government had not denied these claims). In the *May Hearings*, after Porter had questioned the *Famiglia Cristiana* "interview" (noting that the Cambodian government has repeatedly estimated the population at 7.7 million), John Barron attempted to defend his use of the alleged interview, with the following claims: (1) "other Cambodian officials at approximately the same time had stated that there were 5 or 5.2 million inhabitants of Cambodia"; (2) "The figure of 7.7 million mentioned by Mr. Porter I have seen stated one time, and that was in a claim made shortly after the first anniversary of the revolution" denying massacre claims; (3) "I don't know of anybody in the world who has ever contended that the population of Cambodia ever was that large." As for (1), Barron cites no examples and we know of none. As for (2), he was probably referring to the Ministry of Information communique cited in note 104, which estimated the population at 7.7 million, a figure that has been repeated often. But the most surprising claim is (3). Ponchaud, Barron's major nongovernmental source, writes that "in 1970 the population of Cambodia was usually estimated at 8 million" (including 400,000 Vietnamese); *op. cit.*, p. 70. The UN estimated the population in mid-1974 at 7.89 million (see below, p. 264) and in mid-1976 at 8.35 million (cf. *UN Monthly Bulletin of Statistics*, February 1978). Swedish visitors to postwar Cambodia have reported that the population is 8 million and that efforts are being made to increase it to 15 million. Estimates in the 7-8 million range are standard. In their book, Barron and Paul write that "no one heretofore had contended that the prewar population of Cambodia was more than seven million ..." (p. 202n.)

118. It has also been cited on television, e.g., by Leo Cherne of the International Rescue Committee, on the *MacNeil/Lehrer Report* (see note 53). He claims that when Khieu Samphan "was asked what is the population of Cambodia, he said five million. The population of Cambodia used to be 8 million." Cherne notes that this estimate of five million is inconsistent with a population estimate offered by Pol Pot in "Peiping" (the name used for Peking by Dean Rusk, Leo Cherne and others of their political persuasion). This "disparity in the population of Cambodia" is offered as the sole example of "the most remarkable revelations" by Pol Pot. It is, of course, only a "remarkable revelation" to someone who relies on such sources as *Famiglia Cristiana* for his knowledge of international affairs. Recall that it is this "remarkable revelation" that Cherne relied upon to explain why executions have diminished (see note 37, this chapter). The above appears to be the intended sense of some rather confused remarks by Cherne. We rely on the written transcript, Library no. 702, Show no. 3242, 6 June 1978.

119. *Economist* (London), 26 February 1977.

120. *FEER*, 23 September 1977.

121. Kenneth M. Quinn, "Cambodia 1976: Internal Consolidation and

External Expansion," *Asian Survey*, January 1977. Torben Retbøll has brought to our attention that in this article, Quinn claims that Khieu Samphan "offered a partial explanation" for the reduction in population on grounds of war dead and the return of "600,000 ethnic Vietnamese" to Vietnam. But in fact nothing of the sort appears in the cited "interview." If this "interview" is indeed an intelligence fabrication, as appears not unlikely, it may be that it went through several versions before being placed in *Famiglia Cristiana*, to be picked up by the world press.

122. *Op. cit.*, p. 212.

123. "Cambodia 1977: Gone to Pot," *Asian Survey*, January 1978.

124. See Volume I, chapter 3, section 5.4.

125. To add an unnecessary little extra, the same issue of *Famiglia Cristiana* contains an insert on Sihanouk, referring to "a suspicion, expressed in *Le Monde* August 8, that the entire family of the Prince has been exterminated." Retbøll (*op. cit.*) points out that the reference is to a fabricated "appeal" published in good faith by *Le Monde* with the signatures of well-known French leftists. Two days later, *Le Monde* published an apology when it discovered that the signatures were forged—a fact not mentioned in the *Famiglia Cristiana* report. This fact alone might have suggested that this journal is hardly a trustworthy source, had the question been of any concern.

126. See chapter 2 of this volume, p. 29-30, for one of many examples. It is difficult to imagine that the CIA, with its long history of deception in Indochina, has suddenly ceased its disinformation campaigns. Ed Bradley of CBS news, asked on the *MacNeil/Lehrer Report* to comment on the "allegation that there is a disinformation network at work spreading these allegations" of Cambodian atrocities, responded: "I don't have any doubts that there is some element of truth in it...," a plausible surmise. The alleged "interview" is not found in the regular FBIS translations though it does appear in a special "For Official Use Only" supplement to the *Daily Report* for *Asia and Pacific*. Thus it is not available to regular library subscribers, but presumably is available to selected individuals to whom it can be "leaked." We are indebted to Stephen Heder for this information.

127. Barron and Paul, *op. cit.*, p.197.

128. 18 February 1976.

129. Paul defends the translation in a letter to the *Far Eastern Economic Review*, 9 December 1977, citing the research colleague who claims to have been in almost daily contact with Ponchaud (see note 113, this chapter). He ignores the question of the actual source of this alleged quote, to which we turn directly—something that should have been known to a person in almost daily contact with Ponchaud, who allegedly approved this specific translation.

130. Such claims, for which no specific evidence is offered, are emphatically denied by at least some refugees. See below, p. 243. They are also

denied by the State Department's leading specialist, Charles Twining. See *July Hearings*, p. 21. See also Quinn's comment on the austerity of the cadres, above, p. 178.

131. *Op. cit.*, pp. 60-61.

132. *Op. cit.*, p. 97 of the French original; see note 2, this chapter.

133. See the references in note 82, this chapter, and the text at note 82.

134. Ponchaud, "Cambodge: deux ans après la libération," *Revue d'Etudes comparatives Est-Ouest*, Volume 8, no. 7, 1977, pp. 143-156.

135. Ponchaud, *Cambodge Libéré*. Dossier no. 13, Echange France-Asie, January 1976, p. 17.

136. See note 17, this chapter. In *Nouvel Observateur*, 2 October 1978, Lacouture gave the same wording as a quote, attributed to Khmer Rouge cadres: the new generation charged with the building of Cambodia *"needs only a million and a half to two million Cambodians to construct the country,"* (his emphasis). This article is an excerpt from Lacouture's October 1978 book *Survive le peuple cambodgien!*, Seuil, 1978. As we shall see directly, this reference appears in print over a year after Ponchaud, a close associate of Lacouture's, had withdrawn the quote and his interpretation of it as apparently without credible source.

Quite apart from the discrepancy of source and the changes in numbers and text (not to speak of the dubious source, to which we return), it is hardly clear that Khmer Rouge military commanders or whoever might have been the source for this remark, if anyone, "talk of Marxism." Specialists have noted that the Khmer Rouge leadership tended to stress independence, nationalism, manual labor, equality, etc., but not Marxism. According to Carney, Marxism-Leninism made its appearance in domestic radio broadcasts only in 1976. Timothy M. Carney, "Continuity in Cambodian Communism," in Carney, ed., *Communist Party Power in Kampuchea (Cambodia)*, Data Paper number 106, Southeast Asia Program, Department of Asian Studies, Cornell University, January 1977, p. 23.

137. See note 112, this chapter.

138. See note 2, this chapter.

139. Something unknown in the history of industrialization in the West or elsewhere in the "developing world," of course.

140. Our emphasis. Penguin, 1978, p. 92.

141. The subsequent (1978) Norwegian translation (*Kambodsja Ar Null*, Tiden Norsk Forlag, p. 84), retains the quote and the implication that the "formidable boast" is being put into execution. This translation was evidently supervised by Ponchaud, since there are some revisions of the French original as well as new material. See note 395, this chapter.

Skepticism about the source of this alleged quote had already been expressed by Gareth Porter (May *Hearings*, pp. 51-52), properly, it is now clear. Ponchaud's qualifications in his letter regarding the quote are noted by Malcolm Caldwell (*Manchester Guardian*, 8 May

1978). He comments: "Yet, without a move on Ponchaud's part to correct the misuse, the construction of threatening a systematic massacre is the one still put on it by authors determined to slander Kampuchea at any cost to honesty and integrity." This comment takes on added weight now that Ponchaud has deleted from the American edition both the "quote" and the inference drawn from it.

142. This passage is given separately in small print, apparently indicating that it is a quote, or standard report of refugees, or something of the sort. *July Hearings*, p. 12.

143. FBIS *Daily Report*, Asia and Pacific, 12 May 78, p. H3.

144. 23 September 1977.

145. This egregious comment is typical of the colonialist mentality. While the friends and associates of Westerners in Phnom Penh may have been "fun-loving" and "easy-going" as they enjoyed themselves at the expense of the peasant population, the latter appear to have endured a rather different existence, a matter to which we return.

146. *FEER*. 25 August 1978. Note that Wise is reviewing the British edition.

147. In the same review, Wise claims that Ponchaud dismisses the excuse that Phnom Penh was emptied to avoid famine as "rubbish" because "there was enough stocked rice to feed between 2.5 million and three million people ..." Compare what Ponchaud actually wrote: This explanation for the evacuation, "given as the essential one, is not fully convincing." The "more than 1.5 million peasants" who had been driven into Phnom Penh "were all eager to return to their homes without being forced to go" and as for the rest of the population, stocks of rice on hand "might have fed it for two months, with careful rationing" (at which point, presumably, they would have starved to death). *Op. cit.*, pp. 20-21. Note further that on inquiry Ponchaud concedes that his estimate may have been exaggerated. See below, p. 312. But for Wise, Ponchaud has shown the explanation to be "rubbish." This explanation was, as Ponchaud states, commonly given as the essential one. See the comments by Ieng Sary, reported from Tokyo, AP, *Washington Post* (14 June 1978) for one example.

Wise also makes the following curious remark: Ponchaud "eloquently smothers the naive theories of alleged experts who—even *before* Ponchaud's book appeared—had decided there were *no* massacres after the communists took Phnom Penh in 1975 ..." (his emphasis). He cites no such "experts." Note also Wise's curious implication that prior to the appearance of Ponchaud's book in January 1977 it was somehow illegitimate to draw conclusions—at least, the unauthorized ones—about Cambodia.

148. See note 136, this chapter.

149. AP, "UN chief invited to Cambodia," *Christian Science Monitor*. (14 October 1978). See also Frederic A. Moritz, "Critics crack Cambodia's closed door," *ibid.*, 16 October 1978, noting also the visit of a "left-wing

China-oriented Hong Kong" newspaper reporter in September, one of the many whose reports received no coverage in the Western media.

150. See *New York Times,* 7 March 1976, and for a review, Laura Summers, "Defining the Revolutionary State in Cambodia." Cambodia circulated photographs of the incident, but they do not seem to have been published in the U.S. press, which much prefers faked photos produced by Thai intelligence to illustrate alleged Khmer Rouge atrocities. See Heder, "Thailand's Relations with Kampuchea," pp. 27-28, 77-79 (cited in note 90, above).

151. Ross H. Munro, "Envoy Touring Cambodia Finds a No-Wage System," *New York Times,* (9 March 1976), dateline Peking.

152. Elsewhere, he is quoted more positively as saying that he had seen "enormous numbers of children who looked quite healthy and quite lively." *Toronto Globe and Mail,* (8 March 1976), cited by Porter in the *May Hearings,* p. 28. In the *Times* account he is quoted as saying, in response to a query about starvation: "How can I judge? I saw no signs of starvation."

153. Number 2, 1976. We quote from the German translation in *Befreiung,* June 1976.

154. Similar impressions can be derived from a reading of Ponchaud's book, though rarely from the secondary references.

155. The official Cambodian government estimate was 200,000. See Ieng Sary's interview in *Spiegel* (cited in note 117.) It is probable that this estimate was intended to include the suburbs, which according to visitors were more populated than the city itself.

156. Recall that according to Ponchaud's 1978 book, the worst terror was over by the time of Lundvik's trip; see note 37.

157. *Sydney Morning Herald* (Australia, 30 December 1977); cited in *News from Kampuchea,* Vol. I, no. 5, December 1977. The Committee of Patriotic Kampucheans, which published the journal, at that time included Ben Kiernan, an Australian specialist on Cambodia; Shane Tarr, a New Zealander who lived in Cambodia until April 1975; and a group of Cambodians in Australia, three of whom lived in areas under Khmer Rouge administration in 1970 and 1975. In keeping with the theory of the Free Press, it was not subject to censorship and the information it presented about Cambodia was available to the Western reader, journalists included. In further confirmation of the same theory, its documentation and positive accounts of postwar Cambodia reached an audience of about 500 people throughout the world.

158. Both on 23 January 1978.

159. Henry Kamm, *New York Times* (3 February 1978).

160. Lewis M. Simons, "Cambodians Reported to be Well-Fed," *Washington Post,* (28 April 1976).

161. See note 40 of this chapter.

162. 19 May 1978.

163. The text appears in *News From Kampuchea,* vol. 2, no. 1, May 1978.

164. *SWB, Far East,* 5801/B, 3-9, 29 April 1978.
165. Michael Dobbs, "The New Cambodia: Phones, TV, Cars on Rubble Heaps," *Washington Post,* (23 March 1978).
166. AP, *Boston Globe* (29 March 1978).
167. See the reference in note 198 below and Ponchaud, *op. cit.,* p. 113.
168. *Cambodge,* published by the Ministry of Information of the Royal Government of Cambodia, Phnom Penh, 1962, p. 116.
169. "Yugoslavs, After Rare Tour, Tell of a Primitive Cambodia," 24 March 1978.
170. Henry Kamm, "Cambodian Refugees Depict Growing Fear and Hunger," *New York Times,* 13 May 1978. As both the *Post* and *Times* correctly reported, the Yugoslav journalists said they saw no signs of food shortages. Once again Kamm notes that some of the refugees he interviewed were in a "small cage" in a police station, others in a "disused prison" and refugee camps, where "their bearing and comportment recall concentration camp survivors in the Europe of 1945"—a fact that conceivably relates to the conditions of their detention. See p. 162 above.
171. The same "implicit restrictions" prevented them from raising questions about atrocities, he explains. Kamm's remarks on "communist fraternalism" are no doubt appropriate, though Yugoslavia has been known on occasion to exhibit some slight degree of independence, one recalls. But more to the point, Kamm neglects to mention the "implicit restrictions" imposed by "capitalist fraternalism." For example, those that enable a Pulitzer-Prize winning specialist on the misery of refugees to inform his reading public that refugees in Timor are fleeing from the mountains where they have been "forced to live" by FRETILIN guerrillas; this apparently on the authority of a kindly Indonesian general, not—perish the thought—interviews with refugees. Unlike Cambodian refugees in Thai prisons, these unlucky souls are not proper subjects for a reporter of such independence of mind. See Volume I, chapter 3, section 5.4.
172. William Shawcross also reports that "The Yugoslav journalists were shocked by the extent of child labor," and reports the same account of the filming. "Cambodia Today: a Land of Blood and Tears," *New Times,* 13 November 1978. The subheading of this story (which is featured on the front cover) includes the statement that "Cambodia today is a 'hell on earth.'" As the story itself indicates, this is a quote from Hanoi radio, which has rarely been regarded as a reliable source in Western journalism, but is taken quite seriously when it provides negative information about Cambodia in the midst of a bitter war. See note 18, above.

The concern of Western journalists over child labor is rather selective. A rare report on the topic filed from Thailand received little publicity in the United States and aroused no noticeable outrage: Amport Tantuvanich, AP, "Slavery the fate of these children," *Boston Globe* (24 September 1978). The report describes children working in Thai factories "hour after hour without a break around furnaces that generate 1450-degree heat. Their arms and hands bear scars from burns and cuts..." There are tens of thousands of illegally employed children, some "sold by their parents to factory owners" and working as "virtual slaves." "A recent survey by the International Labor Organization in Geneva showed that of 52 million children under age 15 at work around the world, 29 million are working in South Asia." Many of the Thai laborers are under 10. "Labor specialists say that a combination of wide-open free enterprise and a lack of labor-union power contributes to the child labor problem. Under laws laid down by Thailand's military government, strikes and other labor union activities are forbidden." On the U.S. role in creating this situation, see Volume I, chapter 4, section 2. See also the preface to this volume.

Another example is the notable exploitation of child labor from the occupied territories in Israel. At the "Children's Market at the Ashkelon junction" one finds children aged six or seven trucked in by labor contractors at 4 a.m. to work on the private or collective farms in the vicinity, helping to make the desert bloom for their prosperous employers who pay them "a meager subsistence wage" though "often they are cheated even on that." Ian Black, "Peace or no peace, Israel will still need cheap Arab labor," *New Statesmen*, 29 September 1978. The miserable conditions of child labor (and Arab labor from the occupied territories in general) have been discussed and deplored in Israel (see, for example, Amos Elon, "Children's market at the Ashkelon junction," *Ha'aretz*, 2 August 1978), with no effect on the practice, however. The matter has yet to be discussed in the mainstream U.S. press, to our knowledge, surely not by those who are so deeply offended by child labor in Cambodia, a major atrocity that evokes memories of Hitler and Stalin.

Visiting Cambodia in the summer of 1978, Gunnar Bergstrom reports that he saw children working in the fields, mixing work with play in a manner not unfamiliar in peasant societies. See note 180, below. See also the reports cited in note 190, below.

173. François Rigaux, "Un socialisme à la spartiate: le Kampuchéa démocratique," mimeographed, Centre Charles de Visscher pour le droit internationale, College Thomas More, Louvain, 1978.

174. Denzil Peiris, "Phnom Penh's long march back," *Far Eastern Economic Review*, 13 October 1978. See the *Asia 1979 Yearbook* for further discussion of "the apparent achievements of Cambodian agriculture."

175. There were Third World visitors, but their reports are unknown or discounted. Several reports can be found in *News from Kampuchea*. See also Summers, "Defining the Revolutionary State in Cambodia." See also note 149 of this chapter.

176. "US Leftist Editor Says Cambodians Are Thriving," *New York Times* (12 May 1978). Six months later, a column by Burstein appeared on the Op-Ed page of the *Times* ("On Cambodia: But, Yet," 21 November 1978), two days after the *New York Times Magazine* published a major

story by Henry Kamm, to which we return. Burstein's brief statement based on what he says he saw is "opinion"; Kamm's lengthy account of what he says he heard from refugees is "fact." Professor David Sidorsky of Columbia University denounced the *Times* for printing this "propagandistic opinion on questions of fact," (letter, 5 December). He did not criticize the *Times* for publishing Kamm's article with its faked photos, allegations about starvation taking no account of direct testimony to the contrary by visitors, etc. Nor did he criticize the *Times* for withholding evidence provided by visitors. Rather, his criticism was limited to the Burstein Op-Ed statement for not presenting factual evidence, as was obviously impossible in the space provided him.

In contrast to the coverage in the United States, visits by Danish Communists received substantial publicity in the Danish press, we are informed by Torben Retbøll. (Note that some of the visitors whose reports were suppressed in the Free Press were non-Communists, and there is little doubt that they would have been treated rather differently had their reports conformed to the propaganda line.) A detailed report by these visitors appears in *The Call* (P.O. Box 5597, Chicago Ill. 60680), May 15, 22, 29, June 5, 12, 1978; *The Young Communist,* June/July 1978; *Class Struggle,* Summer 1978. There was also a report in the *Guardian* (New York, 7 June 1978). See also *Kampuchea Today, Call* Pamphlets, December 1978, and a "photo-record" of their visit by David Kline and Robert Brown, *The New Face of Kampuchea.* Liberator Press, 1979. They say their trip covered 700 miles with frequent stops and discussions with government leaders and others.

177. We regret that we cannot comment here on television news, since we have no records. We have cited the *MacNeil/Lehrer Report* on Cambodia on the basis of a transcript. Burstein informs us privately that lower-echelon reporters and editors were helpful and sympathetic, but that the idea was apparently killed at a higher level, a process not exactly unfamiliar to us personally. See the prefatory note to Volume I.

178. Henry Kamm, "The Agony of Cambodia," *New York Times Magazine,* 19 November 1978. See note 101 on the accompanying illustrations.

179. See Volume I, chapter 3, section 5.4; this volume, chapter 4. Note that his distortions are systematic; his extreme bias is consistently towards service to the U.S. government propaganda system, whether he is dismissing the testimony of refugees and other victims in Timor and relying on Indonesian generals, or dismissing the testimony of visitors to Cambodia and relying on what he claims to hear from refugees in Thai police cages, or grossly misrepresenting the available evidence from Vietnam.

180. We rely on an hour-long taped interview in English, readily available to enterprising reporters, no doubt. Bergstrom has a number of interesting things to say, and seems careful and qualified in his account. For example, he visited areas where there was alleged to be insurrection, but saw no signs of disturbance and no security presence. Reports by

U.S. journalists to the same effect many months later were front page news. As already noted, the work pace seemed to him moderate by European standards. He gives many details of the life he observed, and in general, reports a peasant society rebuilding with some success from the ruins, noting, however, that his access was limited.

181. Mary McGrory, "Slow reaction to Cambodia bloodbath," *Boston Globe*, 27 November 1978. As the title indicates, the central point is that "for a while, Cambodia was hardly discussed," though finally, by mid-1978, it is receiving some attention. The statement is totally false, but, as we have seen, in keeping with the constant pretense of writers who send this message to their mass audience in the *Reader's Digest*, *TV Guide*, and the major journals, or in the more select periodicals.

182. *Boston Globe*, 19 November 1978. On the same day, the *Globe* reports that "the Inter-American Human Rights Commission yesterday accused the Nicaraguan National Guard of murdering scores of unarmed civilians" in September, charging that "entire families were machine-gunned to death in their homes," that unarmed youths "were allegedly forced to dig their own graves before they were executed," along with other atrocities. This story made page 78. The preceding day a brief AP report noted that "despite pleas from the Nicaraguan opposition the Carter Administration has decided against trying to prevent Israel from supplying light arms to the regime of Nicaraguan dictator Anastasio Somoza Debayle, Administration sources said yesterday." None of this is major news, however and it elicited no editorial or other comment. On November 18 the *New York Times* reported (also not prominently, and in this case with no descriptive detail at all) that the Commission had accused the Nicaraguan Government "of flagrant, persistent abuses of human rights, including summary executions, torture, arbitrary detention, indiscriminate bombing of unarmed civilians and obstructing the humanitarian efforts of the Red Cross"; the government's "practices had victimized all sectors of the population but particularly the poor and people between the ages of 14 and 21." Nothing is said about the long-standing relation between the United States and Nicaragua. See Volume I, chapter 4, section 5.2.

183. Cf. *Philadelphia Inquirer* (19 November 1978).

184. See note 130.

185. The *New York Times* is also not noted for outraged denunciations of gross differences in living standards in the United States. In New York City, for example, one can easily discover wealth that surpasses description only a short distance away from hovels where a grandmother stays awake through the night with a club to prevent rats from killing a child who will go to school the next day without breakfast.

186. See note 172, above.

187. It is not clear that he understands what is required to establish his case. See the serious error in logic discussed below, p. 322-23.

188. Jack Anderson, "Lon Nol in Exile: Sad Symbol of Cambodia," *Washington Post* (1 October 1978). Some of Lon Nol's exploits in this "serene little country" in the 1970s are well-known. See, for example, Volume I, chapter 3, section 2. Anderson's mythical picture of prewar Cambodia is a very common one. Among many examples, an advertisement for a CBS news special on Cambodia reads: "Once, Cambodia was a very special place. Lively, Happy, Peaceful." *New York Times* (1 June 1978). The myth provides a useful backdrop for the picture of merciless horror and madness. See note 232, below.

189. Cited in Jack Anderson, "In Cambodia, Obliterating a Culture," *Washington Post* (2 May 1978).

190. Richard Dudman published an edited version of his series in a special supplement to the *St. Louis Post-Dispatch* (15 January 1979): "Cambodia: A land in turmoil." Elizabeth Becker's series appeared in the *Washington Post*, December 26, 27, 28, 29, 30, 31, 1978 (along with a December 24 story on Malcolm Caldwell's assassination in Phnom Penh). These accounts were serialized in many journals in the United States and elsewhere as they appeared in late December. Our quotes from Dudman are from the edited version cited.

191. Bernard Weinraub, "High-Level Purge in Cambodian Regime Reported," *New York Times* (29 December 1978). Weinraub attributes this opinion to "American analysts." *Times* ideologists continued to disregard the reports by the U.S. journalists, just as they had dismissed earlier testimony from reputable non-Communist observers that was unacceptable on doctrinal grounds. Thus Dudman reports that "with good opportunity for observation" he found "an assurance of apparently adequate food" and no signs of malnutrition, confirming the reports of earlier visitors. But for Henry Kamm it is a matter of dogma that Communist policy has caused starvation ("Although the growing of rice was declared the supreme national objective and almost the entire nation was set to work at this task, the Cambodian people, for the first time in their history, learned hunger"—and contradicting himself in the very next sentence: "Until the war disrupted their lives, [hunger] was perhaps the one scourge of life that Cambodians had always been spared," which is false as well as inconsistent with what precedes). To maintain the dogma with its accompanying "mystery" already noted, it is necessary to ignore the reported facts, as Kamm does, in this article written a month after the accounts by the visiting U.S. journalists were widely circulated. Henry Kamm, "The Cambodian Dilemma," *New York Times Magazine*, 4 February 1979, an "analysis" with accompanying moral lecture that merits no further comment.

192. *Livre Noire, Faits et preuves des actes d'agression et d'annexion du Vietnam contre le Kampuchéa*, Phnom Penh, September 1978.

193. Becker states that the information in the *Livre Noir* "closely paralleled US intelligence estimates" of 1970. We know of no evidence that U.S.

intelligence estimated in 1970 that there were 1.5-2 million "Vietcong" in Cambodia. Similarly, much of the other material in it does not parallel U.S. intelligence estimates, at least so far as the public record indicates. See Nayan Chanda, "The Black Book of Hatred," *Far Eastern Economic Review,* 19 January 1979, for some discussion of the *Livre Noir* and also of conflicting Vietnamese claims in the two-volume *Kampuchea Dossier* published in Hanoi. See Heder's articles cited in note 19 of the preface to this volume for detailed discussion of the background, including the longstanding conflict between Vietnamese and Cambodian Communists.

194. They do, however, regularly accept documents and assessments produced in Hanoi and Phnom Penh prejudicial to the adversary, in the midst of a bitter conflict, on the principle that any negative information concerning a Communist regime, however questionable the source, must be accurate. See notes 18, 172 of this chapter.

195. Elizabeth Becker, "Inside Cambodia," *Newsweek,* 8 January 1979. Her story deals only with Caldwell's assassination, the border war, the alleged support of the *Livre Noir* for U.S. intelligence estimates, atrocity stories from refugees, and the condition of Angkor Wat. It studiously avoids any report on what she actually observed of life in Cambodia.

196. "Cambodia: Silence, Subterfuge and Surveillance," *Time,* 8 January 1979.

197. See the preface to this volume.

198. David P. Chandler, with Ben Kiernan and Muy Hong Lim, "The Early Phases of Liberation in Northwestern Cambodia: Conversations with Peang Sophi," *Working Papers,* no. 10, Monash University (Melbourne), undated (1976 apparently).

199. We have already commented on the localized nature of atrocity reports noted by a number of analysts, Twining included. Chandler observes that the reason may be that conditions elsewhere are better, or that it is more difficult to escape from other areas. Ponchaud (in his author's note for the English translation) states that most of his reports come from the provinces near the Thai border, though "quite a few came from further away" (p. xv.). In an article published in January 1976 (N.B. after the worst atrocities; see above, note 37), Ponchaud wrote that Battambang-Siem Reap (i.e. the Northwest) is a region of "bloody violence more than any other"; cited by Porter, *May Hearings,* p. 24.

200. See Summer's report, note 63.

201. David P. Chandler, "Transformation in Cambodia," *Commonweal,* 1 April 1977. See also his comments in the *May Hearings* (in part cited above, p. 176-77), where this article appears as a supplement.

202. The French also continually readjusted the border in a manner prejudicial to Cambodia. See the preface to this volume, note 20. On the vicious and barbaric French colonial impact on Vietnam, see the references cited in chapter 4, note 40; also note 67. Matters were little different in Cambodia. Chandler's comments on the mythic "happiness"

of the Cambodian peasants as seen by imperial interpreters can be supplemented by the studies cited in notes 2, 18; also Malcolm Caldwell
and Lek Hor Tan, *Cambodia*, Monthly Review Press, 1973, and sources
cited there, particularly Milton E. Osborne, *The French Presence in Cochinchina and Cambodia*, Cornell, 1969. Ponchaud, in contrast, writes
that "to any Western visitor Cambodia was a land of smiles" (the standard cliché; see Meyer, *op. cit.*): "There did not seem to be any major
social or agrarian problems" and "French colonization brought order
and peace" though there were injustices that could be "exploited" by
"an intelligent propaganda campaign," *Cambodia: Year Zero*, pp. 140f.)
203. Ponchaud writes: "During the reign of Sihanouk and then under Lon
Nol, methods used by the government forces in dealing with their
Khmer Rouge enemies were no less savage than those subsequently
employed by Democratic Kampuchea: between 1968 and 1970 prisoners from Samlaut or Dambar, the cradles of the Khmer revolution, were
bound to trees with their stomachs cut open and left to die; others,
hurled off the cliffs of Bokor, agonized for days: enemy villages were
razed and the villagers clubbed to death by local peasants who had
been set against them." *Ibid.*, 140. This account is corroborated from
other sources. The events elicited no reaction in the West, and are now
generally dismissed or ignored (by Ponchaud as well as others) as a
possible reason for subsequent savagery.
204. See the references of notes 2, 45, 202. For a review of press reports,
see Chomsky, *At War With Asia*, chapter 3.
205. Recall Elizabeth Becker's puzzlement over the lack of any "philosophical basis" for the policies of autarky, self-reliance, egalitarianism and
decentralization. On these matters, see Laura Summers, "Democratic
Kampuchea," in Bogdan Szajkowski, *Marxist Governments: A World
Survey*, Macmillan, London, forthcoming. Also her introduction to her
translation of Khieu Samphan, *Cambodia's Economy and Industrial Development*, Cornell 1979, and the text itself, written in Paris in 1959 for
a *Doctorat* in economics. See also Malcolm Caldwell, "Cambodia—Rationale for a Rural Policy," a five-part study presented at the Seminar
"Underdevelopment and Subsistence Reproduction in Southeast Asia,"
University of Bielefeld, 21-23 April 1978. This is a preliminary draft,
never completed, which we hope will be published with Caldwell's papers. See also the report on Thailand cited by Michael Vickery, p. 253,
below. Also Denzil Peiris, "The student principles," *Far Eastern Economic Review*, 2 June 1978, explaining how the "economic restructuring"
of Cambodia had been following Khieu Samphan's ideas in his thesis,
and also outlining these ideas.
206. *Cambodia: Year Zero*, pp. 75-82, 112-21, and elsewhere.
207. On this matter, Ponchaud writes: "The economy inherited by Democratic Kampuchea had been totally devastated by the war." The South
Vietnamese "unhesitatingly demolished a large part of the economic

infrastructure of the Cambodian territory," and the United States bombed the rubber plantations, while the soldiers of the Lon Nol regime, "following their instructors' example, buried their own country under their bombs and shells" and the Khmer Rouge "razed everything in their path that could in any way be connected with the West." *ibid.*, p. 85.

208. See notes 202, 207, above. Ponchaud's reference to "their instructors' example" is more accurate.

209. Michael Vickery, "Looking Back at Cambodia," *Westerly*, December 1976. Citations below are from the original manuscript, dated 10 August 1976.

210. Vickery's observation on the contradictory character of refugee stories reflects his personal experience in refugee camps; see above, p. 168. The contradictory character will naturally not emerge from accounts by reporters who proceed in the manner we have described. Note that when Vickery wrote in August 1976, refugee stories were, as he says, "the only first-hand source of news," though the situation was gradually to change, as we have seen. It should also be noted that the "blackout on information" followed years of censorship under the Lon Nol government.

211. "Anti-French maquis cum bandits, who controlled much of the countryside and in some cases probably had contact with the Viet Minh."

The exact history and character of the Cambodian revolutionary movement and its antecedents is the subject of controversy that we will not attempt to review. Laura Summers informs us (personal communication) that the Issarak movement was supported by the Thai resistance opposing the Japanese in World War II (the allies refused assistance, fearing their reformist social programs). Based in the Thai-occupied provinces of the northwest, it was officially recognized by the Thai resistance government in 1944 and received support from both Siamese and Vietnamese. "Prior to joining the Independence movement most Khmer Issarak were peasants, monks or intellectuals (teachers)." Summers further comments that Lon Nol had been involved in Battambang politics in earlier years, having been appointed to reestablish the local Khmer administration in the region in 1946 and serving as Provincial Governor of Battambang from 1947 to 1949. As for the scale of the military activity of the 1953-54 period, Summers informs us that there were 10,000 armed guerrillas operating in Cambodia in January 1953, 8,000 of them Issaraks divided into several tendencies, less than 2,000 Viet Minh.

212. On political violence perpetrated by the Sihanouk regime, see Heder's forthcoming article in the *Bulletin of Concerned Asian Scholars* (cited in the preface, note 19) where he describes, for example, a speech by Sihanouk in August 1968 "in which he claimed to have put to death over 1,500 communists since 1967 and stated that, if necessary, he would persist in such a policy of merciless extermination until the [Commu-

nist Party] submitted" (we quote from the manuscript). This statement, and others like it, aroused no more outcry in the West than the violent repression carried out by the regime.

213. The reference, clearly, is to the leadership in Phnom Penh and their supporters, not to the peasants driven into the city by the war. T.D. Allman had described Phnom Penh as a city "shared by two separate nations: the poor, the refugees, the ordinary people, their lives torn and complicated by the war beyond imagination; and the political elite for whom the war has meant promotions and a revived sense of their own importance ..." ("Forever Khmer," *Far Eastern Economic Review,* 4 September 1971).

214. Timothy Carney notes that "sometime in 1973 the party apparently decided to accelerate its program to alter Khmer society...," for no cited reason. Carney, ed., *op. cit.,* p. 21. The most interesting material in this collection is a translation of Ith Sarin, "Nine months with the maquis," excerpted from a 1973 book written in an effort to rally opposition to the Khmer Rouge. It gives some insight, from a very hostile source, into the success of the Khmer Rouge in gaining popular support by conscientiously following the maxims of "serve the people," "study from the people in order to be like the people," etc. We have been informed that the sections of Ith Sarin's book that do not appear in Carney's excerpts give a rather favorable description of Communist social and economic programs and that the book was banned by the Lon Nol government as being more harmful than beneficial to its cause.

215. Kissinger succeeded in duping the compliant media into believing that he was simply seeking a "decent interval" after the U.S. departure from Vietnam, but some attention to his actual statements as well as to the unfolding events reveals quite clearly that the aim was military victory in defiance of the Paris Agreements of January 1973, as was pointed out at once, though generally ignored by the press. See the references of chapter 1, note 1.

216. A secondary goal was no doubt to eliminate a rear base for the resistance in Vietnam. According to Snepp, intelligence gathered in 1970 revealed that nearly 80% of the supplies for Communist forces in the southern half of South Vietnam were sent through Cambodia. *Op. cit.,* p. 20.

217. See chapter 1, section 2.

218. Laura Summers, "Cambodia: Model of the Nixon doctrine," *Current History,* December 1973. For more information on the Nixon-Kissinger rejection of a possible settlement in Cambodia at the time of the Paris agreements of January 1973 and thereafter, see Laura Summers and D. Gareth Porter, "Cambodia: Was there an Understanding?," submitted to supplement testimony at the Hearings before the Committee on Foreign Relations, U.S. Senate, on S. 1443, ninety-third Congress, first session, 1973, pp. 457-63.

219. *May Hearings,* p. 14. See the citations on pp. 176-77, above.

220. Laura Summers, "Consolidating the Cambodian Revolution," *Current History,* December 1975.

221. See note 60 of this chapter.

222. Personal communication.

223. See p. 16, above.

224. *Wall Street Journal,* editorials, 31 August 1978, 16 April 1976.

225. On this matter, Vickery writes (personal communication): "I am convinced, however, that a good bit of Cambodian policy since the end of the war has been inspired by good old-fashioned vengeance and that the revolution could have been carried out more gently. This possibly gratuitous violence would have no connection with a 'Communist,' or 'Marxist,' or 'Maoist' orientation of the new leaders, but, I believe, would be well within the limits of traditional Cambodian personality and culture as I came to understand them during a residence of five years there." Cf. Meyer, *op. cit.,* (see note 2) for an analysis of Cambodia that lends support to this interpretation, which, however, is unhelpful for the needs of current propaganda.

226. We quote from the transcript, for which we are indebted to Torben Retbøll, who is preparing a study of the Hearings. We have changed only spelling, punctuation and some obvious misprints and grammatical errors.

On Meyer's own reaction to the hearings, see *Dagens Nyheter* (Stockholm), 23 April 1978 (translated in FBIS, 27 April 1978, Cambodia, H2), where he is quoted as saying: "I know I have been lured into a trap here in Oslo. It has been a question of judging and condemning the new Cambodia and not of trying to understand what has happened there." Of the various participants, Meyer was undoubtedly the one most familiar with Cambodian history, society and culture, in fact the only one to have written on Cambodia apart from the war and postwar period, to our knowledge.

227. See note 2. In a review of Meyer's book in the *Journal of the Siam Society* (January 1973, volume 61, Part I, pp. 310-25), Laura Summers describes him as "one of Sihanouk's closest associates" and "without doubt the most prominent of [Sihanouk's large contingent of French advisors] because of his enormous influence in all areas of foreign and domestic policy making and notably in domestic economic planning... By 1961, it was widely acknowledged that he was almost as powerful as Sihanouk." Summers raises serious questions about Meyer's interpretation of the Khmer peasantry and in particular "his psychologizing of essentially social phenomena [which] prevents him from fully understanding the emergence of leftist movements ..." She notes particularly his avoidance of "any implication of French colonialism" and the "colonial bias" of his account, and his implicit rejection of the possibility that the Khmer peasants might have been capable of making rational decisions for themselves on the basis of their perception

of social reality. We need hardly add that it is not because of these characteristics of his writing that Meyer's book and the statement to which we turn have been ignored in the United States. In fact, like Sihanouk himself, Meyer was regarded as a dangerous radical by U.S. officials, we have been informed.

228. Context suggests that he has in mind the Vietnamese. He writes: "However, it must not be so that the accusations against the regime in Cambodia—even if they to a certain extent are justified—become the pretext of a Vietnamese intervention for a pretended liberation of the Khmer people." On this warning and the failure to heed it, see the preface to this volume.

229. Compare Ambassador Bjork's reactions, cited above, p. 215.

230. "Human Rights in Cambodia," see note 18.

231. About this event, Ponchaud writes only that "until recently the general tone of relations between Khmers and French was one of mutual friendship. With one exception: the measures adopted by Charles Thomson in 1884, during the Jules Ferry government, which made the Khmers very angry. The effect of the measures was to deprive the sovereign of all but symbolic power, and this led to a full-scale rebellion." That seems a little thin for the massacre of 20% of the population. *Cambodia: Year Zero*, p. 145.

232. Elsewhere, she points out that yields were considerably lower than those of Cambodia's Southeast Asian neighbors before the war. "Consolidating the Cambodian Revolution."

See also Virginia Thompson, *French Indo-china* (Macmillan, 1942). She comments on the misery of the Khmers despite the country's potential and actual wealth, the decimation of the population by foreign and internal strife, the indebtedness and lack of credit facilities other than usury for the small proprietors, and the fact that "the population is ever on the edge of starvation" (pp. 338ff.). See also Ben Kiernan, "Peasant life and society in Kampuchea before 1970," mimeographed, Monash University (Australia), 1978. He reports that the official termination of slavery in 1897 had little impact in some districts and that even for peasants who were free, the majority throughout the period were at a subsistence level, with low yields, frequent hunger and even starvation, and a sharp decline in landholdings for about 80% of farmers from 1930 to 1950. In short, hardly a picture of "order and peace" in a land without "any major social or agrarian problems" (Ponchaud) for the "fun-loving, easy-going Cambodians" (Donald Wise), or a land that had never known hunger until it fell into the hands of the evil Communists (Henry Kamm), a "gentle land" of "happy smiles" as depicted by many Western journalists and casual visitors.

233. Ben Kiernan, "The Samlaut Rebellion and its Aftermath, 1967-70: the Origins of Cambodia's Liberation Movement," *Working Papers* of the Centre of Southeast Asian Studies, Monash University, Melbourne, nos. 4 and 5 (undated; apparently 1976).

234. Ben Kiernan, "The 1970 Peasant Uprisings in Kampuchea," unpublished ms., 1978. Ponchaud writes that "with the support of the Khmer revolutionaries, [the Vietcong and North Vietnamese] incited the frontier peasants to march on Phnom Penh and overthrow the Lon Nol regime" (*op. cit.*, p. 166).

235. "Cambodia in the News: 1975-76," *Melbourne Journal of Politics*, volume 8, 1975-76; "Social Cohesion in Revolutionary Cambodia," *Australian Outlook*, December, 1976.

236. Note that this exposure of the fakery was long before the international publicity afforded these fabrications, which still continues unaffected by fact, as we have seen.

237. Barron and Paul visited refugee camps in October and November, and also interviewed refugees elsewhere. See above, p. 162, on their mode of access to refugees. Ponchaud's interviews with refugees were also from the same period. Ponchaud based his book, he writes, on written accounts by 94 Khmer refugees, 77 in Thailand and 17 in Vietnam, and interviews with hundreds of illiterate refugees, mostly from the "laboring classes." He identifies only the 94 literate refugees: all middle or upper class with the possible exception of "seven ordinary soldiers," "four Khmer Rouge," "three bonzes," "two fishermen," "a provincial guard," "a truck driver," "a warehouseman." *Cambodia: Year Zero*, p. x.

238. He notes that Western and Thai journalists in Bangkok as well as U.S. officials in the refugee camps concur with this analysis.

239. Sophi's account; see above, p. 243.

240. Ponchaud writes that in some areas agricultural work was dangerous after the war "because of the unexploded bombs and shells lurking in the grass or brush." In one region northwest of Phnom Penh, "a day never went by without several villagers being injured or killed by explosions." *Cambodia: Year Zero*, p. 56. These deaths and injuries, like those from starvation, disease, and overwork caused by the killing of draught animals, are included among "Khmer Rouge atrocities" in the fanciful tabulations offered by the Western media. When he was evacuated from Phnom Penh in May, 1975, Ponchaud passed through villages where he saw "vestiges of the dreadful American air warfare." In conversation, villagers referred to T-28 bombing (including napalm) as the most terrible part of the war, worse than the B-52s. He also passed "a huge cemetery where thousands of revolutionary fighters were buried," a testimony to the nature of the war. *Ibid.*, pp. 37-38. Such observations rarely found their way to commentary on the book.

241. Recall that Ponchaud's book is known primarily through second- or third-hand accounts. Much of Kiernan's article in *Australian Outlook* is based on interviews with refugees in Bangkok and camps in Thailand from December 1975 to February 1976. As noted above, there were 10,200 Cambodian refugees in Thailand in August 1976; the January 1976 figure was about 9,300 (Kiernan, personal communication).

242. There is unlikely to be a serious and comprehensive study of refugees, in part because of Thai refusal to permit serious scholars to conduct research among refugees (see p. 168, above), in part because of the changed situation after the Vietnamese invasion.

We hope that further comment is unnecessary on the significance of Kiernan's analysis for investigation of the workings of the Western propaganda system with regard to Cambodia. Later events and discoveries, whatever they may be, quite plainly—as a simple point of logic—have no bearing on an evaluation of what the media have been churning out on the basis of research in 1976.

Subsequent analysis of the later period, should it be undertaken, would have to consider the impact of a two-front war that was particularly violent on the Vietnamese side in 1977 and involved continued attacks by the CIA-trained Khmer Serei on the Thai side (cf. R.-P. Paringaux, *Le Monde*, 28-29 August 1977). For a skeptical view about events on the Thai border, see Norman Peagam, *Far Eastern Economic Review*, 11 February 1977; for an eyewitness account of Cambodian atrocities on the Vietnamese side of the border see Nayan Chanda, *FEER*, 31 March 1978, and for a prescient analysis of "the seriousness of Cambodia's predicament" in a highly unequal battle see Chanda, *FEER*, 11 August 1978. The border conflicts undoubtedly had a severe impact within Cambodia. It is quite senseless to exclude them from consideration in interpreting internal events in Cambodia in the postwar period, as is not uncommon. See Heder's papers cited earlier for extensive discussion.

243. Nayan Chanda, "When the killing has to stop," *FEER*, 29 October 1976; "Cambodge: Après deux ans d'isolement complet, Premiers signes d'une timide ouverture au monde extérieur," *Le Monde diplomatique*, May 1977. See also the *FEER Asia Yearbook*, 1977.

244. Note that his estimate is at the lower end of Twining's estimated "thousands or hundreds of thousands. Recall also the estimates by Carney and Holbrooke cited above as well as those by Cambodia watchers cited by Simons (p. 182).

245. Here there is a footnote reference to a communication by W.J. Sampson to which we return.

246. See note 80, this chapter.

247. *FEER*. Whether Chanda is correct in attributing the use of force to uneducated peasants, we are not qualified to say. We should remark, however, that modern history offers little basis for the belief that uneducated peasants are more given to savagery, violence or terror than sophisticated Western intellectuals. Quite the contrary. Similarly, we wonder whether there is any source of peasant origin that offers justification for massacre and annihilation in the manner, say, of Guenter Lewy's highly praised *America in Vietnam*, on which we have commented several times. For further discussion, see our review of this

book in *Inquiry,* 19 March 1979.

248. See notes 82 and 293, this chapter.

249. For more on these matters see the ignored study by Hildebrand and Porter, cited in note 9, this chapter.

250. For more on these matters, briefly noted in the revised English translation of Ponchaud's book, see also *Far Eastern Economic Review,* December 1976, 7 October 1977, and 2 June 1977; and the articles by Summers in *Current History* cited above, notes 63, 220.

251. W.J. Sampson, letter, London *Economist,* 26 March 1977; reprinted in *May Hearings,* as an Appendix.

252. Recall Barron's attempt to defend his 5 million figure; note 117, above. In an unpublished paper, Sampson arrives at an estimate of about 8.4 million for the population at the end of 1978, noting many uncertainties. The *FEER Asia 1979 Yearbook* estimates the population at 8.2 million.

253. This figure presumably includes wartime deaths.

254. See his review of Ponchaud and the "corrections," where the charge is withdrawn. See notes 17, 48.

255. See note 348, below.

256. *May Hearings,* p. 37.

257. William Shawcross, "Third Indochina War," *New York Review of Books,* 6 April 1978.

258. Note that this communication is subsequent to Shawcross's phone call.

259. "An Exchange on Cambodia," *New York Review of Books,* 20 July 1978.

260. George C. Hildebrand, "Kampuchean refugee challenges terror stories circulated in U.S.A.," *News from Kampuchea,* June 1977; also *Guardian* (New York), 30 March 1977. In the same report, Hildebrand states that he "spoke personally with Cambodians who were approached by U.S. agents seeking to recruit them into...armed bands [that "raided Cambodia from bases in neighboring Thailand"] during 1975."

261. Cf. the eyewitness account by Sydney H. Schanberg (New York Times, 9 May 1975): the Khmer Rouge were "peasant boys, pure and simple— darker skinned than their city brethren, with gold in their front teeth. To them the city is a curiosity, an oddity, a carnival, where you visit but do not live...When they looted jewelry shops, they kept only one watch for themselves and gave the rest to their colleagues or passersby." On the peasant army, see also the comments by Peang Sophi and by Jean-Jacques Cazaux, cited below, p. 331-32. On how apparent efforts to prevent looting have been transmuted by the international press into looting, savage repression, brutality and revenge, see note 101, above.

262. Chou Meng Tarr, "Our experiences during the liberation of Phnom Penh, April 1975, Part I," *News from Kampuchea,* volume 1, no. 1, April 1977; Chou Meng Tarr and Shane Tarr, "Part II," *ibid.,* volume 1, no. 2, June 1977.

263. Methods aside, most observers believe it to have been a necessity. See, e.g., the comments by Poole (p. 176) and many others. See also notes

273, 313, and p. 191.

264. Their observations are corroborated by other sources; see Hildebrand and Porter, *op. cit.*, pp. 50f. See also the eyewitness report of the situation in the hospitals at the time of the Khmer Rouge takeover by Jon Swain, *Sunday Times* (London), 11 May 1975: "Hundreds of people were being subjected to a hideous death" at a hospital where doctors "had not reported for work for two days, and there was no one to treat the two thousand wounded." People were bleeding to death in the corridors or in wards caked with blood and thick with flies. A nurse explained that the doctors simply stayed away, while "the dead and dying lay in pools of their own blood," including a Khmer Rouge "who had somehow been brought there for treatment." In dismay, Swain and his journalist colleagues "sloshed our way through the blood to the exit." Reports by Swain and others indicate that the subsequent Khmer Rouge evacuation of the hospitals was a brutal affair, but perhaps the scene they observed is relevant to understanding the evacuation policy.

Swain's lengthy and horrifying account contrasts with the brief mention by his companion, Sydney Schanberg of the *New York Times*, who describes the evacuation vividly and notes that many of the miserable patients forcefully evacuated will have little chance of survival, but of the situation in Phnom Penh he says only that "many of the wounded were dying for lack of care" (*New York Times*, 9 May 1975; in an accompanying dispatch headed "American's Brief Brush With Arrest and Death," he writes: "Doctors and surgeons, out of fear, had failed to come to work and the wounded were bleeding to death in the corridors"). He believes that the Khmer Rouge who threatened him and his companions as they left the hospital may have been angry because "they wanted no foreign witnesses" to the evacuation, though a reading of Swain's account of the same visit raises questions about the alternatives.

265. Richard Boyle, *Flower of the Dragon*, Ramparts Press, 1972. Boyle filed a story on the exodus from Phnom Penh for Pacific News Service (30 June 1975). In it he reports having seen the Calmette hospital "now administered by the Khmer Rouge," "relay station and rest stops along the road out of Phnom Phenh, where Khmer Rouge troops—mostly women—and Buddhist monks supplied refugees with food and water" and "an orderly exodus, in which refugees moved at a leisurely pace on bicycles, ox-carts and on foot." He states that "not one of the 1100 foreign nationals, including about 20 journalists, who left on the two convoys provided by the Khmer Rouge ever witnessed any bodies abandoned on the roadside," contradicting a White House intelligence memo cited by Jack Anderson, *Washington Post*, 23 June 1975. He believes the evacuation to have been justified by horrendous conditions in Phnom Penh, which he describes: squalid refugee camps, severe malnutrition and disease, patients in hospitals dying from gangrene and suffering from lack of treatment unless they were wealthy, lack of doc-

tors (who fled), destruction of water filtration plants and power lines by "secret police agents" ("By the evening of 17 April, there was no power in many parts of the city, and the water supply was running out"), "a dwindling food supply." French medical doctors at Calmette, the only functioning hospital, told him that they "feared an epidemic of bubonic plague, or even worse, cholera or typhoid." He claims further that the Khmer doctors who remained treated patients "too sick to make the journey into the countryside" and that the evacuation was "systematic and well-planned" so far as he could see. He questions the charge in *Newsweek* by its photographer Dennis Cameron that the Khmer Rouge mistreated civilians, noting that "the magazine failed to produce a single photo from Cameron to substantiate his charge." Boyle's account did not appear in the national media, or elsewhere in the press, to our knowledge. Other reports from European journalists giving a similar account of the evacuation are cited by Retbøll ("Kampuchea and 'the *Reader's Digest'*"), who notes that given the resources of the *Reader's Digest,* their omission of evidence inconsistent with the Barron-Paul report "is not a matter of inadvertence but rather a conscious attempt to suppress evidence which might disprove or modify their own conclusions." Retbøll also cites a statement by Lim Pech Kuon, one of the witnesses at the Oslo Hearings, who challenged Anthony Paul from the floor, saying "it is obvious that Paul does not know anything at all about Cambodia. Therefore it is not up to him to judge this country."

266. *Guardian* (New York) (28 May 1975). Barron and Paul report the story that Boyle asserts was censored by AP, *op. cit.,* p. 10.

267. Reporters quoted Dr. Bernard Piquart, chief surgeon at the Calmette Hospital, as having "seen hundreds of bodies with their throats cut in the central market" and having "affirmed that he had been forced to operate on wounded Communist soldiers at gunpoint and that he had cared for French women who had been raped." When he crossed the Cambodian border to Thailand with the convoy from the French Embassy, however, Piquart "seemed embarrassed over the wide publicity given to his reports" and "said he had talked too much and had never seen all of that." AFP, *New York Times* (10 May 1978).

268. 7 October 1977.

269. *TLS,* 28 October 1977.

270. *Ibid.,* 4 November 1974.

271. *Ibid.,* 25 November 1977.

272. *Ibid.,* 2 December 1977.

273. It is not easy to reconcile Leifer's praise for the Barron-Paul book with his own observations and scholarly work. See, for example, his "Economic Survey" of Cambodia in *The Far East and Australasia,* Europa, 1976, pp. 431f., in which he observes that "the onset of war in Cambodia completely disrupted the economy...By April 1975, there was not a Cambodian economy, only the importation of foodstuffs financed by the United

States government." Thus the "first priority" for the Khmer Rouge "was declared to be the restoration of the national economy. Partly to this end, the urban centres, including the capital, were cleared of their inhabitants who were driven into the rural areas to work on the land and in other tasks of economic reconstruction. The initial rigours of the collectivization of agriculture were sustained at human cost but a good first harvest and the virtual rehabilitation of Cambodia's small industrial sector, with Chinese technical assistance, placed the economy in a viable condition." Given these facts, how can one give a favorable review to a book that excises from history all that precedes April 1975 and attributes the Draconian measures then instituted solely to Communist villainy?

274. 30 April 1977.

275. Phil Gailey, "Don't Withhold Aid from Chile Junta Because of 'Mistakes,' Panel Is Told," *Miami Herald* (6 August 1974). His *TV Guide* article, based largely on Barron-Paul, is entitled "The Cambodian Blood Bath and The Great Silence." The major theme is the "appalling" refusal of the media to take seriously "the murder of a million innocent people," to be explained by the tendency of the media to overlook crimes that "are inflicted in the name of revolution." Dr. Lefever "directs the Ethics and Public Policy Program of the Kennedy Institute of Georgetown University in Washington, D.C., and teaches international politics there," *TV Guide* informs us. It should be borne in mind, difficult as it is to imagine, that material of this sort not only inundates a mass audience but is also taken seriously in allegedly "sophisticated" circles in the United States.

276. Donald Wise, *Far Eastern Economic Review*, 23 September 1977. This is the review already cited, which began with the probably fabricated *Famiglia Cristiana* interview and ended with the "quote" about one million people being enough to build the new Cambodia; each example forms part of the impeccable documentation in the Barron-Paul book. Wise also cites with approval Barron-Paul's explanation of the more extreme policies as a consequence of Khieu Samphan's alleged "impotence," and other deep remarks.

277. Paul Grimes, "Books of the Times," *New York Times*, 31 August 1977. The word "however" refers to the Barron-Paul subtitle, "the untold story of Communist genocide in Cambodia." The story "hasn't been untold at all," Grimes correctly observes, referring to a July 1975 story by Henry Kamm in the *New York Times*, one of the innumerably many since. See also the review in the *New York Times Book Review*, 11 September 1977, by Jean Lacouture, which again makes this point.

278. *Economist*, 10 September 1977.

279. For one of many examples, see Editorial, *Christian Science Monitor*, 26 January 1977, reporting the Barron-Paul conclusions with no question as to their authenticity, while deploring the "indifference in America and elsewhere to the fate of freedom under what appears to be one of

the most brutal and concentrated onslaughts in history...in the lovely land and among the engaging people of Cambodia." Like the authors of the book, the editors have conveniently forgotten an earlier onslaught on this lovely land. Their earlier concern for "the fate of freedom" for Cambodian peasants remains a closely-guarded secret.

280. In the *Nation*, 25 June 1977, we commented on some of the more obvious inadequacies of the book.

281. *Manchester Guardian Weekly*, 18 September 1977. Excerpts from the longer *Guardian* article appear in the *Boston Globe* (2 October 1977).

In conformity with the standard line, Woollacott alleges that Cambodian atrocities had previously been disregarded. "The American Right did not want to examine at all closely the kind of fate to which they had abandoned 'their' Cambodians. The whole array of Left-wing and liberal groups in the United States, France, and Britain, who had supported the Khmer Rouge cause, after some sophistry about the evacuation of the cities and some suggestions that the stories of executions were CIA 'plants,' more or less dropped Cambodia." He does not refer us to sources for "the whole array of Left-wing and liberal groups" who took this stand, or explain how the regular condemnations of Cambodian genocide from mid-1975 in the mainstream press (*New York Times, Time,* etc.) comport with this version of the facts. He also states that "only when a figure as impressive as Jean Lacouture spoke out, as he did earlier this year, did a few Left-wingers timidly follow," referring to the article by Lacouture that condemned Cambodian "autogenocide" on the basis of gross misrepresentation of Ponchaud. This paragraph was dropped by the *Boston Globe*, who were aware of the facts; see note 348, below. Woollacott also expresses his astonishment that the Cambodian revolutionaries had not "picked up...the essential humaneness of French life and thought," as exemplified in Indochina for so many years, or in Algeria at the time when they were studying in Paris.

282. *New Statesman,* 23 September 1977. Shawcross is impressed by the consistency of refugee reports, without, however, inquiring into the extent to which this is an artifact based on the selection process, not a small matter, as we have seen, particularly in the case of the book under review.

283. *Manchester Guardian Weekly* (30 July 1978), reprinted from the *Washington Post*.

284. *Op. cit.*, p. viii.

285. This scholarly criticism did not extend to the citations from his own work, as we have seen. Cf. pp. 203ff., above.

286. *Op. cit.* pp. 211-212.

287. *Ibid.*, p. xiv.

288. For example, Jon Swain's comments, cited below. Barron and Paul refer in passing to the "fratricidal war" in which civilians were "caught up in the crossfire between government and insurgent battalions or killed by bombings" (p. 6). Now here is there any indication that the United States had

anything to do with the destruction of the countryside. Equally scandalous is the reference to the U.S. "limited incursion" and the "devastating B-52 raids" which they depict, in accordance with government propaganda, as directed against North Vietnamese and Vietcong sanctuaries (p. 54). Missing from their "impeccable documentation, to cite only one relevant example, are the eyewitness reports by several U.S. correspondents (e.g., Richard Dudman, then a Khmer Rouge captive) of the impact of the U.S. "incursion" and aerial attack on Cambodian civilians. Nor do they take note of the subsequent destruction caused by the United States, or of course, the earlier U.S. interventions, military and otherwise, in Cambodia. See the references cited in notes 2, 45, 202, 204, for ample detail.

The absurdity of their assumption about the irrelevance of history was noted by William Shawcross (*New York Review of Books*, 4 March 1976), referring to their book then under preparation, evidently, with little effect.

289. *Op. cit.*, p. 203.

290. In striking contrast with their freewheeling estimates about deaths in the postwar period (by definition, at the hands of *Angka*), they are properly skeptical about the figures of wartime casualties, which, they sternly admonish, are offered with no stated basis (p. 6n). To appreciate the humor of this remark, one must read through the "methodology" they offer for counting postwar casualties on pp. 203f. Carney, for what it is worth, takes the figure of one million to be a "close" estimate of wartime "killed or wounded." *July Hearings*, p. 22.

291. Our emphasis. *Op. cit.*, p. 206.

292. To be precise, their numbers are 430,000 or more from disease and starvation in the latter half of 1975 and 250,000 or more in 1976, plus 400,000 or more "during the first exodus," presumably from disease and starvation.

293. See Ponchaud, *Cambodia: Year Zero*, p. 71, citing "American Embassy sources," which, he privately informs us, means the Bangkok Embassy. We write "allegedly produced" because no qualified person at the U.S. Embassy ever produced that figure, so we are informed. Charles Twining, who was the Indochina watcher at the U.S. embassy in Bangkok from 1975 to 1977, writes that there was never any "Embassy figure" of 1.2 million "or of any other dimension" and that although people in Bangkok naturally tried to arrive at estimates in their own minds as to the number of Cambodians who died from execution, or from disease or malnutrition, "these were purely private, and mostly short-lived, attempts." Letter, 20 November 1978.

294. See note 82.

295. *Op. cit.*, pp. 6, 28, 208.

296. Perhaps the percentage of the population that voluntarily supported the Communists was as small as the minority that supported the American rebels in 1776-1783; see chapter 2, section 2.

297. *Op. cit.*, pp. 3-4.
298. On this matter see note 418, below.
299. That the Communists depicted the North Vietnamese as "our teachers" seems hardly likely, given their constant emphasis on independence and self-reliance and the long history of conflict between Cambodian and Vietnamese Communists. On the development of Cambodian Communist policy during this period, see Heder's papers cited in the preface, note 19.
300. *Op. cit.*, pp. 54-55.
301. *Ibid.*, p. 61.
302. For a serious account of how the Communist forces were built up from an estimated 5-10,000 in the pre-coup period (January 1968 to March 1970), despite opposition from the Vietnamese and Chinese, who opposed the armed struggle line of the Khmer Communist Party, see Heder, *op. cit.*
303. Even the limited range of sources they cite in their "impeccable documentation" hardly supports their case. Thus under "paucity of popular support for the communists" (p. 214) we find the study edited by Carney, *op. cit.*, which does indeed include the statement by a hostile critic who lived with the Khmer Rouge that the masses do not support them, though it also contains laments from the same source concerning their popularity and success. See note 214 above. Under the same heading they also cite Quinn's study (see note 60), which gives ample evidence suggesting the contrary conclusion, as we have noted.
304. *Op. cit.*, p. 28.
305. Recall that the Tarrs report having seen dead bodies on the streets. As many journalists have noted, it was difficult to decide whether dead that were seen were victims of the last stages of the fighting or postwar executions. Barron and Paul are quite certain, however. Their primary source, Ponchaud, saw no dead bodies (*Cambodia: Year Zero*, p. 24). See also the report by Lim Pech Kuon cited above, p. 167.
306. *Op. cit.*, p. 215.
307. Not surprisingly, reports transmitted under such circumstances have low reliability. For example, Swain also reports that surgeon Bernard Piquart reported several atrocious acts by Khmer Rouge in the Calmette Hospital, a report corroborated by "other witnesses." But Piquart seems to have had second thoughts. See note 267.
308. Cf. chapter 2, section 2.
309. Recall that people who have a considerable knowledge of Cambodia do not find these fellows so "un-Cambodian like"—cf., e.g. Meyer, p. 255, above; Vickery, note 225—though they are undoubtedly quite unlike those whom Meyer calls the "Western colonials" in Phnom Penh.
310. Compare Barron and Paul, who keep strictly to the government propaganda line: whatever the facts, the U.S. was simply striking "communist sanctuaries" (p. 54), i.e., Vietnamese Communists, as the context

makes clear.

311. This is not the only example. To take another, while they quote Swain's horrified account of the evacuation of the hospitals, they omit his equally horrified account of what he saw in a hospital before evacuation. See above, note 264.

312. Cazaux and Juvenal, *Washington Post* (9 May 1975).

313. This is in response to a surmise by some foreigners that only the strong will survive, so that the forced march is "genocide by natural selection." Others, they say, "believe the depopulation of the cities was a necessary race against time to prepare the rice fields for a new planting. Food is very short now, and much farmland had been devastated by the war."

314. The *Washington Post* (9 May 1975) carries a story filed from Aranyaprathet (not Bangkok) compiled from unidentified news dispatches that contains reports that many refugees saw decomposing bodies or people who had been shot or apparently beaten to death, citing also Olle Tolgraven of Swedish Broadcasting who said "he did not believe there had been wholesale executions" though the Khmer Rouge may have shot people who refused to leave their homes when ordered to evacuate.

315. *Washington Post* (9 May 1975). Paul takes care of this annoying fact as follows, in a letter to the *Far Eastern Economic Review* (9 December 1977): "I'm afraid that the evidence is overwhelming that these people, whoever they were, were either the rare exceptions or were not telling the truth," appealing to the testimony of "scores of Cambodian refugees" most of whom "witnessed summary executions" and all of whom, to his recollection, saw "corpses during the long exodus"—as did some foreigners, though the more scrupulous among them pointed out that it was impossible to know whether they were victims of the recent bloody fighting or of executions. Ponchaud writes that he saw no dead bodies in or near Phnom Penh (*Op. cit.*, p. 24).

316. *New York Times* (9 May 1975).

317. *Le Monde* (May 8-10). See the *Manchester Guardian Weekly* (17 May 1975) and a brief report in the *Washington Post* (8 May 1975), which notes correctly that his account "lent no substance to reports that a massive and bloody purge of anti-Communists is under way in Cambodia." He saw no bodies en route and found the streets of Phnom Penh empty on leaving the city. His report "was generally favorable to the Khmer Rouge," and thus not to be discussed further.

318. Recall that the second-hand report of the French teacher which they cite from Swain provides no evidence for the horrible consequences of summary executions that "virtually everybody" saw, but rather serves as an example of the "summary executions" themselves, furthermore, an example that does not support their conclusion, as noted.

319. John Barron, letter, *Economist* (5 November 1977); response to Retbøll's letter of October 15. Anthony M. Paul, letter, *FEER*, 9 December 1977; response to Retbøll's letter of October 28.

320. See note 17, above.

321. See note 2, above. Even "scoops" have been avoided by the press when they convey an unwanted picture. For example, in 1972 Serge Thion was invited to visit the liberated zones in Cambodia, reporting on his experiences in *Le Monde* (26, 27, 28 April 1972). His reports provided a unique insight into the character of an unknown, though evidently very successful and significant movement. His story was offered to the *Washington Post*, but rejected. It appeared nowhere in the U.S. media, to our knowledge. For some excerpts, see *For Reasons of State*, pp. 190ff.

322. Several are cited in Hildebrand and Porter, in their ignored study.

323. See, for example, the testimony of Peter Poole, *May Hearings*, pp. 18-19. He points out that "I don't think there is a great deal we can do" to improve the situation though we might easily worsen it, and that even speaking out will do little good in this case. The point was commonly emphasized by people who know and care about Cambodia, as was the fact that the kind of irresponsible and sometimes hysterical "speaking out" that was being done, with its falsifications and unsupported allegations, could cause serious harm. See note 228 of this chapter, and the preface to this volume.

324. Far easier, in fact. Throughout the protest against the U.S. war in Indochina, the Soviet Union was quite reluctant to back or tolerate strong condemnations of the United States, specifically of Nixon, a fact that led to continual controversy at international meetings.

325. Not really "perfectly" because of the condemnation of the United States and the major theme that Khmer Rouge policies have roots and reason in the domestic society. But few will actually read the book, discovering these elements, and the commentary that reaches a mass audience can be counted on, by and large, to keep to atrocity stories. Lacouture takes note of the Western responsibility but ignores the second major theme of the book, as do other reviewers.

326. Author's note for the American translation, p. xiii.

327. William Shawcross, review of *Cambodia: Year Zero, Inquiry,* 16 October 1978.

328. *Economist*, 1 July 1978.

329. The *Economist* is correct, though not for the reasons it probably had in mind, in describing Lacouture's published corrections as "a bizarre episode." In what passes for intellectual discourse in the West, political discussion included, correction of errors is rare indeed, as a glance at review journals will indicate. Lacouture deserves credit for departing from the general norm. We think that his corrections are inadequate and disagree with some of the conclusions expressed in them, but we want to stress that it is no crime to misread—it is a rare review that avoids error—and it is only proper to issue corrections when errors are discovered. One of us (Chomsky) played a role in this, which though

entirely a matter of private correspondence has for some reason been the subject of considerable discussion (and distortion) in the press. We see no point in commenting on any of this.

330. The *Economist* thinks otherwise, for interesting reasons to which we return directly.

331. See, e.g., Leo Cherne's comment on the *MacNeil/Lehrer Report*, referring to Ponchaud as "very sympathetic to the Khmer Rouge." See note 53. Similarly, the review in *Foreign Affairs* stresses that Ponchaud "was initially sympathetic to the Khmer Rouge" (Winter, 1978-1979), as have many others who take this alleged fact to add to the credibility of his account (reasonably, if it is true). Shawcross also writes that Ponchaud "originally welcomed the prospect of a revolutionary change" (*New York Review*, 6 April 1978). See also note 338.

332. *New York Review*, 31 March 1977; thus he writes that he can read Ponchaud's book "only with shame."

333. *New York Times Book Review*, 11 September 1977.

334. For Sihanouk's own account, see the preface to this volume.

335. See chapter 2, p. 26.

336. See chapter 4, p. 128.

337. *Cambodia: Year Zero*, p. 22.

338. Reed Irvine of Accuracy in Media, Inc. (See note 33), letter, *Boston Globe* (15 October 1978).

339. Lacouture's original charges, in fact, have continued to circulate widely even after they were withdrawn. To cite only one case, Homer Jack, Secretary-General of the World Conference on Religion and Peace, produced a *WCRP Report* entitled "Can the United Nations stop human massacre in Democratic Kampuchea" (20 November 1978) which is full of fanciful charges, including Jean Lacouture's estimate "of the number of persons killed" as "one-quarter of the population," referring to Lacouture's *New York Review* article in which he stated that the regime "boasted" of this achievement, but not to his "Corrections" where he stated that the charge had no basis. It is striking that the credible evidence of substantial atrocities never seems to suffice for human rights activists of this type. Jack surely knew of Lacouture's corrections; indeed, in the course of a series of undocumented slanders directed at "the political right wing" and "the left wing," he denounced our review in which the facts were mentioned. Even when the falsehood was specifically called to his attention, among many others in the document, he felt no need to correct it (or others). Recall Orwell's statement on what is true "in the sight of God" in the Stalinist school of falsification; p. 196, above. The example is not untypical.

340. Editorial, "'Cambodia in the Year Zero,'" 26 April 1977.

341. In contrast, its foreign correspondents have often been outstanding.

342. For a few examples of its countenancing certain acts of barbarism and remaining silent about others, see Chomsky, *American Power and the*

New Mandarins, pp. 14f., 185, 244, 277.

343. See note 279.

344. 21 March 1977.

345. *New York Times* (21 April 1975). The preceding sentence tells us that "the early American decisions on Indochina can be regarded as blundering efforts to do good. But by 1969..." See p. 17, above. More recently Lewis has warned that "America should do nothing" regarding Rhodesia, because, "if we remember Vietnam, we know that intervention, however well-intended, may do terrible harm if it is uninformed." (*New York Times*, 1 February 1979). The inability of the intelligentsia to inform themselves about what their government is up to truly defies comment.

346. Chomsky, letter, 1 June 1977.

347. 12 May 1977.

348. We know of only one case of honest retraction: Matthew Storin, *Boston Globe* (13 May 1977), correcting a report of 7 April based on Lacouture. Storin was also unique in his willingness to at least mention contrary evidence that was privately provided to journalists who had relied on Lacouture, along with conclusive evidence that their references were without basis. Alexander Cockburn expressed the hope—in vain—that "such liberal journalists as Lewis" who had relied on Lacouture's derivative account would see "that 'details' do indeed matter" (*Village Voice*, 16 May 1977). After Lacouture's corrections appeared, a letter was sent to the *New York Review* by a well-known scientist (Nobel Laureate) commenting that in his field, when conclusions are published based on certain evidence and it then turns out that the cited evidence is incorrect, the scientist does not retract the evidence while reiterating the conclusions—but evidently matters are different in journalism. The letter was not published.

349. As we have mentioned (note 48), in the *Nouvel Observateur*, where Lacouture's review was originally published, the corrections never appeared. But this fact, which we find rather surprising, is perhaps of little moment given that in the United States, where they did appear, they have been ignored and what remains in the media record are the original errors. A misstated reference by Lacouture to a quote that has been deleted from the American edition appears on the cover of the British edition of Ponchaud's book. A different quote from Lacouture's review appears on the cover of the American edition, with no concern over the fact that the conclusions expressed were based on no accurate citation. See note 339.

350. Somewhat misleadingly. He writes that "My reference to the death of 'one quarter' of the population in a single year must be corrected"—he had spoken of "boasts" and killing—citing Ponchaud's text, which gives a Cambodian estimate of 800,000 dead during the war and a U.S. embassy (Bangkok) estimate of 1.2 million dead (not killed) since the war; adding the two, we obtain the two million figure, about one quarter of the popu-

lation, that has since been used with abandon in the press and Congress, very likely with this source. See note 293, above, on Ponchaud's 1.2 million estimate allegedly based on "American embassy sources," though the embassy offered no such estimate. Thus Lacouture's statement that the Khmer Rouge boast of having eliminated some 2 million people is based on a misreading of a claim by Ponchaud that is dubious to begin with. Ponchaud mentions other estimates attributed to various vaguely-identified sources, but there is little reason to suppose that these claims have any more validity than the single one which is subject to check, and which, as is the way with verifiable claims, turns out to be inaccurate. Lacouture continues to refer to the 2 million figure (dropping the "boast"); "...the hundreds of thousands, indeed 2 million victims ..." of the Pol Pot Regime (*Nouvel Observateur*, 2 October 1978), an excerpt from his book *Survive le peuple cambodgien!* He gives no source, and does not explain how such charges will help the Cambodian people to survive.

351. See pp. 72-73 of the French original, pp. 50-51 of the American translation.

352. We do not know why Ponchaud dropped the quotes in the translation in this case. Perhaps because of the focus on the question after Lacouture's review and corrections. Or perhaps the reason lies in a debate over translation from Khmer on which we are not competent to comment. In *News from Kampuchea,* August 1977, Stephen Heder challenged several of Ponchaud's translations, including this one. He asserts that in this case, the correct translation of the Khmer phrase (which he says is openly used) is something like "to have no more of this kind of person (e.g., imperialists, oppressors)." In a privately circulated document ("Vicissitudes de la linguistique au service de l'Idéologie abstraite," Ponchaud rejects these challenges to his translations. In this case he states that Heder's proposed translation is "false," but also says that his own translation was "hasty," and would require more time to justify and polish. His own account of the meaning seems to us to leave the correct interpretation rather ambiguous over a certain range, with his specific formulation at the harsher extreme. In any event, even if there is a quote, contrary to what the American edition suggests, it would seem that Lacouture's conclusions from a possible rhetorical flourish are distinctly questionable.

353. The quote as Lacouture gives it in his *Nouvel Observateur* review is inaccurate, and further errors are introduced in the English translation. We will drop this matter, keeping to Ponchaud's text.

354. P. 73 of the French original.

355. This translation, which is sufficiently accurate, is what appears in the British edition, p. 70.

356. Heder provided us with an English translation; Ponchaud with a French translation and the Thai original.

357. Our apologies to the editors of *Prachachat* for the comparison.

358. *News from Kampuchea*, August 1977.

359. Cf. note 273, above. Also, note 82.

360. There is a problem in that the French translation given in Ponchaud's book differs from the French translation that he sent us, which includes the context omitted in the book. We will assume that the translation that he sent us is accurate. It corresponds closely to the English translation provided by Heder. We have not taken the trouble to verify the translations from the Thai original, since the main points emerge fairly clearly even without this further step.

361. The phrase reads: "il peut même arriver qu'on n'y arrive pas partout, et les autorités se trouvent alors chargées d'un fardeau très lourd."

362. American edition, p. 51, a fair translation of the French text in Ponchaud's book.

363. This exercise in verification raises some further questions. It is striking that those passages in the original French text that drew attention because of Lacouture's review have been softened, deleted, or changed in the American translation, or where they remain, are extremely misleading or outright misrepresentations. Note that this is true of each of the four cases just discussed, including the first, where a look at Ponchaud's text shows that estimates of roughly a million dead (the most crucial of which lacks any credible source) become, a few lines later, allegations that many millions are being eliminated, most of the population in fact. These passages were selected for investigation at random, in effect; that is, they were not selected on any basis other than the fact that they seemed to be the passages that Lacouture had in mind in his misrepresentations of (i.e., references to) the book. The facts suggest some obvious questions about the remainder. We have not carried out a thorough line-by-line comparison but a fairly careful reading has not brought to light any other changes from the French original to the American translation (apart from some new material and some rearrangement). If this impression is correct, it also suggests obvious questions.

    Ponchaud's book is almost completely lacking in verifiable documentation. The *Prachachat* reference is one of a handful of examples. It is therefore of more than passing interest to see how it fares upon examination.

364. For a review, see Chomsky, *For Reasons of State*, chapter 2, where there are references for the citations here.

365. Roger Hilsman, *To Move a Nation*, Dell, 1967, pp. 436f.

366. *New York Times* (20 March 1964).

367. See chapter 1.

368. *Cambodia: Year Zero*, p. 164.

369. *Ibid.*

370. See below, p. 288. It has been alleged that Sihanouk was being hypocritical in his denunciation of the U.S. bombing and that he had in fact secretly authorized it. This has been occasionally argued in defense

of the failure of the U.S. media, like Ponchaud, to make public Sihanouk's impassioned criticism of the bombing of the civilian society of
Cambodia. Two points deserve notice. First, even if Sihanouk secretly
authorized bombing of "Vietcong bases," he surely did not authorize
bombing of Khmer peasants, and his protests were directed against
the latter crime. Second, while commentators and media analysts may
draw whatever conclusions they please from the conflicting evidence
available, this does not entitle them to suppress what is, by any standards, crucial evidence, in this case, Sihanouk's attempt to arouse international protest over the U.S. bombing of the civilian society.

371. *Cambodia: Year Zero*, pp. 165, 169.
372. *Ibid.*, p. 170.
373. *Ibid.*, p. 167.
374. *Ibid.*
375. *Ibid.*, p. 164.
376. See notes 146, 147 above.
377. *Ibid.*, p. 21.
378. See above, p. 183.
379. See pp. 175 and 191 above.
380. *Ibid.*, p. 50.
381. *Ibid.*, p. 28.
382. See Peang Sophi's testimony, p. 243 above. See also several reports
     cited by Kiernan, "Social Cohesion," from the *Bangkok Post*, report-
     ing the statements of refugees that an order to stop reprisals was an-
     nounced at the end of May 1975.
383. See note 237, above, for a review of their scope and character.
384. *Cambodia: Year Zero*, pp. 16, 53. Ponchaud does not explicitly state that
     this is the same man, but it appears so from his description.
385. *Le Monde* (17 February 1976).
386. Sometimes in more detail, as we have noted in the case of the alleged
     "quote" about 1-2 million young Khmers being sufficient to build the
     new Cambodia.
387. *Cambodia: Year Zero*, p. 125.
388. *Ibid.*, p. 162. See also notes 203 and 240, above.
389. *Ibid.*, p. xiv.
390. But given Ponchaud's carelessness with fact, already noted in several
     cases, some caution is in order here as well. Thus, the author's note to
     the American translation, dated 20 September 1977, contains a refer-
     ence to a letter dated 19 October 1977.
391. See note 352, above.
392. We omit reference to other slight discrepancies.
393. We have kept to published material, omitting discussion of personal
     correspondence mentioned by Ponchaud, who presumably obtained it
     from the editor of the *New York Review*. His references to this personal
     correspondence, apart from being irrelevant, are incorrect. What he calls

"a polemical exchange" leading to Lacouture's corrections consists of personal letters pointing out errors and urging correction; Lacouture's published corrections reveal how little it was "polemical." It is difficult to imagine a less polemical response to the discovery of serious errors, and it was so understood, as the correspondence clearly shows. Nor is there anything in this correspondence to support Ponchaud's false statements, though even if there were, it would be irrelevant in this context, as should be obvious. We should perhaps mention that in his book cited above and in articles and interviews elsewhere, Lacouture has been presenting grossly false versions of Chomsky's views, invariably without the slightest effort at documentation, and indeed, quite inconsistent with what he knows to be true. This too deserves no further comment.

394. See note 329. Ponchaud's fakery has also found its way into what purports to be "scholarship." In a review of Ponchaud's book in *International Affairs*, journal of the Royal Institute of International Affairs (January 1979), Dennis Duncanson writes that "The author reports, without rancour, that after the French edition came out it was attacked by Professor Noam Chomsky and Mr. Gareth Porter for relying on refugees' stories, on the grounds that refugees can be assumed to warp the truth, that we ought to give the Phnom Penh Politburo the benefit of its secrecy, and that as a positive fact no massacres took place in Cambodia." This is an embellishment of Ponchaud's false statements in the British translation, presented here simply as fact—to this scholar, it is of no concern that Ponchaud's charges are presented not only "without rancour" but also without a particle of evidence, and that, as can be easily verified, the charges are not only false but indeed were conscious falsehoods, as we have seen. Duncanson proceeds with further falsehoods and undocumented slanders that give some insight into what is regarded as "scholarship" in this domain but are otherwise not worthy of comment.

395. Tiden Norsk Forlag, 1978, p. 210. See note 141, above. We are indebted to Torben Retbøll for providing us with the relevant pages.

396. *Inquiry*, 16 October 1978. See note 327, above, and text.

397. *Cambodia: Year Zero*, p. xiv.

398. *Ibid.*, p. 136.

399. Shawcross regards this question as not just serious, but the most crucial question, and he believes that the evidence has firmly established central direction and intent. See note 187, above, and text. In his published work, he appears to rely largely on Ponchaud, quite uncritically.

400. *Cambodia: Year Zero*, p. xvi.

401. The lapse on Ponchaud's part is perhaps far from accidental. Thus in the British translation, the comparable passage in the author's note (p. 16) clearly implies that the "accusing foreigners" are the ones to whom he has already referred: namely, Chomsky and Porter, who "say there have been no massacres" and regard refugees as "not a valid source," an allegation that he knows perfectly well to be false, as we have seen. Recall again that the British version is not available in the United

States, where the merits of his allegations can readily be determined.

402. Much the same is true of Ponchaud's rhetorical question: "How many of those who say they are unreservedly in support of the Khmer revolution would consent to endure one hundredth part of the present sufferings of the Cambodian people" (p. 193), immediately following the familiar accusation that few voices have been "raised in protest against the assassination of a people." He fails to enumerate those who are unreservedly in support of the Khmer revolution, though the list would be small enough so that it could easily have been given at this point. Note also that another question might easily be raised: how many of those who virulently condemn the Khmer revolution would consent to endure one hundredth part of the suffering of the peasants of the traditional society of Cambodia?—a society that was hardly improving their lot in its latter days.

403. In fact, we know of no specialist who takes such an estimate seriously, including Ponchaud in his more sober moments.

404. *Washington Post* (21 September 1978).

405. See note 9. Ponchaud mentions it in the author's note to the American translation without comment, postdating it by a year.

406. *Asia*, March-April 1977.

407. July/August 1977.

408. See notes 237, 259 above.

409. 22 November 1976.

410. 16 April 1976.

411. 20 September 1976.

412. Recall the predictions by U.S. government sources of impending starvation that will take a million lives, or by the Western doctors cited by Hildebrand and Porter (see p. 184, above) in a book which for this reason alone must be kept from public notice.

413. *New York Times* (19 April 1977), our emphasis.

414. 26 April 1977. The implication here, and explicit statement commonly, is that Cambodia did or would refuse any shipments of food. Is that correct? The crew of the Mayaguez saw two Chinese freighters unloading rice in the port of Kampong Som in May 1975. See Roy Rowan, *The Four Days of Mayaguez*, Norton, 1975, p. 153.

415. See chapter 5, note 30.

416. Bertrand Russell, *The Practice and Theory of Bolshevism*, Allen and Unwin, 1920, pp. 68, 55.

417. The specific instances cited are not B-52 attacks.

418. *Bombing in Cambodia*, Hearings before the Committee on Armed Services, U.S. Senate, Ninety-third Congress, first session, July/August, 1973, U.S. Government Printing Office, Washington, 1973, pp. 158-160. See note 370.

419. Cf. Chomsky, *At War With Asia*, 1970, pp. 121ff.

420. *Ibid.*, pp. 122-123.

421. In the Watergate hearings the alleged "secrecy" of the bombing became

an issue but not the bombing itself. Nixon's crime, we must assume, was not that he sent his bombers to destroy a relatively peaceful country with which the United States had "friendly" relations, but that he kept the matter from Congress. On the hypocrisy of the Watergate proceedings and the press reaction quite generally, see Chomsky, introduction to Blackstock, ed., *Cointelpro*.

422. William Beecher, "Raids in Cambodia by U.S. unprotested," *New York Times* (9 May 1969). Recall Ponchaud's comment that Sihanouk's protest against the bombing of North Vietnamese and Vietcong sanctuaries deceived no one. As we pointed out in note 370, Sihanouk's protests were primarily against the bombing of Khmer civilians. In regard to the bombing of Vietnamese concentrations near the border, while there is conflicting evidence as to Sihanouk's attitude, it is not up to the press or others to decide what it "really was" and then to withhold reference to his explicit appeal just cited on grounds that no one is deceived by it. What is more, recall that the bombings of the "Vietcong and North Vietnamese" sanctuaries were undoubtedly aimed at Vietnamese who had been driven across the border by murderous U.S. military operations in Vietnam, primarily since early 1967. And finally, recall that direct observation by Western reporters and others confirms that the B-52 raids were by no means aimed at the Vietnamese. See for example, Swain, *op. cit.*; p. 284-85, above. While the precise scale of these atrocities could not have been known in 1969, and is not known now in the West, a free press could have surmised and perhaps learned a great deal had it chosen to do so. It is remarkable that Beecher's unique though quite inadequate account is now held up as evidence that the press maintained its honor throughout this period, despite the crimes of Richard Nixon.

423. See *At War With Asia,* pp. 121-22.

424. Jean-Jacques Cazaux and Claude Juvenal, AP, *Washington Post,* 9 May 1975.

425. See above, pp. 255-56.

426. "Defining the Revolutionary State in Cambodia."

427. See the accounts surveyed above, as well as the assessment in the *FEER Asia 1979 Yearbook.*

7 Final Comments

1. On these matters, see Alex Carey, "Reshaping the Truth: Pragmatists and Propagandists in America," *Meanjin Quarterly* (Australia), vol. 35, no. 4, 1976; Carey and Truda Korber, *Propaganda and Democracy in America,* forthcoming.

2. In particular, the singular failure of significant segments of the French intelligentsia to come to terms with the true nature of Stalinism and its roots in Leninist ideology and practice.

3. See David Caute, *The Great Fear,* Simon & Schuster, 1978, pp. 19, 35.

Index

ABC (American Broadcasting Co.), 139, 165, 229
AFL-CIO, 117
Agee, Philip, 30
AID. *See* United States Agency for International Development
Aikman, David, 187
Albania, 139
Alexander-de-Rhodes Center, 122
Allende, Salvador, 275
American Broadcasting Co. (ABC), 139, 165, 229
American Civil War, 46, 79
American Friends Service Committee (AFSC), 103, 104
American Revolution, 45–52
Amphoux, Nancy, 316
Andelman, David A., 223
Anderson, Jack, 165, 236
Angka Loeu, 187, 279, 280
Angola, 22
Arakan, 56, 57
Aron, Robert, 42
ARVN (Army of the Republic of Viet Nam), 119
Asahi, 93
ASEAN, 5–6, 12–13
Asian Development Bank, 95–96
Asian Survey, 202
Associated Press (AP), 121, 158, 222, 223, 272, 273, 285–86, 327–28

Association Belgique Kampuchea, 224
Australia, 194, 196, 242

Ban Me Thuot, 31
Bangkok Post, 165, 194, 252
Bangladesh, 11, 56, 57
Barron, John, 161–64, 168, 198–208, 210, 211, 215, 229, 235, 245, 259, 261, 264–65, 268, 272, 273, 275–89, 295, 304, 305, 312, 324, 325
Bataan death march, 36
Battambang Province, 221, 222, 244, 247, 249, 255, 259, 260
BBC (British Broadcasting Corporation), xxiii, 220
Becker, Elizabeth, 213, 237, 240, 241, 276
Beecher, William, 330–31
Beer, Patrice de, 164, 260, 287
Bennett, Joseph, 31
Bergstrom, Gunnar, 227, 231
Beria, Lavrenti, 298, 303
Berlin, Isaiah, 26
Bigart, Homer, 19
Bjork, Kaj, 214
Boorstin, Daniel, 52
Boret, Long, 183
Boston Globe, 233
Boston World Affairs Council, 61
Boupha, Khamphay, 149

447

Boyle, Richard, 271
Britain. See Great Britain
British Broadcasting Corporation.
    See BBC
Brown, Harold, 5, 20
Bryce, Viscount, 27
Bryce Report, 27–29, 109, 164
Buchanan, Patrick, 165
Buckley, William, 181
Buddhism, 221–22
Burma, 56, 57, 60
Burstein, Daniel, 228, 229
Bush, George W., xiii
Butterfield, Fox, 70–71, 74–76, 79,
    82, 88–92
Buttinger, Joseph, 9
Buu, Tran Quoc, 112, 114

Caldwell, Malcolm, 213, 241
Call (Chicago), 228
Cambodia/Kampuchea, viii–xii, xv,
    xvi, xvii, xix, xx, xxii, xxiii,
    xxv–xxvi, 2, 4, 5–6, 53, 84, 93,
    137, 155–337
Canada, 37
Carney, Timothy, 183, 198
Carter, Jimmy, 20–23, 65, 106, 276
Cartesian logic, 181
Casella, Alexander, 80, 81–85, 87,
    90
Castro, Fidel, 308
Catholic University of Louvain, 224
Cazaux, Jean-Jacques, 286–87
CBS (Columbia Broadcasting Sys-
    tem), 159, 164, 179
Center for International Law, 224
Center for International Studies
    (MIT), 69
Central America, xii
Central Intelligence Agency. See
    CIA
Central School of Psychological
    Warfare, 119
Chanda, Nayan, x, xx, 76–80, 85,
    90, 147–48, 151, 152, 261–64

Chandler, David P., 176–77, 242–
    46, 251
Chemical Warfare Center, 41
Cherne, Leo, 170
Chi Hoa Prison, 103
Chile, 139
Chilean Junta, 275
China, xvii, xviii, xxii, xxiii, xxvi,
    xxvii, 57, 58, 84, 139, 145
Choice, 326
Chomsky, Noam, 318, 320, 321
Chou Try, 164
Christian Science Monitor, 145–47,
    180, 294–97, 328
Churchill, Winston, 43
CIA (Central Intelligence Agency),
    xii–xiii, xvii, 3, 10, 22, 29–31,
    34, 58, 72, 84, 112, 114,
    137–41, 144, 150, 165, 197,
    203, 258, 259, 272, 306
Clay, Lucius, 38
Clinton, Bill, ix
Coatsworth, John, xii
Colby, William, 16
Collett, Wallace, 100
Columbia Broadcasting System
    (CBS), 159, 164, 179
Commonweal, 243
Con Son, 83
Cong Tum, 70–71
Costa Rica, 60
Cremin, Lawrence, 52
Cuba, xviii, 96
Cullen, Sen., 28
Czechoslovakia, 135

Dac Lac, 70–71
Dachau, 171
Dahl, Birgitta, 105
Daily Mail, 27
Daily Mirror (London), 283, 285
de Gaulle, Charles, 7, 43
Debris, Catherine, 104
Debris, Jean-Pierre, 103–4
Decornoy, Jacques, 133, 170

Defense Department, U.S., 277
Denmark, 217, 227
DeYoung, Karen, 63
Diem, Ngo Dinh, 18, 69, 71, 113, 114, 119, 306
Dissent, 18
Distel, Barbara, 44
Dobbs, Michael, 222
Draper, Theodore, 21
Dresden, 11, 39
Dudman, Richard, 85–86, 189, 213, 237–42
Duncanson, Dennis, 72, 130

East Timor, viii–xii, 58, 117, 156, 159, 188, 202, 230, 289, 336, 340
Economist (London), xxi, 55–58, 60, 63–64, 69, 115–16, 198, 201, 275, 279, 287, 291, 320
Ecrits de Paris, 42
Ediger, Max, 100–103
Eisenhower, Dwight, 23, 43
Emerson, Gloria, 18–19
Encounter, 302
Europe, xxix, 5, 7, 20
Evangelical Church of Vietnam, 108
Everingham, John, 137–38

Fall, Bernard, 10, 45
Fallaci, Oriana, 158
Fallows, James, xi
Famiglia Cristiana, 198–203, 215, 265, 277
Far Eastern Economic Review (FEER), xvii, 56, 139, 201–3, 210, 261–64, 281–82, 287
Faulk, Henry, 39
Finland, 217
Food for Peace, 96, 147
Foreign Policy, 80
"Foreign Report," 198
Forsythe, Julia, B., 122
Fort Kearney, 40–41
Foster, Douglas, 196

France, xxiv, xxviii, xxix, 1, 42–43, 45, 51, 143, 193, 194
Frankel, Max, 308–9
Fraser, John, 132, 133, 167, 259
Fraternité Vietnam, 98–99
Free Trade Union News, 117
Free World, x, xviii, 2, 7
Freedom House, 33–34
French Foreign Legion, 8
Fulbright, William, 9
FUNK (National United Front of Kampuchea), 249

Gansberg, Judith, 39–40
Gelinas, Father André, 120–31, 293
Geneva, 1, 2, 15
German-Bolshevik Conspiracy, 29
Germany, xviii, 43, 44, 194
Gia Lai, 70–71
Globe and Mail (Toronto), 99, 120, 132, 167
Goering, Herman, 44
Gollobin, Ira, 61
Goodfellow, William, 183–84
Goodling, Rep. William F., 177
Gourou, Pierre, 93
Government Junta of Chile, 275
Great Britain, 5, 27, 39, 45, 51
Green Berets, 107, 272
Greene, Nathanael, 48–49
Guam, 79, 86–87
Guardian (New York), 271–73
Guatemala, 134

Haiti, 61–65
Hanoi Radio, 106
Harlem, 86–87
Hawaii, 35
Heder, Stephen, xxv–xxvi, 168–69, 213, 252
Hickey, Gerald, 72–73
Hiebert, Linda and Murray, 139, 153
Hildebrand, George, 184, 260, 265–68, 325

Hilsman, Roger, 307–8
Himmler, Heinrich, 298, 303
Hiroshima, 37, 44
Hirsch, Amy, 123
Hitler, Adolf, 17, 44, 158
Hmong (Meo), 3, 138, 140, 141, 144, 145
Ho Chi Minh, 30
Hoan, Nguyen Cong, 111, 113–19
Hoang Van Chi, 29, 123
Holbrooke, Richard, 61, 183
Homage to Catalonia, 25
Honduras, 60
Honey, Patrick, 69–70, 130
Hong Kong, 70, 109
Hughes, Richard, 123–24
Hungary, 135

Immigration and Naturalization Services (INS), 62–64
India, 226
Indochina, xv, xvii, xviii, xxix, 1, 5, 7, 8
Indochina Resource Center, 194
Indonesia, viii, xix
International Bulletin, 194–95
International Declaration of Human Rights, 254
International Red Cross, 148, 184–85
Iran, 226
Israel, 25
Issaraks, 248

Jackson, Karl D., 202
Jacqueney, Theodore, 117–19
Japan, xviii, 5, 35, 284
Jefferson, Thomas, 48
Johnson, Lyndon Baines, 2, 14, 128–29
Juvenal, Claude, 286

Kahin, George, 326–27
Kamm, Henry, xxviii, xxix, 51, 66, 92–93, 107, 116–17, 144–45,

163, 164, 169, 217–18, 223–24, 228–34
Kearney, Fort, 40–41
Kennedy, John F., 23, 307
Key, Dr. Penelope, 185
Kham, Chit, 152
Khanh, Nguyen, 3
Khmer Rouge, viii, xii, 155–337
Khoun Sakhon, 267
Khoung, Tran Dinh, 98
Kiernan, Ben, 257–62
Kim il-Sung, 13
King, Mackenzie, 37
King, Martin Luther, Jr., 119
Kissinger, Henry, x, 8, 15, 16, 22, 249, 250, 329
Klassen, James, 107–8
KNUFNS, xxvii, xxviii
Kolko, Gabriel, 93
Komer, Robert, 10
Kon Tum. *See* Cong Tum
Konoe, 36
Kriangsak, General, 13
Kubicka, Louis and Eryl, 103, 152–53

Labor, Dept. of, 79
Lacouture, Jean, 85, 93–94, 97, 121, 161, 171–73, 192, 207–9, 211, 265, 289–305, 315–18, 332
Lacouture, Simonne, 85, 93–94, 97, 121
Lam Dong, 70–71
Laos, xv, xvii, 2–4, 53, 103, 133, 137–55, 246
Latin America, xii–xiii
Le Monde, 131–35, 164, 165, 170, 204–7, 216, 260, 262, 287, 314, 316, 317
Le Soleil (Quebec), 98
Lebanon, 59–61
Lefever, Ernest, 275
Leifer, Michael, 273–75
Lenin, Vladimir, 264

Lewis, Anthony, 17, 295–97
L'Express (France), 120, 121, 128
Liberation News Service, 267
Lim Pech Koun, 167
Livre Noir, 240–41
Lodge, Henry Cabot, 2
Lon Nol, 160, 165, 179, 228, 236,
    242, 259–62, 281, 292–93,
    310, 312
*London Daily Mirror. See Daily
    Mirror*
London *Economist. See Economist*
London *Observer. See Observer*
London *Sunday Telegraph. See
    Sunday Telegraph*
*London Sunday Times. See Sunday
    Times*
London Times, 165–66, 273
Loyalists (American Revolution),
    15, 46–47, 51. *See also* Tories
Luce, Don, 114
Lundvik, Jan, 215, 216
Ly Chanh Trung, 104, 112
Lynhiavu, Lytek, 141

Mabuchi, Naoki, 218
MacNeil/Lehrer Report, 228
Malaysia, 55, 58, 113
Malik, Adam, 202, 203
Marcos, Ferdinand, 13, 65
Marine Corps. U.S., 159
Martin, Graham, 32
Martin, Earl, 126
Marx, Karl, 188–89, 264
Mattern, William, 56
May Hearings, 164, 175
McArthur, George, 106, 107
McGovern, George, 158–60,
    173–75, 179
McGrory, Mary, 232
McNaughton, John, 307
Mekong Delta, 77, 78
Meng, Chou, 268–71
Meo. *See* Hmong
Meyer, Charles, xx, 254–56, 290,

306, 333
MIAs, 96, 146
Middle East, 22
Minnear, Richard, 36, 37
Monash Univ., 176
Montagnards, 70
Montreal Star, 125
Moscow, xviii, 31
Moss, Robert, 198, 199
Moynihan, Daniel P., xi
MPLA (People's Movement for the
    Liberation of Angola), 22
My Lai Massacre, 94, 171, 193
Myrdal, Jan, 227

Naccache, Ursula, 278
Nagasaki, 37
Nation, 292, 301, 326
National Conference of Christians
    and Jews, 16
National Liberation Front for
    South Vietnam. *See* NLF
National Security Council, 202,
    251, 277
National United Front of
    Kampuchea (FUNK), 249
Native Americans, 51–52
Nazis, 5, 171, 186
Nehru, Jawaharlal, 39
New Economic Zones, 113, 114, 133
New Republic, 17, 22
New Times, 234
New York Review of Books, 120, 121,
    124, 126, 128–30, 237, 267,
    289, 291, 293, 294, 318, 326
New York Times, xxix, 10, 14, 17,
    19, 33, 41, 44, 45, 57, 62,
    64–66, 70, 71, 73–77, 79,
    82, 91–96, 98–100, 103–7,
    120–24,
    126–28, 134, 140, 144–46,
    162, 166, 183, 197, 202, 214,
    223, 228, 232, 237, 241, 269,
    273, 295, 308, 328, 330–31
New York Times Magazine, 190,

198, 230
New Yorker, 180
New Zealand, 268, 273
News from Kampuchea, 273, 274
Newsday, 66
Newsweek, 86–88, 190, 195, 196, 229, 241
Ngo Cong Duc, 86, 105
Nicaragua, 134
Niedergang, Marcel, 134
Nixon, Richard, x, 8, 88, 240, 249–51, 329, 330
Nkrumah, Kwame, 309
NLF (National Liberation Front for South Vietnam), 3, 4, 7, 11, 73, 81, 281
North Korea, 21, 22
North Vietnam, 3–4, 11, 21, 84, 96, 139
Nouvel Observateur, 291
Nuremberg trials, 38

Oberg, Jean-Christopher, 216
Observer (London), 12–13
Onn, Hussein, 13
Orwell, George, 25, 34, 196
O'Shaughnessy, Hugh, 134
Oslo Hearings on Human Rights Violations, 166–67

Pacific Affairs, 110
Pacific News Service, 196, 271
Palmer, Robert R., 46
Panama, 134
Paraguay, xviii
Paringaux, R.-P., 131–33, 179
Paris Match, 190
Parks, Michael, 233–34
Pathet Lao, 2, 137–38, 141–42, 144, 148, 151
Paul, Anthony, 161–64, 168, 198–208, 210, 211, 215, 229, 235, 245, 259, 261, 264–65, 268, 272, 273, 275–89, 295, 304, 305, 312, 324, 325

Payne, Les, 66
Peagam, Norman, 142, 144
Peking, xxiii
Pentagon, 22, 34
Pentagon Papers, 72, 307
Persian Gulf, 20, 22
Peters, Charles, 14–16
Peterson, H.C., 27, 28
Philippines, 35, 58, 60, 61, 65, 86–87, 284
Phoenix Program, 10, 80, 85, 89
Pike, Douglas, 158, 175, 179
Pilger, John, 11
Plain of Jars, 150–53
Pleyber-Grandjean, 42
Pol Pot, ix, xii, xxii, xxiii, xxvii, xxviii, 13, 202, 220, 242
Politika, 222
Pomonti-Thion, 290, 306, 310
Ponchaud, François, 155, 161–62, 164, 169, 181, 190, 198, 199, 204–11, 216, 235, 245–46, 256, 259–61, 264–65, 268, 275, 277–78, 289–95, 298–306, 309–17, 319–25, 332
Poole, Peter A., 175–76
Porter, Gareth, 158, 163, 164, 184, 185, 261, 265–68, 318–20, 325, 326
Prachachat, 298, 300–301, 303–4, 316, 317
Pravda, 134–35, 170
PRG (Provisional Revolutionary Government of the Republic of South Vietnam), 7–9, 80, 110, 111
Provisional Revolutionary Government of the Republic of South Vietnam. *See* PRG

Quang Ngai Rehabilitation Center, 103, 104
Quinn, Kenneth M., 177–78, 201–2, 251–52
Quinn-Judge, Sophie, 103

Race, Jeffrey, 92
Ranchic, 222, 223
Rattankiri Province, 255
Read, James Morgan, 27, 28
Reader's Digest, 198, 203, 215, 228,
    237, 267, 275, 288–89
Reasoner, Harry, 139, 152
Red Cross. See International Red
    Cross
Reischauer, Edwm, 30
Retbøll, Torben, 164, 273, 274
Rigaux, François, 224–27
Röling, Bert V., 37, 44
Roosevelt, Franklin D., 43
Rosenberg, Harold, 25
Rosenfeld, Stephen S., 22–23
Ross, Mitchell S., 14
Rostow, Walt, 15
Rusk, Dean, 12
Russell, Bertrand, 18, 328–29

Safran, Nadar, 59
Samphan, Khieu, 158, 187, 190,
    197–203, 215, 276, 279, 282,
    327
Sampson, W.J., 264–67
San Francisco, 65
Sangkum Party, 247–49
Santo Domingo, 86–87
Sapper, Douglas, 272
Schanberg, Sydney, 269–72, 287
Schlesinger, Arthur, 12
School for Oriental and African
    Studies, 130
Seven Days, 219
Shaplen, Robert, 180
Shaw, George Bernard, 188
Shawcross, William, xi, 200, 234–36,
    265–67, 276, 291, 292, 321–24,
    326
Shoeshine Boy Foundation, 122
Shy, John, 45, 49
Siem Reap Province, 259
Sihanouk, Norodom, xx–xxiii, xxv,
xxix, 4, 223, 237, 247, 249,
    250, 256–58, 309–11, 329–31
Silvers, Robert, 318
Simons, Lewis, M., 141–42, 182,
    183, 190–93, 198, 203, 212
Singapore, 30, 153
Snepp, Frank, 10, 31–32, 84, 114
Snepp, Joseph, 31
Social Democrats, U.S., 60
Solarz, Stephen, 158, 175, 265, 266
Solzhenitsyn, Alexander, 189
Somoza, Anastasio, 60
Sonnefeldt Doctrine, 249–50
Sophi, Peang, 242–44
South Asia, 225
South Korea, 86
Soviet Union, xii, xxviii, 21, 139,
    145, 188
Spanish Civil War, 15
SPEEDY EXPRESS, Operation, 171
Spencer, Susan, 179–80
St. Louis Post-Dispatch, 85
Stalin, Joseph, 171
Stanic, Slavko, 220, 221, 235
State Department, U.S., xi, xii, 149,
    175, 182, 184, 186, 190, 196,
    198, 202, 209, 211, 214, 277
Strout, Richard, 17
Suharto, General, 13, 65, 345
Sukarno, Achmed, 309
Summers, Laura, 250, 251, 256,
    257, 333
Sumter, Thomas, 48
Sunday Telegraph (London), 120
Sunday Times (London), 283
Swain, Jon, 269–71, 273, 274, 279,
    283–85
Sweden, 80, 217, 227
Swedish-Kampuchea Friendship
    Association, 231
Swift, Jonathan, 329
Sygma Photo News Agency, 195,
    196

Tarr, Chou Meng and Shane,

268–71, 273, 274
Taylor, Maxwell, 3
Taylor, Telford, 38
Teltsch, Kathleen, 99
Tertrais, Hughes, 97
Thailand, xi, xxiv, xxv, 55, 113,
    142–45, 162, 165, 179, 182,
    190, 191, 216, 217, 228–29,
    247, 260, 268, 270
Thanh, Tran Huu, 119
Thanh, Ngo Ba, 98, 105–7, 110–12
Tharp, David, 116
Thieu, Nguyen Van, 104, 110–14,
    119
Third World, xxv, 12, 19, 21, 23,
    52–53, 63, 189
Thuan, Nguyen Van, 115
Tibbets, Paul, 44
Time, 166, 187–90, 195, 196, 229,
    241, 258
Time-Life, 134
Times (London). *See London Times*
Times of India, 96–97
Tin Sang newspaper, 108
Tinh, Tran Tam, 98, 125
Tokyo, 36, 38
Tories (American Revolution), 47,
    49–51. *See also* Loyalists
Toronto *Globe and Mail*. *See Globe
    and Mail*
Trilateral Commission, 5
Truman, Harry, 342
Turley, William S., 110, 111
Tuyen, Tran Van, 119
TV Guide, 165, 166, 275
Twining, Charles, 163, 169, 175,
    177, 183, 209, 216

Uniform Code of Military Justice,
    36
United Nations (UN), xi, xxi, xxii,
    xxiii, 79, 90, 99–100, 107, 139,
    148, 153, 197
    Food and Agricultural Organiza-
        tion, 97

Security Council, xxix
United States
    Expeditionary Force, 8
    Immigration and Naturalization
        Services (INS), 62–64
United States Agency for Interna-
    tional Development (USAID),
    117, 184
Uppadit, Foreign Minister, 217–18
U.S./Indochina Report, 194
USSR. *See* Soviet Union

Van Doren, Carl, 46, 47
Van Tyne, Claude Halstead, 49–50
Vickery, Michael, 168, 218–19,
    246–53, 259, 301
Viet Cong. *See* NLF
Viet Minh, 30–31, 247
Vietnam, xv–xvii, xxi, xxv–xxvii, 2–4,
    8–9, 14–17, 32–34, 42, 55, 58,
    66–67, 69–135, 137, 143, 155,
    179, 180, 230, 259, 262, 278
Vietnam Bulletinen, 215
*Vietnam South East Asia Interna-
    tional*, 133
Vietnamese Federation of Labor,
    112
Voice of America, xxiii

Waldheim, Kurt, 213
Wall Street Journal, 21, 22, 120,
    128–29, 173, 186, 275, 340–42
Washington, D.C., vii, ix, xii, 11
Washington Monthly, 14
Washington Post, 16–17, 22, 44, 63,
    120, 124, 165, 182, 190, 193,
    194, 196, 217, 229, 240
Weinraub, Bernard, 237
West, Richard, 8
West Bank, 59
Westmoreland, William, 3, 51, 89
Winners and Losers, 18–19
Wise, Donald, 201–4, 312
Woollacott, Martin, 81, 276
World Bank, xxiv, xxv, 78, 79, 90,

99, 148–49
World Health Organization
    (WHO), 95, 184
World Peace Council (WPC), 278
World Vision Organization, 185
World War I, 23, 26–27, 161
World War II, xviii, xxix, 1, 5, 6,
    35–43, 70, 251
Worldview, 101–2

Yamashita, Tomoyuki, 35
Yang Pao, Gen., 141
Yathai, Pin, 164–66
Yew, Lee Kan, 13
Yoshida, Taroichi, 96
Young, Gavin, 12–13
Young Communist League, 78
Yun Yat, 221, 222

Zaire, 22, 60, 65

Also available by Noam Chomsky from Haymarket Books

On Palestine
with Ilan Pappé
$11.95, ISBN: 9781608464708

Culture of Terrorism
$23, ISBN: 9781608463985

The Fateful Triangle
The United States, Israel,
and the Palestinians
(Updated Edition)
Foreword by Edward Said
$22, ISBN: 9781608463992

Gaza in Crisis
Reflections on the US-Israeli War
Against the Palestinians
with Ilan Pappé
$16.95, ISBN: 9781608463312

Hopes and Prospects
$17, ISBN: 9781931859967,
trade paperback
$39.95, ISBN: 9781931859974,
unabridged audiobook

Intervenciones
Foreword by Eduardo Galeano
$16, ISBN: 9781931859592

Masters of Mankind
Essays and Lectures, 1963–2013
Introduction by Marcus Raskin,
$12.95, ISBN: 9781608463633

On Power and Ideology
The Managua Lectures
$16, ISBN: 9781608464005

Pirates and Emperors, Old and New
International Terrorism in the
Real World
$18, ISBN: 9781608464012

Propaganda and the Public Mind
with David Barsamian
$18, ISBN: 9781608464029

Powers and Prospects
Reflections on Nature and
the Social Order
$18, ISBN: 9781608464241

Rethinking Camelot
JFK, the Vietnam War,
and U.S. Political Culture
$16, ISBN: 9781608464036

Rogue States
The Rule of Force in World Affairs
$18, ISBN: 9781608464043

Turning the Tide
U.S. Intervention in
Central America
and the Struggle for Peace
$19, ISBN: 9781608464050

The Washington Connection and Third World Fascism
The Political Economy of Human
Rights: Volume I
with Edward S. Herman
$19, ISBN: 9781608464067

About the Authors

© Don Usner

Noam Chomsky is widely regarded as one of the foremost critics of U.S. foreign policy in the world. He has published numerous ground-breaking books, articles, and essays on global politics, history, and linguistics. Among his recent books are *Masters of Mankind* and *Hopes and Prospects*. This book and its companion volume, *The Washington Connection and Third World Fascism*, are part of a collection of twelve new editions from Haymarket Books of Chomsky's classic works.

Edward S. Herman is professor emeritus of finance at the Wharton School, University of Pennsylvania and has written extensively on economics, political economy, and the media. Among his books are *Corporate Control, Corporate Power, The Real Terror Network,* and *Manufacturing Consent* (with Noam Chomsky).

CPSIA information can be obtained
at www.ICGtesting.com
Printed in the USA
JSHW032212180222
22972JS00005B/5

9 781608 463978